D1600233

*Women State and Territorial
Legislators, 1895–1995*

Women State and Territorial Legislators, 1895–1995

A State-by-State Analysis, with Rosters of 6,000 Women

by ELIZABETH M. COX

McFarland & Company, Inc., Publishers
Jefferson, North Carolina, and London

Frontispiece: the first women state legislators in the United States were elected November 6, 1894, and sworn into the Colorado House of Representatives on January 2, 1895: Clara Cressingham, R–Denver, Arapahoe County [top left]; Carrie Clyde Holly, R–Vineland, Pueblo County [top right]; Frances S. Klock, R–Denver, Arapahoe County [bottom left]. (Courtesy Colorado Historical Society.)   Martha Hughes Cannon D–Salt Lake City [bottom right], the first woman state senator in the United States, was elected November 3, 1896, and sworn into the Utah Senate on January 11, 1897. (Photograph Archives, Utah State Historical Society.)

British Library Cataloguing-in-Publication data are available

Library of Congress Cataloguing-in-Publication Data

Cox, Elizabeth M., 1939–
    Women state and territorial legislators, 1895–1995 : a state-by-state analysis, with rosters of 6000 women / by Elizabeth M. Cox.
       p.   cm.
    Includes bibliographical references (p.) and index. ∞
    ISBN 0-7864-0078-1 (lib. bdg. : 50# alk. paper)
    ✓1. Women legislators—United States. ✓2. Legislative bodies—United States.   I. Title.
    E176.C77   1996
    328.73′082—dc20   95-32652
                                                                              CIP

Manufactured in the United States of America

McFarland & Company, Inc., Publishers
   Box 611, Jefferson, North Carolina 28640

In memory of Ann London Scott (1929–1975),
poet, feminist, wife and mother

Contents

Preface

Nearly a decade ago, I sought the answer to a seemingly simple question: "What has been the experience of American women running for office as state legislators?" I soon discovered that finding the answer would not be simple. No sources existed which could tell me how many women had served in state legislatures, who they were, how they were elected, and what they accomplished. This book is the first comprehensive attempt to list all women who have served in state and territorial legislatures.

In 1986, after completing a commission to study and analyze women voters, I was engaged as a consultant in a woman's state legislative campaign. I decided to review material available at nearby libraries on women running for state legislative offices. Despite a wealth of public and university libraries in the area, I found very little on the subject. *A History of the National Order of Women Legislators, 1939–79* by former legislator Emma R. Poeter at the Library of Congress included founding members and former presidents. I called the Center on American Women in Politics at Rutgers Institute of Politics and learned that they had no data prior to 1971, the year the Center was founded. I was interested in trends over a longer historical period.

This initial exploration of the subject aroused my curiosity even further, as I repeatedly read that before 1970 there were few women legislators, and most of those succeeded their deceased husbands. Somehow that did not ring true and I began to spend any free time I had to research the matter.

Initially, I hoped that I could satisfy my curiosity by consulting works that had already been published. I discovered several different lists of aggregate totals of women state legislators compiled at different times by different people covering various periods. Some were readily available in books (*Women in the Twentieth Century* by Sophonisba P. Breckinridge in 1930, and *Understanding Politics* by Louise M. Young in 1950) or articles ("Women in State Legislatures" by Emmy M. Werner in *Western Political Quarterly*, March 1968), but others were privately published by organiza-

1

tions and more difficult to locate. I was helped in my search by many people who gave generously of their time and energy.

I learned that the Democratic Congressional Wives had published a *History of Democratic Women* in the 1960s but I could not find a copy. I called the Democratic National Committee, who suggested I call Bethine Church, who had been president of the club, but emphasized that I should not waste time as she was packing and moving back to Idaho. I called her at her home in Bethesda, Maryland, and she invited me over and said she would dig it out of a box for me to copy.

I found two copies of lists published in the fifties by the Women's Division of the National Republican Committee in the Library of Congress. These books included a history of Republican women in politics, and rosters of women state legislators for two election cycles. I learned that the Women's Bureau in the Department of Labor had in the past published the numbers of women and it was suggested that I might possibly locate something in their files. Once again, I was just in the nick of time. I found a whole room of file cabinets about to be shipped off to storage. They contained a wealth of information and I was given time and space to search them. I also discovered that the Department of Labor library was a good resource.

Again, just in the nick of time, I learned that the Women's Education Fund, which had started in 1971, was closing down. Rosalie Whelan, the director, searched for pertinent material as she packed the boxes. I also obtained copies of all the old directories compiled by the National Women's Political Caucus (NWPC) since 1981 at the Women's Campaign Fund and the NWPC offices in Washington, D.C..

From these early sources, I attempted to compile the data for the number of women state legislators as a percentage of state legislators nationally from 1920 to the present. I hoped to analyze some of the trends and to compare them with findings from the women voter study that I completed in 1986. I discovered so many discrepancies in the numbers of women legislators cited in various sources that I realized I could not rely on them for analysis. Sophonisba P. Breckinridge came to some of the same conclusions in 1930 when compiling a chapter on women elected officials in her book *Women in the Twentieth Century*. Some counts of women state legislators include only those elected and not the holdovers, and some counts do not state clearly whether women serving in territorial legislators are included. Breckinridge's warning that "news about women in state government has been assembled and is presented . . . but hope of reporting the complete roster cannot be cherished" is posted on the wall by my computer.

I had no choice but to count the women legislators myself.

To count the women who were serving after the even-year election cycle, I realized I would first have to identify them. The oldest collection of state legislative members is in the *Book of States*, published biennially by the Council of State Governments. I looked up the first volume, 1935, and turned to the first roster ever published of the names of the state legislators in the 48 states, "The Men Behind the Laws." This title, along with Breckinridge's warning, illustrates a large part of the problem. In addition, the rosters in the *Book of States* included only names until resident city was added in 1945 , addresses in 1947, party affiliation in 1959, and district numbers in 1979.

I began consulting agencies, offices and records of each of the 50 states and the various territories of the United States. In the process, I gained an even deeper appreciation of the enormous diversity in government procedures among our states and the way they have evolved over time.

In order to keep track of my information, I decided to develop a computer data base with the names of women state legislators and their terms of service. I eventually expanded the database to include pertinent information about each legislator, such as party identification, legislative district, and certain personal information. This book is a result of that effort. The investigation has proven exciting, interesting, and arduous.

Along the way, I learned that one of my cousins had only a few months to live. He was the member of my generation who knew the family history and sent me a chart he had compiled in hopes that I might pursue some of the history in the National Archives. I went to the National Archives to search for my maternal grandparents and experienced the amazement of finding the family listed in the Census. I was hooked and began a new adventure to try to capture as much of the family history as I could before my cousin died. At the time I had no idea that the skills and knowledge I would acquire in this very personal research project would come in handy in the professional project on women state legislators to identify gender and first names.

I decided to research two states that I was somewhat familiar with from my work on women voters, New York and Pennsylvania. During my first visits to the Library of Congress, one could apply for a daily stack privilege and personally go down into the numerous underground floors to view the miles of stacks. These visits were overwhelming. Finding information on one state is not so difficult, but when I began to realize that I would need the other 49, the task began to appear awesome. For these first two states, Pennsylvania and New York, I found that some of the biennial state manuals were not in the Library of Congress. I spent a day at Benjamin Franklin's Free Library on a business trip to Philadelphia to review the missing Pennsylvania manuals. For New York, I dovetailed this research with my own genealogical research when I visited Cattaraugus County where my paternal great-grandparents, a French Canadian great-grandfather and Scottish great-grandmother, met and married after the Civil War. I spent an evening at the St. Bonaventure University Library to review the missing New York manuals. Eventually I found "Women in the Pennsylvania Legislature 1922–1984," compiled by Carol Y. Blake and was able to compare the two lists. At the same time as my own search in New York, the New York legislative Women's Caucus was compiling the "Law Makers: Biographical Sketches of the Women of the New York State Legislature, 1918–1988."

Just before the 1988 elections, I decided to collect the names of the women legislators from the 50 states and after the elections, collect the names of the newly elected women legislators. Even though I was very aware of differences in state service and information from my work in electoral politics and voter information, this seemingly small task proved to be even more challenging. Every state holds elections, but I found that not many states could readily and accurately identify their most recently elected legislators by gender. Some states could send the information, some sent inaccurate lists, some did not include party affiliation or district numbers, others sent their complete roster leaving for me the task of determining who were female.

In many cases, the only indicator of the gender of the legislator was the name. Unfortunately, this is not always a reliable indicator. Johnny Cash's popular song "A Boy Named Sue" is not that far-fetched. I had known men named Joyce and Beverly, and a famous local male sportswriter was named Shirley. I knew women named Casey, Chris, and Kim. In the course of my research I was to learn many more names that might be used by either males or females. In "Mothers of Men As Legislators of States," a title any modern day woman can appreciate, *The National Suffrage News* announced there were 11 female legislators in five states in April of 1917. The article includes interviews with all but one of the named females, Mrs. Alma Greenwood of Utah, a name that I did not have from any source. I looked up Alma Greenwood in the Utah *House Journal* and the Census and discovered Alma was a male who lived long beyond 1917 and therefore was not replaced by his widow.

After the 1990 elections the NWPC commissioned me to compile their 20th anniversary *Directory of Women Elected Officials*. This project included women members of Congress, those holding statewide office, state legislators, mayors, county commissioners and party officials for each of the 50 states. The NWPC directory also includes statistics on the number of women candidates for Congress and state legislatures. I began the project in January 1991 and had only 12 weeks to complete it. This increased my knowledge of the differences among states for tabulating candidate returns and publishing the results, including the fact that some states do not include in their returns candidates who had no opposition in the general election. This makes it difficult to determine who are all the newly elected officials.

I moved to north Texas in the summer of 1991 and decided to spend the fall on the women state legislators research before I began teaching American government at Mountain View Community College in 1992. I surveyed the 50 states to collect the names of women legislators before 1970. Once again, the experience was as diverse as the 50 states, and so were the results. In some states I had to write three or four offices or institutions before I received any information. In one state where an intern had been assigned the responsibility of answering my letter, she took an interest and I received copies of all the photographs and biographical entries for each of the women legislators for every term they had served from 1923 to 1971. In another state, I received from the state women's commission, a copy of a handwritten list of a few names and years from 1920 to 1980. From Utah I received the wonderful book compiled by former state legislator Delila M. Abbott, and from some states I received nothing.

After two months of no response from one state, I called to inquire whether the information was available and discovered that the support staff was compiling the list on their break time because the institution had not approved the research. I am happy to report that their work was eventually assumed by a state office and the list completed and published.

During business trips to Austin, I spent some time in the Texas Legislative Reference Library which has a large collection of recent state legislative manuals from a variety of states. In north Texas, I used the Texas Women's University Library in Denton, Texas, and the Dallas Public Library. By the time I moved back to Washington, D.C., in January 1993, I had a rather extensive data base of names. I relocated near George Washington University where I used the library frequently, and near the Foggy Bottom Metro stop which got me on the line that goes to the Library of Congress.

As the research progressed, I had to increase the storage capacity of my computer and write programs to manipulate the data.

In the spring of 1993, I began work again at the Library of Congress to compile lists for states that I had not been able to research elsewhere, and validate the lists I had collected. I quickly learned that while I was in Texas the Library had reversed the stack privilege policy and this has made the research much more difficult and lengthy. Computer searches were not always helpful in locating the state manuals and legislative journals, and even card searches sometimes did not indicate material I eventually found.

About this time I realized that I would have to establish who the first female legislator was in each state in order to begin at the beginning. This was particularly important for the earliest female legislators in the U.S. who were elected in three western states, Colorado, Utah and Idaho. I began reading some of the volumes of the *History of Women Suffrage* by Susan B. Anthony and Ida Husted Harper which contain lengthy reports from each of the states on the status of the suffrage drive and sometimes information about the election of women to public office.

I found a wealth of information on the Utah women, "Gentle Persuaders, Utah's First Women Legislators" by Jean Bickmore White and "'The Goose Hangs High': Excerpts from the Letters of Martha Hughes Cannon" by Constance L. Lieber in the *Utah Historical Quarterly*, but nothing on the Colorado women legislators. I set up shop in the Manuscript Division of the Library of Congress where I spent several weeks sifting throughout the collections of the National American Women Suffrage Association, the National Women's Party, the League of Women Voters, the Carrie Chapman Catt papers, the Susan B. Anthony papers and others. I moved into the Current Periodical Division where a variety of newspapers from the 50 states are kept on microfilm.

I began reading the Colorado *Rocky Mountain News* in 1893. I called the Colorado Women's Commission and was directed to the Committee on Women's History which was organized to commemorate the 100th anniversary of Colorado women suffrage in 1893. I was given the name of Mary Renstrom in Denver who had researched the first Colorado women legislators. I talked to Mary, an experienced genealogist and professional legislative analyst, and discovered that she had spent hours searching for photographs of Carrie Clyde Holly, Clara Cressingham, and Frances S. Klock, who were elected to the Colorado General Assembly in 1894 and the first women legislators in the United States. Fortunately for us all, she had found the photographs of these "lost women" in a Colorado Historical Society file box. The Committee sent me a copy of their booklet *Colorado Suffrage Centennial, 1893–1993*, and the Colorado Historical Society sent me a copy of the special issue on suffrage of the *Colorado Heritage*. These publications are excellent resource material for Colorado suffrage, they provide the only photographs Mary found of the first female legislators but no biographical sketch of their personal and public life.

On the Idaho search, I received a letter from the Idaho State Historical Society Library and Archives researcher, Elizabeth Jacox, responding to my query about the first women legislators whose photograph I had found reproduced in the *Idaho Blue Book, 1989*. We began six months of communication via mail, fax, and telephone to reconstruct the lives of the three Idaho women.

The Colorado search became the central part of my research for about three months because I discovered that there was nothing written about the very first three women legislators. It seemed impossible, and I kept thinking I would find something. The same occurred for the three women in Idaho. And the experience was repeated for many of the states.

What I have found in this search of the "first" women is that sometimes biographical information has survived, but there is a serious absence of political analysis of how these women attained office and what they did while they were legislators. I have had to dedicate much more time than I would have believed necessary just to document who were the first women, locate a photograph, and reconstruct some of their political life. The search has led me to write and phone local libraries and county historical and genealogical societies, spend hours reading newspapers on the microfilm machine as well as the *House* and *Senate Journals* and the *Session Laws* of the respective states.

What I learned from my own research of the first women legislators is that they were important people in their own right. Very few of them, as recurring myth would have it, succeeded their deceased husbands. Many of them were successful at business or in other endeavors before entering the legislature. They also proved to be effective legislators, often wielding an influence far beyond what might be expected from their limited numbers. Alice Stone Blackwell, editor of *The Woman's Journal* in Boston, provided much coverage of the early elected women officials. When the *Journal* merged with *The National Suffrage News*, Carrie Chapman Catt's suffrage newspaper in New York City, to form *The Woman Citizen*, Stone and Mary Sumner Boyd became the experts in the country on elected women officials. They launched essay contests with monetary prizes for winning essays on women in elections. Reviewing their columns, I readily identified with their difficulties in identifying gender of candidates and winners, as well as who was "first." Several issues after each election they were still printing "corrections."

Nevertheless, I found that attitudes which dismiss the contributions of these women are remarkably persistent. Many times, a librarian I contacted would ask if I had checked this or that book and when I replied yes and that I had not found anything on this woman, the reply would be that "she must not be very important if you didn't find anything."

One local public library referred me to the local historical museum. The woman who answered the phone knew the name I gave her and said, yes, she had a whole box of things that were brought to her from a professional house cleaning service who found them in an attic of a house they had been cleaning. She noticed that one of the pieces of correspondence had the capitol on the letter head and read through to discover it was signed by a female legislator. She sent me copies of all the material, which provides more information than the state library or the state legislature had for this particular woman, who was the first in her state.

The photograph of one of the first woman legislators is available only because a father wanted his daughter to know that a woman had been elected from their home town. He discovered that at some time in the past her portrait had hung in the capitol but was not there presently. He persisted until it was located in the basement and he was given permission to take a camera into the basement and photograph the portrait. His photograph now hangs in the local museum for his daughter and everyone else to see, but the original portrait is still in the basement of the capitol building.

Another photograph of a first woman legislator that had been "lost" for twenty years was finally found misfiled in a state archives by my son, Benjamin L. Cox. In another state, I am still trying to locate the photograph that the legislature passed a resolution to hang in the capitol. No one knows where it is and so far it has not been uncovered.

In compiling the information in this book, I have tried to be as complete as possible. I have attempted to include all women who have ever served, including those who were appointed or elected in special elections, as well as those who were elected in the regular election cycle. My objective has been to identify all the women behind the numbers that are used in most studies of women legislators. The bibliography entries are limited to resources that list names and therefore do not include a wealth of published studies and books on the broader topic of women in elective office. I have been told by more than one scholar that their study did not include the roster of names because there might be errors and that would compromise the credibility of the conclusions. In some of the lists I first obtained from states, I discovered what I thought were omissions or errors and corresponded with many of the states in an attempt to resolve these differences. Some of the discrepancies have been resolved to both our satisfaction, but others await an in depth history of women legislators in each state. These problems may have contributed to the long overdue compilation and publication of a book like this one. Because of differences in the way these matters are handled in various states and my reliance on records available at the Library of Congress and elsewhere that I have been able to visit or to contact local experts, there may be errors and omissions. I apologize in advance for any errors or omissions, and ask that all of them be brought to my attention.

If there is a male "Sue" or "Alma" or "Florence" included, they or their descendants can rejoice in this extra publicity.

Many early legislative rosters and lists did not include party affiliation. This was especially true for material found in the literature of women's organizations and I suspect that they believed there was a political advantage in appearing nonpartisan. But it is also true that many official state publications omit this information. This is unfortunate, because partisanship is an integral part of our political system and therefore the information is necessary to provide a more complete understanding of trends and events. It would have been easier to leave the party column blank for many women, but long hours reading newspapers on microfilm yielded a complete column of party affiliation. This book is multipartisan.

Many women were listed as "Mrs." with their husband's name, and described as the wife of, daughter of, or widow of. Additional time and effort was dedicated in determining each woman legislator's given name by searching the Census at the National Archives, reading newspapers and local histories, and going to local sources. There were times that the local historian and I became convinced that the woman we were researching had "wife of" on her gravestone.

Much research and analysis remains to be done. The stories are there, and with a good bit of sleuthing, they can be ferreted out. Each of these now forgotten women legislators is a worthy subject for more exhaustive research. The same is true of many of their successors, who did not have the distinction of being first but who distinguished themselves in other important ways. There are several collections of biographies of women legislators in a particular state, but very few comprehensive historical and political analyses. Joanne Varner Hawks and Carolyn Ellis researched the history of women state legislators in some Southern states and have published valuable articles on their findings. Ann Rathke in North Dakota, Emily Steir Adler and Stanley Lemons in Rhode Island, Rita Mae Kelly in Arizona, Katheryne and Richard McCormick in New Jersey, and Suzanne O'Day Schenken in Iowa have completed excellent books on women state legislators in their respective states.

Like many women of my generation, I first met a woman state legislator while I was organizing and lobbying for ratification of the Equal Rights Amendment in the early seventies as a political consultant for the National Organization for Women Legislative Office. I learned a great deal about these women legislators during the drive for the ERA, their isolation in the political arena, their commitment to achieving political goals, and their extraordinary courage and leadership in conquering blatant acts of sexism. Today, we can look at the state of Washington, where women comprise 40 percent of the state legislators, and we can see the future.

In addition to a note of appreciation to the hundreds of state offices and local public librarians who tried to answer my queries, I am particularly grateful to Anselmo Arellano and Kathy Flynn for their assistance in New Mexico, and to James Dompier and the Baraga County Historical Society in Michigan. Special thanks and appreciation go to Mary Beth Koechlin, Joanne Varner Hawks, Ilene Cornwell, Suzanne Schenken, Enerida Rivero, and Elizabeth Jacox for reviewing some of the states.

I have discovered that many books begin just as this one did, with an attempt to answer a question. First the question, then a few answers, then a growing number of answers, and then a vision of a book. Along the way, my colleagues, friends and family have provided much support and encouragement. To Dave, my husband, thank you for believing in this quest, for the technical assistance you gave so generously to compile this book, and the years of living with state file boxes stacked in every nook and corner of office and home.

No single researcher could possibly complete an in-depth research and analysis of the accomplishments of every woman legislator, placing them in the historical and political context of their time as well as in the context of the political role of women as it has developed over time.

The starting point, however, is to answer the first question: "Who were these women?" I hope that this work will help other researchers who want to recapture the lost history of women legislators and their political accomplishments in each state.

Introduction

The year 1995 is the 100th anniversary of the service of women in state legislatures in the United States. The story begins in the West, where three women legislators were elected to the Colorado General Assembly in 1894 and sworn in on January 2, 1895. Their experience provides an example of the interrelation between women legislators and the historical, cultural and political currents of their time.

The year 1995 is also the 75th anniversary of the ratification of the Nineteenth Amendment, granting women's suffrage nationally.

By the time the Nineteenth Amendment passed, the expansion of the electorate was widely accepted, and generally welcomed. By that time, women in Wyoming had been voting for half a century, and those of Colorado for 25 years. Twelve states had granted full political rights to women, and 17 additional states had some form of women's suffrage for presidential elections. In fact, solicitation of women voters for the 1920 presidential race was already underway when the Nineteenth Amendment passed the Congress.

The 36 states without full political rights for women had seen the workings of suffrage and generally understood that it was not a great political threat. After all, when women voted, no existing voters lost their voting rights.

This was not necessarily universally understood at the beginning. Ellis Meredith, a Colorado suffragist and journalist, described a case of misunderstanding after the women's suffrage referendum in Colorado in 1893. As described in the chapter on Colorado by Ellis Meredith and her mother in Susan B. Anthony's *History of Woman Suffrage*, volume 4, page 520:

> The day after the election a German woman came out of her house and accosted one of the members of the club with the exclamation, "Ach, Yon he feel so bad; he not vote any more; me, I vote now!" When assured that John had not been deprived of any of his rights, with more generosity than can be attributed to many of the Johns, she called her husband, exclaiming delightedly: "Yon, Yon, you vote too; we bofe vote!"

Running for political office or holding positions of political power and influence was another matter entirely. Positions of influence were inherently scarce and existed in a "closed" system of "back room" politics of the political parties and their nominating conventions. In that environment, if a woman achieved elected office or other position of influence, that deprived a man of the position.

Carrie Chapman Catt, president of the National American Women's Suffrage Association (NAWSA), was keenly aware of this reality. She, more than any other national figure, encouraged women to participate in the political party of their choice, including running for elective office, and not to be dismayed that men did not welcome them.

Ellis Meredith described her earlier experience in Colorado political parties in 1927 in "Women's Contribution" in Leroy R. Hafen's *Colorado and Its People*:

> certainly [the men] had no intention of allowing women to "tinker" with the political machine. They tried to make it clear that women were welcome to occupy the pleasant "parlor" cars, but under no circumstances would they be permitted to suggest destinations to the engineers or investigate the running-gear.

More than any other single factor, it is the closed nature of the political structure that has impeded the election of women to political office. From the outset, the success of women candidates has required an unusual combination of ability, perseverance, self confidence and favorable circumstance. The obstacles faced by women legislative candidates became apparent from the very beginning, a century ago in Colorado.

The Beginning

"Go West, young woman; go to Colorado!" suffragist leader Carrie Chapman advised the gathering in Boston's Faneuil Hall celebrating the 120th anniversary of the Boston Tea Party on December 16, 1893. "There you will have the 'sovereignty of citizenship,' for last month the men in Colorado voted to enfranchise the women of Colorado."

Carrie Clyde Holly, a native of New York City who was active in the New York suffrage movement, heard the call as early as 1889 when she "came out to Colorado with strong beliefs in the advantages of a public life for women." Within five years she ran successfully for the Vineland school board, supported the Colorado suffrage referendum, and in 1894 was elected one of the three first women state legislators in the United States. Frances S. Klock, the oldest of the three pioneer legislators, was a native of Massachusetts who became a skilled organizer working for the Sanitary Commission during the Civil War in Wisconsin, and after moving to Denver became active in veterans affairs. Clara Cressingham, the youngest of the trio, was a native of Brooklyn, New York, who left a career in elocution to work in her family's failing business, married and moved her ailing husband to Colorado for his health, where she wrote articles for newspapers back East and cared for her two children.

Holly, Klock and Cressingham, all Republicans, blazed a trail that was followed two years later when a Democratic Utah doctor became the first woman elected to a state senate. By the turn of the century, 16 women had served in the state legislatures of Colorado, Idaho and Utah. The three Colorado women set precedents concerning women legislators, acting as a model for those who followed. In the process, they encountered attitudes, prejudices and obstacles that are still familiar today, a century later.

Colorado Suffrage

Unlike neighboring Wyoming, where the legislature granted full suffrage and political rights to women in 1869 to attract women settlers, Colorado women actively organized and campaigned for suffrage by popular referendum. After losing a suffrage referendum in 1877, they redoubled their efforts. Following the 1892 gubernatorial victory by the Populist Party, which advocated women's suffrage in its platform, a new referendum was held in November 1893, passing by a two-to-one margin.

The election of women to public office was not a primary goal of the suffrage movement. Advocates claimed that suffrage would raise the education level of the electorate, clean up polling places, improve candidates, and insure that politicians paid more attention to the public welfare. Movement leaders denied that suffrage would lead to women in public office, and antisuffragists claimed that legislatures would be paralyzed if women were elected because the men would be so inhibited by their presence. Two key decisions by Colorado women proved both predictions false, and set precedents for Colorado and the states that followed.

The first decision was to neutralize a major argument of suffrage opponents that women did not want to vote, as evidenced by allegedly poor turnout at school elections, where women were already allowed to vote. Denver women decided to demonstrate the "desire for enfranchisement" by launching a campaign for one of their own activists, Ione T. Hanna, for school director in the 1893 spring nonpartisan school elections. Hanna won a bitterly fought campaign by a large turnout of women voters, thus demonstrating not only women's desire for suffrage, but also that a woman candidate could attract more women voters. This demonstration was particularly significant because one fourth of Colorado's population lived in

Denver, and 40 percent of them were women. This was a bloc of voters large enough to capture the attention of the political parties.

After winning the suffrage referendum, the Colorado Suffrage Association met to celebrate and to discuss future goals. The major question was whether they should continue pursuing their goals as an independent group or by working as individuals through the political parties of their choice. The Association voted for members to go into their chosen parties to pursue their joint goals in public policy.

Partisan Politics

The women faced many new challenges. For the first time, they encountered the hurdles of voter registration. Furthermore, they had to learn about and gain access to their party's nomination process. In each precinct, each county and at the state level, party leaders welcomed the new *voters*, but created barriers to equal *participation* and leadership in party business.

Women began to organize in each of the major parties for voting, but had to maneuver through factions to gain access to nominating conventions. They had no experienced suffragists from other states as models or mentors. Their lack of experience was somewhat offset by a fluid political situation in Colorado, where both Republican and Democratic parties were split over the use of silver or gold as a monetary standard, and the Populist party was split by controversy over their incumbent governor. The situation opened more doors to women in this first election than otherwise would have been possible.

The political parties, for their own part, positioned themselves to gain adherents from the newly enfranchised women. In February, the Populist Party opened a new office in Denver for the education and training of the new voters. They sent in a paid full time organizer, Phoebe Couzins, an attorney who had been a deputy marshall from St. Louis.

There was, however, dissension within the party that was to affect the opportunities for women. The controversy centered around incumbent Populist Governor Davis H. Waite. Waite had alienated many in his own party as well as in the population as a whole by using the militia to protect striking miners against security agents hired by mine owners. Other parties accused Waite of misrule and anarchy. Opponents within his own party accused Waite of establishing a machine in contravention of Populist principles.

During the Populist convention in the fall of 1894, more than 150 delegates walked out and opened an anti–Waite convention. Attacking Waite supporters for packing the convention and not allowing free discussion, the anti–Waite convention organized to topple Waite. Prominent Populist women were among the leaders in unsuccessful anti–Waite movement, including Ellis Meredith Stansbury, Minnie Reynolds, Dr. Minnie T. Love, and many others.

The Republican State Chairman appointed Angenette Peavey (who had organized Denver women for the suffrage referendum) to name women to serve on state and county committees, in equal number to the men, and appointed a woman to organize Republican women's clubs throughout the state in June 1894. The Arapahoe County (Denver) Central Committee vehemently refused to allow *any* women on the committee. A compromise at the state convention allowed for one woman on each committee, one woman nominee for the state school office, and three women for the legislature. One delegate made the case for diversity in his nomination speech. As reported in the *Rocky Mountain News*, he observed that the delegates "had nominated men of legal ability and a man of executive ability . . . a man with one leg and another with one arm, and it would only be proper to complete the ticket by placing a woman on it."

The Democratic Party split over the silver issue into "White Wings" and "Silver" factions. Both factions offered women "auxiliary" status, which they refused. Mary C. C. Bradford, who organized Democratic women in the state, led a women's delegation to both conventions. She announced that women would not support them unless the two factions agreed to a unified slate. She won agreement for a unified statewide slate as well as the nomination for state superintendent of public instruction. On the county level, Democrats eventually joined with Populists to form a Fusion Ticket for state legislative races.

Even though each major party presented a different problem to newly enfranchised women, the result was similar. Each party nominated one woman on the statewide ticket (out of 6 offices), and three women for the state legislature (out of 65 house seats and 18 senate seats). The Prohibition Party nominated a woman for state senate as well as three for the house.

The First Campaign

The Republican election strategy challenged the Populists on law and order, claimed credit for women's suffrage, and avoided their internal differences on gold and silver altogether. During Holly's legislative campaign, she charged Populist Governor Waite with "mis-rule" and "anarchy" in the state, and claimed he was not a true friend of women because he had only called for municipal women's suffrage (in his inaugural address) rather than full rights. Although she did not support prohibition as a political issue, she refused to attend a meeting "called by the whiskey men" and said "they fought me, and I ran behind my ticket on that account." Judith Ellen

Forster, sent from the National Republican Committee to speak throughout the state, pushed for straight Republican ticket voting by suggesting to
the new women voters that if they "scratched (split) the ticket on the ballot
they might lose their vote.

As the first state election in which women could vote drew near, there
was a run on hats in the Denver millinery shops—the store owners had
been unprepared for the increased demand for hats in the fall. Just as
women had bought all the Fisk's *Civil Government* books in the spring in
hopes of preparing for full political participation, they bought new hats in
the fall so they would be properly attired for the serious political act of
voting in their first state election.

On the eve of the election, an innovative get out the vote activity by
Denver women received national attention. The *New York Times* reported:

> A novel demonstration . . . by the Republican women in Denver on the
> night previous to the election. They chartered a number of electric cars
> on the tramway line, decorated them profusely with flowers and bunting
> brilliantly lighted the open cars with hundreds of incandescent lights, and
> sped through the principal street of the city . . . these trains of cars were
> run in section and not a man was aboard except the motormen . . . the
> novel parade had been duly advertised, and large crowds filled the streets
> through which the merry making campaigners proceeded.

The Republican strategy proved successful, for the three Republican women were swept into office on the coattails of the successful state
Republican ticket. While fewer women voted than men (53 percent men,
47 percent women), 78 percent of eligible women voters turned out com-
pared to only 56 percent of eligible men (statistics compiled from data in
Equal Suffrage by Helen L. Sumner, 1908 [New York: Arno Press, 1972]).
The defeated Populist governor, who had fought openly for the suffrage
referendum, told a Populist convention in Minnesota the following month
that women had defeated him and predicted (inaccurately) the end of
Populist support for suffrage.

The Legislature

Election of women members did not immediately result in equal access to power and equal treatment in the legislature. For example, by tradi-
tion, wives of legislators were allowed on the floor for the opening session.
When newly elected Holly arrived for the first session, accompanied by her
husband and her daughter, the doorkeeper said only she could enter. Holly
demanded that her husband be given equal rights with wives of male
members. She won the argument, and her family entered.

The women did in fact clean up both the language and the air in the house chamber. They insisted on enforcement of the no smoking rule on the floor even when the legislature was not in session, and they pushed for a ruling to disallow lobbying on the floor during the session.

> The lady members of the house are causing the strict enforcement of the rule against smoking on the floor of the house, whether that body is in session or not. When a member forgets himself, he is at once apprised of the fact by the sergeant at arms, who is sent to them by the fair member.

In the Senate, where women worked as clerks and had requested that the rule be enforced, they were ignored. Holly concluded that it was "a question of position quite as much as of sex."

Early in the session, when a Republican man introduced an amendment during debate on provision for separate sleeping accommodations for jury members with "coarse levity," Representative Klock jumped to her feet. "Mr. Chairman," she objected, "I protest against such language upon the floor of the house." *The Rocky Mountain News* reported, "The offending member immediately withdrew the amendment, the few faces that had expanded in a half smile instantly straightened themselves, and the offense has never been repeated." Perhaps because her protest was successful, she chose to characterize the incident as a "mistaken desire to be funny rather than a desire to offend the women members."

Cressingham was elected secretary of the Republican Caucus. A crisis came when male politicians complained the three women had packed the patronage clerkships. She held her ground, observing that if they would pay attention they might know what was happening. "You make motions, amend them, quarrel over them, add substitutes, and when the final vote comes you don't know what you are doing. If, then, you have prevented the selection of your candidates as cleared, don't you dare lay the blame on me! I won't stand it."

The women proved more adept on the floor of the House than many had expected. One incident was reported by *The Rocky Mountain News* with headlines trumpeting, "SAVED BY A WOMAN—REPRESENTATIVE HOLLY COMES TO THE RESCUE." The Populist Party introduced an anti-corporation resolution and Republicans responded by shouting protests and interrupting the clerk so that a first reading could not be accomplished, invalidating the introduction. The Populists requested that the protests be read into the record. Republicans then attempted filibustering and introduced delaying motions until Holly solved the impasse. At her behest, the Republicans introduced a resolution expunging both the proposed resolution and the protest from the House Journal. It passed by a partisan vote.

U.S. Senate Vote

Since U.S. senators were elected by state legislatures prior to 1913, Holly, Cressingham and Klock became the first women to vote for a U.S. senator when the Colorado House and Senate met in joint session on January 16, 1895. The scene was described by the *Colorado Chieftain*:

> The women's gallery was well filled, but the ladies were not confined to the distant opera chairs above the heads of the law-makers. . . . chairs were arranged around the walls, and gallant representatives vacated their comfortable places behind their high desks so that the stranger would have supposed that at least a third of the house was made up of woman legislators, if it had not been for the absence of the bonnets from the heads of the three duly elected.

The Republicans had a majority in the joint session to re-elect the junior Republican senator from Colorado, Edward O. Wolcott, but his ambiguous suffrage record was attacked by Populists and many women. He had voted against a U.S. Senate resolution for women's suffrage in the Oklahoma territory, and had voted against a suffrage bill in the Colorado senate. After Colorado suffrage passed, Wolcott introduced a resolution in the U.S. Senate calling for a suffrage amendment to the U.S. Constitution. Despite the opposition of many women who doubted his conversion, the three Republican women seconded Wolcott's nomination, and he was elected.

Holly's Bill

Many women were upset at Representative Holly for having seconded the nomination of Wolcott and having voted for him. The following week, however, these same women came to praise her for her fine leadership in introducing and securing passage of the first successful bill sponsored by a woman legislator.

Holly's bill, to raise the "age of consent" for girls from 16 to 18, was controversial, and guaranteed to lead to a spirited debate. The gallery was full in anticipation of fiery and possibly ribald speeches. At stake were issues of public morality against the future of the rather substantial prostitution industry. While the Republicans spoke against the bill and attempted to kill it with amendments, there was a lot of Populist support since it had been in their platform. One of the more imaginative amendments was to have the law apply to "chaste woman only." Holly "kept her head and never failed to detect a fallacy" in opposing arguments and the bill passed.

The passage of Holly's legislation was a nationwide sensation. After

Holly guided the bill through the legislature, the delegates to the annual National American Women's Suffrage Association convention, meeting in Atlanta, immediately voted to send a telegram to congratulate the Honorable Mrs. Holly. Holly, at the end of the session, referred to the hundreds of letters from women in every state of the Union who had written to her at the House. Most wanted to know, "How does it work?"

Press reaction across the nation was not, however, uniformly favorable. The *Michigan Herald* declared that the Colorado experience with women legislators was "Not a Success" and *The Arizona Republic* reported that the women "have not been conspicuous in any way except that one of them arose frequently to demand the enforcement of the rule against smoking . . . the only bills they were able to get through were pushed through by the courtesy of the men . . . ."

The Liquor Question and Independence

After Holly successfully ushered her bill through the House, she began to assert some independence from her party. She had campaigned stating that prohibition should not be considered a political question. When the House began debate on a Populist sponsored "local option" bill which would also regulate the sale of liquor at club houses, she broke ranks with fellow Republicans, including the two other women. Parliamentary maneuvers and filibusters filled the afternoon session with many votes breaking along party lines (Republicans against and Populists for). Holly, joined by nine male Republicans, voted with the Populists against the fatal amendments and kept the bill alive. Republican Party regulars fought to kill the bill. One Republican threatened Holly, announcing that "if the women of Colorado took a decided stand on this question they would array the entire whisky power of the Unites States against woman suffrage." The bill passed to the Senate by a 30–26 vote. Holly observed that "if the women were going to sacrifice principle to expediency, just as men had always done, their presence in politics would not elevate it any, and they might as well stay out." She also broke with her party by supporting a street car vestibule bill, opposing a church taxation bill, and by supporting a bill to abolish capital punishment.

One of Holly's bills required educational qualifications for voting. Principally an anti-immigrant measure, it faced early opposition among Mexican Americans. She thought she had negotiated a compromise and put in a motion to reconsider. During debate, the alleged compromise fell apart as Holly referred to Representative Garcia of Conejos County as the "gentleman from Mexico," claiming that "he wanted Mexicans excepted" and that she had agreed to this modification. Garcia objected that he "was not from Mexico and never was," pointing out that he was a natural born citizen.

Holly's further allusions to Garcia brought that member to his feet with a point of order. The chair decided for him. Garcia explained that "I disapprove of anyone being disfranchised who pays taxes." The motion was killed by a vote of 24 to 15.

Klock and Cressingham

Frances S. Klock, the oldest of the three women legislators, had not been active in the suffrage movement and was surprised when she was asked to run, but quickly became "convinced that in legislative assemblies women have a position where they can do a great deal for humanity. Three can do something — if necessary we can protest." Her accomplishments included more than protesting to clean up the language in the legislature. She chaired the powerful Military and Indian Affairs Committee, successfully got a new facility for the Soldier's Home, and secured passage of her own bill creating a home for friendless and incorrigible girls.

Klock concluded that the greatest lesson women have to learn is "that of taking rebuff and defeat, and encountering difference of opinion with cool philosophy, as men do . . . you will see the men fighting each other with the most bitter opposition , and at recess you will find them in a group all having a good time together . . . women can't do that yet, but they have got to learn it if they are going to be in politics, and they will; contact with the world is all that is necessary . . . politics isn't just like anything else . . . one needs great tact and judgment of human nature." She expressed great pride that she had never been approached by a "lobbyist."

Clara Cressingham, the youngest of the trio, found service in the legislature "exhilarating and exciting." She introduced several bills to encourage the sugar beet industry, which was in the experimental stages in Colorado at that time, and won passage of one of them. Speaking as one of the first three women state legislators, she told a *New York World* reporter that they were all aware "that the suffrage movement may be injured by indiscreet actions on our part, and we have to be very careful. What would pass unnoticed in men will be made prominent enough when we are to be considered so that the position we occupy is not the most easy to fill." She held that one half of the legislators should be women, but that women ought not to introduce radical measures or take radical positions on reform questions. She opposed any prohibition, claiming that her research on such measures in Maine and Kansas confirmed that they had not worked well there.

Accomplishments

The 1895 session of the Colorado Legislature was a momentous session. For the first time in the United States, women served as lawmakers. Despite the arguments of naysayers across the nation, it is apparent that these women served effectively, and that their presence made a difference. Although newspapers paid great attention to issues of decorum, it is apparent in retrospect that the beneficial influence of these three women went far beyond decorum. They took their responsibilities seriously, and did their best to insure that the body did so as a whole.

Most apparent was their emphasis on social welfare. There were male members equally concerned over such issues, but the presence of the three women in the chamber and the close observation of the proceedings by women voters strengthened their hand considerably. Reports in some papers that women proved ineffective legislators were plainly wrong.

None of these first women elected to the Colorado legislature ran for a second term, but other women were elected in their place. Each of them went on to prominence in other areas of public life. The fact that they were not reelected is less significant than it might appear. During this period of political upheaval, few male legislators ran for more than one term either (only four of the 1894 men returned to the Colorado house in 1896). In some respects, legislative service was seen as somewhat akin to jury duty, that is, an occasional obligation for good citizens, but not a permanent occupation.

What was significant is the legacy that these women left behind them. They proved that women legislators could serve effectively in public office. It was a small beginning. These first women were elected during the height of the populist movement and they were part of the experiment to broaden the political arena after the Civil War. With the dawn of the twentieth century, populism was dead politically, and the national suffrage movement entered a dormant period, not to re-emerge until the second decade with the Progressive movement.

In tandem, the number of women state legislators decreased significantly. After the Populist bubble burst, Democratic and Republican men felt little political pressure to nominate women in their conventions where the slates were made behind closed doors. Women politicians were, for all practical purposes, shut out, and turned their efforts to non-partisan election reform. With the passage of direct primary election laws, women were again nominated and elected to state legislatures.

Two years after the three Colorado women were elected to the legislature, on November 3, 1896, Utah elected the first woman state senator in the country, Dr. Martha Hughes Cannon, a Democrat from Salt Lake City. Cannon, a practicing medical physician, mother, and fourth wife in a polygamous marriage, won on a Democratic slate by defeating the Republican slate which included her husband.

State Senator Cannon, and Representatives Sarah Anderson, Democrat, and Eurithe LaBarthe, Democrat, were each nominated for the U.S. Senate by fellow legislators attempting to break a deadlock during the 53 ballots in 1897.

Cannon chaired the Committee on Public Health and introduced legislation to establish a Utah State Health Board. She was appointed as one of the first members of the new board by the governor. Senator Cannon was pregnant with her third child during the second half of her four year senate term and gave birth to a daughter two weeks after the session ended in April 1899.

Two years later, on November 8, 1898, Idaho elected Mary A. Wright, a Populist and teacher from Rathdrum, Harriet F. Noble, a Democrat and businesswoman from Idaho City, and Clara Permilia Campbell, a Republican and former teacher in Boise to the Idaho House of Representatives. Wright, who was elected chair of the Populist Caucus, became the first woman to serve as a minority leader and to be nominated for speaker. All three women chaired committees, Wright chaired Engrossment, Campbell chaired Elections and Privileges, and Noble chaired Enrollment.

By the end of the nineteenth century, 16 women had served in state legislatures, all in the west: Colorado, Utah, and Idaho.

National Suffrage

By 1918, many of the arguments that opponents had raised against women's suffrage were losing their power. The liquor question had been settled (temporarily) with the passage of the of a constitutional amendment and the suffrage movement was strengthened by virtue of the service of many of its adherents in support of the war effort, as nurses, "yeomanettes," in bond drives, and other patriotic efforts. In addition, by 1919, 29 of the 48 states allowed women some form of voting for presidential electors, either in party primaries or in presidential elections.

It is often thought that women had little power or influence over passing of the proposed Suffrage Amendment and that the male electorate could have prevented ratification. Of course, the Nineteenth Amendment, like all of the U.S. constitutional amendments, was not ratified by the electorate at large, but by the state legislatures. The role of women in that ratification was larger than is often remembered.

On January 10, 1918, when the Suffrage Amendment was passed by the U.S. House of Representatives, the general debate was opened by Congresswoman Jeanette Rankin of Montana, the first woman to serve in the

United States Congress. It was thought that the Senate would pass the Amendment as well, but a number of members died, affecting the vote count adversely. The Amendment finally passed in 1919 at the end of the session.

Women were serving in at least 11 state legislatures when those legislatures voted to ratify the Nineteenth Amendment. In Arizona, for example, the participation of women in the state's political life was so generally accepted that there was no controversy when the governor called a special session to vote on ratification. The session convened at noon February 12, 1920, and adjourned at 9:30 P.M. the same day. The resolution of ratification was introduced jointly by the four women members and passed both houses without a single dissenting vote.

The vote was not as easy in other states, but at least two dozen women members of their respective state legislatures took part in the ratification in Kansas, New York, Montana, Utah, California, Colorado, Oregon, Nevada, Idaho and Washington, as well as in Arizona. Women were also eligible to serve Wyoming, but none were present at the special sessions called to consider ratification.

Women Legislators, 1921–1937

Suffrage advocates were anxious for the states to ratify the Nineteenth Amendment before opposition had time to build. One of the most frustrating obstacles was that the Congress had passed the amendment late in its session after most state legislatures had closed their sessions. This provided an additional obstacle because the expense of calling a special session delayed ratification even in states where there was no controversy.

A further obstacle was that states which already had complete political rights for women were in no particular hurry to ratify. Despite these obstacles, in August 1920, the 36th state to ratify, Tennessee, put the amendment over the top and woman suffrage became the law of the land. This did not mean, however, that women were immediately eligible to run for office in every state.

In those states where eligibility for public office was described as the same as that for electors of the most numerous house, there was no problem. In some states, however, eligibility included a gender qualification. This required a further state constitutional amendment before women were eligible to run for the legislature. This was the case, for example, in Missouri, where women were not eligible to run until 1922.

In addition, in many states, ratification of the Nineteenth Amendment came after the filing deadline for candidates. As a result, women were excluded as candidates for the 1920 elections in a number of states. In the

Percentage of Women as Legislators in States as Women Became Eligible, 1895–1995

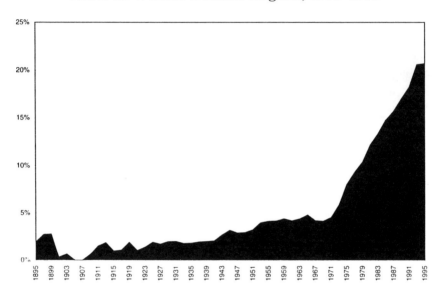

South, payment of the poll tax was a state requirement for voting and running for office, and in some states had to be paid in January at the beginning of the year. In 1920, women voted in the presidential elections in all but two states, Georgia and Mississippi, but were not eligible to run for state offices in several states. Finally in 1928, thirty-five years after the first women legislators were elected, the last state, Iowa, allowed women to run for the state legislature. It was eight more years, in 1936, when the 48th and last state, Louisiana, elected its first woman to the state legislature, Doris Lindsey Holland. This was 42 years after election of the first women legislators in Colorado. Doris Lindsey Holland Rhodes is still living and was recently inducted into the Louisiana Women's Hall of Fame.

Ideally, it was thought, women would increase their numbers each election until they attained parity in state legislatures with their fathers, husbands, brothers, and sons. In 1920, women in both major parties made a grand start by gaining legislative seats in each of the first three elections with a total of 141 women serving by 1925. Two years later, in 1927, this early growth came to an abrupt end when the total number of women in both major parties decreased, but women in both parties regained their losses and more in the 1929 state legislatures. In ensuing years, the growth of women legislators was interrupted when women became susceptible to the same partisan electoral pattern as men, gaining when their party gained and losing when their party lost. These interruptions

tions slowed down the drive to attain female representation in the state legislatures.

Women Legislators, 1937–1973

It is often argued that, after the initial surge of women legislators, there was a decline, which is variously attributed to a perception that women legislators were ineffective (1927), a perception that women were not sufficiently versed in business to be able to handle the economic issues of the Great Depression (1933), and a perception that with a growing danger of war, men were better suited to serve (1941), and after the war men should return to the civilian work force and women return to the home (1947).

The data compiled from the rosters in this book indicate that the total number of women have increased their numbers in all but six of the 38 legislative years from 1921 to 1995 (1927, 1933, 1947, 1961, 1967, 1969). Historically, the party that wins the White House also increases their numbers in the U.S. Congress and the state legislatures, the coattail effect. Two years later, in the Congressional elections, the opposition party usually enjoys increases in the Congress and the state legislatures. Between 1921 and 1995, state legislative returns deviated only five times from this partisan pattern (1935, 1961, 1977, 1989, 1993).

Women's historical pattern from 1920 to the present has been different. The number of women legislators of both major parties increased in 19 of the 38 legislative years, and decreased in two (1927, 1967). In the remaining 17 legislative years, women were more susceptible to the partisan coattails, with Democratic women failing to increase eight times alongside Democratic men, and Republican women failing to make gains nine times with Republican men. The overall percentage remained low, however, reaching 5 percent for the first time in 1973, more than seventy-five years after the first women were elected.

Women Legislators, 1973–1995

Since 1973, there has been a much more pronounced increase in the percentage of women legislators. Beginning in 1971, women legislators of both major parties registered gains six consecutive times, creating the longest trend of this phenomenon in the data, and tripling the percentage of women in the legislatures from 4 percent in 1971 to 12 in 1981. What caused this increased rate?

The Equal Rights Amendment passed the U. S. Congress in 1972 and was sent to the states for ratification. This issue, more than any other, propelled women into the state legislative political arena over the next ten years. In 1983, as the time period for ratification of the amendment by the states expired, two states short of ratification, the trend of increased numbers of women state legislators every two years in both major parties ended.

Between 1973 and 1993, the percentage increased from 5 to 20 percent, or about a one and a half percent improvement in each two year cycle. This contrasts with the preceding fifty years that it took to reach 5 percent, or less than half a percent per election cycle.

Until recently, if your name was Charlene and your nickname was "Charlie" and you were running for office, your campaign consultant would have advised you to use "Charlie" on the ballot because you might be able to take advantage of the bias to elect male candidates. Today that same consultant would tell you to use "Charlene" to take advantage of your "natural base" of women voters. This reflects fundamental changes in demography and voting behavior.

The 1960 elections were the last in which the majority of the electorate was male, but since there were more women than men of the voting age population, this meant that the percentage of women who voted, the voter participation rate, was lower than that of men. In other words, in forty years of full suffrage, women's numbers had grown, but so had their life expectancy rate, creating a substantial demographic advantage in the universe of eligible voters. If women were to reach the level of the male participation rate, there would be an even larger number of women voters than male voters.

The Women's Vote Analysis (Cox, Foreman, Heidepriem, and Lake, 1986) tracked the baby boomer generation that started voting in 1968. We found that each new cohort of women voted at a higher rate than men. In the past, this had not been true of first time voters as they entered the voting age population. This gigantic wave of baby boomers, as they have matured, have been more willing to elect women candidates, and they were replacing older voters with a long-standing bias favoring male candidates. The year 1980 marked a significant milestone, because for the first time nationwide the voter participation rate of women was equal to that of men. Since then, women have voted at a higher rate than men, and a continuous difference in voting has developed between women and men on a variety of issues, the gender gap.

Partisan Trends

Republican women dominated the suffrage movement. In the early period, they tended to be better educated and to have better financial resources than their Democratic counterparts. As a result, after the passage of national suffrage, Republican women legislators represented a higher percentage of all Republican legislators than did Democratic women of Democratic legislators.

Percentage of Women Among State
Legislators per Political Party, 1895–1995

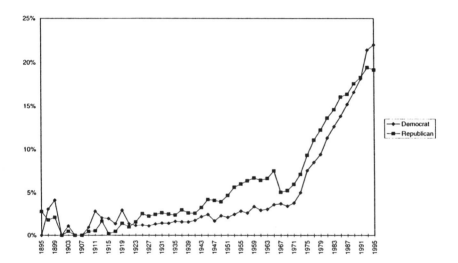

This trend lasted from 1921 until 1993 when, for the first time, the figures for Democratic women legislators exceeded those for the Republican women legislators. Results from the 1994 election indicate that Democratic women, even though they decreased in numbers for the first time since 1971, further increased their percentage of Democratic legislators because their losses were proportionately less than Democratic men.

Republican women have not kept pace. After 18 years of continuous increases in their numbers, they failed to gain in 1982 in the first Congressional year elections after Ronald Reagan became president. In the next Congressional year elections, in 1986, Republican women decreased their numbers. In the most recent election, even though they increased their numbers, Republican women shrank in their percentage of Republican legislators.

The partisan trend in the nineties appears to be more like that in the eighties than the dual increases for women in both parties in the seventies. The percentage of all women legislators barely increased in 1995, by only one-tenth of one percentage point, because so many Democratic women lost and so few Republican women won. In 1990, the report that, for the first time, more people lived in the suburbs than in a rural or urban setting was thought to be good news for women, since suburban voters tend to be younger and more willing to elect women. With a record number of newly drawn districts in 1992, women legislators in both parties gained and registered a 12 percent increase in the national total.

The 1994 elections were the most partisan elections in almost 50 years, rendering a turnover of control from the Democrats to the Republicans in both the U.S. House and the Senate. In the states, Republicans, for the first time since 1957, gained control of more state legislatures, 19, than Democrats, 18, while sharing control in the other 12. Preliminary data reveal some clues to the losses by women candidates in these political circumstances. Some independent women voters who supported the Democratic tickets in 1992 supported Republican tickets in 1994, and many other women did not vote, depriving Democratic women candidates of their basic constituencies of past elections. Republican women candidates fared better than the Democratic women, but did not win at the same rate as Republican men, creating the reduction of the increase from 12 percentage points in 1993 to less than one tenth of one percentage point in 1995.

House Membership by Gender and Party, 1995

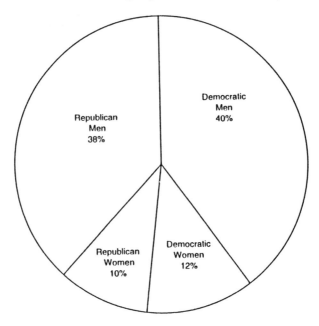

Republican Men 38%

Democratic Men 40%

Republican Women 10%

Democratic Women 12%

Senate Membership by Gender and Party, 1995

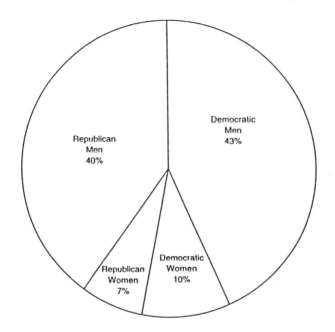

These partisan trends are important to the future of women state legislators who, having passed the 20 percent threshold, are more visible in the political arena. Many are now seeking leadership positions, and this partisan trend in 1995 seems encouraging for Democratic women but may slow the advance for Republican women in achieving these new goals.

Regional Trends

As we have seen, the West led the nation in granting suffrage and in electing women to legislative positions. Soon after the granting of women's suffrage nationally, however, the North caught up. From 1933 until 1987, the North had a higher percentage of women legislators than any other region. In 1987, the West once again surpassed the North and continues to be the region with the highest percentage of female legislators.

The Midwest has had a lower percentage of women legislators than the West, but since 1971 has had about the same rate of increase as the West. The South has the lowest percentage of women legislators and this percentage is increasing at a slower rate than any other region.

National women's suffrage in 1920 was simultaneous with another

Percentage of Women Among
Western State Legislators, 1895–1995

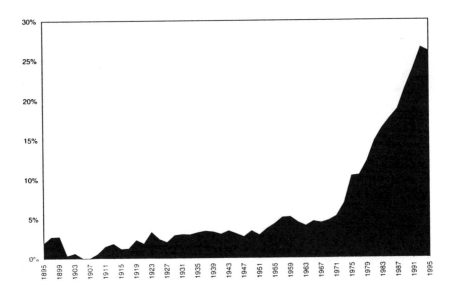

Percentage of Women Among
Northern State Legislators, 1919–1995

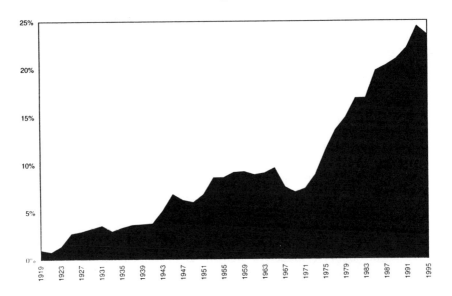

Percentage of Women Among
Midwestern State Legislators, 1919–1995

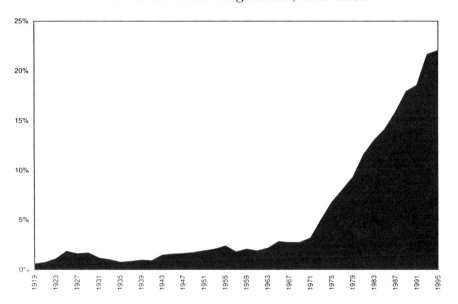

Percentage of Women Among
Southern State Legislators, 1921–1995

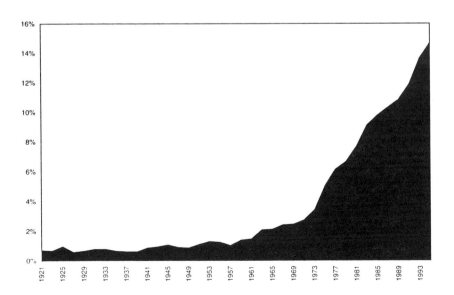

Comparison of Women State
Legislators, by Region, 1921–1995

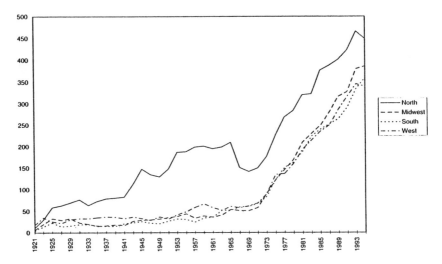

important event in U.S. political history. For the first time, the U.S. Census reported, a majority of the population lived in urban areas. Nevertheless, the imbalance of political power favoring rural areas remained in effect through a system based on small towns in the North and on counties in the other regions. Forty years later, the "one man one vote" in *Baker vs. Carr* (1962) and *Reynolds vs. Sims* (1964) rulings finally forced proportional political representation for the urban population. In those cases, the Supreme Court ruled that representation must be based on population and not the geographical lines used by many states. Alongside these adjustments for representation, the 1965 Voting Rights Act gained voting and political rights for African Americans, who had long been disenfranchised and not represented in an entire region, the South.

These two events, representation of population, and minority voting rights, greatly impacted the gender composition of the state legislatures in 1967 and 1969. Women still constituted less than 5 percent of the legislators, and very few ever reached leadership positions. When the battles began in state legislatures to draw the new lines, women were too few in numbers and too weak politically to hold onto their seats. The national total of women plummeted 15 percentage points in 1967 and continued to decline in 1969.

The decrease in numbers was greatest in the North, where women established strong traditions of public service in the town based representation. More than half the country's women legislators were in the North from 1935 to 1965. In 1965 Northern women constituted 55 percent of all women legislators, and that percentage dropped 10 points to 45 percent in 1969, and to 26 percent in 1995. Downsizing of the legislatures by almost one-third, as part of the reforms in Vermont, Connecticut, and Ohio, reduced the number of seats available to both women and men, but women legislators decreased proportionately more than men in those states in the succeeding elections.

While the number of women legislators in the North and Midwest declined during the reform years, women made gains in the South and the West. After the initial restructuring, women began to make larger gains outside the North, especially minority women who had been excluded in the South and were absent from the underrepresented urban centers in the other regions. It may be that the political reforms played a key role in the large decrease of women in the legislatures in the sixties *and* the large increases that followed in the seventies. There is a great need for a thorough examination of the impact of these two political events on the history of women in elections in each state.

Future Trends

The question of representation, both in Congress and the state legislatures, has been debated and changed throughout U.S. history. At the constitutional convention in 1787, it was decided to "count" women, children, Native Americans, aliens and three-fifths of all slaves for purposes of representation in the Congress, even though almost all of them could not vote. State constitutions varied widely on the issue of suffrage. For example, aliens could vote but not hold office in several states.

After women won suffrage in a referendum in Colorado in 1893, the Colorado Populist Party added newly enfranchised women to their county and state party committees in equal numbers to men, but the Republicans and Democrats added only one woman to each committee. Colorado women pushed for successful state legislation to require equal representation on party committees and direct primary elections. The Colorado model became known as the "50/50" plan and was adopted by both national committees and some states when the Nineteenth Amendment was ratified.

The membership of state legislatures has been adjusted by expansion or reduction numerous times for partisan, racial, or demographic reasons, but there was no advocacy to expand state legislatures in conjunction with the coming of national suffrage for women in the United States. A few countries have experimented with gender based plans for their democratically elected legislatures. President Anwar Sadat initiated set aside seats for women candidates in the Egyptian national parliament, and Brazil instituted

State Legislators by Region and Gender, 1995

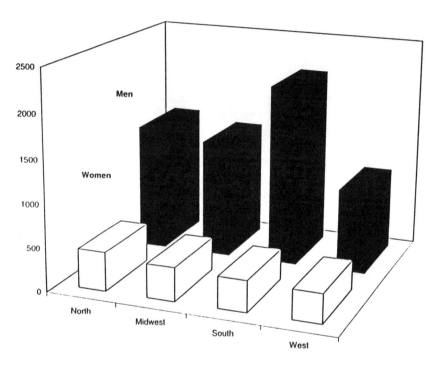

a gender allocation for party nominations to the national parliament last year.

The movement to limit terms of state legislators in the United States is becoming a reality and may provide a new opportunity for increased gender representation. According to a report by the National Conference of State Legislatures, 20 states have passed laws or constitutional amendments to restrict the number of terms or years of service in their legislatures. The new laws go into effect in the first two states, California and Maine, in the 1996 elections. Since many incumbents will be prevented from running, the number of "open seats" available to newcomers may increase. Recent studies by Barbara Burrell in 1994 (*A Woman's Place Is in the House*) and the National Women's Political Caucus in 1994 (*Perception and Reality* by Jody Newman) have shown that women candidates are just as successful as men when they are running in open seats. These latest reforms may result in more women running and more women winning elections to the state legislatures.

Organization of the Book

This book recognizes the public service of more than 6,000 women in the 50 state and seven territorial legislatures from 1895 to 1995. From the first three women in Colorado in 1895 to the 1,535 women in 1995.

The layout of the book is simple. States and territories are arranged alphabetically in one sequence. A brief introduction for each state or territory includes the history of suffrage and political rights for women in that state or territory and the legislature's size and terms of the members. A summary of the total number of women who have served is listed and followed by a graph depicting the percentage of women every two years. The senate and house rosters of women legislators include their name, city and county of residence, party affiliation, and years of service with notes for partial terms.

Behind the simple layout, however, lie a number of complex issues. Readers can make better use of the book if they understand those issues.

Elections and Appointments

I have attempted to include all women who were ever elected or appointed even though some may never have participated in a legislative session. Election laws and rules of procedure in the legislature differ from state to state. In some cases, members may be sworn in and then unseated after an election dispute. Anna S. Larkin (H-R) was elected in New Mexico in November 1924, seated and participated in the legislature when it convened in January 1925, but was unseated in February after an election investigation determined that there had been fraud in her district. Although she was fully exonerated from any knowledge of or participation in the fraud, she and another Republican were replaced by two male Democrats.

States use a variety of methods to determine how to fill legislative vacancies and these laws changed from time to time throughout the period

covered in this book. In Oregon, for example, the governor has the power
to appoint an interim legislator who holds the office until a special election
is called. In some states, local political party officials nominate the candidate to fill a vacancy. In most states the vacancies are filled by appointment by the governor or by special election, but sometimes the vacancy is
not filled if the regularly scheduled election is near. Often, an appointment
is made to fill a vacancy when a special session is called. Margaret Bognet
Pike, a Democrat from Boise City, Ada County, was appointed to the Idaho
Senate on July 28, 1936, to serve in two special sessions, and again on November 28, 1938, to the House to serve in a special session.

Names

In the past, women were often listed in the official state rosters with
a title, either "Mrs." or "Miss," a practice that helped me identify just who
was female. However, there were females on these rosters who had no title
and who were missed by earlier researchers. Married women were often
listed with their husband's names, and this led to some confusion when I
tried to determine the given name of a woman. I discovered that Mrs. Lacy
Stewart in Texas was named Maribelle and her husband Lacy, and that Mrs.
Douglas Cook Webb in Kentucky was named Douglas. All women are
listed with their given first name and their last name at the time of their
service. If a last name change is known, reference is made to the additional
listing under the second last name.

Legislatures

Forty-nine states have two chambers. The lower chamber is usually
named the House and the upper chamber, Senate. Some have different
titles. The Assembly is the lower chamber of the New York Legislature, the
General Assembly in Colorado is the state legislature. Members of the New
Jersey Legislature who are in the lower house, the General Assembly, are
called delegates. The lower house of the Maryland General Assembly is
called the House of Delegates.

Nebraska, since 1936, is the only state with a unicameral legislature.
Guam adopted a unicameral legislature in 1951 and the Virgin Islands, in
1954. Most women who served in both chambers were in the lower chamber first and then the upper chamber. There are, however, a few women
who reversed this order of service.

Presently, the smallest state legislature is Nebraska's unicameral legislature with 49 members, followed by Alaska with 60, Delaware with 62,

and Nevada with 63. The largest state legislature is New Hampshire with 424, followed by Pennsylvania with 253, Georgia with 236, Minnesota with 201, and Massachusetts with 200. Connecticut downsized from 294 to 187, Vermont from 246 to 180, and Ohio from 169 to 132 during the reforms of the 1960s, and Massachusetts from 280 to 200 in 1978 and Illinois from 235 to 177 in 1982.

Because of the large differences in size and changes in size, data for women legislators are presented as a percentage of all legislators for comparative analysis in a graph for each state. The reader should keep in mind that one female legislator will yield more than one percentage point in the smaller legislatures and less than a quarter of a percentage point in the larger. It takes four to five women in New Hampshire to yield the same percentage as one in Nevada.

The total number of legislators in states where women were eligible to run for the state legislature in 1895 was 155 for Colorado and Wyoming. By 1929 when women could run in all 48 states, the number of legislators expanded to 7,556, and to 7,771 when Alaska and Hawaii were added in 1959. The highest number of both male and female legislators between 1895 and 1995 was reached in 1965 when the total was 7,854 mainly as a result of the fact that states kept adding seats in unsuccessful attempts to comply with the legal challenges on representation and civil rights in the 1950s and 1960s. In 1995 the total number of legislators was 7,424 (since 1993); the number was 7,461 from 1983 to 1991.

City and County of Residence

The city and county of residence is listed with each woman state legislator because they are the most consistent geographic identifiers throughout the period. State legislatures redraw district lines after the decennial national census and a legislator may serve in several different districts as a result. In 1894, representation in the state legislatures in the North was based on small towns, and in other regions of the United States the county was the basic unit of representation. In the West when a new county was created the inhabitants sometimes acquired a seat in the lower house no matter how sparsely populated the area might be at the time. In the North, communities were eligible to become towns and acquire a seat in the lower house when the number of inhabitants reached a certain level. Since the political reforms of the 1960s, representation has been based on population and districts have usually been identified by a number.

Terms

Most states hold legislative elections in November of even years, and convene the legislative session in the following odd year. The two years from November to November in even years is commonly referred to as the election cycle. The two years from January to January in the odd years is commonly referred to as the legislative cycle. A graph is printed for each state showing the percentage of women who served in the legislature in the spring of the odd year following the even year elections. Six states have a different pattern. Mississippi, New Jersey, and Virginia hold legislative elections in odd years and convene sessions in even years. Kentucky held elections in odd years until 1984, when they switched to even years. Maryland held elections in odd years until 1924, when they instituted four year terms for both chambers to be elected every fourth even year. Louisiana held elections and a convening session in even years until 1975, when they began holding elections in odd years but continued to convene sessions in even years.

As of 1995, terms of the senate and house in all states are either two or four years. In the past, two states held annual elections for their lower chamber: New York until 1936 and New Jersey until 1946. Today, all lower house members are elected at the same time in all the states. Most senates with four year terms have staggered elections with one half being elected every two years. Nine states with four year senate terms elect all their senators at the same time (Alabama, Kansas, Louisiana, Maryland, Minnesota, Mississippi, New Mexico, and South Carolina, and Virginia). Some states adjust their four year senate terms to the U.S. census decennial years: New Jersey has a two year term and two four-year terms to add up to the 10 years between the U.S. censuses. Illinois senators draw lots for three categories: 2-4-4 year terms, 4-2-4, and 4-4-2.

The number of terms or years for service is now limited in 20 state legislatures. The limited number of terms or years of service varies from state to state and information about this is included at the beginning of each state's section of the book.

In the rosters, all terms of service are listed for each woman in two year increments, except New York and New Jersey, where the one year terms are listed. Legislative service begins with election day in some states, the beginning of the next calendar year in some states, and the first day of the session with the administering of the oath of office. For uniformity, all listings begin with the odd year except for Louisiana, Mississippi, New Jersey, Virginia, and Kentucky until 1984, where the term begins in the even years.

Some women changed party designations. This is indicated in the roster. The listing of terms of office will be interrupted by a semicolon followed by the abbreviation for the new party for which the candidate ran in the term[s] that follow.

Partial terms are noted with asterisks. Dates of appointment and special elections, or resignation or death while in office are listed in the notes at the end of the rosters. The dates are followed by the name in parentheses of the legislator who is being replaced by a woman entering the legislature. A bracketed [F] follows the name in the parentheses to indicate a female. For a woman leaving the legislature, the same procedure is used for her replacement. This information is supplied to assist the reader in determining how many women were serving at specific points in time and to prevent "double counting" when a woman resigns and is replaced by a woman.

Graphs

The percentage of women legislators depicted in the graphs is based on the number who were serving in the spring of the legislative year. By April all states have convened their sessions, and most vacancies resulting from election or appointment to other state or U.S. offices have been filled. If a woman was elected in November but resigned before spring, she was not included for the total that year. If a woman was appointed or won a special election in February, she is counted for that year.

Party

All women are listed with their party affiliation, including Nonpartisan and Independent. The party graph shows the percentage of women within their own party, Democrat and Republican, as women became eligible to serve in each state. Women who served with minor party labels, Populist, Progressive, Farm Labor, Socialist, and those who are Nonpartisan or Independent are grouped together in one category as "Independent" (sometimes called "minor party" or "other") and are not included in the partisan graph. Nebraska is included in the partisan statistics until 1937, when nonpartisan elections were implemented and their membership was moved into the "Independent" category. North Dakota members are included in the "Independent" category until 1937, when party alignment data for Democrats and Republicans are available. Minnesota is included in the "Independent" category until 1973, at which time partisan elections were implemented. Territories are not included in the partisan graphs.

Information on the political composition of the legislatures was compiled from numerous sources: state manuals, *Senate* and *House Journals*, *Session Laws*, and newspapers, and in one state from the office of the Clerk of the Senate. In addition, since 1937, the Council of State Governments has included a state legislative chart showing the political composition of the state legislatures in their biennial publication *The Book of the States*.

National Graph

States were added to the national total as women were eligible to serve in the legislature, beginning in 1895 with Colorado and Wyoming. On the eve of national suffrage, in 1919, there were 12 states that allowed women in the state legislatures. By 1929, women could serve in all 48 state legislatures. Alaska and Hawaii were added as states in 1959.

Regional Graphs

Regional graphs depict the gender composition of state legislatures in the four standard U.S. census regions. This provides a way to compare the state graphs with trends in their own region as well as with overall national trends. The Northern Region includes the following nine states: Connecticut, Massachusetts, Maine, New Hampshire, New Jersey, New York, Pennsylvania, Rhode Island, and Vermont. The Midwestern Region has 12 states: Iowa, Illinois, Indiana, Kansas, Michigan, Minnesota, Missouri, North Dakota, Nebraska, Ohio, South Dakota, and Wisconsin. The Southern Region has 16 states: Alabama, Arkansas, Delaware, Florida, Georgia, Kentucky, Louisiana, Maryland, Mississippi, North Carolina, Oklahoma, South Carolina, Tennessee, Texas, Virginia, and West Virginia. The Western Region has 13 states: Alaska, Arizona, California, Colorado, Hawaii, Idaho, Montana, New Mexico, Nevada, Oregon, Utah, Washington, and Wyoming.

Bibliography

This bibliography is divided into two parts: Rosters of Women State Legislators by Election Year, and Rosters of Women State Legislators and Historical Rosters of State Legislators by State.

The first part includes lists of women state legislators by election year cycle. In the early years, there were no "lists" so I have included some articles about these early women lawmakers. *The Woman's Journal* (later, *The Woman Citizen*) has the most comprehensive national coverage up to 1931, when it ceased publication. *The Woman's Journal* published in Boston by Alice Stone Blackwell merged with Carrie Chapman Catt's *National Suffrage News* of New York in 1917 and was renamed *The Woman Citizen*. Although their reports sometimes contained errors and omissions, these are the most comprehensive lists of women legislators that I have found for the early period. The selections that follow are not comprehensive but are an attempt to provide sources for the names of women legislators by election years. *The Woman's Journal* and *The Woman Citizen* are available on microfilm and microfiche.

The last section of the first part of the bibliography is a selection of national rosters, directories and biographies of state legislators and sources for state rosters of legislators by year.

The second part of the bibliography is dedicated to rosters of women state legislators in each of the states and territories. Many of these lists are now updated by a state office after elections; some of them, however, are not. The first listing for each state is the most recent list of women state legislators, followed by older lists. A second entry is included for an historical roster of the state legislature in the states where they have been compiled. Although these general rosters do not include gender identification, they are an excellent resource for determining dates of service and other types of information.

Chart of First Women

A chart of the first women in each state and territorial legislature provides an historical overview of the history of women in public office in the United States. Additional charts have been compiled from the research for this book of the first women in leadership positions, the first to serve from political parties, the longest serving, and the first women of color in the state legislatures.

Much is known about the first African American women state legislators, but more research is needed about Asian American political women.

Dolly Lucille Smith Cusker Akers of the Assiniboine Tribe who served in Montana in 1933 is often listed as the first Native American woman state legislator. In answer to my query about Cora Belle Reynolds Anderson, the first woman to serve in the Michigan House in 1925, I received a letter from James Dompier, president of the Baraga County Historical Society in which he mentioned that there was some indication that she was Native American. Over the course of two years, with the help of the society, and examination of the Census and records at the National Archives, I was able to confirm that Cora Anderson's maternal family was La Pointe Band, Chippewa.

The search for the first Hispanic woman state legislator proved to be the longest and most complicated. I found no claim of who was first. By a process of elimination, I determined that the first most likely served in New Mexico. I narrowed the possibilities to two women, Mrs. Ezequiel Gallegos and Mrs. P. Saiz who were elected in 1930. I asked Dr. Anselmo F. Arellano, Director of the Center for Regional Studies at the University of

New Mexico about Gallegos. He had relatives in Wagon Mound, and subsequently learned that her name was Fedelina Lucero Gallegos and interviewed her descendants for the Oral History Program. Mrs. Saiz proved more elusive for she was from Mangas, a town that no longer exists. Ms. Kathy Flynn, editor of the *New Mexico Blue Book* in the office of Secretary of State Stephanie Gonzales, finally solved the mystery. She located a senior citizen now living in a neighboring town who remembered that Porfirria Hidalgo Saiz came from Mexico to attend convent school in Socorro and then taught school in Mangas.

List of Abbreviations

Legislature

H   House

S   Senate

Party

D   Democratic
DFL   Democratic Farm Labor
      (Minnesota)
F-L   Farm-Labor
I   Independent
IR   Independent Republican
      (Minnesota)
IVA   Independent Voters
      Association (North
      Dakota)

Np   Nonpartisan
NPL   Non Partisan League
      (North Dakota)
Pop   Populists
Pro   Progressive
R   Republican
Soc   Socialist
SR   Silver Republican
TSR   Teller Silver Republican
      (Colorado)

Political Parties in Puerto Rico

ER   Republican Statehood;
      Partido Estadista Re-
      publicano
Lib   Liberal; Partido Liberal
PNP   New Progressive (R); Par-
      tido Nuevo Progresista
Pop   Popular; Partido Popular

PPD   Popular Democrat (D);
      Partido Popular Demo-
      cratico
URS   Republican Socialist Union;
      Union Republicana-
      Socialista

Territories

AS   American Samoa
GU   Guam
NI   Northern Mariana Islands

PR   Puerto Rico
VI   Virgin Islands

Women Legislators

Arranged alphabetically by state or territory

ALABAMA (1923–1995)

Alabama women gained suffrage on August 26, 1920. Payment of the poll tax was waived for women to allow them to vote in the November 1920 federal elections. Women first voted in state elections in 1922 and Harriet Hooker Wilkins (D–Selma, Dallas County) won election to the House of Representatives.

State elections are held every four years for 35 senators and 105 representatives. The last elections were in 1994, and the next elections were scheduled for 1998. Vacancies are filled by special election.

24 women have served in the Alabama Legislature:
   3 in the Senate
   23 in the House
   (2 in the House and Senate)

Women as Percentage of Alabama Legislators

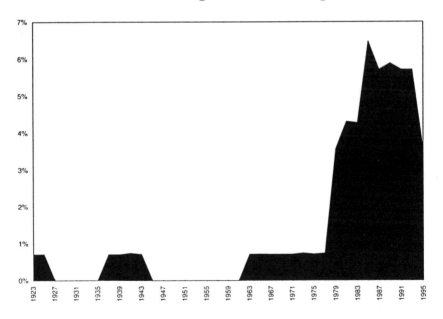

Senate
4 Year Terms

Name	City, County	Party	Legislative Year
Bedsole, Ann	Mobile, Mobile	R	1983 1985 1987 1989 1991 1993
Russell, Sundra Escott see Escott	Birmingham, Jefferson	D	1993* 1995
Strong, Frances	Demopolis, Marengo	D	1983* 1985

House
4 Year Terms

Name	City, County	Party	Legislative Year
Bedsole, Ann	Mobile, Mobile	R	1979 1981
Berryman, Kylie Terry	Moulton, Lawrence	D	1969*
Boyd, Barbara Bigsby	Anniston, Calhoun	D	1995
Bugg, June	Gadsden, Etowah	D	1983* 1985 1987 1989 1991 1993*
Davis, Patricia	Birmingham, Jefferson	D	1983 1985 1987 1989*
Escott, Sundra E. see Russell	Birmingham, Jefferson	D	1981* 1983 1985 1987 1989
Fields, Clara Stone	Mobile, Mobile	D	1963 1965 1967 1969
Graham, Betty Carol	Alexander City, Tallaposa	D	1995
Gullatt, Jane	Phenix City, Russell	D	1989* 1991 1993
Hall, Laura	Huntsville, Madison	D	1993* 1995
Kennedy, Yvonne	Mobile, Mobile	D	1979* 1981 1983 1985 1987 1989 1991 1993 1995
Marietta, Beth	Theodore, Mobile	D	1983* 1985 1987 1989
McDowell, Bobbie Will Greene	Bessemer, Jefferson	D	1983* 1985 1987 1989 1991 1993
Pool, Sybil	Linden, Marengo	D	1935* 1937 1939 1941 1943 1945*
Quarles, Marilyn	Springville, Calhoun	D	1975 1977
Rockhold, Lois	Mobile, Mobile	D	1991 1993
Russell, Sundra Escott see Escott	Birmingham, Jefferson	D	1991 1993*
Smith, Martha Jo	Huntsville, Madison	D	1979 1981
Thomas, Louphenia	Birmingham, Jefferson	D	1977*
Thornton, Jarushia	Birmingham, Jefferson	D	1983*
Ward, Shelby Dean	Opelika, Lee	D	1977* 1979 1981
Wilkins, Harriet Hooker	Selma, Dallas	D	1923 1925

Alabama House, continued

Name	City, County	Party	Legislative Year
Wynot, Retha Deal	Gadsden, Etowah	D	1971 1973
Zoghby, Mary S.	Mobile, Mobile	D	1979 1981 1983 1985 1987 1989 1991 1993

*Notes:

Berryman, Kylie Terry—Elected Oct. 21, 1969 (Berryman)
Bugg, June—Elected reapportionment Nov. 1983. Died May 19, 1993 (Page)
Davis, Patricia—Expelled 1990
Escott, Sundra E.—Elected Jan. 27, 1981 (Hillard), resigned March 1993 elected to Senate (Hillard)
Gullatt, Jane—Elected 1989
Hall, Laura—Elected Aug. 13, 1993 (Grayson)
Kennedy, Yvonne—Elected Jan. 1, 1979 (Cooper)
Marietta, Beth—Elected reapportionment Nov. 1983
McDowell, Bobbie Will Greene—Elected reapportionment Nov. 1983
Pool, Sybil—Appointed July 1935, elected Nov. 3, 1936 (Harrison), resigned 1944
Russell, Sundra Escott *see Escott*
Strong, Frances—Elected reapportionment Nov. 1983
Thomas, Louphenia—Elected July 1977 (Porter)
Thornton, Jarushia—Lost reapportionment election Nov. 1983
Ward, Shelby Dean—Elected May 11, 1977 (Higginbotham)

ALASKA, Territory of (1937–1958)

Alaska women gained suffrage in 1913 and the right to run for state office in 1934 from the territorial legislature. In 1936, Nell Scott (D–Seldovia) was the first woman elected to the Alaska Territorial Legislature.

State elections were held every two years for 24 representatives who served two year terms and 16 senators who served four year terms. In 1945 the Senate was doubled to 16 and the House increased to 24. There are no counties in Alaska. Vacancies were filled by Governor's appointment.

16 women served in the Alaska Territorial Legislature:
  3 in the Senate
  16 in the House
  (3 in the House and Senate)

Women as Percentage of
Alaskan Territorial Legislators

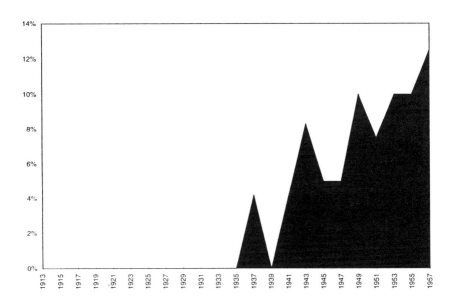

Senate
4 Year Terms

Name	City, County	Party	Legislative Year
Barnes, Doris M.	Wrangell	R	1953 1955
Bullock, Edith R.	Kotzebue	R	1957
Garnick, Anita	Juneau	I	1949 1951

House
2 Year Terms

Name	City	Party	Legislative Year
Awes, Dorothy	Anchorage	D	1957
Barnes, Doris M.	Wrangell	R	1949 1951
Bullock, Edith R.	Kotzebue	R	1953 1955
Cross, Bess	Kotzebue	D	1945
Dale, Essie R.	Fairbanks	D	1949
Dimock, Barbara D.	Anchorage	R	1953
Engstrom, Thelma Catherine	Juneau	R	1947

Territory of Alaska House, continued

Name	City, County	Party	Legislative Year
Fischer, Helen	Anchorage	D	1957
Garnick, Anita	Juneau	R	1947
Gunderson, Amerlia A.	Ketchikan	D	1949 1951
Jenne, Crystal S.	Juneau	D	1941 1943
Linck, Alaska S.	Fairbanks	D	1943 1945
Prior, Dorothy M.	Anchorage	R	1953
Ryan, Irene E.	Anchorage	D	1955 1957
Scott, Nell	Juneau	D	1937
Sweeney, Doris M.	Juneau	D	1955 1957

ALASKA, State of (1959–1995)

In the first elections after statehood was granted in 1958, Senator Irene E. Ryan (D–Anchorage) and Representatives Helen Fischer (D–Anchorage) and Doris M. Sweeney (D–Juneau) were elected and were joined by Representative Blanche L. McSmith (D–Anchorage), who was appointed April 26, 1959 to fill a vacancy.

Women as Percentage of Alaska State Legislators

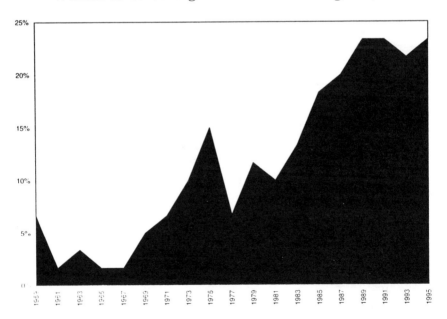

State elections are held every two even years for 40 representatives who serve two year terms and 20 senators who serve four year terms. Vacancies are filled by governor's appointment. There are no counties in Alaska.

52 women have served in the Alaska Legislature:
    14 in the Senate
    44 in the House
    (6 in the House and Senate)

Senate
4 Year Terms

Name	City	Party	Legislative Year
Banfield, Mildred H.	Juneau	R	1963*
Chance, Genie	Anchorage	D	1975
Collins, Virginia M.	Anchorage	R	1991
Devris, Edna B.	Palmer	R	1985
Fahrenkamp, Bettye	Fairbanks	D	1979 1981 1983 1985 1987 1989 1991
Faiks, Jan	Anchorage	R	1983 1985 1987 1989
Green, Lyda	Wasilla	R	1995
Lincoln, Georgianna	Rampart	D	1993 1995
Little, Suzanne R.	Soldotna	D	1993
Pearce, Drue	Anchorage	R	1989 1991 1993 1995
Polland, Kathryn	Kodiak	D	1969* 1971 1973 1975 1977
Ryan, Irene E.	Anchorage	D	1959
Salo, Judith E.	Kenai	D	1993 1995
Sturgulewski, Arliss	Anchorage	R	1979 1981 1983 1985 1987 1989 1991

House
2 Year Terms

Name	City	Party	Legislative Year
Banfield, Mildred H.	Juneau	R	1967 1969 1971 1973
Barnes, Ramona L.	Anchorage	R	1979 1981 1983 1987 1989 1991 1993 1995
Beirne, Helen D.	Spenard	R	1969 1973 1975
Branson, Margaret Cooper	Landing	R	1979
Brown, M. Kay	Anchorage	D	1987 1989 1991 1993 1995
Bruckman, Betty	Anchorage	D	1991
Buchholdt, Thelma	Anchorage	D	1975 1977 1979 1981
Cato, Bette M.	Valdez	D	1981 1983 1985 1987 1989*
Chance, Genie	Anchorage	D	1969 1971 1973
Collins, Virginia M.	Anchorage	R	1985 1987 1989
Davis, Bettye J.	Anchorage	D	1991 1993 1995

State of Alaska House, continued

Name	City	Party	Legislative Year
Davis, Cheri	Ketchikan	R	1989 1991
Fischer, Helen	Anchorage	D	1959 1971 1973 1975*
Hanley, Alyce A.	Anchorage	R	1985 1987 1989
Herrmann, Adelheid	Naknek	D	1983 1985 1987
Hurley, Katherine T.	Wasilla	D	1985
Itta, Brenda T.	Barrow	D	1975
James, Jeanette A.	N. Pole	R	1993 1995
Johnson, Grace	Nome	D	1961*
Kelley, Ramona M.	Anchorage	D	1975 1977*
Lacher, Barbara	Palmer	R	1983
Lincoln, Georgianna	Rampart	R	1991
MacLean, Eileen Panigee	Cantwell	D	1989 1991 1993 I 1995
Masek, Beverly	Willow	R	1995
McSmith, Blanche L.	Anchorage	D	1959*
Miller, Jo Ann	Chugiak	R	1973
Miller, Mary	Chugiak	R	1991
Munson, Joyce	Anchorage	D	1979
Nicholia, Irene Kay	Tanana	D	1993 1995
Ostrosky, Kathryn	Anchorage	D	1975
Pearce, Drue	Anchorage	R	1985 1987
Phillips, Gail	Homer	R	1991 1993 1995
Pinkerton, Lucille	Ketchikan	D	1965
Robinson, Caren	Juneau	D	1995
Rudd, Lisa	Anchorage	D	1975* 1977
Salo, Judith E.	Soldotna	D	1989*
Smith, Sarah J.	Fairbanks	D	1977 1979 1981
Spohnholz, Ann	Anchorage	D	1989*
Sullivan, Susan	Anchorage	D	1975
Sweeney, Doris M.	Juneau	D	1959 1961 1963
Tischer, Mae	Anchorage	R	1983
Toohey, Cynthia D.	Anchorage	R	1993 1995
Ulmer, Fran T.	Juneau	D	1987 1989 1991 1993
Wallis, F. Kay	Fort Yukon	D	1985 1987 1989

*Notes:
Banfield, Mildred H. — Appointed 1963 (Engstrom)
Cato, Bette M. — Resigned Jan. 8, 1990
Fischer, Helen — Resigned June 30, 1976
Johnson, Grace — Appointed Dec. 1961 (Johnson)
Kelley, Ramona M. — Resigned Jan. 9, 1977
McSmith, Blanche L. — Appointed April 26, 1959 (Rader)
Polland, Kathryn — Appointed March 1970 (Polland)
Rudd, Lisa — Appointed Jan. 12, 1976 (Bowman)
Salo, Judith E. — Appointed June 25, 1990
Spohnholz, Ann — Appointed Jan. 9, resigned April 5, 1989

AMERICAN SAMOA (1953–1995)

Mabel C. Reid of Maoputasi and Zilpher Jennings of Swains Island were the first women elected to the territorial legislature in 1952.

Territorial legislative non-partisan elections are held every two years for 21 representatives who serve two year terms and 18 senators who serve four year terms.

4 women have served in the American Samoa Territorial Legislature:
    0 in the Senate
    4 in the House

Women as Percentage of American Samoa Legislators

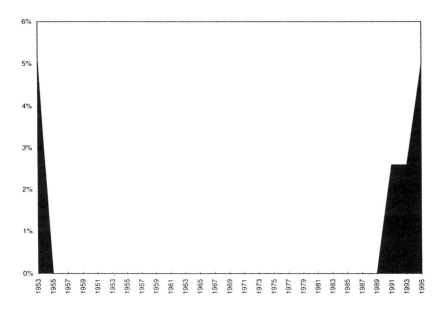

American Samoa, continued

House
2 Year Terms

Name	City, County	Party	Legislative Year
Haleck, Fiasili Puni E.	Pago Pago, Maoputasi	Np	1991 1993 1995
Jennings, Zilpher	Swains Island	Np	1953
Reid, Mabel C.	Maoputasi	Np	1953
Thompson, Eliza Jennings	Swains Island	Np	1995

ARIZONA (1915–1995)

Arizona women gained school suffrage from the Territorial Legislature in 1887 and full suffrage after statehood by a constitutional amendment placed on the ballot by referendum petition in 1912. Women first voted in state elections in 1914 and elected Senator Frances Willard Munds (D–Prescott, Yavapai) and Represenative Rachel Emma A. Berry (D–St. Johns, Apache). Berry's daughter, Mary Alice Patterson (D–Phoenix) served as a representative in 1929.

Women as Percentage of Arizona Legislators

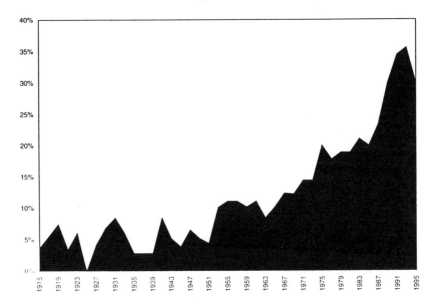

From 1912 to 1953 the House had only 35 members and the Senate 19. By 1964, the House had increased to 80 and the Senate to 28. In 1966, the membership was decreased to the present 30 senators and 60 representatives who serve two year terms. State legislative service is limited to four consecutive terms. Vacancies are filled by governor's appointment and special election.

131 women have served in the Arizona Legislature:
  33 in the Senate
  116 in the House
  (18 in the House and Senate)

Senate
2 Year Terms

Name	City, County	Party	Legislative Year
Alston, Lela	Phoenix, Maricopa	D	1977 1979 1981 1983 1985 1987 1989 1991 1993
Bollinger, Thelma C.	Kingman, Mohave	D	1959* 1961
Brewer, Janice Kay	Glendale, Maricopa	R	1987 1989 1991 1993 1995
Burgess, Isabel	Phoenix, Maricopa	R	1967 1969*
Burns, Brenda	Glendale, Maricopa	R	1995
Bush, Nellie T.	Parker, Yuma	D	1935
Camping, Gertrude	Phoenix, Maricopa	R	1971 1973 1977 1979
Davidson, Lucy	Tucson, Pima	D	1975
Day, Ann	Tucson, Pima	R	1991 1993 1995
Dye, Sue	Tucson, Pima	D	1975 1977
English, Karen L.	Flagstaff, Coconino	D	1991
Getzwiller, Polly	Casa Grande, Pinal	D	1977 1979 1981 1983
Harelson, Juanita	Tempe, Maricopa	R	1983 1985
Hartley, Mary	Phoenix, Maricopa	D	1995
Hermon, Beverly	Tempe, Maricopa	R	1993
Hill, Nancy L.	Phoenix, Maricopa	D	1991
Kennedy, Sandra	Phoenix, Maricopa	D	1993 1995
Lindeman, Anne	Phoenix, Maricopa	R	1977 1979 1981 1983 1985
MacDonald, Carol Lee	Stafford, Graham	R	1987
Morrison, Betty	Phoenix, Maricopa	D	1975
Munds, Frances L.	Prescott, Yavapai	D	1915
Noland, Patricia A.	Tucson, Pima	R	1993 1995
O'Connor, Sandra	Paradise Valley, Maricopa	R	1969* 1971 1973
Resnick, Cindy L.	Tucson, Pima	D	1991 1993
Solomon, Ruth	Tucson, Pima	D	1995
Springer, Carol	Prescott, Yavapai	R	1991 1993 1995
Steiner, Jacque	Phoenix, Maricopa	R	1981 1983 1985 1987 1989

Arizona Senate, continued

Name	City, County	Party	Legislative Year
Stinson, Bess B.	Phoenix, Maricopa	R	1971 1973
Thode, Edna Blowden	Casa Grande, Pinal	D	1965 1967 1969 1971
Van Arsdell, Madelene	Phoenix, Maricopa	D	1975
Walker, Carolyn	Phoenix, Maricopa	D	1987 1989 1991*
Weeks, Marica	Phoenix, Maricopa	D	1975 1977 1981
Wright, Patricia	Glendale, Maricopa	R	1987 1989 1991 1993

House
2 Year Terms

Name	City, County	Party	Legislative Year
Adams, Ruth	Scottsdale, Maricopa	R	1953 1955 1957 1965 1967 1969 1971
Aguirre, Linda G.	Phoenix, Maricopa	D	1993 1995
Allen, Carolyn S.	Scottsdale, Maricopa	R	1995
Anderson, Evelyn	Warren, Cochise	D	1953 1955*
Bailey, Josephine	Tumcacori, Santa Cruz	D	1955*
Beezley, Linda	Phoenix, Maricopa	D	1991* 1993
Berry, Rachel	St. Johns, Apache	D	1915
Bevan, Jessie E.	Bisbee, Cochise	D	1931 1933
Blake, Pat	Mesa, Maricopa	R	1991 1993
Boehringer, C. Louise	Yuma, Yuma	D	1921
Botzum, Clara Osborn	Parker, Yuma	D	1943 1945 1947 1949 1959 1961
Brewer, Janice Kay	Glendale, Maricopa	R	1983 1985
Brienholt, Ione L.	Phoenix, Maricopa	R	1929
Brubaker, Maxine P.	Phoenix, Maricopa	D	1941 1943
Burgess, Isabel	Phoenix, Maricopa	R	1953 1957 1961 1963 1965*
Burns, Brenda	Glendale, Maricopa	R	1987 1989 1991 1993
Bush, Nellie T.	Parker, Yuma	D	1921 1923 1927 1931 1933 1941
Cajero, Carmen F.	Tucson, Pima	D	1973* 1975 1977 1979 1981 1983 1985 1987 1989 1991 1993 1995
Campbell, Annie	Prescott, Yavapai	D	1929 1931 1933
Carlson, Donna J. *see* Carlson-West	Phoenix, Maricopa	R	1975 1977 1979
Carlson, Helen Grace	Phoenix, Maricopa	D	1971 1973
Carlson-West, Donna J. *see Carlson*	Phoenix, Maricopa	R	1981
Cauthron, Jo	Tucson, Pima	D	1975
Cavness, Blanche	Glendale, Maricopa	D	1931
Cullinan, Anna J.	Tucson, Pima	D	1975

Daniels, Lori S.	Chandler, Maricopa	R	1993 1995
Decker, Eva O.	Snowflake, Navajo	R	1947 1949
Dunn, Clare	Tucson, Pima	D	1975 1977 1979 1981*
Dwyer, Mary	Phoenix, Maricopa	R	1951 1953
Earl, Marie S.	Phoenix, Maricopa	D	1957 1959
Eden, Catherine	Phoenix, Maricopa	D	1991* 1993
Eliot, Geraldine	Phoenix, Maricopa	R	1957 1959 1961 1963
Ellis, Mabel S.	Prescott, Yavapai	D	1953* 1955 1957 1959 1961 1963
English, Karen L.	Flagstaff, Coconino	D	1987 1989
Eskesen, Ruth E.	Tucson, Pima	R	1989 1991
Foster, Kathi	Phoenix, Maricopa	D	1995
Francis, Mary	Phoenix, Maricopa	D	1931* 1933
Gardner, Gladys	Prescott, Yavapai	R	1965 1967 1969 1971 1973
Gerard, Susan Muir	Phoenix, Maricopa	R	1989 1991 1993 1995
Getzwiller, Polly	Casa Grande, Pinal	D	1963 1965 1967 1969 1971 1973 1975
Godfrey, Rose F.	Phoenix, Maricopa	D	1931*
Grace, Sue	Phoenix, Maricopa	R	1991 1993 1995
Graham, Lisa	Paradise Valley, Maricopa	R	1991 1993
Haberl, Clara S.	Phoenix, Maricopa	D	1953
Harelson, Juanita	Tempe, Maricopa	R	1973 1975 1977 1979 1981
Harris, Virginia	Wenden, Yuma	D	1929
Hayes, Priscilla H.	Phoenix, Maricopa	R	1959 1961 1963 1965
Hayward, Nellie	Douglas, Cochise	D	1919
Hermon, Beverly	Tempe, Maricopa	R	1983 1985 1987 1989 1991
Hershberger, Winifred	Oro Valley, Pima	R	1993 1995
Horton, Herschella	Tucson, Pima	D	1991 1993 1995
Hull, Jane Dee	Phoenix, Maricopa	R	1979 1981 1983 1985 1987 1989 1991 1993*
Hunt, Ruth I.	Phoenix, Maricopa	D	1955
Hutcheson, Etta Mae	Tucson, Pima	D	1953* 1955 1957 1959 1961 1963 1965 1967 1969 1971
Ivey, Vernettie O.	Phoenix, Maricopa	D	1923 1927 1929
James, Susan Louise	Phoenix, Maricopa	D	1975
Jarrett, Marilyn	Mesa, Maricopa	R	1995
Jennings, Emogene M.	Phoenix, Maricopa	R	1957 1959
Johnson, Leslie Whiting	Mesa, Maricopa	R	1983 1985 1987 1989 1991 1993
Jordan, Becky	Glendale, Maricopa	R	1993 1995
Jordan, Lillian	Phoenix, Maricopa	R	1977 1979 1981
Kelly, Mary Elizabeth	Miami, Gila	D	1933*
Kennedy, Sandra	Phoenix, Maricopa	D	1987 1989 1991
Knaperek, Laura	Tempe, Maricopa	R	1995

Arizona House, continued

Name	City, County	Party	Legislative Year
Kuntz, Ruth C.	Phoenix, Maricopa	R	1953
Larson, Augusta T.	Lakeside, Navajo	R	1955 1957 1959 1961
Laybe, Sue	Phoenix, Maricopa	D	1989 1991*
Leeper, Gertrude B.	Phoenix, Maricopa	D	1931*
Lindeman, Anne	Phoenix, Maricopa	R	1973 1975
Lockwood, Lorna E.	Phoenix, Maricopa	D	1939 1941* 1947
Lynch, Sue	Prescott, Yavapai	R	1993 1995
Macy, Elizabeth Lew	Tucson, Pima	R	1981
Marks, Freda	Phoenix, Maricopa	R	1923
Marsh, Theodora	Nogales, Santa Cruz	D	1917
Maynard, Ethel	Tucson, Pima	D	1967 1969 1971
McCarthy, Diane B.	Glendale, Maricopa	R	1973 1975 1977 1979
McCune, Debbie	Phoenix, Maricopa	D	1979 1981 1983 1985 1987 1989 1991 1993
McGrath, Jean	Phoenix, Maricopa	R	1995
McKay, Rosa Jane	Bisbee, Cochise	D	1917 1919 1923
McRae, Laura Morris	Phoenix, Maricopa	D	1939 1941 1943 1945 1947 1949 1951 1953 1955
Mills, Karen R.	Glendale, Maricopa	R	1985 1987 1989 1991
Moore, Louise A.	Phoenix, Maricopa	D	1941
Nagel, Candice	Phoenix, Maricopa	R	1989 1991*
Noland, Patricia A.	Tucson, Pima	R	1989 1991
Norton, Jenny	Tempe, Maricopa	R	1987 1989
O'Neill, Pauline Mary	Phoenix, Maricopa	D	1917 1919
Ollson, Marjory	San Manuel, Maricopa	D	1979
Patterson, Mary Alice	Phoenix, Maricopa	D	1929
Peck, Ruth	Phoenix, Maricopa	R	1959 1961 1963 1965 1967 1969 1971 1973 1975
Phelps, Claire	Chandler, Maricopa	D	1941 1943 1945 1947
Pickens, Marion	Tucson, Pima	D	1991 1995
Porter, Bridgie M.	Miami, Maricopa	D	1931 1933 1935 1937
Preble, Lou-Ann M.	Tucson, Pima	R	1993 1995
Resnick, Cindy L.	Tucson, Pima	D	1983 1985 1987 1989
Retzloff, Lillian	Phoenix, Maricopa	D	1955 1957
Richardson, Elaine	Tucson, Pima	D	1993 1995
Rios, Rebecca	Dudleyville, Pinal	D	1995
Rockwell, Elizabeth Adams	Phoenix, Maricopa	R	1965 1967 1969 1971 1973 1975 1977 1979 1981 1983 1985 1987
Rosenbaum, Edwynne C. Polly	Globe, Maricopa	D	1949* 1951 1953 1955 1957 1959 1961 1963 1965 1967 1969 1971 1973 1975 1977 1979 1981 1983 1985 1987 1989 1991 1993
Schorr, Eleanor D.	Tucson, Pima	D	1989 1991

Shaw, Robin	Phoenix, Maricopa	R	1995
Solomon, Ruth	Tucson, Pima	D	1989 1991 1993
Sprague, Harriet	Phoenix, Maricopa	D	1931*
Steffey, Lela	Mesa, Maricopa	R	1983 1985 1987 1989 1991 1993
Steiner, Jacque	Phoenix, Maricopa	R	1975* 1977 1979
Stinson, Bess B.	Phoenix, Maricopa	R	1967 1969
Struckmeyer, Fritzi	Phoenix, Maricopa	D	1937
Thode, Edna Blowden	Casa Grande, Pinal	D	1953 1955 1957 1959 1961
Thomas, Rhonda	Phoenix, Maricopa	R	1981 1983
Updike, Margaret	Phoenix, Maricopa	R	1989
Varn, Doris R.	Tucson, Pima	R	1961 1963 1965
Walker, Carolyn	Phoenix, Maricopa	D	1983 1985
Walker, Gladys	Togales, Santa Cruz	D	1927
Wessel, Nancy K.	Phoenix, Maricopa	R	1983 1985 1987 1989 1991 1993*
Westover, Anna R.	Yuma, Yuma	D	1919
Willis, Juliette C.	Tucson, Pima	R	1951 1953 1955 1957
Wright, Patricia	Glendale, Maricopa	R	1977 1979 1981 1983 1985

*Notes:

Anderson, Evelyn—Resigned Oct. 24, 1955 (Lewis)
Bailey, Josephine—Appointed Dec. 20, 1954 (Brown), resigned Oct. 24, 1955 (Hathway)
Beezley, Linda—Appointed Jan. 19, 1991 (Raymond)
Bollinger, Thelma C.—Appointed Jan. 22, 1960 (Bollinger)
Burgess, Isabel—Resigned 1969 (O'Connor)[F]
Cajero, Carmen F.—Appointed 1973 (Cajero)
Dunn, Clare—Died July 30, 1981
Eden, Catherine—Appointed March 25, 1991 (Laybe)[F]
Ellis, Mabel S.—Appointed 1953 (Rush)
Francis, Mary—Appointed Feb. 20, 1931 (Francis)
Godfrey, Rose F.—Appointed Dec. 28, 1931 (Jennings)
Hull, Jane Dee—Resigned Oct. 4, 1993 (Wong)
Hutcheson, Etta Mae—Appointed 1953 (Woods)
Kelly, Mary Elizabeth—Appointed June 5, 1933 (Kelly)
Laybe, Sue—Resigned March 13, 1991 (Eden)[F]
Leeper, Gertrude B.—Resigned Dec. 1931 (Sprague)[F]
Lockwood, Lorna E.—Resigned 1942
Nagel, Candice—Resigned 1991
O'Connor, Sandra—Appointed Oct. 30, 1969 (Burgess)[F]
Rosenbaum, Edwynne C. Polly—appointed 1949 (Rosenbaum)
Sprague, Harriet—Appointed Dec. 28, 1931 (Leeper)[F]
Steiner, Jacque—Appointed July 1976
Walker, Carolyn—Expelled March 20, 1991 (Ruiz)
Wessel, Nancy K.—Resigned April 12, 1993 (Eberhart)

ARKANSAS (1922–1995)

Arkansas women gained primary suffrage by legislative enactment in 1917 and full suffrage on August 26, 1920. Women first voted in state elections in 1920, but the Attorney General ruled that women were not eligible to run for the legislature. The state legislature passed a law in 1921 to allow women to serve and the first woman legislator, Representative Frances Hunt (D–Pine Bluff, Jefferson) was appointed to fill a vacancy in the Arkansas house on April 11, 1922. Women first ran in the 1922 state elections and elected Representative Hunt to a full term along with a second woman, Miss Erle Chambers (D–Little Rock).

State elections are held every two years for 100 representatives who serve two year terms and 35 senators who serve four year terms. State legislative service is limited to three two year terms for representatives and two four year terms for senators. Vacancies are filled by Governor's appointment and special election.

46 women have served in the Arkanasas General Assembly:
　5 in the Senate
　42 in the House
　(1 in the House and Senate)

Women as Percentage of Arkansas Legislators

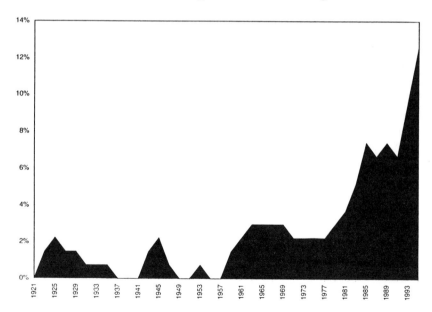

Senate
4 Year Terms

Name	City, County	Party	Legislative Year
Allen, Dorothy	Brinkley, Monroe	D	1965* 1967 1969 1971 1973
Chaffin, Charlie Cole	Benton, Benton	D	1985 1987 1989 1991 1993
Jeffries, Peggy	Fort Smith, Sebastian	R	1995
Shield, Vada	Mountain Home, Baxter	D	1977 1979 1981 1983
Watson, Gladys	Monette, Mississippi	D	1989

House
2 Year Terms

Name	City, County	Party	Legislative Year
Ammons, Evelyn	Waldron, Scott	D	1995
Autry, Lucille S.	Burdette, Mississippi	D	1967*
Balton, Nancy Crain	Wilson, Mississippi	D	1985 1987 1989
Bennett, Dee	N. Little Rock, Pulaski	D	1993 1995
Brown, Irma Hunter	Little Rock, Pulaski	D	1981 1983 1985 1987 1989 1991 1993 1995
Brown, Maude	Monroe, Monroe	D	1929
Brownlee, Christene	Gilmore, Crittenden	R	1991 1993
Buchanan, Helen May E.	Prescott, Nevada County	D	1945
Bush, Ann	Blytheville, Mississippi	R	1993* 1995
Cabe, Gloria B.	Little Rock, Pulaski	D	1979 1983 1985 1987 1989
Calhoun, Shirley Meacham *see* *Meacham*	Monroe, Monroe	D	1985 1987 1989
Chambers, Erle Rutherford	Little Rock, Pulaski	D	1923 1925
Cunningham, Ethel	Yell County	D	1931 1933*
Ferrell, Lisa	Little Rock, Pulaski	D	1995
Hackett, Mattie	Stamps, Lafayette	D	1959 1961 1963*
Hartness, Peggy	Monticello, Drew	D	1983 1985*
Horn, Barbara	Foreman, Little River	D	1993* 1995
Hunt, Frances	Pine Bluff, Jefferson	D	1921* 1923 1925
Hurst, Ella B.	Fayettville, Washington	D	1935 1943 1945
Jones, Myra	Little Rock, Pulaski	D	1985 1987 1989 1991 1993 1995
Kizer, Bernice Lighty	Fort Smith, Sebastian	D	1961 1963 1965 1967 1969 1971 1973
Lynn, Becky	Heber Springs, Baxter	D	1995

Arkansas House, continued

Name	City, County	Party	Legislative Year
Madison, Sue	Fayetteville, Washington	D	1995
Martin, Gladys *see*			
Oglesby	Stamps, Lafayette	D	1963* 1965
McCastlain, Doris	Brinkley, Monroe	D	1961* 1963 1965
McRaven, Florence	Little Rock, Pulaski	D	1927 1929
Meacham, Shirley *see*			
Calhoun	Monroe, Monroe	D	1975 1977 1979 1981
			1983
Mulkey, Dove Tolland	Nashville, Howard	D	1961 1963
Northcutt, Wanda	Stuttgart, Arkansas	D	1985 1987 1989 1991
			1993 1995
Oates, Will Etta L.	Little Rock, Pulaski	D	1959
Oglesby, Gladys Martin *see Martin*	Stamps, Lafayette	D	1967 1969
Owens, Marian D.	Warren, Bradley	D	1993 1995
Petty, Judy	Little Rock, Pulaski	R	1981 1983
Pollan, Carolyn	Fort Smith, Sebastian	R	1975 1977 1979 1981
			1983 1985 1987
			1989 1991 1993
			1995
Roberts, Jacqueline	Pine Bluff, Jefferson	D	1991 1993 1995
Rowlette, Lera Jean	Texarkana, Miller	D	1953
Schexnayder, Charlotte T.	Dumas, Desha	D	1985 1987 1989 1991
			1993 1995
Shield, Vada	Mountain Home, Baxter	D	1967 1969 1971 1973
			1975 1993
Smith, Judy Seriale	Camden, Ouachita	D	1991 1993 1995
Thompson, Elizabeth H.	Phillips County	D	1925
Thompson, Norma	Marked Tree, Craighead	D	1981*
Wigstrand, Mary B.	Polk County	D	1927
Wilkins, Josetta	Pine Bluff, Jefferson	D	1993 1995
Word, Arlene	Osceola, Mississippi	D	1943 1945 1947

*Notes:

Allen, Dorothy—Elected 1964 (Allen)
Autry, Lucille S.—Elected Jan. 30, 1968 (Autry)
Bush, Ann—Appointed Sept. 6, 1993 (Day)
Cunningham, Ethel Cole—Resigned May 10, 1933
Hackett, Mattie—Died June 1963 (Martin)[F]
Hartness, Peggy—Resigned Nov. 1, 1985 (Murphy)
Horn, Barbara—Appointed Aug. 20, 1993 (Horn)
Hunt, Frances—Appointed April 11, 1922
Martin, Gladys—Elected June 18, 1963 (Hackett)[F]
McCastlain, Doris—Elected 1962 (McCastlain)
Thompson, Norma—Appointed Aug. 1981 (Thompson)

CALIFORNIA (1919–1995)

California women gained suffrage by popular referendum in 1911. Women first voted in state elections in 1912 and first ran for the state legislature but did not win until 1918 when Assemblywomen Esto B. Broughton (D–Modesto), Grace S. Dorris (R–Bakersfield), Elizabeth Hughes (R–Oroville), and Anna L. Saylor (R–Alameda) were elected.

State elections are held every two years for 80 assembly members who serve two year terms and 40 senators who serve four year terms. State legislative service is limited for the Assembly to three two year terms and for the Senate to two four year terms. Vacancies are filled by special election.

63 women have served in the California Legislature:
  8 in the Senate
  60 in the Assembly
  (5 in the Assembly and Senate)

Women as Percentage of California Legislators

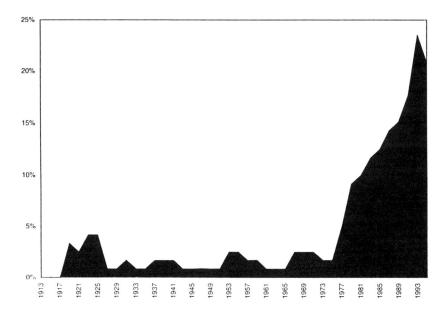

Senate
4 Year Terms

Name	City, County	Party	Legislative Year
Bergeson, Marian	Newport Beach, Orange	R	1985 1987 1989 1991 1993 1995*
Hughes, Teresa P.	Los Angeles, Los Angeles	D	1993 1995
Killea, Lucy	San Diego, San Diego	D	1989* 1991 I 1993 1995
Morgan, Rebecca Q.	Menlo Park, Santa Clara	R	1985 1987 1989 1991 1993
Solis, Hilda L.	El Monte, Los Angeles	D	1995
Vuich, Rose Ann	Dinuba, Tulare	D	1977 1979 1981 1983 1985 1987 1989 1991
Watson, Diane E.	Los Angeles, Los Angeles	D	1979 1981 1983 1985 1987 1989 1991 1993 1995
Wright, Cathie	Simi Valley, Ventura	R	1993 1995

Assembly
2 Year Terms

Name	City, County	Party	Legislative Year
Alby, Barbara	Sacramento, Sacramento	R	1993* 1995
Allen, Doris	Cypress, Orange	R	1983 1985 1987 1989 1991 1993 1995
Alpert, Deidre	Del Mar, Imperial	D	1991 1993 1995
Archie-Hudson, Mar-guerite	Los Angeles, Los Angeles	D	1991 1993 1995
Bentley, Carol	San Diego, San Diego	R	1989 1991
Bergeson, Marian	Newport Beach, Orange	R	1979 1981 1983
Boland, Paula L.	Granada Hills, Los Angeles	R	1991 1993 1995
Bornstein, Julie	Palm Desert, Imperial	D	1993
Bowen, Debra	Marina Del Ray, Los Angeles	D	1993 1995
Brathwaite, Yvonne W.	Inglewood, Los Angeles	D	1967 1969 1971
Brewer, Marilyn C.	Irvine, Orange	R	1995
Bronshvag, Vivien	Kentfield, Marin	D	1993
Broughton, Esto	Modesto, Stanislaus	D	1919 1921 1923 1925
Brown, Valerie K.	Sonoma, Sonoma	D	1993 1995
Daley, Jeanette E.	San Diego, San Diego	D	1937 1939 1941
Davis, Pauline L.	Portola, Plumas	D	1953 1955 1957 1959 1961 1963 1965 1967 1969 1971 1973 1975

Davis, Susan	Sandiego, San Diego	D	1995
Donahoe, Dorothy	Bakersfield, Kern	D	1953 1955 1957 1959
Dorris, Grace S.	Bakersfield, Kern	R	1919 1923 1925
Ducheny, Denise Moreno	Chula Vista, San Diego	D	1993* 1995
Eastin, Delaine	Union City, Alameda	D	1987 1989 1991 1993
Egeland, Leona H.	San Jose, Santa Clara	D	1975 1977 1979
Escutia, Martha M.	Huntington Park, Los Angeles	D	1993 1995
Eu, March K.	Fong Oakdale, Stanislaus	D	1967 1969 1971 1973
Figueroa, Liz	Alameda, Santa Clara	D	1995
Friedman, Barbara	Los Angeles, Los Angeles	D	1993 1995
Hallett, Carol	Atascadero, San Luis Obispo	R	1977 1979 1981
Hansen, Bevan P.	Santa Rosa, Sonoma	R	1987 1989 1991
Honeycutt, Kathleen M.	Hesperia, Kern	R	1993
Hughes, Elizabeth	Oroville, Butte	R	1919 1921
Hughes, Teresa P.	Los Angeles, Los Angeles	D	1975* 1977 1979 1981 1983 1985 1987 1989 1991
Hunter, Tricia Rae	Escondido, Imperial	R	1991
Karnette, Betty	Long Beach, Los Angeles	D	1993
Kelogg, Sarah E.	Los Angeles, Los Angeles	R	1929* 1931
Killea, Lucy	San Diego, San Diego	D	1983 1985 1987 1989*
Kuehl, Sheila James	Santa Monica, Los Angeles	D	1995
LaFollette, Marian W.	Northridge, Los Angeles	R	1981 1983 1985 1987 1989
Lee, Barbara	Oakland, Alameda	D	1991 1993 1995
Martinez, Diane	Monterey Park, Los Angeles	D	1993 1995
Mazzoni, Kerry	Nevada, Marin	D	1995
McDonald, Juanita M.	Carson, Los Angeles	D	1993 1995
Miller, Eleanor	Pasadena, Los Angeles	R	1923 1925 1927 1929 1931 1933 1935 1937 1939 1941
Mojonnier, Sunny	San Diego, San Diego	R	1983 1985 1987 1989
Molina, Gloria	Los Angeles, Los Angeles	D	1983 1985 1987*
Moore, Gwen	Los Angeles, Los Angeles	D	1979 1981 1983 1985 1987 1989 1991 1993
Moorehead-Duffy, Jean	Sacramento, Sacramento	R	1979 1981 1983 1985
Napolitano, Grace F.	Norwalk, Los Angeles	D	1993 1995
Niehouse, Kathryn T.	San Diego, San Diego	R	1943 1945 1947 1949 1951 1953
Roybal-Allard, Lucille	Los Angeles, Los Angeles	D	1987* 1989 1991
Ryan, Marilyn	Palo Verdes, Los Angeles	R	1977 1979 1981

California Assembly, continued

Name	City, County	Party	Legislative Year
Sankary, Wanda	San Diego, San Diego	D	1955
Saylor, Anna L.	Alameda, Alameda	R	1919 1921 1923 1925
Seastrand, Andrea	Salinas, Monterey	R	1991 1993
Snyder, Margaret E.	Modesto, Stanislaus	D	1993
Solis, Hilda L.	El Monte, Los Angeles	D	1993
Speier, Jacqueline K.	South San Francisco, San Mateo	D	1987 1989 1991 1993 1995
Tanner, Sally	El Monte, Los Angeles	D	1979 1981 1983 1985 1987 1989 1991
Waters, Maxine	Los Angeles, Los Angeles	D	1977 1979 1981 1983 1985 1987 1989
Woodbridge, Cora	Nevada, Nevada	R	1923 1925
Wright, Cathie	Simi Valley, Ventura	R	1981 1983 1985 1987 1989 1991

*Notes:
Alby, Barbara—Elected Aug. 2, 1993 (Collins)
Bergeson, Marian—Resigned Jan. 1995
Ducheny, Denise Moreno—Elected April 1994 (Peace)
Hughes, Teresa P.—Elected July 15, 1975
Kelogg, Sarah E.—Elected 1930 (Kelogg)
Killea, Lucy—Resigned, elected Dec. 5, 1989 to Senate (Stirling)
Molina, Gloria—Resigned 1987 (Roybal-Allard) [F]
Roybal-Allard, Lucille—Elected April 12, 1987 (Molina)[F]

COLORADO (1895-1995)

Colorado women gained school suffrage in the first state constitution in 1876, and won full suffrage in a popular referendum in 1893. Women voted in 1894 state elections the next year and elected the first female state legislators in the United States: Representatives Carrie Clyde Holly (R–Vineland, Pueblo County), and Frances S. Klock (R–Denver, Arapahoe County) and Clara Cressingham (R–Denver, Arapahoe County).

State elections are held every two years for 65 representatives who serve two year terms and 35 senators who serve four year terms. State legislative service is limited for the house to four consecutive two year terms and for the senate to two consecutive four year terms. Vacancies are filled by governor's appointment.

146 women have served in the Colorado General Assembly:
  28 in the Senate
  131 in the House
  13 in the House and Senate

Women as Percentage of Colorado Legislators

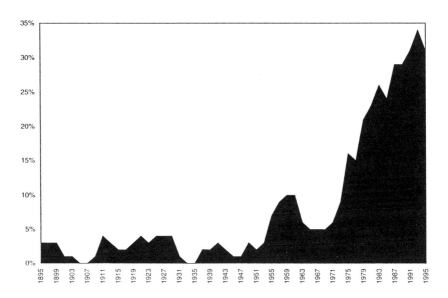

Senate
4 Year Terms

Name	City, County	Party	Legislative Year
Allison, Bonnie J.	Edgewater, Jefferson	R	1989 1991
Arnold, Kathy Spelts *see Spelts*	Littleton, Jefferson	R	1983* 1985
Baca-Barragan, Polly	Thornton, Adams	D	1979 1981 1983 1985
Ball, Roseanne	Denver, Denver	R	1973*
Bandy, Amanda	Cortez, Montezuma	D	1993*
Darby, Lorena E.	Longmont, Boulder	D	1973 1975
Dennis, Ginette	Pueblo West, Pueblo	R	1995
Ezzard, Martha M.	Englewood, Denver	R	1981 1983 1985 1987*
Finley, Thelma	Center, Rio Grande	D	1959*
Holme, Barbara S.	Denver, Denver	D	1975 1977 1979 1981 1983
Hopper, Sally	Golden, Jefferson	R	1987 1989 1991 1993 1995

Colorado Senate, continued

Name	City, County	Party	Legislative Year
Johnson, Joan	Denver, Adams	D	1991 1993 1995
Lacy, Elsie	Aurora, Arapahoe	R	1993 1995
Mendez, Jana Wells	Longmont, Boulder	D	1985 1987 1989 1991 1993 1995*
Pascoe, Pat	Denver, Denver	D	1989 1991 1995
Powers, Linda	Crested Butte, Gunnison	D	1993 1995
Riddle, Agnes L.	Denver, Arapahoe	R	1917 1919
Robinson, Helen R.	Denver, Denver	D	1913 1915
Rupert, Dorothy	Boulder, Boulder	D	1995*
Saunders, Allegra	Denver, Denver	D	1959 1961 1967 1969
Smith, Eudochia Bell	Denver, Denver	D	1941 1943 1945*
Stockton, Ruth S.	Lakewood, Jefferson	R	1965 1967 1969 1971 1973 1975 1977 1979 1981 1983
Tanner, Gloria Travis	Denver, Denver	D	1993* 1995
Taylor, Rena Mary	Palisade, Mesa	R	1959 1961
Tebedo, Mary Anne	Colorado Springs, El Paso	R	1989 1991 1993 1995
Traylor, Claire	Wheat Ridge, Jefferson	R	1983 1985 1987 1989 1991 1993
Wham, Dottie	Denver, Denver	R	1987* 1989 1991 1993 1995
Wilson, Hestia	Nucla, Montrose	D	1957*1959 1961

House
2 Year Terms

Name	City, County	Party	Legislative Year
Adkins, Jeanne M.	Parker, Douglas	R	1989 1991 1993 1995
Agler, Vickie	Littleton, Jefferson	R	1991 1993 1995
Allen, Debbie	Aurora, Arapahoe	R	1993 1995
Allison, Bonnie J.	Edgewater, Jefferson	R	1983 1985 1987
Anderson, Norma V.	Lakewood, Jefferson	R	1987 1989 1991 1993 1995
Armstrong, Vickie L.	Grand Junction, Mesa	R	1981 1983 1985 1987
Arnold, Kathy Spelts see Spelts	Littleton, Jefferson	R	1983*
Artist, Jane	Greeley, Weld	R	1985*
Baca-Barragan, Polly	Thornton, Adams	D	1975 1977
Bain, Jean K.	Denver, Denver	R	1961 1963 1965 1967 1969 1971
Baker, Mabel Ruth	Denver, Denver	R	1919 1921 1923
Barry, Mary F.	Pueblo, Pueblo	TSR	1899
Beck, Lucille L.	Denver, Denver	D	1955 1957
Benavidez, Betty L.	Denver, Denver	D	1971 1973

Benavidez, Celina	Denver, Denver	D	1991* 1993
Bigelow, May T.	Denver, Denver	R	1919
Blue, Mary	Longmont, Boulder	D	1993
Brighton, Kitty	Trinidad, Las Animas	D	1927 1929 1931
Burrows, Pat	Broomfield, Jefferson	D	1975
Butler, Olive C.	Denver, Arapahoe	SR	1897
Carr, Eleanor	Denver, Denver	R	1953
Chronic, Betty	Boulder, Boulder	R	1959*
Clark, Ruth B.	Fort Collins, Larimer	R	1955 1957 1959 1961 1963 1965
Conine, Martha A. B.	Denver, Arapahoe	Np	1897
Cowperthwaite, Blanche	Denver, Denver	R	1955
Cressingham, Clara	Denver, Arapahoe	R	1895
Cresswell, Mildred	Denver, Denver	R	1967
Dambman, Mary	Colorado Springs, El Paso	R	1983 1985 1987
De Herrera, Laura	Denver, Denver	D	1977 1979 1981
Degette, Diana	Denver, Denver	D	1993 1995
Dick, Nancy E.	Aspen, Pitkin	D	1975 1977
Dittemore, Betty Ann	Englewood, Denver	R	1969 1971 1973 1975 1977
Dunning, Annabelle	Aurora, Arapahoe	D	1983
Dyer, Candace	Longmont, Boulder	D	1981 1983
Edmonds, Carol R.	Grand Junction, Mesa	D	1979
Epps, Mary Ellen	Colorado Springs, El Paso	R	1987 1989 1991 1993 1995
Ezzard, Martha M.	Englewood, Denver	R	1979
Faatz, Jeanne	Denver, Denver	R	1979 1981 1983 1985 1987 1989 1991 1993 1995
Fine, Eunice W.	Greeley, Weld	R	1979 1981 1983
Fischer, Sara L.	Colorado Springs, El Paso	R	1955
Fish, Marleen M.	Lakewood, Jefferson	R	1985 1987 1989 1991
Fleming, Faye L.	Thornton, Adams	D	1983 R 1987 1989 1991 1993
Flett, Nancy	Arvada, Jefferson	D	1975
Ford, Judy	Arvada, Jefferson	R	1981*
Frank, Barbara	Denver, Denver	D	1967
Fry, Mae Carroll	Denver, Denver	R	1927
Gaylord, Madge	Pueblo, Pueblo	D	1959
Gilbert, Lela S.	Denver, Denver	D	1957* 1959 1961
Gorsuch, Anne McGill	Denver, Denver	R	1977 1979
Green, Joan	Aurora, Arapahoe	R	1985 1987
Greenwood, Daphne T.	Colorado Springs, El Paso	D	1991 1993
Groff, Jo Ann	Westminster, Adams	D	1983 1985 1987 1989
Hastings, Melba	Sterling, Logan	D	1979 1981
Heartz, Evangeline	Denver, Denver	Pop	1897 1901; D 1915 1917

Colorado House, continued

Name	City, County	Party	Legislative Year
Hendie, Dorothy	Denver, Denver	R	1943
Holly, Carrie Clyde	Pueblo, Pueblo	R	1895
Hume, Gwenne Sandy	Boulder, Boulder	R	1977 1979 1981 1983
Jackson, Josie J.	Denver, Denver	R	1921 1925
Jones, Lee Richardson	Boulder, Boulder	R	1977 1979
Jones, Louise U.	Denver, Denver	D	1911
June, Vi	Westminster, Adams	D	1991 1993 1995
Keller, Maryanne	Wheat Ridge, Jefferson	D	1993 1995
Kerns, Peggy	Aurora, Arapahoe	D	1989 1991 1993 1995
Kerwin, Louise M.	Denver, Denver	D	1911
Killian, Pat	Wheat Ridge, Jefferson	D	1989 1991
Klock, Frances S.	Denver, Arapahoe	R	1895
Kramer, Florence H.	Denver, Denver	D	1937 1939 1941
Kramer, Shirley M.	Denver, Denver	D	1949
Kreutz, Martha Hill	Littleton, Jefferson	R	1993 1995
Lafferty, Alma V.	Denver, Denver	D	1909 1911
Lamm, Peggy	Louisville, Boulder	D	1995
Larson, Jean M.	Colorado Springs, El Paso	R	1979 1981 1983
Lawrence, Joyce R.	Pueblo, Pueblo	R	1995
Lawrence, Michelle	Arvada, Jefferson	R	1991 1993
Lee, Frances S.	Denver, Arapahoe	D	1899 1913
Littler, Kathleen P.	Greeley, Weld	R	1961 1963
Lock, Selma	Denver, Denver	D	1981*
Long, Martha E.	Denver, Denver	R	1925 1927
Love, Minnie C. T.	Denver, Denver	R	1921 1925
Lyle, Glenda Swanson	Denver, Denver	D	1993 1995
Markert, Margaret	Aurora, Arapahoe	D	1983 1985
Marks, Jean	Northglenn, Adams	D	1975 1977 1979 1981
Mason, Margaret	Crawford, San Miguel	R	1987 1989
Mattingly, Mildred	Pueblo, Pueblo	D	1993*
Mead, Hattie A.	Pueblo, Pueblo	R	1929
Miller, Betty	Littleton, Jefferson	D	1965
Miller, Laura A.	Littleton, Jefferson	R	1971 1973 1975
Miller, Patricia	Arvada, Jefferson	R	1991
Morrison, Marcy	Manitou Springs, El Paso	R	1993 1995
Munson, Kay	Colorado Springs, El Paso	R	1969 1971 1973 1975
Musgrave, Marilyn	Fort Morgan, Larimer	R	1995
Neale, Betty Irene	Denver, Denver	R	1975 1977 1979 1981 1983 1985 1987 1989 1991
Nichol, Alice J.	Denver, Adams	D	1993 1995
Noland, Helen Beatty	Durango, La Plata	R	1929
Orten, Betty	Westminster, Adams	D	1975 1977 1979 1981
Patterson, Louise M.	Pueblo, Pueblo	D	1923 1925
Pellet, Elizabeth E.	Rico, San Miguel	D	1941 1949 1951 1953 1955 1957 1959 1961 1963

Pettee, Annah G.	Denver, Denver	R	1927 1929
Phillips, Barbara	Colorado Springs, El Paso	R	1985 1987 1989
Prendergast, Ruth	Denver, Denver	R	1981 1983
Reeser, Jeannie G.	Thornton, Adams	D	1985 1987 1989 1991 1993 1995
Reeves, Peggy	Fort Collins, Larimer	D	1983 1987 1989 1991 1993 1995
Riddle, Agnes L.	Denver, Arapahoe	R	1911 1913
Ruble, Alice M.	Denver, Arapahoe	D	1903
Rupert, Dorothy	Boulder, Boulder	D	1987 1989 1991 1993 1995*
Scherling, Beverly	Aurora, Arapahoe	R	1979 1981
Sears, Virginia La Coste	Greeley, Weld	R	1973 1975 1977
Smith, Eudochia Bell	Denver, Denver	D	1937 1939
Smith, Montana F.	Lake City, Denver	D	1947 1949
Snyder, Carol	Northglenn, Adams	D	1991 1993 1995
Spelts, Kathy see Arnold	Littleton, Jefferson	R	1979 1981
Stockton, Ruth S.	Lakewood, Jefferson	R	1961 1963
Sullivan, Kathleen	Meeker, Rio Blanco	D	1981
Swenson, Betty	Longmont, Boulder	R	1985 1987 1989 1991
Tanner, Gloria Travis	Denver, Denver	D	1985 1987 1989 1991 1993*
Taylor, Arie P.	Denver, Denver	D	1973 1975 1977 1979 1981 1983
Taylor, Rena Mary	Palisade, Mesa	R	1951 1953 1955 1957
Taylor-Little, Carol	Arvada, Jefferson	R	1983 1985 1987 1989
Tebedo, Mary Anne	Colorado Springs, El Paso	R	1981* 1983 1985 1987
Tempest, Carol	Denver, Denver	R	1973
Thompson, Anne M.	Rocky Ford, Otero	R	1957 1959
Traylor, Claire	Wheat Ridge, Jefferson	R	1979 1981
Tucker, Shirleen	Lakewood, Jefferson	R	1987 1989 1991 1993 1995
Webb, Wilma J.	Denver, Denver	D	1981 1983 1985 1987 1989 1991
West, Betty Kirk	Pueblo, Pueblo	D	1955 1957 1959 1961 1963 1965
Wham, Dottie	Denver, Denver	R	1985 1987*
Williams, Kathi	Westminster, Adams	R	1985 1987 1989
Wilson, Mary E.	Victor, Teller	R	1921 1923
Witherspoon, Dorothy K.	Lakewood, Jefferson	D	1975 1977 1979
Woodhouse, Janet	Denver, Denver	D	1957 1959
Wright, Harriet G. R.	Denver, Arapahoe	Pop	1899
Wright, Ruth	Boulder, Boulder	D	1981 1983 1985 1987 1989 1991 1993

Colorado, continued

*Notes:
Arnold, Kathy Spelts—Resigned, appointed April 6, 1983 (Schaefer) to Senate
Artist, Jane—Appointed Sept. 11, 1986 (Artist)
Ball, Roseanne—Appointed July 30, 1973 (Bermingham)
Bandy, Amanda—Appointed May 21, 1994 (Cassidy)
Benavidez, Celina—Appointed Aug. 22, 1991 (Hernandez)
Chronic, Betty—Appointed Nov. 1960 (Crawford)
Ezzard, Martha M.—Resigned July 25, 1987
Finley, Thelma—Appointed Sept. 17, 1959 (Finley)
Ford, Judy—Appointed Oct. 21, 1981 (Tancredo)
Gilbert, Lela S.—Appointed Feb. 11, 1957 (Cobb)
Lock, Selma—Appointed Oct. 13, 1982 (Eberle)
Mattingly, Mildred—Appointed May 1993 (Thiebaut)
Mendez, Jana Wells—Resigned Dec. 1994 (Tuppa)
Rupert, Dorothy—Resigned Dec. 3, 1994, appointed to Senate (Weissman)
Smith, Eudochia Bell—Resigned 1946
Spelts, Kathy *see Arnold*
Tanner, Gloria Travis—Resigned, elected April 1, 1994 (Groff) to Senate
Tebedo, Mary Anne—Appointed Jan. 25, 1982 (Becker)
Wham, Dottie—Resigned, appointed Nov. 25, 1987 (Dodge) to Senate
Wilson, Hestia—Appointed 1957 to fill unexpired term (Hestia)

CONNECTICUT (1921-1995)

Women as Percentage of Connecticut Legislators

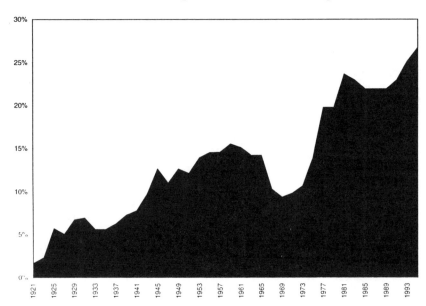

Connecticut women gained school suffrage in 1893 and full suffrage on August 26, 1920. Women first voted and ran for state office in the 1920 state elections when they elected Representatives Emily Sophie Brown (R–Naugatuck), Rev. Grace I. Edwards (I–New Hartford), Lillian M. S. Frink (R–Canterbury), Mary M. Hooker (R–Hartford) and Helen A. Jewett (D–Tolland).

State elections are held every two years for 36 senators and 151 representatives who serve two year terms. In 1966 the Connecticut House membership was decreased from 280 members to 177, and to the present 151 in 1972. Vacancies are filled by special election.

419 women have served in the Connecticut General Assembly:
    32 in the Senate
    400 in the House
    (13 served in the House and Senate)

Senate
2 Year Terms

Name	City, County	Party	Legislative Year
Beck, Audrey P.	Storrs, Tolland	D	1975 1977 1979 1981 1983*
Berry, Louise E.	Danielson, Windham	R	1973
Cook, Catherine W.	Mystic, New London	R	1993 1995
Daily, Eileen M.	Westbrook, Middlesex	D	1993 1995
Diloreto, Virginia	New Britain, Hartford	D	1965*
Eads, M. Adela	Kent, Litchfield	R	1981 1983 1985 1987 1989 1991 1993 1995
Fahey, Marcella C.	East Hartford, Hartford	D	1979 1981
Farmer, Marjorie Dilley	Darien, Fairfield	R	1961
Finney, Florence D.	Cos Cob, Fairfield	R	1955 1957 1959 1961 1963 1965 1967 1969 1971 1973 1975
Freedman, Judith G.	Westport, Fairfield	R	1987 1989 1991 1993 1995
Hammer, Lucy T.	Branford, New Haven	R	1961 1963 1965 1967 1969 1971
Harp, Toni N.	New Haven, New Haven	D	1993 1995
Herbst, Marie A.	Vernon, Tolland	D	1987 1989 1991
Hudson, Betty	Madison, New Haven	D	1975 1977
Hurley, Margaret C.	Windham, Windham	D	1943 1945
Johnson, Nancy Lee	New Britain, Hartford	R	1977 1979 1981
Martin, Mary A.	Groton, New London	D	1975 1977 1979 1981 1983

Connecticut Senate, continued

Name	City, County	Party	Legislative Year
Matthews, Cynthia A.	Wethersfield, Hartford	D	1983 1987 1989 1991
Merritt, Alice P.	Hartford, Hartford	R	1925 1927
Morton, Margaret E.	Bridgeport, Fairfield	D	1981 1983 1985 1987 1989 1991
Mustone, Amelia P.	Meriden, New Haven	D	1979 1981 1983 1985 1987 1989 1991 1993
Peters, Melodie	Quaker Hill, New London	D	1993 1995
Prague, Edith G.	Columbia, Tolland	D	1995
Reimers, Barbara D.	Branford, New Haven	R	1977
Rowland, Alice V.	Ridgefield, Fairfield	R	1943 1945 1947 1949
Scarpetti, Angelina	Trumbull, Fairfield	R	1985 1989 1991 1993 1995
Schaffer, Gloria	Woodbridge, New Haven	D	1959 1961 1963 1965 1967 1969
Smith, Regina R.	Northford, New Haven	D	1979 1981 1983
Streeter, Anne P.	West Hartford, Hartford	R	1983 1985
Tracy, Kathleen M.	Rocky Hill, Hartford	D	1967
Truex, Ruth O.	Wethersfield, Hartford	R	1973
Weaver, Mary B.	New Milford, Litchfield	R	1929

House
2 Year Terms

Name	City, County	Party	Legislative Year
Abercromblie, Florence	Stratford, Fairfield	R	1939 1941 1943
Ahlberg, Nellie M.	Cromwell, Middlesex	R	1955
Alsop, Corinne Robinson	Avon, Hartford	R	1925 1929 1931
Anderson, Ruth Leah	Cromwell, Middlesex	R	1957
Arnold, Anne H.	Westport, Fairfield	R	1939 1941 1943
Arrigoni, Mary R.	Durham, Middlesex	R	1945 1947
Auburn, Laura M.	New Hartford, Litchfield	R	1951 1953
Baker, Shelia A.	Bridgeport, Fairfield	D	1987
Baldwin, Elizabeth G.	Cheshire, New Haven	R	1951 1953
Balstad, Blanche E.	Monroe, Fairfield	R	1961 1963 1965
Barnes, Dorothy D.	Farmington, Hartford	R	1977 1979 1981
Baronian, Maureen M.	West Hartford, Hartford	R	1981 1983 1985
Barrett, Susan	Fairfield, Fairfield	D	1983
Bartlett, Dorothy J.	Putnam, Windham	D	1933 1935 1937 1939 1941 1943
Beals, Nancy	Hamden, New Haven	D	1993 1995
Beck, Audrey P.	Storrs, Tolland	D	1969 1971 1973
Beckett-Rinker, Pegge	Branford, New Haven	R	1983 1985

Name	Town, County	Party	Years
Beckwith, Laurette J.	New London, New London	D	1955
Begg, Claire H.	Waterbury, New Haven	D	1971*
Belaga, Julie D.	Westport, Fairfield	R	1977 1979 1981 1983 1985
Benson, Arline M.	Newington, Hartford	R	1951 1953 1955 1957
Berman, Rosalind	New Haven, New Haven	R	1977 1979 1981 1983
Bertinuson, Teresalee	Melrose, Tolland	D	1975 1977 1979 1981 1983 1985 1987 1989
Bishop, Mary G.	Niantic, New London	R	1961 1963 1965
Bixler, Sylvia W.	Ledyard, New London	R	1961 1963 1965
Blacker, Bessie M.	Cheshire, New Haven	R	1961 1963 1965
Blackman, Beulah L.	Bridgeport, Fairfield	R	1949 1951 1953 1955 1957 1959 1961
Blood, Virginia L.	Darien, Fairfield	R	1941 1943
Boatwright, Mary H.	Stonington, New London	R	1963 1965
Bolster, Sally McCarthy	Rowayton, Fairfield	R	1987* 1989 1991
Boukus, Elizabeth A.	Plainville, Hartford	D	1995
Bouteiller, Marie S.	Middletown, Middlesex	R	1957
Brennan, Mary M.	Somers, Tolland	D	1951
Brown, Elizabeth Crichton	Waterbury, New Haven	D	1987 1989 1991
Brown, Emily Sophie	Naugatuck, New Haven	R	1921*
Brown, Gertrude E.	Plymouth, Litchfield	D	1959 1961 1963 1965
Brown, Ida Baldwin	Southbridge, Tolland	R	1959 1961 1963 1965
Bryant, Josephine E.	E. Hartford, Hartford	R	1929
Buckingham, Hattie M.	Seymours, New Haven	R	1927 1929
Buckley, Muriel W.	Groton, New London	R	1981 1983 1985 1987
Budd, Elizabeth H.	Wethersfield, Hartford	R	1955 1957 1959 1961
Burns, J. Agnes	Hartford, Hartford	D	1931 1933 1935
Buys, Bernice T.	Prospect, New Haven	R	1937
Bysiewicz, Susan	Middletown, Middlesex	D	1993 1995
Cappelletti, Norma L.	Waterbury, New Haven	R	1981 1985
Carini, Helen J.	Haddam, Middlesex	R	1961
Carrozzella, Jeanette	Wallingford, New Haven	D	1971*
Carter, Annette Wheeler	Hartford, Hartford	D	1987* 1989 1991 1993 1995
Castro, Illia	Hartford, Hartford	D	1993* 1995
Chatfield, Emily B.	Voluntown, New London	R	1927
Cheney, Marjory	Manchester, Hartford	R	1925 1927 1929 1931
Clark, Hannah E. *see Russell*	Orange, New Haven	R	1961
Clark, Harriet L.	Litchfield, Litchfield	R	1957 1959 1961 1963 1965
Clark, Mary V.	Avon, Hartford	R	1961
Clark, Ruth H.	Branford, New Haven	R	1971 1973
Clarke, Hilda S.	Stamford, Fairfield	R	1955 1957 1967 1969 1971

Connecticut House, continued

Name	City, County	Party	Legislative Year
Clemons, Thomasina	Vernon, Tolland	D	1995
Cocco, Jacqueline M.	Bridgeport, Fairfield	D	1987 1989 1991 1993 1995
Coe, Alice Lee	Winsted, Litchfield	R	1927 1929 1931
Coe, Blanche M.	Durham, Middlesex	R	1949 1951
Coe, Elizabeth W.	Waterbury, New Haven	R	1925
Cohen, Naomi K.	Bloomfield, Hartford	D	1983 1985 1987 1989 1991
Collins, Beatrice S.	Unionville, Hartford	R	1963 1965
Colton, Bertha W.	Granby, Hartford	R	1947 1949
Concannon, Terry	Haddam, Middlesex	D	1993 1995
Cone, Carolyn L.	Lyme, New London	R	1943 1945 1953 1961
Conniff, Lucy C.	Danbury, Fairfield	D	1949 1951
Connolly, Virginia S.	Simsbury, Hartford	R	1971 1973 1975 1977 1979
Considine, Ella	N. Canaan, Litchfield	R	1931 1933
Cook, Edith Valet	New Haven, New Haven	R	1927 1957
Cook, Mabel F.	West Willington, Tolland	R	1949
Cooley, Ruth M.	Vernon, Tolland	D	1941
Crawford, Julia P.	Manchester, Hartford	R	1947
Crawford, Sara B.	Westport, Fairfield	R	1925 1927 1931 1933 1935 1937
Cronk, Helen H.	Woodbury, Litchfield	R	1957 1959 1961
Croumey, Elizabeth M.	East Haven, New Haven	R	1953 1955 1957
Crouse, Annie E.	Granby, Hartford	R	1931 1933
Cunningham, Mary Van Zile	New Canaan, Fairfield	R	1951 1953 1955 1957 1959 1961 1963 1965
Currey, Melody A.	East Hartford, Hartford	D	1993 1995
Curtis, Sarah Frances	Sandy Hook, Fairfield	R	1953 1955 1957 1963 1965 1967 1969 1971 1973
D'Aguilla, Angelina	East Haddam, Middlesex	R	1951 1953
Daly, Casey M.	Bridgeport, Fairfield	R	1981 1985
Dandrow, Ann P.	Southington, Hartford	R	1987 1989 1991 1993 1995
Davids, Georgina B.	Greenwich, Fairfiels	R	1929
Delbianco, Doreen M.	Waterbury, New Haven	D	1983 1987 1989 1991
Demarinas, Nancy A.	Groton, New London	D	1993 1995
Depaolo, Juanine S.	Plantsville, Hartford	D	1955 1959 1961 1963 1965
Dickinson, Signa C.	New Hartford, Litchfield	R	1947
Diefenderfer, Eva P.	Wethersfield, Hartford	R	1963 1965
Diel, Mildred A.	Trumbull, Fairfield	R	1963*
Dillon, Patricia A.	New Haven, New Haven	D	1985 1987 1989 1991 1993 1995
Downing, Edith Hunt	Clinton, Middlesex	R	1947 1949 1951 1953

Doyle, Julia H.	Enfield, Hartford	D	1931 1935
Draper, Nancy Carroll	Ridgefield, Fairfield	R	1953 1955 1957 1959
Dunn, Barbara B.	East Hartford, Hartford	R	1967 1969
Dunne, Antoinette M.	Farmington, Hartford	D	1937
Durrell, Jacquelyn C.	Fairfield, Fairfield	R	1977
Dworak, Marie D.	Hartford, Hartford	D	1967
Eads, M. Adela	Kent, Litchfield	R	1977 1979
Eberle, Mary U.	Bloomfield, Hartford	D	1993 1995
Edgarston, Edna A.F.	Stamford, Fairfield	R	1943 1945 1947
Edwards, Grace I.	New Hartford, Litchfield	I	1921
Elloitt, Geraldine	Danielson, Windham	R	1985
Emery, Julia	Stamford, Fairfield	R	1925 1927 1929
Emmons, Linda N	Madison, New Haven	R	1977 1979 1981 1983 1985 1987 1989 1991
Emmons, Marie P.	Hartland, Hartford	R	1923
Erb, Lillian	Noank, New London	R	1963 1965 1967 1969 1971*
Erk, Anna P.	Naugatuck, New Haven	R	1943
Evarts, Katharine A.	Kent, Litchfield	R	1959 1961 1963 1965
Fahey, Mary Q.	Torrington, Litchfield	R	1957
Fahrbach, Ruth C.	Windsor, Hartford	R	1981 1983 1985 1987 1989 1991 1993 1995
Farmer, Marjorie Dilley	Darien, Fairfield	R	1931 1933 1935 1953 1955 1957 1959
Faulise-Boone, Dorothy	Norwich, New London	D	1975 1977 1979
Favreau, Irene B.	New Britain, Hartford	D	1983 1985 1987
Fenniman, Edna C.	Naugatuck, New Haven	R	1925
Fillmore, Mildred A.	Hebron, Tolland	R	1937 1939
Finney, Florence D.	Cos Cob, Fairfield	R	1949 1951 1953
Fisher, Evelyn S.	Southbury, New Haven	D	1959 1961
Flanagan, Ruth W.	Windsor Locks, Hartford	D	1959 1961 1963 1965
Flynn, Mary E.	Southington, Hartford	D	1937 1945 1947 1949
Foote, Annie	Andover, Tolland	R	1945
Francis, Kathryn G.	Durham, Middlesex	R	1975
Frankel, Esther	Amston, Tolland	D	1959
Freer, Frances A.	Bridgeport, Fairfield	R	1981
Frink, Lillian M. S.	Canterbury, Windham	R	1921 1923 1953 1955 1957
Fritz, Mary G.	Yalesville, New Haven	D	1983 1987 1989 1991 1993 1995
Frost, Violet A.	Cromwell, Middlesex	D	1959
Fuchs, Josephine S.	Westport, Fairfield	R	1987 1989 1991 1993 1995
Fulgham, Margaret	Waterbury, New Haven	R	1955
Galbraith, Marie W.	Thomaston, Litchfield	D	1987
Garcia, Edna L.	Bridgeport, Fairfield	D	1993 1995
Garvey, Jeanne W.	New Milford, Litchfield	R	1993 1995
Gedrim, Sophia	Broad Brook, Hartford	D	1955 1959 1961

Connecticut House, continued

Name	City, County	Party	Legislative Year
Genest, Eraine L.	Prospect, New Haven	D	1959
Gerratana, Theresa B.	New Britain, Hartford	D	1993 1995
Giannini, Agnes E.	Bridgeport, Fairfield	D	1969
Gibson, Betsy Burg-hardt	Waterford, New London	D	1981 1983
Gill, Margaret S.	Wilton, Fairfield	R	1987 1989 1991
Gillie, Elizabeth B.	New Haven, New Haven	R	1947
Goldsmith, Fannie P.	Branford, New Haven	R	1931*
Goodwin, Dorothy C.	Mansfield, Tolland	D	1975 1977 1979 1981 1983
Googins, Sonya	Glastonbury, Hartford	R	1995
Granger, Beula P.	East Granby, Hartford	R	1945 1947 1949 1951
Grasso, Ella T.	Windsor Locks, Hartford	D	1953 1955
Green, Elizabeth	Tolland, Tolland	D	1923
Green, Eloise B.	Southbury, New Haven	R	1961 1963 1965 1967 1969 1971 1973 1975 1977
Green, Helen A.	Granby, Hartford	R	1925
Greenbacker, Lena W.	Middlefield, Middlesex	R	1927 1929
Griffin, Anna E.	Trumbull, Fairfield	R	1943 1945 1947
Griffin, Sadie K.	Trumbull, Fairfield	Soc	1939
Griswold, Mary R.	New Haven, New Haven	D	1967 1969 1971 1973
Gutmann, Myrtle Perri *see Perri*	Shelton, Fairfield	D	1967
Gyle, Norma	New Fairfield, Fairfield	R	1985 1987 1989 1991 1993 1995
Hall, Evelyn E.	Granby, Hartford	R	1963 1965
Halstedt, Alice M.	Cromwell, Middlesex	R	1963 1965
Hamerman, Wilda S.	Orange, New Haven	D	1975
Hammer, Lucy T.	Branford, New Haven	R	1955 1957 1959
Hanazalek, Astrid T.	Suffield, Hartford	R	1971 1973 1975 1977 1979
Harris, Eva M.	Lisbon, New London	D	1959 1961 1963 1965
Harris, Fannie	Norwalk, Fairfield	R	1953 1955
Hartley, Joan V.	Waterbury, New Haven	D	1985 1987 1989 1991 1993 1995
Hendel, Patricia T.	New London, New London	D	1975 1977 1979
Herskowitz, Carol A.	Southbury, New Haven	R	1981 1983 1985 1987
Heser, Bertha G.	Killingworth, Middlesex	D	1939 1941
Hess, Marilyn A.	Greenwich, Fairfield	R	1993 1995
Hill, Mary	New London, New London	D	1959 1961 1963 1965 1967 1969 1971
Hiltgen, Mildred C.	Coventry, Tolland	D	1961
Hoare, Ann Cleary	New London, New London	D	1949
Hoffman, Mildred O.	Cromwell, Middlesex	R	1953
Holmgren, Theresa	Stratford, Fairfield	R	1933 1935 1937

Hooker, Mary M.	Hartford, Hartford	R	1921 1925
Hubbard, Clemon- tine D.	Higganum, Middlesex	R	1949 1951
Hull, Sylvia G.	Bridgeport, Fairfield	R	1933 1935 1951
Hurley, Margaret C.	Windham, Windham	D	1935 1937 1939 1941
Hutton, Dorothy S.	Somers, Tolland	R	1961 1963 1965
Hutton, Lillian E.	Winsted, Litchfield	R	1949 1951 1953 1957
Hyde, Alice E.	Hamden, New Haven	R	1957
Ireland, Barbara M.	Ridgefield, Fairfield	D	1987 1989 1991 1993
Jackson-Brooks, Andrea	New Haven, New Haven	D	1993
Jagger, Lina W.	Washington Depot, Litchfield	R	1949 1951 1953
James, Mary P.	Fairfield, Fairfield	R	1957
Jansen, Jane M.	Ridgefield, Fairfield	R	1985*
Javorski, Helen B.	Thompsonville, Hartford	D	1957
Jerman, Beatrice C.	Westport, Fairfield	R	1949 1951
Jewett, Helen A.	Tolland, Tolland	D	1921
Jones, Natalie B.	Hebron, Tolland	D	1951
Jones, Ruth A.	Waterbury, New Haven	R	1947 1957
Jorgensen, Annie Follet	Norwichtown, New London	I	1955
Kamemski, Steph- anie R.	Berlin, Hartford	R	1941 1943 1945 1947
Katona, Mary A.	Fairfield, Fairfield	D	1959
Keeler, Mary J.	Ridgefield, Fairfield	R	1959*
Keeney, Julia Allen	Somers, Tolland	R	1935 1937 1939 1941 1943 1945
Kelly, Mary Jane	West Haven, New Haven	D	1983
Kemler, Joan R.	West Hartford, Hartford	D	1975 1977 1979 1981 1983
Kennedy, May McC.	Washington Depot, Litchfield	R	1955 1957
Kenney, Mary Catherine	New Britain, Hartford	D	1949
Kerensky, Nancy E.	South Windsor, Hartford	D	1995
Kezer, Pauline	Plainville, Hartford	R	1979 1981 1983 1985
Kipp, Phyllis T.	Mystic, New London	R	1973 1975 1977 1979
Kirkley-Bey, Maria Lopez	Hartford, Hartford	D	1993 1995
Kirschner, Dorothy	Harwinton, Litchfield	R	1961 1963 1965
Kitchel, Helen B.	Sound Beach, Fairfield	R	1931 1933 1935 1937
Kline, Sophie Z.	Meriden, New Haven	D	1945 1949
Koskoff, Gertrude F.	Plainville, Hartford	R	1953 1955 1957
Kusnitz, Adele	Monroe, Fairfield	R	1981 1983 1985 1987 1989
Laplace, Helen D.	Deep River, Middlesex	R	1957
Leonard, Elizabeth M.	Ridgefield, Fairfield	R	1977 1979 1981
Leopold, Alice K.	Westport, Fairfield	R	1949
Lester, Helen M.	Litchfield, Litchfield	R	1957 1959 1961 1963 1965

Connecticut House, continued

Name	City, County	Party	Legislative Year
Lewis, Clara Wentworth M.	Bridgeport, Fairfield	R	1933 1935 1937 1949 1951
Lewis, Helen E.	Stratford, Fairfield	R	1923 1925 1927 1929 1931
Lewitz, Loretta	Norwich, New London	D	1959
Liss, Sophie G.	New Britain, Hartford	D	1945
Little, Eleanor H.	Guilford, New Haven	R	1941 1945
Lockton, Janet K.	Greenwich, Fairfield	R	1991 1993 1995
Lojzim, Ruth E.	Tolland, Tolland	R	1959 1961 1963 1965
Lord, Florence S.	East Hampton, Hartford	D	1951 1953 1955 1957 1959 1961
Lyons, Moira K.	Stamford, Fairfield	D	1981 1983 1985 1987 1989 1991 1993 1995
Mackie, Helen H.	Westport, Fairfield	R	1957 1959
Maher, Annie H.	New Haven, New Haven	D	1929 1931
Malloy, Jeanette A.	Avon, Hartford	R	1965*
Maloney, Ruth Ryan	Lebanon, New London	D	1951
Mansfield, Carrie F.	Preston, New London	R	1953 1955 1957 1959 1961 1963 1965
Martin, Mary A.	Preston, New London	D	1971
Maschal, Sara C.	Norwalk, Fairfield	R	1939
Matarese, Lucille A.	Hartford, Hartford	D	1967
Matrascia, Patsy R.	Torrington, Litchfield	D	1947 1949 1951
Maxwell, Florence P.	Rockville, Tolland	R	1929
Maynard, Bernadette C.	Norwich, New London	R	1955 1957
McCluskey, Dorothy S.	Northford, New Haven	D	1975 1977 1979 1981
McBee, Doris	Willington, Tolland	R	1935 1937
McCue, Margaret L.	Windsor Locks, Hartford	D	1951
McDonald, Anne B.	Stamford, Fairfield	D	1991 1993 1995
McDonnell, Mary H.	Northford, New Haven	R	1947 1949
McGrattan, Mary K.	Gales Ferry, New London	D	1993 1995
McKeehan, Martha M.	Old Greenwich, Fairfield	R	1947
Mead, Julia B.	Greenwich, Fairfield	R	1941
Merrill, Denise W.	Mansfield Center, Tolland	D	1993* 1995
Meyer, Alice V.	Easton, Fairfield	R	1975* 1977 1979 1981 1983 1985 1987 1989 1991
Miller, Charlotte E.	East Haven, New Haven	R	1939 1941 1943 1945 1947 1949
Miller, Dorothy R.	Bolton, Tolland	R	1959 1961 1969 1971 1973 1977
Miller, Edith V.	Hartland, Hartford	R	1929 1931 1933
Miller, Georgana C.	Norwich, New London	R	1941 1943 1945 1947 1949
Miller, Leone Holman	New Britain, Hartford	R	1947

Mills, Janet Marsico	Norwalk, Fairfield	R	1985
Mills, Lotus M.	Stamford, Fairfield	D	1959
Moore, Marie P.	Northford, New Haven	R	1955
Moriairty, Ruth Beckwith	East Hampton, Middlesex	R	1963 1965
Morton, Margaret E.	Bridgeport, Fairfield	D	1973 1975 1977 1979
Moynihan, Rosemary L.	East Hartford, Hartford	D	1991
Murdock, Beatrice	Avon, Hartford	R	1979* 1981 1983 1985 1987
Mushinsky, Mary M.	Wallingford, New Haven	D	1981 1983 1985 1987 1989 1991 1993 1995
Nardello, Vickie O.	Prospect, New Haven	D	1995
Negron, Edna	Danbury, Fairfield	D	1991
Nevius, Clarissa	New Fairfield, Fairfield	R	1923 1925 1927 1929 1931 1933 1935 1937 1939 1941 1943 1945 1947 1949 1951
Nichols, Finette B.	Fairfield, Fairfield	R	1931 1933 1935 1937 1939 1941 1943 1945
Niedermeier, Christine M.	Fairfield, Fairfield	D	1979 1981 1983 1985
Nolan, Florence H.	West Haven, New Haven	R	1953
Norton, Helen L.	Durham, Middlesex	R	1953 1955
Nucci, Ella M.	Deep River, Middlesex	D	1963 1965
O'Connell, Ruth S.	Sharon, Litchfield	R	1963 1965
O'Shea, Clara P. L.	Beacon Falls, New Haven	D	1945 1947 1949 1951 1953 1955 1957 1959
O'Sullivan, Mary Ann	Torrington, Litchfield	D	1993
Olander, Alice Swanie	Marlborough, Hartford	D	1943 1945
Orcutt, Geil	New Haven, New Haven	D	1975 1977 1979 1981
Osiecki, Clarice A.	Danbury, Fairfield	R	1973 1975 1977 1979
Osler, Dorothy K.	Riverside, Fairfield	R	1973 1975 1977 1979 1981 1983 1985 1987 1989 1991
Otterness, Naomi W.	Ledyard, New London	D	1979 1981
Pallanck, Anna Mae	Stafford Springs, Tolland	R	1953 1955 1957
Parker, Antonina B.	Glastonbury, Hartford	R	1977 1979 1981 1983
Parker, Belle R.	Newington, Hartford	R	1949
Parker, Catherine M.	New Haven, New Haven	D	1977 1979 1981
Parker, Jannette	New Haven, New Haven	D	1991
Parmelee, Alice E.	East Hartland, Hartford	R	1943 1953
Pearson, Marilyn	Stratford, Fairfield	R	1969 1971 1973
Perri, Myrtle S. *see* Gutmann	Shelton, Fairfield	D	1959 1961 1963 1965
Perry, Carrie Saxon	Hartford, Hartford	D	1981 1983 1985 1987
Peterson, Alice T.	Short Beach, New Haven	R	1949 1951 1953

Connecticut House, continued

Name	City, County	Party	Legislative Year
Pierson, Olive D.	Cromwell, Middlesex	R	1933
Pitney, Blanche	S. Glastonbury, Hartford	R	1945
Pitt, Harriet Sampson	Woodstock, Windham	R	1955 1957 1959 1961
Platt, Caroline T.	Milford, New Haven	R	1929 1931
Polinsky, Janet C.	Waterford, New London	D	1977 1979 1981 1983 1985 1987 1989 1991
Poss, Janet C.	Guilford, New Haven	D	1991 1993
Powers, Claudia M.	Riverside, Fairfield	R	1993 1995
Powers, Nora A.	Plainville, Hartford	D	1959 1961 1963 1965
Prague, Edith G.	Columbia, Tolland	D	1983 1985 1987 1989 1991*
Pratt, Blanche F.	Essex, Middlesex	R	1953
Pratt, Clara E.	Plainville, Hartford	R	1951
Prokop, Rose E.	Stratford, Fairfield	R	1945 1947 1949 1951 1953 1955 1957
Quimby, Marguerite	New London, New London	D	1953 1955
Radzwillas, Aldona	Bridgeport, Fairfield	D	1975
Rapoport, Natalie	Waterbury, New Haven	D	1973 1975 1977 1979
Raymond, Edith M.	Lyme, New London	R	1925
Redick, Frances	Newington, Hartford	R	1941
Reed, Mary S.	Bethel, Fairfield	R	1953 1955 1957
Reinhardsen, Margaret S.	West Redding, Fairfield	R	1959 1961 1963 1965
Rell, M. Jodi	Brookfield, Fairfield	R	1985 1987 1989 1991 1993
Renshaw, Elizabeth P.	Darien, Fairfield	R	1937 1939
Richards, Muriel	Milford, New Haven	D	1959
Roberts, Dorothy F.	Barkhemsted, Litchfield	R	1937 1939
Roberts, Marian Green	Hartford, Hartford	D	1929
Roche, Marilyn M.	Wilton, Fairfield	R	1983 1985
Rock, Isabel K.	Wilton, Fairfield	R	1961 1963 1965 1967
Rockwood, Florence J.	Franklin, New London	R	1941 1943
Romanoff, Sally	Canterbury, Windham	R	1961 1963 1965
Rossi, Virginia N.	Torrington, Litchfield	D	1941 1943 1945
Rothman, Martha D.	Ridgefield, Fairfield	R	1981* 1983 1985
Rowland, Alice V.	Ridgefield, Fairfield	R	1931 1933
Rowley, Rosabelle	Riverton, Litchfield	R	1947 1949 1951
Russ, Alice W.	Shelton, Fairfield	R	1929 1931
Russell, Belle D.	Haddam, Middlesex	R	1939 1941 1945
Russell, Hannah E. Clark *see Clark*	Orange, New Haven	R	1963 1965
Ryan, Arline W.	Branford, Hartford	R	1955 1961 1963 1965 1967 1969
Ryan, Ethel M.	Ridgefield, Fairfield	R	1925 1927 1943 1945

Rylander, Isabel C.	Litchfield, Litchfield	R	1941 1943 1945 1947 1949 1951 1953 1955
Sanchez, Maria C.	Hartford, Hartford	D	1989
Satti, Dorothy	New London, New London	D	1945
Sauer, Claire	Lyme, New London	D	1995
Sawyer, Pamela Z.	Bolton, Tolland	R	1993 1995
Scalettar, Ellen	Woodbridge, New Haven	D	1993 1995
Schenherr, Grace H.	Norfolk, Litchfield	R	1935 1937 1939
Schmeltz, Olive-beth E.	Norfolk, Litchfield	R	1947 1949 1951 1953 1955
Schmidle, Mae S.	Newtown, Fairfield	R	1981 1983 1985 1987 1989
Schroeder, Louise	Georgetown, Fairfield	R	1949 1951
Sellers, Helen Earle	Hebron, Tolland	D	1941 1949
Shanley, Helen C.	Thomaston, Litchfield	D	1959
Sharpe, Edna B.	Abington, Windham	R	1949 1951
Shepard, Elizabeth T.	Putnam, Windham	R	1957
Sherlock, Doris M.	Prospect, New Haven	D	1961
Simons, Agnes O.	Bridgeport, Fairfield	D	1967 1969 1971
Smith, Edith W.	Chaplin, Windham	R	1949 1951
Smith, Gertrude	Farmington, Hartford	R	1933 1939
Smith, Helen M.	Milford, New Haven	R	1945 1947 1949
Spallone, Jeanne F.	Deep River, Middlesex	D	1959
Spaulding, Emilie H.	Norfolk, Litchfield	R	1945
Stalsburg, Kathryn	Deep River, Middlesex	R	1943 1945
Stearns, Frances C.	Storrs, Tolland	R	1955
Stevens, Lydia H.	Greenwich, Fairfield	R	1989 1991
Stevens, Marie A.	Bethlehem, Litchfield	R	1961* 1963 1965
Stewart, Nellie D.	New Canaan, Fairfield	R	1931 1933 1935 1937 1939 1941 1943 1945
Stillman, Andrea L.	Waterford, New London	D	1993 1995
Stolle, Doris S.	Broad Brook, Hartford	R	1957
Stratton, Jessie G.	Canton Center, Hartford	D	1989 1991 1993 1995
Strekas, Margaret	Somers, Tolland	R	1953 1955 1957 1959
Strunk, Eleanore	Brooklyn, Windham	R	1957
Sturges, Adella R.	Georgetown, Fairfield	R	1945 1947
Suarez, Ruth F.	Cheshire, New Haven	R	1953 1955 1957
Sullivan, Hazel Thrall	Windsor, Hartford	D	1945 1947
Sutliffe, Edith E.	Plymouth, Litchfield	R	1929
Swensson, Elsie L.	Manchester, Hartford	R	1981 1983 1985
Taborsak, Lynn H.	Danbury, Fairfield	D	1985 1987 1989 1991
Taft, Esther K.	Norwich, New London	D	1959 1961 1963 1965
Taneszio, Theresa	New Haven, New Haven	D	1967 1969 1971
Tanger, Winifred A.	Waterford, New London	D	1975
Taylor, Bessie H.	Redding, Fairfield	R	1941 1943
Tedesco, Jane J.	Bridgeport, Fairfield	D	1945
Temkin, Zena H.	Torrington, Litchfield	D	1959 1961
Ter Kuile, Barbara J.	Litchfield, Litchfield	R	1967 1969

Connecticut House, continued

Name	City, County	Party	Legislative Year
Thornton, Jean T.	Glastonbury, Hartford	R	1963 1965 1967 1969 1971 1973 1975
Tippin, Barbara	Essex, Middlesex	R	1955
Toulson, Diane	Milford, New Haven	R	1955 1957
Townshend, Hannah D.	New Haven, New Haven	R	1925
Tracy, Kathleen M.	Rocky Hill, Hartford	D	1959 1961 1963 1965
Truex, Ruth O.	Wethersfield, Hartford	R	1967 1969 1971
Truglia, Christel H.	Stamford, Fairfield	D	1989 1991 1993 1995
Tyler, Pauline B.	South Coventry, Tolland	R	1953
Tyrol, Olive B.	S. Glastonbury, Hartford	R	1947
Vadnais, Bertha A.	Putnam, Windham	D	1959 1961 1963 1965
Vance, Morag L.	Trumbull, Fairfield	R	1977 1979 1981 1983 1985 1987
Vestal, Ina	Woodbridge, New Haven	R	1955 1957 1959 1961 1963 1965 1967
Vinton, Annie E.	Mansfield, Tolland	R	1923 1925 1931
Von Hagen, Emma M.	Higganum, Middlesex	R	1953 1955 1957 1959 1961
Wakelee, Rose E.	Wolcott, New Haven	R	1943 1945 1947
Warner, Helen L.	Newington, Hartford	R	1943 1945 1947
Warnock, Helen Holme	Westport, Fairfield	R	1945 1947
Wasserman, Julia B.	Sandy Hook, Fairfield	R	1991 1993 1995
Weaver, Mary B.	New Milford, Litchfield	R	1923 1925 1927 1939
Weir, Madelyn R.	Stamford, Fairfield	R	1953
Welles, Arline T.	Old Saybrook, Middlesex	R	1949 1951 1953 1955
Wells, Ruth T.	Coventry, Tolland	D	1943
White, Edith A.	Danbury, Fairfield	R	1953
White, Mildred M.	North Stonington, New London	R	1957 1959 1961 1963 1965
Widlitz, Patricia	Guilford, New Haven	D	1995
Wiedman, Mary S.	Hartford, Hartford	R	1927
Wilber, Elinor F.	Fairfield, Fairfield	R	1973 1975 1977 1979 1981 1983 1985 1987 1989 1991
Wilford, May F.	Cornwall Bridge, Litchfield	R	1929
Winkler, Lenny T.	Groton, New London	R	1987* 1989 1991 1993 1995
Wojtas, Joyce A.	Windsor Locks, Hartford	D	1977 1979
Wood, Elizabeth A.	Litchfield, Litchfield	R	1977
Wood, Gertrude P.	Sommersville, Tolland	R	1947 1949
Woodford, Majorie M.	Marlborough, Hartford	D	1939
Woodward, Lucille M.	Salisbury, Litchfield	R	1939 1941
Woodward, Maud L.	Bolton Notch, Tolland	R	1925 1927 1929 1935 1937 1939 1941 1943 1945

Wright, Julia T.	Orange, New Haven	R	1951 1953 1955 1957 1959
Wrynn, Lucie	Wallingford, New Haven	D	1949 1951 1953 1955
Wyman, Nancy S.	Tolland, Tolland	D	1987 1989 1991 1993
Yacavone, Muriel T.	East Hartford, Hartford	D	1971 1973 1975 1977 1979 1981
Yerrington, Lillian L.	Rocky Hill, Hartford	R	1947
Zbikowski, Helen	Bristol, Hartford	D	1943 1945
Zdunczyk, Elizabeth	Plantsville, Hartford	D	1951 1953
Zemke, Jennie	Wallingford, New Haven	D	1959

*Notes:
Beck, Audrey P.—Died March 11, 1983 (Johnston)
Begg, Claire H.—Elected March 8, 1971 (Begg)
Bolster, Sally McCarthy—Elected 1988 (Esposito)
Brown, Emily Sophie—Resigned April 1921
Carrozzella, Jeanette—Elected 1972 (Carrozzella)
Carter, Annette Wheeler—Elected 1988 (Perry)[F]
Castro, Illia—Elected Nov. 12, 1993
Diel, Mildred A.—Died May 3, 1964 (Dowd)
Diloreto, Virginia—Resigned March 26, 1965 (Amenta)
Erb, Lillian—Died May 17, 1971 (Wright)
Goldsmith, Fannie P.—Died April 6, 1931
Jansen, Jane M.—Elected 1986 (Rothman)F
Keeler, Mary J.—Elected July 2, 1959 (Keeler)
Malloy, Jeanette A.—Elected March 29, 1965 (Malloy)
Merrill, Denise W.—Elected Nov. 2, 1993 (Pelto)
Meyer, Alice V.—Elected 1976 (Manchester)
Murdock, Beatrice—Elected 1980 (Swomley)
Prague, Edith G.—Resigned Jan. 8, 1991
Rothman, Martha D.—Elected 1982 (Leonard)[F]
Stevens, Marie A.—Elected April 17, 1961 (Stevens)
Winkler, Lenny T.—Elected 1988 (Buckley)[F]

DELAWARE (1925–1995)

Delaware women gained school suffrage in 1898 and full suffrage on August 26, 1920. A constitutional amendment allowing women to serve in state offices passed in 1923. Florence M. Hanby (R–Holly Oak) was the first woman elected to the General Assembly in 1924.

State elections are held every two years to elect 41 representatives who serve two year terms and 21 senators who serve staggered two-four-four year terms. Vacancies are filled by special election.

39 women have served in the Delaware General Assembly:
    13 in the Senate
    31 in the House
    (5 in the House and Senate)

Women as Percentage of Delaware Legislators

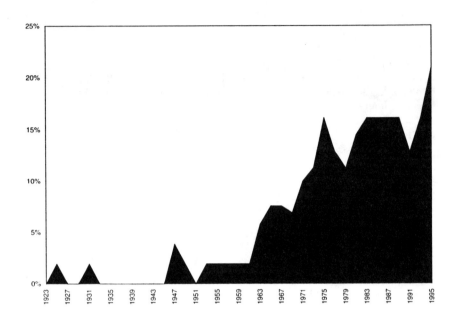

Senate
2 – 4 – 4 Year Terms

Name	City, County	Party	Legislative Year
Bair, Myrna L.	Wilmington, New Castle	R	1981 1983 1985 1987 1989 1991 1993 1995
Bane, Margo Ewing	Wilmington, New Castle	R	1987 1989
Blevins, Patricia M.	Wilmington, New Castle	D	1991 1993 1995
Conner, Louise T.	Delair, New Castle	R	1965 1967 1969 1971
Cook, Nancy W.	Kenton, Dover	D	1975 1977 1979 1981 1983 1985 1987 1989 1991 1993 1995
Davis, Vera G.	Dover, Kent	R	1947 1949
Henry, Margaret R.	Wilmington, New Castle	R	1993* 1995
Lord, Evelyn M.	Wilmington, New Castle	R	1963
Manning, Margaret R.	Wilmington, New Castle	R	1961 1963 1965 1967 1969 1971 1973 1975

Minner, Ruth Ann	Milford, Sussex	D	1983 1985 1987 1989 1991
Reed, Donna	Newark, New Castle	R	1995
Sorenson, Liane M.	Hockessin, New Castle	R	1995
Spence, Winifred M.	Middletown, New Castle	R	1977 1979

House
2 Year Terms

Name	City, County	Party	Legislative Year
Anderson, Marian P.	Newark, New Castle	D	1977 1979 1981 1983 1985
Boykin, Mary Beth T.	Wilmington, New Castle	R	1983 1985 1987 1989 1991
Bradley, Peggy G.	Wilmington, New Castle	D	1993
Capano, Deborah H.	Wilmington, New Castle	R	1995
Davis, Vera G.	Dover, Kent	R	1953
Fallon, Tina	Seaford, Sussex	R	1977* 1979 1981 1983 1985 1987 1989 1991 1993 1995
Gooding, Mary Etta	Woodcrest, New Castle	D	1963 1965 1967
Hanby, Florence M.	Holly Oak, New Castle	R	1925
Heckert, Clarice U.	Highland Woods, New Castle	R	1965 1967 1969 1971 1973
Jester, Katharine M.	Middletown, New Castle	D	1981 1983 1985 1987 1989
Johnson, Henrietta	Wilmington, New Castle	D	1971 1973 1975 1977
Lesher, Lois M.	Claymont, New Castle	R	1973 1975
Lytle, Wilfreda J.	Carcroft, New Castle	R	1947
Maier, Pamela S.	Newark, New Castle	R	1995
Manning, Margaret R.	Wilmington, New Castle	R	1957 1959
Maroney, Jane P.	Wilmington, New Castle	R	1979 1981 1983 1985 1987 1989 1991 1993 1995
Miller, Karen Jennings	Dover, Kent	D	1975 1977
Minner, Ruth Ann	Milford, Sussex	D	1975 1977 1979 1981
Seibel, Marion I.	Newark, New Castle	R	1969 1971 1973 1975
Smith, Gwynne P.	Wilmington, New Castle	R	1975 1977 1979 1981 1983 1985 1987 1989
Soles, Ada Leigh	Newark, New Castle	D	1981 1983 1985 1987 1989 1991
Sorenson, Liane M.	Hockessin, New Castle	R	1993
Spence, Winifred M.	Middletown, New Castle	R	1973 1975
Stone, Donna D.	Dover, Kent	R	1995
Tschudy, Estelle W.	Smyrna, Kent	R	1931
Tunnell, Mildred S.	Georgetown, Sussex	D	1955

Delaware House, continued

Name	City, County	Party	Legislative Year
Ulbrich, Stephanie A.	Newark, New Castle	R	1995
Wagner, Nancy H.	Dover, Kent	R	1993 1995
Wojewodzki, Catherine	Newark, New Castle	D	1993
Worthen, Sandra	Newark, New Castle	D	1973 1975 1977*
Wright, Joan C.	Wilmington, New Castle	D	1971

*Notes:
Fallon, Tina—Elected 1977 (Temple)
Henry, Margaret R.—Elected April 1993 (Holloway)
Worthen, Sandra—Resigned 1978 (Petrillo)

FLORIDA (1929-1995)

Florida women gained suffrage on August 26, 1920. Women first voted in state elections in 1920 and first ran for the state legislature in the 1922 primary

Women as Percentage of Florida Legislators

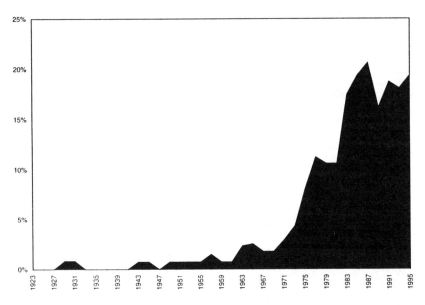

elections. The first woman legislator, Edna Giles Fuller (D–Orlando) was elected to the House in 1928.

State elections are held every two years for 120 representatives who serve two year terms and 40 senators who serve four year terms. Special reapportionment elections were held in 1967 and 1983. State legislative service is limited to eight consecutive terms. Vacancies are filled by special election.

88 women have served in the Florida Legislature:
    23 in the Senate
    76 in the House
    (11 in the House and Senate)

Senate
4 Year Terms

Name	City, County	Party	Legislative Year
Brown-Waite, Ginny	Brooksville, Hernando	R	1993 1995
Castor, Elizabeth Betty	Tampa, Hillsborough	D	1977 1983 1985
Davis, Helen Gordon	Tampa, Hillsborough	D	1989 1991
Fox, Roberta	Coral Gables, Dade	D	1983 1985
Frank, Pat Collier	Tampa, Hillsborough	D	1979 1981 1983 1985 1987
Grizzle, Mary R.	Indian Rock, Pinellas	R	1979 1981 1983 1985 1987 1989 1991
Grogan, Patricia	Merritt Island, Brevard	D	1993
Harris, Katherine	Sarasota, Sarasota	D	1995
Holzendorf, Betty S.	Jacksonville, Duval	D	1993 1995
Jennings, Toni	Orlando, Orange	R	1981 1983 1985 1987 1989 1991 1993 1995
Johnson, Beth	Orlando, Orange	D	1963 1965 1967*
Johnson, Elizabeth J.	Cocoa Beach, Brevard	R	1967 1969 1971
Johnson, Karen	Leesburg, Lake	D	1993 1995
Kurth, Patsy Ann	Palm Bay, Brevard	D	1991 1993 1995
Malchon, Jeanne	St. Petersburg, Pinellas	D	1983 1985 1987 1989 1991
Margolis, Gwen	N. Miami Beach, Dade	D	1981 1983 1985 1987 1989 1991
Meek, Carrie P.	Miami, Dade	D	1983 1985 1987 1989 1991
Ros-Lehtinen, Ileana *see Ros*	Miami, Dade	R	1987 1989*
Thurman, Karen L.	Dunnellon, Marion	D	1983 1985 1987 1989 1991
Walker, Sherry D.	Waukeenah, Jefferson	D	1989 1991
Weinstock, Eleanor	W. Palm Beach, Martin	D	1987 1989 1991

Florida Senate, continued

Name	City, County	Party	Legislative Year
Wilson, Lori	Cocoa Beach, Brevard	I	1973 1975 1977
Woodson, Mariene E.	E. Bradenton, Manatee	R	1987 1989

House
2 Year Terms

Name	City, County	Party	Legislative Year
Bailey, Patricia L.	Pinellas Park, Pinellas	D	1983
Baker, Mary Lou	St. Petersburg, Pinellas	D	1943 1945
Baker, Maxine E.	Miami, Dade	D	1963 1965 1967 1969 1971
Bass, Virginia	Pensacola, Santa Rosa	D	1983 1985 1987
Benson, Lois	Pensacola, Santa Rosa	R	1993
Betancourt, Annie	Miami, Dade	D	1995
Bloom, Elaine	N. Miami Beach, Dade	D	1975 1977 1985* 1987 1989 1991 1993 1995
Brennan, Mary M.	Pinellas Park, Pinellas	D	1991 1993 1995
Brown, Corrine	Jacksonville, Duval	D	1983 1985 1987 1989 1991
Brown, Shirley A.	Sarasota, Sarasota	D	1993 1995
Bullard, Larcenia J.	Miami, Dade	D	1993 1995
Burke, Beryl Roberts	Carol City, Dade	D	1993 1995
Burnsed, Beverly B.	Lakeland, Hillsborough	D	1977 1979 1981 1983 1985 1987
Carlton, Fran	Orlando, Orange	D	1977 1979 1981 1983 1985 1987
Carlton, Lisa	Osprey, Sarasota	R	1995
Cherry, Gwendolyn Sawyer	Miami, Dade	D	1971 1973 1975 1977 1979*
Chestnut, Cynthia Moore	Gainesville, Alachua	D	1991 1993 1995
Chinoy, Kathy Geller	Jacksonville, Duval	D	1991
Coolman, Karen B.	Ft. Lauderdale, Broward	D	1975
Cox, Linda C.	Ft. Lauderdale, Broward	R	1977 1979 1981
Culp, Faye	Tampa, Hillsborough	R	1995
Davis, Helen Gordon	Tampa, Hillsborough	D	1975 1977 1979 1981 1983 1985 1987
Dawson, Muriel	Ft. Lauderdale, Broward	D	1993 1995
Dennis, Willye F.	Jacksonville, Duval	D	1993 1995
Easley, Betty	Clearwater, Largo	R	1973 1975 1977 1979 1981 1983 1985
Edwards, Lori	Auburndale, Polk	D	1993 1995
Evans, Marilyn Bailey	Melbourne, Brevard	R	1977 1979 1981 1983 1985

Figg, Mary	Lutz, Hillsborough	D	1983 1985 1987 1989 1991
Fox, Roberta	Coral Gables, Dade	D	1977 1979 1981
Frank, Pat Collier	Tampa, Hillsborough	D	1977
Frankel, Lois J.	W. Palm Beach, Martin	D	1987 1989 1991 1995
Fuller, Edna Giles	Orlando, Orange	D	1929 1931
Gonzalez-Quevedo, Arnhilda B.	Coral Gables, Dade	R	1985 1987*
Gordon, Elaine	N. Miami, Dade	D	1973 1975 1977 1979 1981 1983 1985 1987 1989 1991 1993
Greene, Addie L.	Mangolia Park, Duval	D	1993 1995
Grizzle, Mary R.	Indian Rock, Pinellas	R	1963 1965 1967 1969 1971 1973 1975 1977
Guber, Susan	Miami, Dade	D	1987 1989 1991
Hanson, Carol G.	Boca Raton, Palm Beach	R	1983 1985 1987 1989 1991 1993
Harrington, Nancy O.	Coral Gables, Dade	D	1975
Hawkins, Mary Ellen	Naples, Collier	R	1975 1977 1979 1981 1983 1985 1987 1989 1991 1993
Heyman, Sally A.	N. Miami Beach, Dade	D	1995
Holzendorf, Betty S.	Jacksonville, Duval	D	1987* 1989 1991
Horan, Debbie	Key West, Dade	D	1995
Irvine, Frances L.	Orange Park, Orange	R	1985 1987 1989 1991
Jacobs, Suzanne	Delray Beach, Palm Beach	D	1993 1995
Jennings, Toni	Orlando, Orange	R	1977 1979
Johnson, Beth	Orlando, Orange	D	1957 1959 1961
Lewis, Marian V.	N. Palm Beach, Palm Beach	R	1987 1989 1991
Lynn, Evelyn	Ormond Beach, Volusia	R	1995
MacKenzie, Anne	Ft. Lauderdale, Broward	D	1983 1985 1987 1989 1991 1993 1995
MacKenzie, Mary Ann	Miami, Dade	D	1963 1965
Margolis, Gwen	N. Miami Beach, Dade	D	1975 1977 1979
McAndrews, Mimi K.	Boca Raton, Palm Beach	D	1993
McClure, Julie G.	Bradenton, Manatee	D	1993
Meek, Carrie P.	Miami, Dade	D	1979* 1981
Merchant, Sharon J.	Palm Beach Gardens, Palm Beach	R	1993 1995
Metcalf, Elizabeth L.	Coral Gables, Dade	D	1983 1985 1987
Mortham, Sandra Barringer	Largo, Pineallas	R	1987 1989 1991 1993
Muscarella, Patricia A.	Clearwater, Largo	R	1991
Patton, Bryant Mary	Apalachicola, Franklin	D	1955 1957
Pearce, Edna	Ft. Basinger, Highlands	D	1949 1951 1953
Prewitt, Debra A.	New Port Richey, Pasco	D	1995
Robinson, Jane W.	Cocoa, Brevard	R	1971 1973 1975

Florida House, continued

Name	City, County	Party	Legislative Year
Rochlin, Irma S.	Hallandale, Dade	D	1983* 1985 1987
Ros, Ileana *see Ros-Lehtinen*	Miami, Dade	R	1983 1985
Rosen, Virginia L.	N. Miami, Dade	D	1979 1981
Sample, Dorothy Eaton	St. Petersburg, Pinellas	R	1977 1979 1981 1983 1985 1987
Sanderson, Deborah P.	Ft. Lauderdale, Broward	R	1983 1985 1987 1989 1991 1993 1995
Sansom, Dixie	Satellite Beach, Brevard	R	1983* 1985 1987 1989 1991
Schultz, Debbie Wasserman	Davie, Broward	D	1993 1995
Shepard, Kimberly M.	Orlando, Orange	D	1993
Simone, Peggy	Bradenton, Manatee	R	1983 1985 1987 1989 1991
Singleton, Mary L.	Jacksonville, Duval	D	1973 1975
Spivey, Helen L.	Crystal River, Citrus	D	1995
Turnbull, Marjorie	Tallahassee, Leon	D	1995
Weinstock, Eleanor	W. Palm Beach, Martin	D	1979 1981 1983 1985

*Notes:
Bloom, Elaine—Elected March 4, 1986 (Kutun)
Cherry, Gwendolyn Sawyer—Died Feb. 7, 1979 (Meeks)[F]
Gonzalez-Quevedo, Arnhilda B.—Died May 9, 1988
Holzendorf, Betty S.—Elected May 1988 (Gaffney)
Johnson, Beth—Elected reapportionment elections, 1967 only
Meek, Carrie P.—Elected March 27, 1979 (Cherry)[F]
Rochlin, Irma S.—Elected March 1984 (Lehman)
Ros-Lehtinen, Ileana—Resigned Aug. 29, 1989, elected US Congress
Sansom, Dixie—Elected April 10, 1984 (Deratany)

GEORGIA (1923–1995)

Georgia women gained suffrage on August 26, 1920. The state refused to waive the poll tax requirement for women to vote in the November 1920 elections. On August 13, 1921, the Georgia General Assembly repealed a law that declared women ineligible for public office. Women first ran for the state legislature in the 1922 state elections and elected Representatives Bessie Kempton (D–Atlanta, Fulton County) and Viola Ross Napier (D–Macon, Bibb County).

State elections are held every two years for 180 representatives and 56 senators who serve two year terms. Vacancies are filled by special election.

93 women have served in the Georgia General Assembly:
  22 in the Senate
  79 in the House
  (8 in the House and Senate)

Women as Percentage of Georgia Legislators

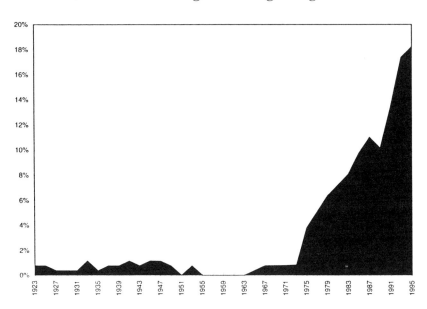

Senate
2 Year Terms

Name	City, County	Party	Legislative Year
Blitch, Iris Faircloth	Homerville, Clinch	D	1947 1953
Blitch, Peg	Homerville, Clinch	D	1993 1995
Cannon, Tassie Kelley	Hiawassee, Rabun	D	1931*
Coffin, Alice Walker	Richland, Stewart	D	1951*
Coxon, Helen Williams	Ludowici, Long	D	1941
Engram, Beverly Leigh	Fairburn, Fulton	D	1981 1983 1985 1987 1989
Glanton, Pam	Riverdale, Fulton	R	1993 1995
Hemmer, Jane	Gainsville, Forsyth	D	1993
Horton, Janice S.	McDonough, Henry	D	1979 1981 1983 1985
James, Donzella J.	College Park, Fulton	D	1995
Johnson, Diane Harvey	Savannah, Chatham	D	1995

Georgia Senate, continued

Name	City, County	Party	Legislative Year
Johnson, Margaret B.	Watkinsville, Oconee	D	1925*
Moore, Susie Tillman	Tifton, Tift	D	1933 1939
Moye, Judy	Fayetteville, Fayette	D	1991
Newbill, Sallie	Atlanta, Fulton	R	1987 1989 1991 1993 1995
Odom, Suzanne Link	Newton, Baker	D	1947
Oliver, Mary Margaret	Atlanta, Fulton	D	1993 1995
Rainey, Rebecca Laing	Dawson, Terrell	D	1945
Shapard, Virginia	Griffin, Spalding	D	1975 1977
Steinberg, Cathey Weiss	Atlanta, Dekalb	D	1991
Stokes, Connie	Decatur, Dekalb	D	1995
Thomas, Nadine	Atlanta, Fulton	D	1993 1995

House
2 Year Terms

Name	City, County	Party	Legislative Year
Aaron, Betty S.	Decatur, Dekalb	D	1981 1983 1985 1987 1989
Ashe, Kathy B.	Smyrna, Fulton	R	1993 1995
Beal, Alveda King	Atlanta, Fulton	D	1979 1981
Blitch, Iris Faircloth	Homerville, Clinch	D	1949
Blitch, Peg	Homerville, Clinch	D	1991
Brooks, Donna Staples	Newnan, Cowetta	R	1993 1995
Buckner, Gail M.	Lake City, Clayton	D	1991 1993 1995
Bunn, Barbara Jean	Conyers, Rockdale	R	1993 1995
Calhoun, Anne C.	Augusta, Richmond	R	1975
Canty, Henrietta Mathis	Atlanta, Fulton	D	1975* 1977 1979 1991 1993 1995
Childs, Peggy	Decatur, Dekalb	D	1975 1977 1979 1981 1983 1985 1987
Clark, Betty Jean	Decatur, Dekalb	D	1973 1975 1977 1979 1981 1983 1985 1987 1989
Coker, Lynda	Marietta, Cobb	R	1991 1993 1995
Couch, Barbara H.	Atlanta, Fulton	D	1981 1983 1985 1987 1989
Cox, Cathy	Bainbridge, Decatur	D	1993 1995
Coxon, Helen Williams	Ludowici, Long	D	1933 1935 1937
Crowe, Lelia	Cartersville, Bartow	D	1961*
Davis, Grace W.	Atlanta, Fulton	D	1987 1989 1991 1993 1995
Falls, Sharon	Macon, Bibb	R	1995

Name	Location	Party	Years
Felton, Dorothy	Atlanta, Fulton	R	1975 1977 1979 1981 1983 1985 1987 1989 1991 1993 1995
Fuller, Cynthia	Atlanta, Fulton	D	1981
Galer, Mary Jane	Columbus, Muscogee	D	1977 1979 1981 1983 1985 1987
Glover, Mildred W.	Atlanta, Fulton	D	1975 1977 1979 1981
Guerry, Ophelia S.	Montezuma, Macon	D	1941 1943 1945
Hamilton, Grace		D	1965* 1967 1969
Towns	Atlanta, Fulton		1971 1973 1975 1977 1979 1981 1983
Harris, Melanie	Woodstock, Cherokee	R	1993 1995
Hart, Bettieanne Childers	Waynesboro, Burke	D	1993 1995
Hegstrom, June	Scottdale, Dekalb	D	1993 1995
Henson, Michele	Stone Mountain, Fulton	D	1991 1993 1995
Herbert, Suzi Johnson see *Johnson*	Orchard Hill, Spalding	D	1987 1989 1991
Hugley, Carolyn F.	Columbus, Muscogee	D	1993 1995
Irwin, Karen Osborne	McDonough, Clarke	D	1989
Jamieson, Jeanette Mary	Toccoa, Stephens	D	1985 1987 1989 1991 1993 1995
Johnson, Diane Harvey	Savannah, Chatham	D	1983 1985 1987 1989 1993
Johnson, Gail	Jonesboro, Rockdale	R	1993 1995
Johnson, Suzi see *Herbert*	Orchard Hill, Spalding	D	1983 1985
Kempton, Bessie	Atlanta, Fulton	D	1923 1925 1927 1929
King, Glynda B	Riverdale, Fulton	D	1991
Lee, Carolyn	Carrollton, Carroll	D	1985
Lowe, Bettye	Atlanta, Fulton	R	1979* 1981
Mankin, Helen Douglas	Atlanta, Fulton	D	1937 1939 1941 1943 1945*
McBee, Louise	Athens, Oglethorpe	D	1993 1995
McClinton, Joann	Atlanta, Fulton	D	1993 1995
McDuffie, Love	Columbus, Muscogee	D	1933
McKinney, Cynthia Ann	Atlanta, Fulton	D	1989 1991
Merritt, Janet	Americus, Sumter	D	1965 1967 1969 1971
Mills, Debra A.	Powder Springs, Cobb	D	1991
Mobley, Barbara J.	Decatur, Dekalb	D	1993 1995
Moore, Martha W.	Evans, Columbia	R	1993
Mueller, Anne	Savannah, Chatham	R	1983 1985 1987 1989 1991 1993 1995
Napier, Viola Ross	Macon, Bibb	D	1923 1925
Oliver, Mary Margaret	Atlanta, Fulton	D	1989 1991
Orrock, Nan Grogan	Atlanta, Fulton	D	1987 1989 1991 1993 1995
Parkman, Lillian H.	Albany, Dougherty	D	1979

Georgia House, continued

Name	City, County	Party	Legislative Year
Pelote, Dorothy B.	Savannah, Chatham	D	1991 1993 1995
Purcell, Ann R.	Rincon, Effingham	D	1991 1993 1995
Rainey, Rebecca Laing	Dawson, Terrell	D	1947 1949
Ramsey, Virginia	Brunswick, Glynn	R	1985 1987
Randolph, Mamie M.	Atlanta, Fulton	D	1993 1995
Richardson, Eleanor Low	Decatur, Dekalb	D	1975 1977 1979 1981 1983 1985 1987 1989
Selman, Helen	Palmetto, Fulton	D	1981* 1983 1985 1987 1989 1991
Sinkfield, Georganna T.	Atlanta, Fulton	D	1983 1985 1987 1989 1991 1993 1995
Sizemore, Earleen	Sylvester, Worth	D	1975 1977 1979 1981 1983 1985 1987
Smith, Willou	Sea Island, Glynn	R	1987 1989 1991 1993 1995
Stanley, Lanett	Atlanta, Fulton	D	1987 1989 1991 1993 1995
Stanley, Pamela A.	Atlanta, Fulton	D	1993 1995
Steinberg, Cathey Weiss	Atlanta, Dekalb	D	1977 1979 1981 1983 1985 1987
Stocks, Nellie M.	Leesburg, Lee	D	1953
Taylor, Maretta Mitchell	Columbus, Muscogee	D	1991 1993 1995
Teague, Sharon Beasley	Red Oak, Fulton	D	1993 1995
Thomas, Mable Able	Atlanta, Fulton	D	1985 1987 1989 1991
Thomas, Nadine	Atlanta, Fulton	D	1991
Thomas, Regina	Savannah, Chatham	D	1995
Trense, Sharon	Atlanta, Fulton	R	1993 1995
Turnquest, Henrietta E.	Decatur, Dekalb	D	1991 1993 1995
Valenti, Rita	Clarkston, Dekalb	D	1991
Watkins, Lottie H.	Atlanta, Fulton	D	1977* 1979
Williams, Betty Jo	Atlanta, Dekalb	R	1979 1981 1983 1985 1987 1989 1991 1993 1995
Williams, Juanita Terry	Atlanta, Fulton	D	1985 1987 1989 1991
Young, Mary M.	Albany, Dougherty	D	1983 1985 1987 1989 1991

*Notes:
Cannon, Tassie Kelley—Elected Jan. 21, 1931 (Cannon)
Canty, Henrietta Mathis—Elected June 10, 1975 (Alexander)
Coffin, Alice Walker—Elected 1951 (Coffin)
Crowe, Lelia—Appointed July 26, 1962 (Crowe)
Hamilton, Grace Towns—Elected reapportionment special election June 16, 1965

Johnson, Margaret B. — Elected Sept. 3, 1927 (Johnson) but never assumed office
Lowe, Bettye — Elected Oct. 23, 1978 (Horton)
Mankin, Helen Douglas — Resigned Feb. 12, 1946, elected US Congress
Selman, Helen — Elected May 11, 1982 (Selman)
Watkins, Lottie H. — Elected April 5, 1977 (Brown)

GUAM (1947–1995)

Rosa Aguigui Reyes (Merizo) was elected to the 7th and 8th Congress of Guam in 1946 during the last years of the U.S. Military Government of Guam. Cynthia J. Torres (I) was the first woman elected to the Guam Territorial Legislature in 1955.

The Territorial Government of Guam was formed in 1950 with a unicameral legislature of 21 senators elected for four year terms. In 1961 the Popular Party affiliated with the national Democratic Party and the Territorial Party with the national Republican Party.

19 women have served in the Guam Congress and Territorial Legislature:
1 in the Congress
18 in the Senate

Women as Percentage of Guam Legislators

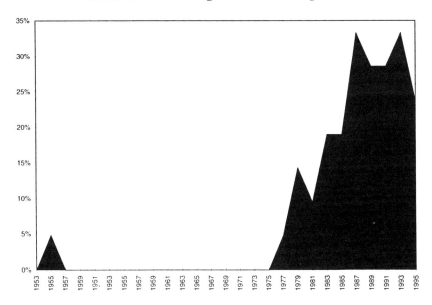

Guam, continued

Congress
1946-1950   2 Year Terms

Name	City, County	Party	Legislative Year
Reyer, Rosa Aguigui	Merizo	I	1947 1949

Senate
1950-1995   2 Year Terms

Name	City, County	Party	Legislative Year
Aguon, Katherine Bordallo	Agana	R	1977 1979
Arriola, Elizabeth P.	Tamuning	D	1983 1985 1987 1989 1991 1993
Bamba, Cecilia C.	Agana	R	1979
Barrett-Anderson, Elizabeth	Chalan Pago	R	1995
Bordallo, Madeleine Mary	Agana	D	1981 1987* 1989 1991*
Brooks, Doris F.	Agana	R	1989 1991 1993
Brown, Joanne	Chalan Pago	R	1995
Cristobal, Hope	Tamuning	D	1995
Dierking, Herminia D.	Tamuning	D	1985 1987 1993
Guerrero, Carlotta Leon	Sinajana	R	1995
Hartsock, Marcia K.	Yona	D	1983 1987
Kasperbauer, Carmen Artero	Agana	R	1979 1981
Lujan, Pilar C.	Chalan Pago	D	1983 1985 1987 1989 1991 1993
Manibusan, Marilyn D. A.	Chalan Pago	R	1983 1985 1987 1989 1991 1993
Ruth, Martha C.	Tamuning	R	1987 1989 1993
Torres, Cynthia J.	Agana	I	1955
Won Pat-Borga, Judith	Inarajan	D	1995

*Notes:
Bordallo, Madeleine Mary—Elected 1987 (Sanchez); elected 1991 to replace Marilyn A. P. Won Pat who was elected but died before taking office.

HAWAII, Territory of (1925-1959)

Hawaii women gained suffrage by territorial legislative enactment in 1921. Rosalie Keliinoi (R–Kapana, Kauai) lost in the 1922 elections but won in 1924 to become the first woman to serve in a territorial legislature.

Territorial elections were held every two years to elect 30 representatives who served two year terms and 15 senators who served four year terms. The last territorial elections were November 1958 and the first statehood elections were July 1959. Vacancies were filled by governor's appointment.

14 women have served in the Hawaii Territorial Legislature:
  7 in the Senate
  9 in House
  (2 in the House and Senate)

Women as Percentage of Hawaiian Territorial Legislators

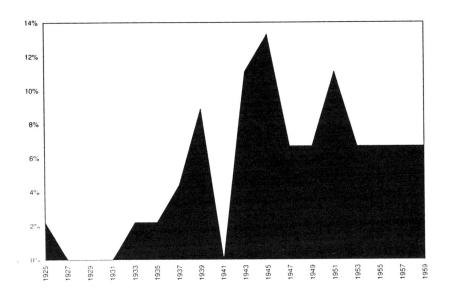

Senate
4 Year Terms

Name	City, County	Party	Legislative Year
Campbell, Alice Kamoki- laikaw	Ewa, Oahu	R	1943 1945
Cunningham, Sarah Todd	Hilo, Hawaii	D	1937; R 1939 1943*
Duponte, Dee	Wailuku Maui	D	1955 1957
Harrison, Thelma Akana	Honolulu, Oahu	R	1945 1947 1949 1951
Mink, Patsy T.	Honolulu, Oahu	D	1959
Robinson, Mary K.	Honolulu, Oahu	R	1951 1953
Wilcox, Elsie H.	Hanalei, Kauai	R	1933 1935 1937 1939

Territory of Hawaii, continued

House
2 Year Terms

Name	City, County	Party	Legislative Year
Devereux, Dorothy L.	Honolulu, Oahu	R	1959
Duponte, Dee	Wailuku, Maui	D	1951 1953
Hayes, Flora K.	Honolulu, Oahu	R	1939 1943 1945 1947 1949 1951 1959
Kahanamoku, Anna F.	Honolulu, Oahu	D	1955 1957
Keliinoi, Rosalie E. L.	Kapaa, Kauai	R	1925
Mink, Patsy T.	Honolulu, Oahu	D	1957
Mossman, Bina N.	Honolulu, Oahu	R	1939 1943 1945
Richardson, Esther K.	Kona, Hawaii	R	1943 1945 1947 1949 1951 1953 1955
Thompson, Isabelle N.	Maui County	D	1945

*Note:
Cunningham, Sarah Todd—Elected to two year unexpired term

HAWAII, State of (1959–1995)

Women as Percentage of Hawaiian State Legislators

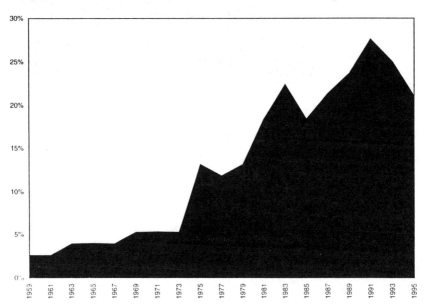

When statehood was granted in 1959, Dorothy L. Devereux (R–Honolulu, Oahu) and Eureka B. Forbes (R–Honolulu, Oahu) won seats in the House.

State elections are held every two years to elect 51 representatives who serve two year terms and 25 senators who serve four year staggered terms. Vacancies are filled by governor's appointment.

46 women have served in the Hawaii Legislature:
  15 in the Senate
  40 in House
  (9 in the House and Senate)

Senate
4 Year Terms

Name	City, County	Party	Legislative Year
Baker, Rosalyn	Lahaina, Maui	D	1993* 1995
Fernandes, Lehua Salling	Kapaa, Kauai	D	1983 1985 1987 1989 1991 1993 1995
Forbes, Eureka B.	Honolulu, Oahu	R	1967 1969 1971 1973
Fukunaga, Carol	Honolulu, Oahu	D	1993 1995
George, Mary	Kailua, Oahu	R	1975 1977 1979 1981 1983 1985 1987 1989 1991 1993 1995
Ikeda, Donna R.	Honolulu, Oahu	R	1987*; D 1989 1991 1993 1995
Kahanamoku, Anna F.	Honolulu, Oahu	D	1965
King, Jean Sadako	Honolulu, Oahu	D	1975 1977
Kobayashi, Ann H.	Honolulu, Oahu	R	1981 1983 1985 1987; D 1989 1991 1993
McMurdo, Mary Jane	Honolulu, Oahu	D	1985 1987 1989 1991
Mink, Patsy T.	Honolulu, Oahu	D	1963
Saiki, Patricia	Honolulu, Oahu	R	1975 1977 1979 1981
Solomon, Malama	Kohala, Hawaii	D	1983 1985 1987 1989 1991 1993 1995
Tungpalan, Eloise Y.	Pearl City, Oahu	D	1987* 1989 1991 1993
Young, Patsy K.	Waipahu, Oahu	D	1975 1977 1979 1981 1983 1985 1987

House
2 Year Terms

Name	City, County	Party	Legislative Year
Amaral, Annelle C.	Ewa Beach, Oahu	D	1989 1991 1993 1995
Anderson, Eve Glover	Waimanalo Oahu	R	1995
Baker, Rosalyn	Lahaina, Maui	D	1989 1991 1993*
Beirne, Ululani	Kanehoe, Oahu	D	1993
Chun, Connie	Honolulu, Oahu	D	1981 1983
Chun, Suzanne N. J.	Honolulu, Oahu	D	1991 1993 1995
Devereux, Dorothy L.	Honolulu, Oahu	R	1959 1961 1963 1965 1967 1969 1971
Duldulao, Julie R.	Waipahu, Oahu	D	1989 1991 1993
Evans, Faith P.	Kailua, Oahu	R	1975 1977 1979
Forbes, Eureka B.	Honolulu, Oahu	R	1959 1961 1963 1965
Fukunaga, Carol	Honolulu, Oahu	D	1979 1981 1987 1989 1991
Hansen, Diana	Kailua, Oahu	R	1971
Hashimoto, Clarice Y.	Pearl City, Oahu	D	1979 1981 1983 1985 1987 1989 1991
Hayes, Joan	Honolulu, Oahu	D	1983 1987 1989
Hirono, Mazie	Honolulu, Oahu	D	1981 1983 1985 1987 1989 1991 1993
Horita, Karen K.	Honolulu, Oahu	D	1987 1989 1991
Ikeda, Donna R.	Honolulu, Oahu	R	1975 1977 1979 1981 1983 1985 1987*
Isbell, Virginia	Kealakekua, Hawaii	R	1981 1983 1985 1987 D 1989 1991 1993 1995
Ishii-Morikami, Paula	Hanalei, Kauai	D	1993
Kamalii, Kinau Boyd	Hanapepe, Oahu	R	1975 1977 1979 1981 1985
Kawakami, Bertha C.	Hanapepe, Oahu	D	1987* 1989 1991 1993 1995
Kim, Donna Mercado	Honolulu, Oahu	D	1983 1985
King, Jean Sadako	Honolulu, Oahu	D	1973
Kiyabu-Saballa, Avia A.	Ewa Beach, Oahu	D	1983
Marumoto, Barbara	Honolulu, Oahu	R	1979 1981 1983 1985 1987 1989 1991 1993 1995
McMurdo, Mary Jane	Honolulu, Oahu	D	1995
Meyer, Colleen	Honolulu, Hawaii	R	1995
Minn, Momi T.	Waihawa, Oahu	D	1967 1969
Naito, Lisa	Honolulu, Oahu	D	1975 1977
Pule, Sarah K.	Halaula, Hawaii	D	1969*
Saiki, Patricia	Honolulu, Oahu	R	1969 1971 1973
Santos, Velma M.	Wailuku, Maui	R	1975
Stanley, Kathleen Gould	Honolulu, Oahu	D	1975 1977 1979 1981 1983
Tatibouet, Jane B.	Honolulu, Oahu	R	1991

Thielen, Cynthia	Kailua, Oahu	R	1991 1993 1995
Tungpalan, Eloise Y.	Pearl City, Oahu	D	1981 1983 1985 1987*
Wong, Norma	Waimanalo, Oahu	D	1983
Yoshinaga, Terry	Waimanalo, Oahu	D	1995
Young, Jackie	Kailua, Oahu	D	1991 1993
Young, Patsy K.	Waipahu, Oahu	D	1971* 1973

*Notes:
Baker, Rosalyn — Resigned Nov. 26, 1993 (White), apppointed to Senate (Blair)
Ikeda, Donna R. — Resigned Dec. 26, 1986, appointed to Senate (Soares)
Kawakami, Bertha C. — Appointed March 13, 1987 (Kawakami)
Pule, Sarah K. — Appointed Nov. 1, 1969 (Pule)
Tungpalan, Eloise Y. — Resigned Dec. 17, 1987, appointed to Senate (J. T. Kuroda)
Young, Patsy K. — Appointed Dec. 23, 1971 (J. T. Kuroda)

IDAHO (1899–1995)

Idaho women gained school suffrage from the Territorial Legislature in 1886 and full suffrage after statehood by state constitutional amendment in 1896.

Women as Percentage of Idaho Legislators

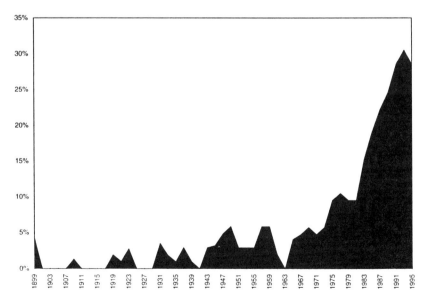

Women first voted in 1898 state elections and elected Representatives Mary
A. Wright (Populist–Rathdrum, Kootenai), Harriet F. Noble (D–Idaho City,
Boise County) and Clara L. Campbell (R–Boise City, Ada). Nellie Cline Steen-
son (D–Pocatello, Bannock) who served in the Idaho Senate from 1945 to 1950
and 1955 to 1962 served earlier in the Kansas House from 1921 to 1926 as Nellie
Cline.

State elections are held every two years to elect 42 senators and 84 representatives who serve two year terms. State legislative service is limited for the
house to eight years during a fifteen year period and for the senate to eight
years in a fifteen year period. Vacancies are filled by special election.

107 women have served in the Idaho Legislature:
   32 in the Senate
   89 in the House
   (14 in the House and Senate)

Senate
2 Year Terms

Name	City, County	Party	Legislative Year
Benson, Betty G.	Moscow, Latah	D	1987* 1991*
Bilyeu, Diane	Pocatello, Bannock	D	1969
Bray, Gail Etheridge	Boise, Ada	D	1983 1985 1987 1989*
Brooks, Mary T.	Carey, Blaine	R	1965 1967 1969*
Calabretta, Martha	Osburn, Shoshone	D	1985 1987 1989 1991
Campbell, Marguerite A.	New Meadows, Adams	R	1947 1949 1951*
Chamberlain, Barbara K.	Post Falls, Kootenai	D	1993
Cooke, Karen	Priest River, Bonner	D	1989*
Danielson, Judith	Council, Adams	R	1995
Davis, Nora L.	Letha, Gem	D	1957 1959
Derr, Hattie	Clark's Fork, Bonner	D	1937*
Dobler, Norma	Moscow, Latah	D	1977 1979 1981 1983 1985
Gilbert, Rachel S.	Boise, Ada	R	1985 1987 1989
Hartung, Mary	Payette, Payette	R	1989* 1991 1993 1995
Klein, Edith Miller	Boise, Ada	R	1969 1971 1973 1975 1977 1979 1981
Lloyd, Mary Ellen	Pocatello, Bannock	D	1991 1993
Manley, Margaret Swan	Coeur D'Alene, Kootenai	D	1971*
McCann, Dorothy H.	Wallace, Shoshone	D	1977*
McDermott, Patricia L.	Pocatello, Bannock	D	1991
McLaughlin, Marguerite	Orofino, Clearwater	D	1983 1985 1987 1989 1991 1993 1995

Name	City, County	Party	Legislative Year
McRoberts, Joyce	Twin Falls, Twin Falls	R	1989 1991 1993 1995
Olsen, Martha E.	Horseshoe Bend, Boise	R	1939
Pike, Margaret Bognet	Boise, Ada	D	1935*
Reed, Mary Lou	Coeur D'Alene, Kootenai	D	1985 1987 1989 1991 1993 1995
Reents, Sue	Boise, Ada	D	1989* 1991 1993 1995
Rydalch, Ann	Idaho Falls, Bonneville	R	1983* 1985 1987 1989
Scanlin, Cynthia	Boise, Ada	D	1991
Snodgrass, Sally E.	Boise, Ada	D	1991
Sorensen, Sheila A.	Boise, Ada	R	1993 1995
Steenson, Nellie Cline	Pocatello, Bannock	D	1945 1947 1949 1955 1957 1959 1961
Wetherell, Claire	Mountain Home, Elmore	D	1983 1987 1989 1991 1993 1995
Williams, Phyllis C.	Idaho Falls, Bonneville	R	1977*

House
2 Year Terms

Name	City, County	Party	Legislative Year
Abercrombie, Katherine L.	Lewiston, Nez Perce	D	1923
Aherns, Pamela I. Bengson *see Bengson*	Boise, Ada	R	1991 1993 1995
Albright, Lora	Arrow, Nez Perce	R	1949*
Allan-Hodge, Elizabeth	Caldwell, Canyon	R	1985 1987 1989
Alworth, Frankie K.	Filer, Twin Falls	D	1937*
Barrett, Lenore Hardy	Challis, Custer	R	1993 1995
Beardmore, Lucy	Priest River, Bonner	R	1923
Beaudoin, Monica	Sandpoint, Bonner	D	1989* 1991 1993*
Bell, Maxine T.	Jerome, Jerome	R	1989 1991 1993 1995
Bengson, Pamela I. *see Aherns*	Boise, Ada	R	1981* 1983 1985 1987 1989
Bergeson, Bonnie	Pocatello, Bannock	R	1971*
Bernard, Myrtle	Nampa, Canyon	D	1931
Bistline, Beverly B.	Pocatello, Bannock	D	1975
Bunting, Peggy	Boise, Ada	R	1973 1975 1977 1979 1981 1983
Calloway, Mary	Boise, Ada	D	1933 1935
Campbell, Clara L.	Boise, Ada	R	1899
Chamberlain, Barbara K.	Post Falls, Kootenai	D	1991
Clouchek, Emma	Twin Falls, Twin Falls	R	1931
Cosho, Maude L.	Boise, Ada	D	1931 1933 1937
Crow, Dolores J.	Nampa, Canyon	R	1983* 1985 1987 1989 1991 1993 1995

Idaho House, continued

Name	City, County	Party	Legislative Year
Crozier, Vivian	Pocatello, Bannock	D	1985* 1987*
Danielson, Judith	Council, Adams	R	1989 1991 1993
Davis, Nora L.	Letha, Gem	D	1943 1945 1947 1949 1951 1953 1955
Dewey, Linda Stein-man	Pocatello, Bannock	D	1983* 1985*
Dobler, Norma	Moscow, Latah	D	1973 1975
Drake, Emma	New Plymouth, Payette	R	1919
Durham, Beth	Lewiston, Nez Perce	D	1957
Edwards, Lydia Justice	Donnelly, Valley	R	1981* 1983 1985
Edwards, Mary	Council, Adams	R	1971*
Field, Frances	Grand View, Owyhee	R	1985 1987 1989 1991 1993 1995
Fitzwater, Beth	Boise, Ada	R	1975
Flandro, Millie L.	Pocatello, Bannock	D	1991 1993 1995
Folkinga, Celia see Gould	Buhl, Twin Falls	R	1987
George, Mary Young	Hailey, Blaine	D	1923
Gilbert, Rachel S.	Boise, Ada	R	1981 1983
Givens, Jeanne	Coeur D'Alene, Kootenai	D	1985 1987
Gould, Celia R. Fol-kinga see Folinga	Buhl, Twin Falls	R	1989 1991 1993 1995
Gurnsey, Kathleen W.	Boise, Ada	R	1975 1977 1979 1981 1983 1985 1987 1989 1991 1993 1995
Hartung, Mary	Payette, Payette	R	1987 1989*
Hay, Janet S.	Nampa, Canyon	R	1985 1987 1989
Hedlund, Vera	Saint Maries, Benewah	D	1965*
Hoagland, Glenna L.	Mountain Home, Elmore	R	1985
Hofman, Elaine	Pocatello, Bannock	D	1991 1993 1995
Hornbeck, Twila	Grangeville, Idaho	R	1995
Horton, Anita Louise	Emmett, Gem	R	1987*
Irwin, Bertha V.	Twin Falls, Twin Falls	R	1921
Jaquet, Wendy	Ketchum, Blain	D	1995
Jenkins, Janet	Coeur D'Alene, Kootenai	D	1991 1993
Johnson, Sadie	Worley, Kootenai	R	1953*
Jones, Donna	Payette, Payette	R	1987* 1989 1991 1993 1995
Judd, June E.	Saint Maries, Benewah	D	1991 1993 1995
Kearnes, Elaine	Idaho Falls, Bonneville	R	1971* 1973 1975 1977 1979 1981
Kellogg, Hilde	Post Falls, Kootenai	D	1983; R 1985 1987 1989 1993 1995
Kent, Pernecy D.	Mackay, Custer	D	1959
King, Robbi Lorene	Glenns Ferry, Elmore	R	1993 1995

Klein, Edith Miller *see*			
Miller	Boise, Ada	R	1965 1967
Lasuen, Leanna	Mountain Home, Elmore	D	1987 1989 1991
Lazechko, Molly	Boise, Ada	D	1991
Lloyd, Mary Ellen	Pocatello, Bannock	D	1987* 1989
McCann, Dorothy H.	Wallace, Shoshone	D	1973 1975 1977* 1983
			1985 1987 1989
McDermott, Patricia L.	Pocatello, Bannock	D	1969 1971 1973 1975
			1977 1979 1981
			1983 1985 1987
			1989
McFadden, Lettie J.	Meridan, Ada	R	1909
McKeeth, Sylvia	Boise, Ada	R	1993 1995
McKinney, Helen	Salmon, Lemhi	R	1965 1967 1969 1971
McLaughlin, Marguerite	Orofino, Clearwater	D	1979 1981
Miller, Edith I. *see*			
Klein	Boise, Ada	R	1949
Miller, Helen J.	Glenns Ferry, Elmore	D	1937 1943 1945 1947
			1949 1951 1953
			1955 1957 1959
Nafziger, Pattie	Wendell, Gooding	D	1991 1993
Neider, Maxine	Coeur D'Alene, Kootenai	R	1975*
Noble, Hattie F.	Idaho City, Boise	D	1899
Pietsch, Carol A.	Sandpoint, Bonner	D	1995
Pike, Margaret Bognet	Boise, Ada	D	1937*
Rambeau, Ione E.	Orofino, Clearwater	D	1957 1959
Reynolds, Dorothy L.	Caldwell, Canyon	D	1975 1977 1979 1983
			1985 1987 1989
			1991 1993 1995
Scott, Donna	Twin Falls, Twin Falls	R	1983 1985
Smith, Virginia D.	Caldwell, Canyon	R	1975* 1977 1979
			1981 1983
Sorensen, Sheila A.	Boise, Ada	R	1987* 1989 1991
Stanger, Marilyn	Idaho Falls, Bonneville	R	1985
Stebbins, Naomi E.	Wardner, Shoshone	D	1957 1959 1961
Steenson, Nellie Cline	Pocatello, Bannock	D	1943
Stone, Ruby R.	Boise, Ada	R	1985* 1987 1989
			1991 1993 1995
Sutton, Gertrude	Midvale, Washington	R	1991* 1993 1995
Swank, Gladys	Lewiston, Nez Perce	D	1965 1967
Taylor, Edith	Grouse, Custer	D	1947*
Tregoning, Margot	Wardner, Shoshone	D	1967 1969 1971
Ungricht, Wendy	Boise, Ada	R	1977 1979 1981*
Vickers, Deanna	Lewiston, Nez Perce	D	1987 1989 1991
White, Carrie Harper	Twin Falls, Twin Falls	R	1919
Wilde, Gayle Ann	McCall, Valley	R	1987 1989 1991 1993
			1995
Wood, Jo An E.	Rigby, Madison	R	1983 1985 1987 1989
			1991 1993 1995
Wright, Mary A.	Rathdrum, Kootenai	Pop	1899
Yearian, Emma R.	Lemhi, Lemhi	R	1931

Idaho, continued

*Notes:
Albright, Lora—Appointed Dec. 20, 1948 (Rosenkranz)
Alworth, Frankie K.—Appointed Nov. 28, 1938 (Powers)
Beaudoin, Monica—Appointed Dec. 12, 1989 (Tucker), resigned Sept. 1, 1993 (Stevens)
Bengson, Pamela I.—Appointed Sept. 10, 1981 (Ungricht)[F]
Benson, Betty G.—Appointed March 6, 1987 (Beitelspacker); appointed Dec. 5, 1990 (Mosman)
Bergeson, Bonnie—Appointed June 21, 1972 (Palmer)
Bray, Gail Etheridge—Resigned Nov. 9, 1989 (Reents)[F]
Brooks, Mary T.—Resigned June 1, 1969 (son, Brooks)
Campbell, Marguerite A.—Resigned April 7, 1951 (Campbell)
Cooke, Karen—Resigned Nov. 6, 1989 (Tucker)
Crow, Dolores J.—Appointed Sept. 28, 1983 (Sharp)
Crozier, Vivian—Appointed Nov. 25, 1985 (Dewey)[F]. Died Jan. 21, 1986 (Lloyd)[F]
Derr, Hattie—Appointed March 1, 1937 (Derr). Resigned Nov.28, 1938
Dewey, Linda Steinman—Appointed Aug. 5, 1983 (Lacy), resigned Nov. 11, 1985 (Crozier)[F]
Edwards, Lydia Justice—Appointed May 6, 1982 (Munger)
Edwards, Mary—Appointed July 14, 1972 (Edwards)
Hartung, Mary—Resigned Jan. 19, 1990, appointed to Senate (Fairchild)
Hedlund, Vera—Appointed Jan. 20, 1965 (Hedland)
Horton, Anita Louise—Appointed May 13, 1988 (Fry)
Johnson, Sadie—Appointed Jan. 15, 1953 (Vetter)
Jones, Donna—Appointed April 20, 1987 (Strasser)
Kearnes, Elaine—Appointed Sept. 3, 1971 (Hyde)
Lloyd, Mary Ellen—Appointed Dec. 12, 1986 (Crozier)[F]
Manley, Margaret Swan—Appointed Feb. 11, 1971 (Swan)
McCann, Dorothy H.—Resigned Nov. 21, 1977 (Horvath), appointed to Senate (Murphy)
Neider, Maxine—Appointed Jan. 26, 1976 (Neider)
Pike, Margaret Bognet—Appointed Senate July 28, 1936 (Yost), appointed to House Nov. 28, 1938 (Lusk)
Reents, Sue—Appointed Nov. 14, 1989 (Bray)[F]
Rydalch, Ann—Appointed Sept. 29, 1983 (Floyd)
Smith, Virginia D.—Appointed March 1, 1976 (Clements)
Sorensen, Sheila A.—Appointed Dec. 17, 1987 (Sorensen)
Stone, Ruby R.—Appointed Jan. 13, 1986 (Stone)
Sutton, Gertrude—Appointed March 21, 1991 (Sutton)
Taylor, Edith—Appointed Dec. 5, 1946 (Taylor)
Ungricht, Wendy—Resigned Sept. 10, 1981 (Bengson)[F]
Williams, Phyllis C.—Appointed March 4, 1977-Feb. 17, 1978 (Williams)

ILLINOIS (1923-1995)

Illinois women gained municipal and presidential suffrage by legislative enactment in 1913, but had to wait until August 26, 1920 for state suffrage. Women first voted in state elections in 1920 and first ran for the state legislature in 1922 and elected Representative Lottie Holman O'Neill (R–Downer's Grove, Dupage). State Senator Laura Kent Donahue is the daughter of former Representative Mary Lou Kent.

State elections are held every two years to elect 118 representatives for two year terms and 59 senators who serve four year terms. Senators draw lots for two-four-four, four-two-four, or four-four-two year terms after the U. S. decennial census every ten years. In 1982 the Illinois house membership was reduced from 177 to 118. Vacancies are filled by governor's appointment and special election.

118 women have served in the Illinois General Assembly:
    28 in the Senate
    105 in the House
    (15 in the House and Senate)

Women as Percentage of Illinois Legislators

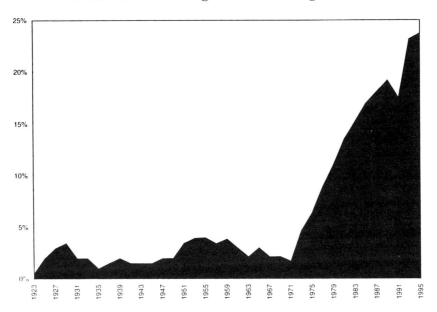

Senate
2 and 4 Year Terms

Name	City, County	Party	Legislative Year
Alexander, Ethel Skyles	Chicago, Cook	D	1987* 1989 1991
Bohrer, Florence Fifer	Bloomington, Monroe	R	1925 1927 1929 1931

Illinois Senate, continued

Name	City, County	Party	Legislative Year
Bowles, Evelyn	Edwardsville, Madison	D	1993* 1995
Collins, Earlean	Chicago, Cook	D	1977 1979 1981 1983 1985 1987 1989 1991 1993 1995
Donahue, Laura Kent	Quincy, Adams	R	1981* 1983 1985 1987 1989 1991 1993 1995
Fawell, Beverly J.	Glen Ellyn, Dupage	R	1983 1985 1987 1989 1991 1993 1995
Geo-Karis, Adeline Jay	Zion, Lake	R	1979 1981 1983 1985 1987 1989 1991 1993 1995
Green, Madge Miller	Palestine, Crawford	R	1963*
Hasara, Karen A.	Springfield, Sangamon	R	1993 1995
Hickey, Vivian Veach	Rockford, Winnebago	D	1975 1977
Holmberg, Joyce	Rockford, Winnebago	D	1983 1985 1987 1989 1991
Joyce, Janet	Reddick, Livingston	D	1991*
Karpiel, Doris C.	Carol Stream, Dupage	R	1985 1987 1989 1991 1993 1995
Keegan, Betty Ann	Rockford, Winnebago	D	1973*
Kent, Mary Lou	Quincy, Adams	R	1981*
MacDonald, Virginia B.	Arlington Heights, Cook	R	1983 1985 1987 1989 1991
Martin, Lynn Morley	Rockford, Winnebago	R	1979
Munizzi, Pamela A.	Chicago, Cook	D	1991*
Netsch, Dawn Clark	Chicago, Cook	D	1973 1975 1977 1979 1981 1983 1985 1987 1989 1991*
O'Neill, Lottie Holman	Downer's Grove, Dupage	R	1951 1953 1955 1957 1959 1961
Palmer, Alice	Chicago, Cook	D	1993 1995
Parker, Kathy	Highland Park, Lake	R	1995
Saperstein, Esther	Chicago, Cook	D	1967 1969 1971 1973 1975*
Schlagenhauf, Lillian E.	Quincy, Adams	R	1953 1955 1957 1959 1961 1963
Severns, Penny L.	Decatur, Macon	D	1987 1989 1991 1993 1995
Smith, Margaret	Chicago, Cook	D	1983 1985 1987 1989 1991 1993 1995
Stern, Grace Mary	Highland Park, Lake	D	1993
Topinka, Judith Barr	North Riverside, Cook	R	1985 1987 1989 1991 1993 1995*

House
2 Year Terms

Name	City, County	Party	Legislative Year
Alexander, Ethel Skyles	Chicago, Cook	D	1979 1981 1983 1985
Balanoff, Miriam D.	Chicago, Cook	D	1979 1981
Barnes, Jane M.	Palos Park, Cook	R	1975 1977 1979 1981 1983 1985 1987 1989 1991
Barnes, Lizzie	Carmi, White	D	1939
Biggert, Judy	Hinsdale, DuPage	R	1993 1995
Breslin, Peg McDonnell	Ottawa, Lasalle	D	1977 1979 1981 1983 1985 1987 1989
Catania, Susan	Chicago, Cook	R	1973 1975 1977 1979 1981
Chapman, Eugenia Sheldon	Arlington Heights, Cook	D	1965 1967 1969 1971 1973 1975 1977 1979 1981
Cheney, Flora Sylvester	Chicago, Cook	R	1929*
Ciarlo, Flora L.	Steger, Cook	R	1995
Clayton, Verna L.	Buffalo Grove, Cook	R	1993 1995
Clements, Floy	Chicago, Cook	D	1959
Cowlishaw, Mary Lou	Naperville, Dupage	R	1983 1985 1987 1989 1991 1993 1995
Currie, Barbara Flynn	Chicago, Cook	D	1979 1981 1983 1985 1987 1989 1991 1993 1995
Curry, Julie A.	Decatur, Macon	D	1995
Davidson, Mary	Carthage, Hancock	D	1931 1933
Davis, Monique D.	Chicago, Cook	D	1987 1989 1991 1993 1995
Dawson, Frances L.	Evanston, Cook	R	1957 1959 1961 1963 1965 1967 1969
Deuchler, Suzanne L.	Aurora, Kane	R	1981 1983 1985 1987 1989 1991 1993 1995
Didrickson, Loleta A.	Flossmoor, Cook	R	1983 1985 1987 1989 1991*
Doederlein, Deloris K.	Algonquin, McHenry	R	1987 1989 1991
Dyer, Goudylock E.	Hinsdale, DuPage	R	1969 1971 1973 1975 1977 1979
Elrod, Rena	Chicago, Cook	R	1925 1927 1929
Erwin, Judy	Chicago, Cook	D	1993 1995
Fantin, Arline M.	Calumet, Cook	D	1995
Fawell, Beverly J.	Glen Ellyn, Dupage	R	1981
Feigenholtz, Sara	Chicago, Cook	D	1995

Illinois House, continued

Name	City, County	Party	Legislative Year
Flowers, Mary E.	Chicago, Cook	D	1985 1987 1989 1991 1993 1995
Frederick, Virginia Fiester	Lake Forest, Cook	R	1979 1981 1983 1985 1987 1989 1991 1993
Gash, Lauren Beth	Highland Park, Lake	D	1993 1995
Geo-Karis, Adeline Jay	Zion, Lake	R	1973 1975 1977
Giolitto, Barbara A.	Rockford, Winnebago	D	1993
Goode, Katherine Hancock	Chicago, Cook	R	1925 1927
Green, Mabel Emerson	Rockford, Winnebago	R	1949 1951 1953 1955 1957 1959 1961
Grow, Dorah	Quincy, Adams	D	1965
Hallstrom, Mary Jeanne	Glennview, Cook	R	1979 1981
Hanely, Sarah Bond	Monmouth, Warren	D	1927 1929
Hasara, Karen A.	Springfield, Sangamon	R	1985* 1987 1989 1991
Howard, Constance A.	Chicago, Cook	D	1995
Hoxsey, Betty J.	Ottawa, Lasalle	R	1977 1979 1981
Hughes, Ann	Woodstock, McHenry	R	1993 1995
Hurley, Jeanne C.	Wilmette, Cook	D	1957 1959
Ickes, Anna Wilmarth	Winnetka, Cook	R	1929 1931 1933
Jones, Lovanna S.	Chicago, Cook	D	1987 1989 1991 1993 1995
Jones, Marjorie	Chicago, Cook	D	1979*
Jones, Shirley M.	Chicago, Cook	D	1987* 1989 1991 1993 1995
Karmazyn, Lillian K.	Chicago, Cook	R	1969 1971
Karpiel, Doris C.	Carol Stream, Dupage	R	1979* 1981 1983
Kaszak, Nancy	Chicago, Cook	D	1993 1995
Kent, Mary Lou	Quincy, Adams	R	1973 1975 1977 1979
Klingler, Gwenn	Springfield, Sangamon	R	1995
Koehler, Judith	Henry, Dupage	R	1981 1983 1985
Krause, Carolyn H.	Mount Prospect, Cook	R	1993 1995
Lindner, Patricia Reid	Aurora, Kane	R	1993 1995
Lyons, Eileen	Western Springs, Cook	R	1995
MacDonald, Virginia B.	Arlington Heights, Cook	R	1973 1975 1977 1979 1981
Markette, Sharon G.	Chicago, Cook	D	1983*
Martin, Lynn Morley	Rockford, Winnebago	R	1977
Martin, Peggy Smith	Chicago, Cook	D	1973 1977
McAdams, Mary C.	Quincy, Adams	D	1927 1929
McCaskrin, Hazel A.	Rock Island, Rock Island	R	1947* 1951 1953 1955*
McCormick, Hope	Chicago, Cook	R	1965
Meany, Mary K.	Chicago, Cook	R	1965 1967

Moore, Andrea S.	Libertyville, Lake	R	1993 1995
Moseley, Vickie	Springfield, Sangamon	D	1993
Moseley-Braun, Carol	Chicago, Cook	D	1979 1981 1983 1985 1987
Mulligan, Rosemary	Des Plaines, Cook	R	1993 1995
Munizzi, Pamela A.	Chicago, Cook	D	1989* 1991*
Murphy, Maureen	Evergreen, Cook	R	1993 1995
Nelson, Diana	Western Springs, Cook	R	1981 1983
O'Neill, Lottie Hol-man	Downer's Grove, Dupage	R	1923 1925 1927 1929 1933 1935 1937 1939 1941 1943 1945 1947 1949
Oblinger, Jose-phine K.	Sherman, Sanamon	R	1979 1981 1983 1985
Palmer, Alice	Chicago, Cook	D	1991*
Pankau, Carole	Roselle, Cook	R	1993 1995
Parcells, Margaret R.	Northfield, Cook	R	1983* 1985 1987 1989 1991 1993
Pebworth, Majorie Hull	Riverdale, Cook	R	1965 1967*
Peffers, Maud N.	Aurora, Kane	R	1937* 1939 1941 1943 1945 1947 1949 1951 1953 1955
Perry, Josephine	Chicago, Cook	R	1931 1933
Pierce, Ferne Carter	Malta, Dekalb	D	1957 1959 1961
Piotrowski, Lillian	Chicago, Cook	D	1951 1953 1955 1957 1959 1961 1963
Prussing, Laurel Lunt	Urbana, Champaign	D	1993
Pullen, Penny Park	Ridge, Cook	R	1977 1979 1981 1983 1985 1987 1989 1991
Raschke-Lind, Paula	Rockford, Winnebago	D	1993*
Reed, Betty Lou	Deerfield, Lake	R	1975 1977 1979 1981
Rinaker, Pauline B.	Carlinville, Macoupin	R	1953 1955
Ronen, Carol	Chicago, Cook	D	1993 1995
Saperstein, Esther	Chicago, Cook	D	1957 1959 1961 1963 1965
Satterthwaite, Helen F.	Champaign, Champaign	D	1975 1977 1979 1981 1983 1985 1987 1989 1991
Schakowsky, Janice D.	Evanston, Cook	D	1991 1993 1995
Smith, Margaret	Chicago, Cook	D	1979* 1981
Stepan, Ann	Chicago, Cook	D	1991*
Stern, Grace Mary	Highland Park, Lake	D	1985 1987 1989 1991
Stewart, Monica Faith	Chicago, Cook	D	1981
Stiehl, Celeste M.	Belleville, St. Clair	R	1973 1975 1977 1979 1981
Sumner, Mary Lou	Dunlap, Peoria	R	1977 1979 1981
Suthers, Marie H.	Chicago, Cook	R	1951
Topinka, Judith Barr	North Riverside, Cook	R	1981 1983

Illinois House, continued

Name	City, County	Party	Legislative Year
Van Der Vries, Bernice T.	Winnetka, Cook	R	1935 1937 1939 1941 1943 1945 1947 1949 1951 1953 1955
Wessels, Pennie L. Von Bergen	Sterling, Whiteside	D	1993
Willer, Anne Walsh	Lagrange, Cook	D	1975 1977 1979
Williamson, Linda-Jean M.	Franklin Park, Cook	R	1985 1987 1989
Wojcik, Kathleen L.	Schaumburg, Cook	R	1983 1985 1987 1989 1991 1993 1995
Younge, Wyvetter H.	East St. Louis, St. Clair	D	1975 1977 1979 1981 1983 1985 1987 1989 1991 1993 1995
Zickus, Anne	Palos Hills, Cook	R	1989 1993 1995
Zwick, Jill	East Dundee, Kane	R	1981 1983 1985

*Notes:

Alexander, Ethel Skyles—Appointed
Bowles, Evelyn—Appointed May 9, 1994 (Delabene)
Cheney, Flora Sylvester—Died April 18, 1929
Didrickson, Loleta A.—Resigned Jan. 1991
Donahue, Laura Kent—Appointed 1981 (Mother)
Green, Madge Miller—Elected 1963 (Green)
Hasara, Karen A.—Appointed Jan. 1986
Jones, Marjorie—Appointed 1980
Jones, Shirley M.—Appointed Sept. 1986
Joyce, Janet—Appointed 1992 (Joyce)
Karpiel, Doris C.—Appointed 1979 (Friedland)
Keegan, Betty Ann—Died 1974
Kent, Mary Lou—Died 1981 (daughter, Donahue)
Markette, Sharon G.—Appointed 1983
McCaskrin, Hazel A.—Elected 1947 (McCaskrin). Died 1955
Munizzi, Pamela A.—Appointed 1989. Resigned 1992, appointed to Senate
Netsch, Dawn Clark—Resigned Jan. 14, 1991
Palmer, Alice—Appointed 1991 (Newhouse)
Parcells, Margaret R.—Appointed April 1984
Pebworth, Majorie Hull—Died 1967
Peffers, Maud N.—Appointed 1936 (Peffers)
Raschke-Lind, Paula—Appointed 1994 (Giorgi)
Saperstein, Esther—Resigned 1975
Smith, Margaret—Elected 1979 (Bullock)
Stepan, Ann—Appointed Feb. 11, 1991
Topinka, Judith Barr—Resigned Dec. 1994, elected State Treasurer

INDIANA (1921–1995)

Indiana women first gained presidential suffrage by legislative enactment in 1917 but had to pass it a second time because of a court decision. Full suffrage came on August 26, 1920. Women first voted in state elections in 1920. Seven women ran for state legislature in 1920, but only Julia D. Reynolds Nelson (R–Muncie, Delaware) won. Reynolds had been selected by the county Republican party to take the place of a deceased nominee.

State elections are held every two years for 100 representatives who serve two year terms and 50 senators who serve four year terms. Vacancies are filled by special election.

105 women have served in the Indiana General Assembly:
  28 in the Senate
  86 in the House
  (9 in the House and Senate)

Women as Percentage of Indiana Legislators

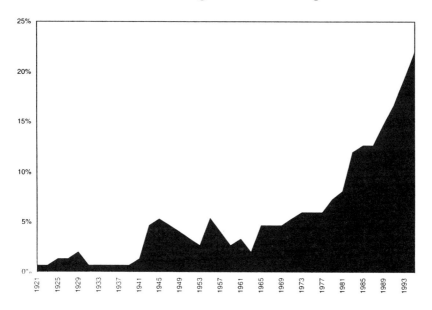

Senate
4 Year Terms (Before 1936, 2 Year Terms)

Name	City, County	Party	Legislative Year
Allstatt, Angeline Patterson	Indianapolis, Marion	D	1973 1975
Antich, Rose Ann	Merrillville, Lake	D	1991 1993 1995
Balz, Arcada S.	Indianapolis, Marion	R	1943* 1945 1947
Blankenbaker, Virginia M.	Indianapolis, Marion	R	1981 1983 1985 1987 1989 1991
Bowser, Anita Olga Albu	Michigan City, La Porte	D	1993 1995
Breaux, Billie J.	Indianapolis, Marion	D	1991* 1993 1995
Burnett, Martha Yeager	Indianapolis, Marion	R	1957* 1959 1961 1963
Carson, Julia	Indianapolis, Marion	D	1977 1979 1981 1983 1985 1987 1989*
Dempsey, Sandra	Munster, Lake	R	1995
Gard, Beverly J.	Greenfield, Hancock	R	1989 1991 1993 1995
Gardner, Dorothy Haberstroth	Ft. Wayne, Allen	R	1947 1949 1951 1953 1955 1957
Garrett, Mary C.	Indianapolis, Marion	D	1949 1951
Gubbins, Joan M.	Indianapolis, Marion	R	1969 1971 1973 1975 1977 1979
Hall, Katie	Gary, Lake	D	1977 1979 1981 1983
Landske, Dorothy Suzanne	Cedar Lake, Lake	R	1985 1987 1989 1991 1993 1995
Lauck, Marie Theresa	Indianapolis, Marion	D	1965 1967 1973 1975
Lawson, Betty M.	South Bend, St.Joseph	D	1989 1991
Leising, Jean	Oldenburg, Franklin	R	1989 1991 1993 1995
Lubbers, Teresa S.	Indianapolis, Marion	R	1993 1995
Miller, Patricia L.	Indianapolis, Marion	R	1983* 1985 1987 1989 1991 1993 1995
Mosby, Carolyn Brown	Gary, Lake	D	1983* 1985 1987 1989
Parent, Lillian M.	Dannville, Hendricks	R	1979* 1981 1983
Rogers, Earline S.	Gary, Lake	D	1991 1993 1995
Simpson, Vi	Bloomington, Monroe	D	1985 1987 1989 1991 1993 1995
Skillman, Becky	Bedford, Lawrence	R	1993 1995
Smith, Kathy	New Albany, Floyd	D	1987 1989 1991 1993 1995
Sullivan, Jessie Jean Keirn	Peru, Miami	R	1975*
Wolf, Katie L.	Monticello, Carroll	D	1987 1989 1991 1993 1995

House
2 Year Terms

Name	City, County	Party	Legislative Year
Achor, Helen E. Martin	Anderson, Madison	R	1969
Atkins, Katharine Lewis Watson	Indianapolis, Marion	R	1945
Barnes, Vanessa Summers	Indianapolis, Marion	D	1993 1995
Barning, Elsie Seiler	Evansville, Vanderburg	D	1949 1955 1961 1963 1967 1971
Becker, Vaneta Liley	Evansville, Vanderburg	R	1981* 1983 1985 1987 1989 1991 1993 1995
Bowser, Anita Olga Albu	Michigan City, La Porte	D	1979* 1983 1985 1987 1989 1991
Brinkman, Joyce	Indianapolis, Marion	R	1985* 1987 1989 1991 1993
Brown, Alice Mathias	Highland, Lake	D	1955
Budak, Mary Kay	Michigan City, La Porte	R	1981 1983 1985 1987 1989 1991 1993 1995
Caesar, Victoria	Gary, Lake	D	1965 1967 1971
Carson, Julia	Indianapolis, Marion	D	1973 1975
Churilla, Mildred Kopack	East Chicago, Lake	D	1955 1957 1959 1961
Conn, Harriette B.	Indianapolis, Marion	R	1967 1969*
Coons, Clara Van Cleave	Crawfordsville, Montgomery	R	1941 1943 1945 1947 1957
Crimmins, Janiece L.	Marion, Grant	R	1971 1973
Crosby, Susan R.	Greencastle, Putnam	D	1991 1993 1995
Currie, Lucille Smith	Indianapolis, Marion	D	1959
Daugherty, Elizabeth Hunt	Wabash, Wabash	R	1925
Dickinson, Mae	Indianapolis, Marion	D	1993 1995
Dorbecker, Doris L.	Indianapolis, Marion	R	1969 1971 1973 1977 1979 1981 1983*
Downey, Nelle Bowman	Indianapolis, Marion	R	1941 1943 1945 1947 1951 1953
Downing, Elizabeth Williams	Indianapolis, Marion	R	1943
Duncan, Cleo	Greenburg, Decatur	R	1995
Dunn, Mabel A.	Indianapolis, Marion	D	1949
Engle, Barbara L.	Decatur, Adams	R	1983 1985 1987 1989 1991 1993 1995
Fay, Wilma J.	Indianapolis, Marion	R	1967 1969 1971*
Ferguson, Lettie McCave	Fort Wayne, Allen	R	1929
Fifield, Esther	East Chicago, Lake	R	1979* 1981 1983 1985 1987 1989

Indiana House, continued

Name	City, County	Party	Legislative Year
Fruits, Katherine	Indianapolis, Marion	D	1965
Gardner, Ella Van Sickle	Indianoplis, Marion	R	1927
Gaylord, Ella Frances	Lafayette, Tippecanoe	R	1967 1969 1971 1973
Goeglein, Gloria J.	Fort Wayne, Allen	R	1991 1993 1995
Hagenwald, Antoinette Colonge	Terre Haute, Vigo	R	1925
Haines, Tella Chloe	Graysville, Sullivan	D	1931
Hall, Katie	Gary, Lake	D	1975
Hawthorne, Marcia M.	Indianapolis, Marion	R	1961
Heffley, Irene	Indianapolis, Marion	R	1995
Henderson, Linda Kay	Bedford, Lawrence	D	1993
Hibner, Janet L.	Richmond, Wayne	R	1977 1979 1981 1983 1985
Kaufman, Bess Robbins see *Robbins*	Indianapolis, Marion	D	1939
Kirk, Naomi J.	New Albany, Floyd	D	1955 1957
Klinker, Sheila Ann J.	Lafayette, Tippecanoe	D	1983 1985 1987 1989 1991 1993 1995
Lambert, Sally Rideout	Boonville, Posey	R	1995
Lauck, Marie Theresa	Indianapolis, Marion	D	1959
Leuck, Claire M.	Fowler, Benton	D	1987 1989 1991 1993 1995
Lloyd, Daisy R.	Indianapolis, Marion	D	1965
Logan, Cecilia M.	Indianapolis, Marion	D	1965
Lowe, Mabel Leota	Indianapolis, Marion	R	1943
Lynch, Irma Stone	Evansville, Vanderburg	D	1945
Mahoney, Donnabelle	Hammond, Lake	D	1973* 1975
Malinka, Bernadine Betty	Gary, Lake	D	1943 1945 1947 1951 1953 1955
Maloney, Anna	Gary, Lake	D	1961 1963 1965 1967 1969 1971
Mason, Clara Harris	Terre Haute, Vigo	R	1927
May, Emma Mary	Terre Haute, Vigo	D	1945
Miller, Patricia L.	Indianapolis, Marion	R	1983*
Misener, Mary Z. Hershey	Michigan City, La Porte	R	1929
Morris, Candy	Indianapolis, Marion	R	1995
Mosby, Carolyn Brown	Gary, Lake	D	1979 1981 1983*
Nelson, Julia D. Reynolds	Delaware, Madison	R	1921
Nicholson, Roberta West	Indianapolis, Marion	D	1935
Noble, Jane Ann	Kokomo, Howard	D	1949
Norris, Fern E.	Indianapolis, Marion	R	1951
Parent, Lillian M.	Dannville, Hendricks	R	1977 1979*
Pettersen, Mary J.	Hammond, Lake	D	1979 1981 1983 1985

Name	Place	Party	Years
Pond, Phyllis J.	New Haven, Allen	R	1979 1981 1983 1985 1987 1989 1991 1993 1995
Rainey, Elizabeth	Indianapolis, Marion	R	1923
Richardson, Kathy Kreag	Noblesville, Hamilton	R	1993 1995
Ricketts, Marvel	Indianapolis, Marion	D	1965
Roach, Grace E.	Milan, Ripley	D	1949
Robbins, Bess see Kaufman	Indianapolis, Marion	D	1933 1937
Rogers, Earline S.	Gary, Lake	D	1983* 1985 1987 1989
Scholer, Sue W.	W. Lafayette, Tippecanoe	R	1991 1993 1995
Schultz, Marilyn F.	Bloomington, Monroe	D	1973 1975 1977 1979 1981 1983 1985
Seyfried, Maryann	Indianapolis, Marion	D	1975
Smelser, Anna Padberg	South Bend, St. Joseph	D	1953 1955
Stout, Harriet Cracraft	Indianapolis, Marion	R	1955 1957
Van Arsdale, Catherine E.	Indianapolis, Marion	D	1975
Willing, Katherine	Lebanon, Boone	R	1993 1995
Wilson, Esther M.	Portage, Porter	D	1977 1979 1983 1985 1987 1989 1991 1993 1995
Wilson, Ida R.	Boonville, Warrick	R	1943 1947
Wolf, Katie L.	Monticello, Carroll	D	1985
Wolf, Sarah Margaret	Greenfield, Hancock	D	1991
Womacks, Martha A.	Indianapolis, Marion	R	1995
Wooffendale, Lucille	Frankfort, Clinton	R	1973
Worman, Marna Jo	Cedar Creek, Allen	R	1977
Wyatt, Margaret L.	Indianapolis, Marion	R	1945 1947
Zimmerman, Bertha A. Goad	Terre Haute, Vigo	R	1929

*Notes:

Balz, Arcada S. — Elected Nov. 3, 1942 (Green)
Becker, Vaneta Liley — Elected Sept. 22, 1981 (Server)
Bowser, Anita Olga Albu — Elected Dec. 28, 1979 (Arnold)
Breaux, Billie J. — Elected Jan. 7, 1991 (Carson)[F]
Brinkman, Joyce — Elected (Burkley)
Carson, Julia — Resigned 1990 (Breaux)[F]
Conn, Harriette B. — Resigned March 24, 1970
Dorbecker, Doris L. — Died March 8, 1984 (Jones)
Fay, Wilma J. — Died Aug. 20, 1972
Fifield, Esther — Elected Oct. 9, 1979 (Fifield)
Mahoney, Donnabelle — Elected Sept. 5, 1973 (Mahoney)
Miller, Patricia L. — Resigned (Cottey), elected Sept. 26, 1983 to Senate (Bosma)
Mosby, Carolyn Brown — Resigned (Rogers)[F], elected Nov. 1982 to Senate (Hall)[F]
Parent, Lillian M. — Resigned (Thompson), elected Jan. 26, 1979 (Swisher) to Senate
Rogers, Earline S. — Elected Dec. 11, 1982 (Mosby)[F]
Sullivan, Jessie Jean Keirn — Elected Jan. 3, 1976 (Sullivan)

IOWA (1929–1995)

Iowa women gained presidential suffrage by legislative enactment in 1919. After the Nineteenth Amendment was ratified on August 26, 1920 for national suffrage and women voted in the 1920 state elections, the Iowa Attorney General ruled that the state constitution which called for "male legislators" would have to be amended before women could run for the state legislature. A constitutional amendment passed in 1926 and in 1928 Carolyn Campbell Pendray (D–Maquosketa, Jackson) was elected to the House.

State elections are every two years to elect 100 representatives who serve two year terms and 50 senators who serve four year terms. Vacancies are filled by special election.

95 women have served in the Iowa General Assembly:
  24 in the Senate
  82 in the House
  (11 in the House and Senate)

Women as Percentage of Iowa Legislators

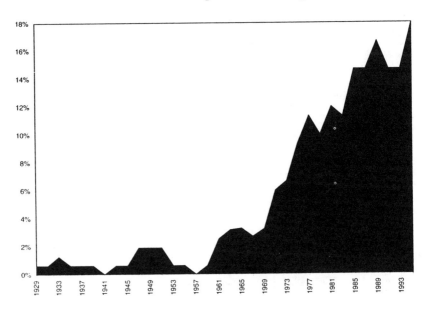

Senate
4 Year Terms

Name	City, County	Party	Legislative Year
Boettger, Nancy	Harlan, Shelby	R	1995
Buhr, Florence D.	Des Moines, Polk	D	1991 1993
Conklin, Charlene W.	Waterloo, Black Hawk	R	1969 1971
Corning, Joy	Cedar Falls, Black Hawk	R	1985 1987 1989*
Doderer, Minnette F.	Iowa City, Johnson	D	1969 1971 1973 1975 1977
Douglas, Jo Ann	Adair, Adair	R	1995
Freeman, Mary Lou	Storm Lake, Buena Vista	R	1993* 1995
Gentleman, Julia B.	Des Moines, Polk	R	1979 1981 1983 1985 1987 1989
Hammond, Johnie	Ames, Story	D	1995
Hannon, Beverly A.	Anamosa, Jones	D	1985 1987 1989 1991
Judge, Patty	Albia, Monroe	D	1993 1995
Kirketeg, Kathlyn M.	Bedford, Taylor	R	1947*
Kramer, Mary E. W.	Des Moines, Polk	R	1991 1993 1995
Lloyd-Jones, Jean	Iowa City, Johnson	D	1987 1989 1991 1993
Lundby, Mary A.	Marion, Linn	R	1995*
Miller, Elizabeth R.	Marshalltown, Marshall	R	1973 1975 1977 1979
Neuhauser, Mary C.	Iowa City, Johnson	D	1995
Orr, Joan Yessler	Grinnell, Iowa	D	1969*1973 1975 1977 1979
Pendray, Carolyn Campbell	Maquoketa, Jackson	D	1933 1935
Shaw, Elizabeth Orr	Davenport, Scott	R	1973 1975 1977*
Shivvers, Vera H.	Knoxville, Marion	R	1963*
Szymoniak, Elaine	Des Moines, Polk	D	1989 1991 1993 1995
Tinsman, Maggie	Bettendorf, Scott	R	1989 1991 1993 1995
Yenger, Sue	Ottumwa, Wapello	R	1979 1981

House
2 Year Terms

Name	City, County	Party	Legislative Year
Adams, Janet	Webster City, Hamilton	D	1987 1989 1991
Baxter, Elaine	Burlington, Des Moines	D	1981*1983 1985
Beatty, Linda L.	Indianola, Warren	D	1985 1987 1989 1991 1993
Bloom, Amy M.	Dayton, Webster	R	1947
Bock, Lenabelle	Garner, Hancock	R	1961 1963
Bogenrief, Mattie B.	Des Moines, Polk	D	1965
Boggess, Effie Lee	Villisca, Montgomery	R	1995
Brandt, Diane	Cedar Falls, Black Hawk	D	1975 1977 1979 1981
Buhr, Florence D.	Des Moines, Polk	D	1983 1985 1987 1989

Iowa House, continued

Name	City, County	Party	Legislative Year
Burnett, Cecelia	Ames, Story	D	1995
Carl, Janet	Grinnell, Iowa	D	1981 1983 1985
Carpenter, Dorothy F.	W. Des Moines, Polk	R	1981 1983 1985 1987 1989 1991 1993
Chapman, Kathleen	Cedar Rapids, Linn	D	1983 1985 1987 1989 1991
Clark, Betty Jean	Rockwell, Cerro Gordo	R	1977 1979 1981 1983 1985 1987 1989
Cohen, Gertrude S.	Waterloo, Black Hawk	D	1965
Conklin, Charlene W.	Waterloo, Black Hawk	R	1967
Crabb, Helen Marget	Jamacia, Guthrie	D	1949 1951
Doderer, Minnette F.	Iowa City, Johnson	D	1963* 1965 1967 1981 1983 1985 1987 1989 1991 1993 1995
Duitscher, Lucile	Wright County	D	1969*
Egenes, Sonja	Story City, Story	R	1971 1973 1975 1977 1979 1981
Elliot, Isabel M.	Bronson, Woodbury	D	1937 1939
Falvey, Katherine M.	Albia, Monroe	D	1957*1959 1961 1963
Franklin, June A.	Des Moines, Polk	D	1967 1969 1971
Garman, Teresa	Ames, Story	R	1987 1989 1991 1993 1995
Garner, Ada Adair	Shell Rock, Butler	D	1933
Gentleman, Julia B.	Des Moines, Polk	R	1975 1977
Glanton, Willie S.	Des Moines, Polk	D	1965
Gregerson, Mary Pat	Council Bluffs, Pottawat-tamie	D	1965
Greiner, Sandra H.	Keota, Keokuk	R	1993 1995
Gruhn, Josephine	Spirit Lake, Dickinson	D	1983 1985 1987 1989 1991
Grundberg, Betty	Des Moines, Polk	R	1993 1995
Hakes, Frances G.	Laurens, Pocahontas	R	1961 1963
Hammitt, Donna	Logan, Harrison	D	1995
Hammond, Johnie	Ames, Story	D	1983 1985 1987 1989 1991 1993
Harper, Mattie	West Grove, Davis	D	1973 1975 1977
Harper, Patricia M.	Waterloo, Black Hawk	D	1987 1989 1993 1995
Hester, Joan L.	Honey Creek, Pottawat-tamie	R	1985 1987 1989 1991 1993
Hoffman-Bright, Betty A.	Muscatine, Muscatine	R	1977 1979 1981 1983
Jacobs, Libby W.	Des Moines, Polk	D	1995
Jochum, Pam	Dubuque, Dubuque	D	1993 1995
Kiser, Emma Jean	Davenport, Scott	R	1973
Larsen, Sonja	Ottumwa, Wapello	R	1979
Lawrence, Edna C.	Ottumwa, Wapello	R	1947 1949
Lipsky, Joan	Cedar Rapids, Linn	R	1967 1969 1971 1973 1975 1977

Lloyd-Jones, Jean	Iowa City, Johnson	D	1979 1981 1983 1985
Lonergan, Joyce	Boone, Boone	D	1975 1977 1979 1981 1983 1985
Lundby, Mary A.	Marion, Linn	R	1987 1989 1991 1993 1995*
Lynch, Mae A.	Pocahontas, Pocahontas	D	1943 1945
Mann, Karen	Scranton, Greene	R	1981
Martin, Mona	Davenport, Scott	R	1993 1995
Mascher, Mary	Iowa City, Johnson	D	1995
McElroy, Lillian	Percival, Fremont	R	1971 1973 1975
Mertz, Dolores M.	Ottosen, Humbolt	D	1989 1991 1993 1995
Metcalf, Janet	Des Moines, Polk	R	1985 1987 1989 1991 1993 1995
Metz, Katheryn C.	Lamoni, Decatur	R	1949 1951
Miller, Elizabeth R.	Marshalltown, Marshall	R	1969 1971
Miller, Opal L.	Rockwell City, Calhoun	D	1975 1977
Mullins, Sue	Corwith, Kossuth	R	1979 1981 1983 1985 1987
Nelson, Beverly	Marshalltown, Marshall	D	1995
Nelson, Gladys Shand	Newton, Jasper	R	1951 1953 1955
Nelson, Linda	Council Bluffs, Pottawattamie	D	1993 1995
Neuhauser, Mary C.	Iowa City, Johnson	D	1987 1989 1991 1993
Nielsen, Joyce	Cedar Rapids, Linn	D	1989 1991
O'Halloran, Mary T.	Cedar Falls, Black Hawk	D	1973 1975 1977
Peick, Doris	Cedar Rapids, Linn	D	1983 1985
Pendray, Carolyn Campbell	Maquoketa, Jackson	D	1929 1931
Poffenberger, Virginia	Perry, Dallas	R	1979 1981
Sargisson, Hallie	Salix, Woodbury	D	1971
Shaw, Elizabeth Orr	Davenport, Scott	R	1967 1969 1971
Shimanek, Nancy J.	Monticello, Jones	R	1977 1979 1981*
Smith, Jo	Davenport, Scott	R	1981
Svoboda, Jane	Clutier, Tama	D	1987 1989 1991
Svoboda, Linda A.	Amana, Iowa	D	1975 1977
Teaford, Jane	Cedar Falls, Black Hawk	D	1985 1987 1989 1991
Thompson, Patricia L.	Des Moines, Polk	R	1977 1979
Thompson, Rose Mary	Marion, Linn	R	1995*
Torrence, Janis I.	Atalissa, Muscatine	R	1983 1985
Trucano, Jo Ann	Des Moines, Polk	R	1981
Van Alstine, Percie E.	Glimore City, Humboldt	R	1961 1963
Walter, Marcia K.	Council Bluffs, Pottawattamie	D	1981
Wolcott, Olga Doran	Rockwell, Cerro Gordo	D	1965
Zimmerman, Jo Ann	Des Moines, Polk	D	1983 1985

*Notes:
Baxter, Elaine—Elected Nov. 3, 1981 (Shimanek) [F]
Corning, Joy—Resigned Nov. 7, 1990

Iowa, continued

Doderer, Minnette F.—Elected Jan. 1964 (Swisher)
Duitscher, Lucile—Elected 1970 (Bailey)
Falvey, Katherine M.—Elected 1957 (Falvey)
Freeman, Mary Lou—Elected Feb. 22, 1994 (Fuhrman)
Kirketeg, Kathlyn—Elected 1947 (Kirketeg)
Lundby, Mary A.—Resigned, elected Dec. 1994 to Senate (Pate)
Orr, Joan Yessler—Elected 1970 (Benda)
Shaw, Elizabeth Orr—Resigned 1978 (Holden)
Shimanek, Nancy J.—Resigned Sept. 10, 1981 (Baxter) [F]
Shivvers, Vera H.—Elected Jan. 10, 1963 (Shivvers)
Thompson, Rose Mary—Elected Jan. 10, 1995 (Lundby)

KANSAS (1919–1995)

Kansas women gained school suffrage in 1861, tax and bond suffrage in 1903, and full suffrage by constitutional amendment in 1912.

Minnie Tamar Johnson Grinstead (R–Liberty, Seward) was the first woman elected to the state legislature in 1918. Nellie Cline (D–Larned, Pawnee County) moved to Idaho where she served in the Idaho State Senate from 1945 to 1950 and 1957 to 1962 as Nellie Cline Steenson.

Women as Percentage of Kansas Legislators

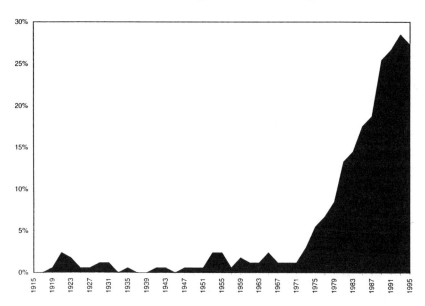

State elections are held every two years for 125 representatives who serve two year terms and 40 senators who serve four year terms. All senators are elected at the same time and will be up for election in 1996. Vacancies are filled by governor's appointment.

128 women served in the Kansas Legislature:
    23 in the Senate
    108 in the House
    (3 in the House and Senate)

Senate
4 Year Terms

Name	City, County	Party	Legislative Year
Beall, Ailene	Clay Enter, Clay	R	1959*
Daniels, Norma L.	Valley Center, Sedgwick	D	1981 1983 1985 1987 1989 1991
Downey, Christine	Newton, Harvey	D	1993 1995
Eldredge, Jane M.	Lawrence, Douglas	R	1981
Frahm, Sheila	Colby, Thomas	R	1989 1991 1993 1995*
Hardenburger, Janice	Haddam, Washington	R	1993 1995
Hoferer, Jeanne	Topeka, Shawnee	R	1985 1987
Langworthy, Audrey	Prairie Village, Johnson	R	1985 1987 1989 1991 1993 1995
Lawrence, Barbara	Wichita, Sedgwick	R	1993 1995
Lee, Janis K.	Kensington, Smith	D	1989 1991 1993 1995
McClure, Janice Lee	Sublette, Meade	D	1989 1991
Meyers, Jan	Overland Park, Johnson	R	1973 1975 1977 1979 1981 1983
Oleen, Lana	Manhattan, Riley	R	1989 1991 1993 1995
Papay, Lillian D.	Great Bend, Barton	R	1993 1995
Parrish, Nancy Elaine	Topeka, Shawnee	D	1979* 1981 1983 1985 1987 1989 1991
Petty, Marge	Topeka, Shawnee	D	1989 1991 1993 1995
Porter, Louise	Miller, Lyon	R	1965 1967 1969
Praeger, Sandy	Lawrence, Douglas	R	1993 1995
Ranson, Pat	Wichita, Sedgwick	R	1993 1995
Reynolds, Marian K.	Dodge City, Ford	R	1993 1995
Salisbury, Alicia Laing	Topeka, Shawnee	R	1985 1987 1989 1991 1993 1995
Solander, Patricia	Osawatomie, Miami	R	1929 1931
Tillotson, Carolyn	Leavenworth, Leaven- worth	R	1993 1995

House
2 Year Terms

Name	City, County	Party	Legislative Year
Adam, Joan E.	Atchison, Atchison	D	1983 1985 1987 1989 1991
Allen, Barbara P.	Prairie Village, Johnson	R	1987* 1989 1991 1993 1995
Anderson, Geneva June	Mulvane, Sedgwick	D	1975 1977 1979
Apt, Denise C.	Iola, Allen	R	1981 1983 1985 1987
Aylward, Jayne Anne	Salina, Saline	R	1979 1981 1983 1985 1987 1989
Baker, Elizabeth	Derby, Sedgwick	R	1983 1985 1987 1989 1991
Ballard, Barbara W.	Lawrence, Douglas	D	1993 1995
Barr, Ginger	Auburn, Shawnee	R	1983 1985 1987 1989
Baughman, Gladys A.	Elk Falls, Elk	D	1959* 1961
Benlon, Lisa	Shawnee, Johnson	R	1991 1993 1995
Borum, Isabel L.	Wichita, Sedgwick	R	1987* 1989
Bradford, Georgia	Wichita, Sedgwick	R	1991
Branson, Jessie M.	Lawrence, Douglas	D	1981 1983 1985 1987 1989
Brown, Nancy	Stanley, Johnson	R	1985 1987 1989 1991 1993
Charlton, Betty Jo	Lawrence, Douglas	D	1979* 1981 1983 1985 1987 1989 1991 1993
Chronister, Rochelle Beach	Neodesha, Wilson	R	1979 1981 1983 1985 1987 1989 1991 1993 1995
Cline, Nellie	Larned, Pawnee	D	1921 1923
Cobb, Reba L.	Galva, McPherson	R	1983
Cornfield, Darlene	Valley Center, Sedgwick	R	1991 1993 1995
Cozine, Ann	Mulvane, Sumner	D	1991
Dawson, Carol	Russell, Russell	R	1991 1993 1995
Dickhut, Rosa Been	Scott City, Scott	D	1953 1955
Donica, Lavonia M.	Scott City, Scott	R	1925
Empson, Cindy	Independence, Montgomery	R	1987 1989 1991 1993 1995
Everhart, Denise	Berryton, Shawnee	D	1989 1991 1993
Flottman, Dorothy H.	Winfield, Cowley	R	1983 1985 1987 1989 1991
Flower, Joann	Oskaloosa, Jefferson	R	1989 1991 1993 1995
Freeborn, Joann	Ames, Cloud	R	1993 1995
Fuller, Wanda L.	Wichita, Sedgwick	R	1981 1983 1985 1987 1989 1991 1993*
Garrett, Mozelle	Derby, Sedgwick	D	1979* 1981
Gilbert, Ruby	Wichita, Sedgwick	D	1991* 1993 1995

Gilmore, Phyllis	Olathe, Johnson	R	1995
Gjerstad, Diane	Wichita, Sedgwick	D	1985 1987 1989 1991
Goodwin, Greta Hall	Winfield, Cowley	D	1993 1995
Graham, Harriet	Wichita, Sedgwick	D	1965 1967
Grant, Jill	Topeka, Shawnee	R	1995
Griffiths, Karen	Newton, Harvey	R	1979* 1981
Grinstead, Minnie Tamar Johnson	Liberal, Seward	R	1919 1921 1923
Hackler, Ruth Ann	Olathe, Johnson	D	1991
Haines, Stella B.	Augusta, Butler	R	1927 1929
Hamilton, Joan	Topeka, Shawnee	D	1991
Hassler, Elaine	Abilene, Dickinson	R	1979 1981 1983 1985 1987
Hess, Sharon	Wichita, Sedgwick	R	1975 1977 1979
Hochhauser, Sheila	Manhattan, Riley	D	1989 1991 1993 1995
Horst, Deena	Salina, Saline	R	1995
Hoyt, Jennie P.	Lyons, Rice	R	1953 1955
Hurt, Katha Connor	Manhattan, Riley	D	1989
Hutchins, Becky	Holton, Jackson	R	1995
Jacquart, Beatrice L.	Satanta, Haskell	R	1957 1959 1961 1963 1965
Jenkins, Martha	Leavenworth, Leavenworth	R	1985 1987 1989
Johnson, Mary Jane	Kansas City, Wyandotte	D	1983 1985 1987 1989 1991
Jones, Glee Carrel	Hamlin, Brown	R	1971 1973 1975 1977
Kennard, Connie Ames	Wichita, Sedgwick	D	1987
Kininmonth, Patricia A.	Winfield, Cowley	R	1947 1949
Kirk, Nancy	Topeka, Shawnee	D	1995
Landwehr, Brenda	Wichita, Sedgwick	R	1995
Lawrence, Barbara	Wichita, Sedgwick	R	1989 1991
Luzzati, Ruth	Wichita, Sedgwick	D	1973 1975 1977 1979 1981 1983 1985
Lynch, Eloise	Salina, Saline	D	1989 1991 1993
Macy, Judith K.	Desoto, Johnson	D	1991 1993*
Matlack, Ardena L.	Clearwater, Sedgwick	D	1975 1977 1979 1981 1983
McClure, Laura L.	Glen Elder, Osborne	D	1993 1995
Minnich, Minnie J.	Wellington, Sumner	R	1921
Morss, Nettie H.	Howard, Elk	D	1935
Murphy, Kathryn	Bethel, Wyandotte	D	1961*
Newell, Dollie E.	Stafford, Stafford	R	1963* 1965
Nichols, Dorothy N.	Ottawa, Franklin	R	1981 1983 1985
Niles, Anita G.	Lebo, Coffey	D	1975 1977 1979 1981 1983
O'Connor, Kay	Olathe, Johnson	R	1993 1995
O'Laughlin, Kathryn	Hays, Ellis	D	1931*
Otis, Mildred	Phillipsburg, Phillips	R	1953 1955
Ott, Belva J.	Wichita, Sedgwick	R	1977* 1979 1981 1995
Pauls, Janice L.	Hutchinson, Reno	D	1991* 1993 1995

Kansas House, continued

Name	City, County	Party	Legislative Year
Pettey, Pat Huggins	Kansas City, Wyandotte	D	1993 1995
Pottorff, Jo Ann	Wichita, Sedgwick	R	1985 1987 1989 1991 1993 1995
Praeger, Sandy	Lawrence, Douglas	R	1991
Renn, Nell Arkansas	City, Cowley	R	1951* 1953 1955
Reynolds, Marian K.	Cimarron, Gray	D	1975
Roenbaugh, Susan	Lewis, Stafford	R	1983 1985 1987 1989
Ruff, L.Candy	Leavenworth, Leaven-worth	D	1993 1995
Runnels, Judith C.	Topeka, Shawnee	D	1983 1985
Sader, Carol H.	Prairie Village, Johnson	D	1987 1989 1991 1993
Samuelson, Ellen Banman	Newton, Harvey	R	1989 1991 1993 1995
Schauf, Debara K.	Mulvane, Sedgwick	R	1987 1989
Sebelius, Kathleen	Topeka, Shawnee	D	1987 1989 1991 1993
Shelton, Cora W.	Salina, Saline	D	1941 1943
Shumway, Bettie Sue	Ottawa, Franklin	D	1989
Standifer, Sabrina	Wichita, Sedgwick	D	1993 1995
Stephens, Stevi	Tonganoxie, Leavenworth	D	1991
Stewart, Mary E.	Stockton, Rooks	D	1959*
Strahm, Nina Jean	Sabetha, Nemaha	R	1979 1981
Sughrue, Kathryn	Dodge City, Ford	R	1977 1979 1981 1983 1985 1987 1989
Swearengen, Fern Catherine	Hill City, Graham	D	1959
Toelkes, Dixie E.	Topeka, Shawnee	D	1995
Thompson, Majorie J.	Winfield, Cowley	D	1977 1979 1981
Thorp, Norma	Desoto, Johnson	D	1993*
Wagle, Susan	Wichita, Sedgwick	R	1991 1993 1995
Wagnon, Joan	Topeka, Shawnee	D	1983 1985 1987 1989 1991 1993
Walker, Ida M.	Norton, Norton	R	1921 1923
Weaver, Patricia	Baxter Springs, Cherokee	D	1983* 1985
Weber, Shari	Herington, Dickinson	R	1995
Weinhold, Carolyn	Salina, Saline	D	1993
Wells, Elaine L.	Carbondale, Osage	D	1987 1989 1991 1993
Welshimer, Gwen	Wichita, Sedgwick	D	1991 1993 1995
Whiteman, Donna L.	Hutchinson, Reno	D	1983* 1985 1987 1989 1991
Wilkin, Ruth W.	Topeka, Shawnee	D	1973 1975 1977 1979 1981
Yoh, Donna	Pittsburg, Crawford	R	1995
Younkin, Josephine	Junction City, Geary	D	1969 1971 1973

*Notes:
Allen, Barbara P.—Appointed 1988 (Fox)
Baughman, Gladys A.—Appointed 1960 (Baughman)

Beall, Ailene—Appointed Nov. 1959 (Beall)
Borum, Isabel L.—Appointed 1988 (Duncan)
Charlton, Betty Jo—Appointed 1980 (Glover)
Frahm, Sheila—Resigned 1994, elected Lt. Governor
Fuller, Wanda L.—Died Oct. 14, 1993 (Farmer)
Garrett, Mozelle—Appointed 1980 (Garrett)
Gilbert, Ruby—Appointed 1992 (Cribbs)
Griffiths, Karen—Appointed 1980 (Gilmore)
Macy, Judith K.—Resigned Aug. 5, 1994 (Thorp)[F]
Murphy, Kathryn—Appointed 1962 (Murphy)
Newell, Dollie E.—Appointed 1963 (Newell)
Ott, Belva J.—Appointed (Reeves)
Parrish, Nancy Elaine—Appointed 1980 (Parrish)
Pauls, Janice L.—Appointed 1992 (Whiteman)[F]
Renn, Nell—Appointed (Renn)
Stewart, Mary E.—Appointed 1959 (Stewart)
Thorp, Norma—Appointed Sept. 6, 1994 (Macy)[F]
Weaver, Patricia—Appointed 1984 (Weaver)
Whiteman, Donna L.—Appointed 1984 (Myers)

KENTUCKY (1922–1995)

Women as Percentage of Kentucky Legislators

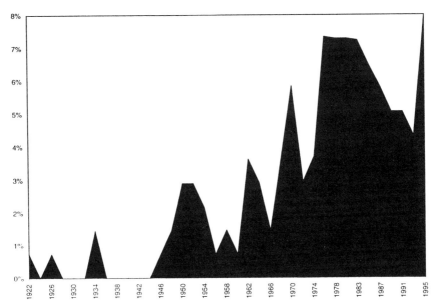

Kentucky widows with school age children who lived in country districts gained the right to vote in school elections in 1838. Taxpaying spinsters and widows who lived outside chartered cities were granted the right to vote in school elections in 1888. Kentucky women gained presidential suffrage in 1920 by legislative enactment and full suffrage on August 26, 1920. Women first voted in state elections in 1921 and elected Representative Mary Elliott Flanery (D–Catlettsburg, Boyd).

State legislative elections were held every two years in the odd years until 1981 when a transition three year term implemented even year elections. Since 1984, elections are held in even years to elect 38 senators who serve four year terms and 100 representatives who serve two year terms. Vacancies are filled by special election.

61 women have served in the Kentucky General Assembly:
   13 in the Senate
   48 in the House

Senate
4 Year Terms

Name	City, County	Party	Legislative Year
Bishop, Lillie	Rockcastle, Rockcastle	R	1970*
Cobb, Hazel Warner	Rickman, Jessamine	D	1962*1964
Davis, Georgia M. *see Powers*	Louisville, Jefferson	D	1968 1970 1972
Davis, Pauline P.	Grayson, Carter	R	1958*1960
Derickson, Van-detta L.	Stanton, Powell	D	1962*1964
Garrett, Helen R.	Paducah, McCracken	D	1978*1980 1983 1985 1987 1989
Johns, Susan D.	Louisville, Jefferson	D	1991 1993
Moore, Carolyn C.	Franklin, Simpson	D	1950*
Powers, Georgia M. Davis *see Davis*	Louisville, Jefferson	D	1974 1976 1978 1980 1983 1985 1987
Rose, Julie Carman	Louisville, Jefferson	R	1995
Thaler, Daisy Wigginton	Louisville, Jefferson	D	1974 1976
Tori, Elizabeth	Radcliff, Meade	R	1995
Weaver, Patti	Waton, Boone	D	1989*
Webb, Douglas Cook	Guthrie, Todd	D	1954*

House
2 Year Terms

Name	City, County	Party	Legislative Year
Bendl, Gerta	Louisville, Jefferson	D	1976 1978 1980 1983 1985 1987
Bevins, Glenna A.	Lexington, Fayette	D	1976
Bleemel, Virginia	Shepherdsvile, Bullitt	D	1970*
Boatwright, Linda	Paducah, McCracken	D	1978*
Bondurant, Kaye	Hodgenville, La Rue	D	1993*1995
Brown, Frances P.	Sandy Hook, Elliott	D	1985*
Bryant, Jo Elizabeth	Williamsburg, Whitley	R	1991 1993
Burnett, Mary Elizabeth	Lexington, Fayette	D	1946 1948 1950 1952
Cantrill, Florence Shelby	Lexington, Fayette	D	1934
Castleman, Robbie	Mayfield, Graves	D	1991*
Colter, Barbara White	Manchester, Knox	R	1995
Craddock, Allene A.	Elizabethtown, Hardin	D	1976 1978 1980 1983
Cruse, Marge	Louisville, Jefferson	R	1968
Flanery, Mary Elliott	Catlettsburg, Boyd	D	1922
Freibert, Pat	Lexington, Fayette	R	1978* 1980 1983 1985 1987 1989 1991
Hale, Kathleen McGary	Owensboro, Daviess	D	1966*
Hall, Ann Butcher	Bypro, Floyd	D	1958
Hogancamp, Kathy	Paducah, McCracken	R	1995
Hoover, Mae	Albany, Clinton	R	1987
Jenkins, Joni L.	Shively, Jefferson	D	1995
Jorris, Ann Grider	Rowens, Russell	R	1926
Kenton, Carolyn L.	Lexington, Fayette	D	1980* 1983
Kidd, Mae Straight	Louisville, Jefferson	D	1968 1970 1972 1974 1976 1978 1980 1983
Kirtley, Mary Louise Gasser	Owensboro, Daviess	D	1962 1964
Linton, Allie Mae	Russellvile, Logan	D	1950 1952
Lyne, June D.	Olmstead, Logan	D	1985 1987 1989 1991 1993
Marzian, Mary Lou	Louisville, Jefferson	D	1993*1995
McGill, Charlotte S.	Louisville, Jefferson	D	1970* 1972 1974 1976
McNamara, Nell Guy	Mt. Sterling, Montgomery	D	1964 1966 1968 1970
McNutt, Alice Dolly H.	Paducah, McCracken	D	1976* 1978 1980 1983 1985
Mills, Frances Jones	Gray, Knox	D	1962
Northup, Anne Meagher	Louisville, Jefferson	R	1987* 1989 1991 1993 1995
Palumbo, Ruth Ann	Lexington, Fayette	D	1991 1993 1995

Kentucky House, continued

Name	City, County	Party	Legislative Year
Priddy, Dorothy	Louisville, Jefferson	D	1970 1972 1974 1976 1978 1980 1983 1985 1987 1989
Riner, Claudia	Louisville, Jefferson	D	1978 1980
Rutherford, Susan Bond	Lawrenceburg, Anderson	D	1948
Scott, Mary Breckinridge	Hoods, Fayette	D	1934
Shacklette, Donna	Louisville, Jefferson	D	1991* 1993 1995
Stewart, Margaret J.	Lexington, Fayette	R	1985
Stine, Katie Kratz	Ft. Thomas, Campbell	R	1995
Stokes, Susan B.	Louisville, Jefferson	R	1987* 1989 1991
Stovall, Thelma L.	Louisville, Jefferson	D	1950 1952 1954
Tobin, Marjorie	Harned, Breckinridge	D	1970
Tobin, Mary Ann	Irvington, Breckinridge	D	1976 1978 1980 1983
Tucker, Amelia M.	Louisville, Jefferson	R	1962
White, Caroline	Barbourville, Knox	D	1983* 1985 1987 1989
Wilson, Cynthia Randolph	Glasgow, Barren	D	1952 1954 1956
Wolchick, Ruth	Paintsville, Johnson	R	1968

*Notes:

Bishop, Lillie — Elected 1971 (Bishop)
Bleemel, Virginia — Elected Feb. 1971 (Bleemel)
Boatwright, Linda — Elected 1978 (Boatwright)
Bondurant, Kaye — Elected Nov. 2, 1993 (Pearman)
Brown, Frances P. — Elected Jan. 1986
Castleman, Robbie — Elected Aug. 1991 (Castleman)
Cobb, Hazel Warner — Elected Jan. 1962 (Cobb)
Davis, Pauline P. — Elected Jan. 1958 (Davis)
Derickson, Vandetta L. — Elected Jan. 1962 (Derickson)
Freibert, Pat — Elected Jan. 1979
Garrett, Helen R. — Elected July 1979 (Garrett)
Hale, Kathleen McGary — Elected 1967 (Hale)
Kenton, Carolyn L. — Elected Jan. 1982 (Kenton)
Marzian, Mary Lou — Elected Nov. 2, 1993 (Ward)
McGill, Charlotte S. — Election Jan. 1971 (McGill)
McNutt, Alice Dolly H. — Elected Nov. 1976 (McNutt)
Moore, Carolyn C. — Elected Nov. 8, 1949 (Moore)
Northup, Anne Meagher — Elected Oct. 1987 (Cowan)
Shacklette, Donna — Elected Sept. 1992
Stokes, Susan B. — Elected 1987
Weaver, Patti — Elected May 1989 (Weaver)
Webb, Douglas Cook — Elected Nov. 3, 1953 (Manafield)
White, Caroline — Elected Nov. 1983

LOUISIANA (1936–1995)

Louisiana women gained tax and bond suffrage in 1898 and full suffrage on August 26, 1920. Doris Lindsey Holland (D–Greensburg, St. Helena) succeeded her deceased husband as the Senate Democratic nominee in 1936 and won in the regular general election on March 27, 1936 to become the first women state legislator.

Before 1975, legislative elections were held in the spring every four years in even years and were followed immediately by the first regular session. Since 1975, 39 senators and 104 representatives are elected in an open primary system every four years in odd years and the first regular session convenes the following even year. The last regularly scheduled state elections were held in 1991 but due to reapportionment, a special election was held in 1992. The next regular election is scheduled for 1995. Vacancies are filled by special election.

33 women have served in the Louisiana Legislature:
  5 in the Senate
  31 in the House
  (3 in the House and Senate)

Women as Percentage of Louisiana Legislators

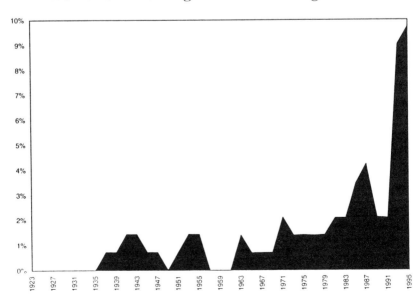

Senate
4 Year Terms

Name	City, Parish	Party	Legislative Year
Bajoie, Diane Elizabeth	New Orleans, Jefferson	D	1990* 1992 1994
Holland, Doris Lindsey	Greensburg, St. Helena	D	1936 1940
Irons, Paulette	New Orleans, Jefferson	D	1994*
Sevier, Irene Jordan	Talluhah, Madison	D	1962*
Shehee, Virginia Kilpatrick	Shreveport, Caddo	D	1976 1978

House
4 Year Terms

Name	City, Parish	Party	Legislative Year
Bajoie, Diane Elizabeth	New Orleans, Jefferson	D	1976 1978 1980 1982 1984 1986 1988 1990*
Blackmon, Evelyn Kinnison	West Monroe, Ouachita	D	1984 1986
Blanco, Kathleen Babineaux	Lafayette, Lafayette	D	1984 1986
Bowler, Shirley D.	Harahan, Jefferson	R	1992 1994
Burns, Bland Cox	New Orleans, Jefferson	D	1950* 1952 1954
Dixon, Irma Muse	New Orleans, Jefferson	D	1988 1990
Dorsey, Yvonne	Baton Rouge, Baton Rouge	D	1992 1994
Durand, Sydnie Mae M.	Parks, St. Martin	D	1992 1994
Farve, Naomi W.	New Orleans, Jefferson	D	1992 1994
Flournoy, Melissa	Shreveport, Caddo	D	1992 1994
Gleason, Mary Smith	Minden, Webster	D	1958*
Holland, Doris Lindsey	Greensburg, St. Helena	D	1940 1942 1944 1946
Irons, Paulette	New Orleans, Jefferson	D	1992* 1994*
Johnson, Louise Brazzel	Bernice, Union	D	1972 1974
Krieger, Suzanne M.	Slidell, St. Tamany	R	1992 1994
Landrieu, Mary L.	New Orleans, Jefferson	D	1980 1982 1984 1986
Laperouse, Helen Grace Landry	New Iberia, Iberia	D	1968* 1970
Lewis, Margaret Russell	DeRidder, Beauregard	D	1962* 1962
Lowenthal, Margaret Welsh	Lake Charles, Calcasieu	D	1980 1982 1984 1986
McCain, Audrey A.	Plaquemine, Iberville	D	1992 1994
Mitchell-Clarkson, Jacquelin	New Orleans, Jefferson	D	1995*
Moore, Beatrice Hawthorne	Shreveport, Caddo	D	1940 1942
Parrot, Mary Baker	Eunice, Acadia	D	1952 1954

Pratt, Renee	New Orleans, Jefferson	D	1990* 1992 1994
Taylor, Dorothy Mae Delavallade	New Orleans, Jefferson	D	1970* 1972 1974
Thompson, Lizzie Price	Doyline, Webster	D	1950*
Walker, Lillian W.	Baton Rouge, Baton Rouge	D	1964 1966 1968 1970
Warren, Naomi White	New Orleans, Jefferson	D	1986* 1988 1990 1992
Weston, Sharon	Baton Rouge, Baton Rouge	D	1992 1994
Wilkerson, Pinkie C.	Grambling, Lincoln	D	1992 1994
Willard-Lewis, Cynthia	New Orleans, Jefferson	D	1992* 1994

*Notes:

Bajoie, Diane Elizabeth—Resigned (Pratt)[F], elected March 1991 to Senate
Burns, Bland Cox—Elected March 27, 1950 (Corcoran)
Gleason, Mary Smith—Appointed July 30, 1959 (Gleason)
Irons, Paulette—Elected Nov. 1992. Resigned Nov. 8, 1994 (Mitchell)[F], elected to Senate.
Laperouse, Helen Grace Landry—Elected July 3, 1969 (Laperouse)
Lewis, Margaret Russell—Appointed Jan. 18, 1962 (Lewis)
Mitchell-Clarkson, Patricia Ann—Elected Feb. 6, 1995 (Irons)[F]
Pratt, Renee—Elected 1991 (Bajoie)[F]
Sevier, Irene Jordan—Elected May 23, 1962 (Sevier)
Taylor, Dorothy Mae Delavallade—Elected March 3, 1971 (Morial)
Thompson, Lizzie Price—Elected May 7, 1951 (Thompson)
Warren, Naomi White—Elected April 5, 1986 (Jackson)
Willard-Lewis, Cynthia—Elected Aug. 1, 1993 (Armstrong)

MAINE (1923–1995)

Maine women gained presidential suffrage by legislative enactment in 1919 and full suffrage on August 26, 1920. Women first voted in state elections in 1920. Women were first eligible to run for the state legislature in the 1922 state elections and elected Dora Pinkham (R–Fort Kent, Aroostook) to the house. The Penobscot Nation has been represented since 1823 and the Passamaquoddy Tribe since 1842 in the Maine State Legislature. The two Native American representatives are non-voting delegates in the House. In 1972, the Penobscot Nation elected Vivian F. Massey as the first woman to fill one of these seats.

State elections are held every two years to elect 35 senators and 151 representatives for two year terms. State legislative service is limited to four consecutive two year terms. Vacancies are filled by governor's appointment.

233 women have served in the Maine Legislature:
    42 in the Senate
    220 in the House
    (29 in the House and Senate)

Women as Percentage of Maine Legislators

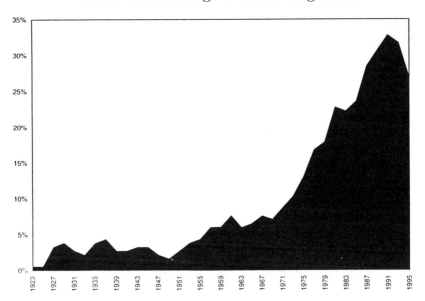

Senate
2 Year Terms

Name	City, County	Party	Legislative Year
Allen, Katharine C.	Hampden, Penobscot	R	1927 1929
Amero, Jane A.	Cape Elizabeth, Cumber-land	R	1993 1995
Berube, Georgette B.	Lewiston, Androscoggin	D	1985 1987 1989 1991 1993 1995
Brawn, Linda Curtis	Camden, Knox	R	1987 1989 1991
Bustin, Beverly Miner	Augusta, Kennebec	D	1981 1983 1985 1987 1989 1991 1993 1995
Cahill, Pamela Leedall	Woolwich, Sagadahoc	R	1987 1989 1991 1993
Carswell, Catherine Hendricks *see Hendricks*	Portland, Cumberland	D	1971

Carter, Claire S.	Auburn, Androscoggin	R	1927* 1929 1931
Chalmers, Jean B.	Rockland, Knox	D	1985
Chisholm, Mary E.	Cape Elizabeth, Cumberland	D	1965
Christie, Augusta K.	Presque Isle, Aroostook	R	1961 1963
Clark, Nancy Randall	Freeport, Cumberland	D	1979 1981 1983 1985 1987 1989 1991
Clough, Ruth Thorndike	Bangor, Penobscot	R	1945 1947
Cummings, Minnette H.	Newport, Penobscot	R	1973 1975 1977
Foster, Ruth S.	Blue Hill, Hancock	R	1991 1993
Gay, Maude Clark	Waldoboro, Lincoln	R	1933
Gill, Barbara A.	S. Portland, Cumberland	R	1979 1981 1983 1985 1987 1989 1991
Goldthwait, Jill M.	Bar Harbor, Hancock	I	1995
Harrington, Ida M.	Patten, Penobscot	R	1963
Holloway, Muriel D.	N. Edgecomb, Lincoln	R	1989 1991
Kany, Judy C.	Waterville, Kennebec	D	1983 1985 1987 1989 1991
Kavanagh, Mary L.	Lewiston, Androscoggin	R	1951 1953
Laughlin, Gail	Portland, Cumberland	R	1937 1939
Longley, Susan W.	Liberty, Knox	D	1995
Lord, Hazel C.	S. Portland, Cumberland	R	1955 1957 1959 1961
Ludwig, Margaret G.	Houlton, Aroostook	R	1987 1989 1991 1993
Luther, M. Ida	Mexico, Oxford	D	1993
Martin, Marion E.	Bangor, Penobscot	R	1935 1937
Maybury, Mary-Ellen	Brewer, Penobscot	R	1985 1987
McCormick, Dale	Monmouth, Kennebec	D	1991 1993 1995
Najarian, Mary	Portland, Cumberland	D	1979 1981 1983 1985
Paradis, Judy A.	Frenchville, Aroostook	D	1993 1995
Pendexter, Joan M.	Scarborough, Cumberland	R	1995
Pingree, Rochelle M.	New Haven, Lincoln	D	1993 1995
Pinkham, Dora	Fort Kent, Aroostook	R	1927 1929
Rand, Anne M.	Portland, Cumberland	D	1995
Sewall, Charlotte Zahn	Newcastle, Lincoln	R	1981 1983 1985 1987
Small, Mary E.	Bath, Lincoln	R	1995
Snowe, Olympia J.	Auburn, Androscoggin	R	1977
Sproul, Margaret	Bristol, Lincoln	R	1963 1965 1967
Titcomb, Bonnie L.	North Haven, Knox	D	1989 1991 1993
Trafton, Barbara M.	Auburn, Androscoggin	D	1979 1981

House
2 Year Terms

Name	City, County	Party	Legislative Year
Aikman, Rosalie Hemond	Poland, Androscoggin	R	1989 1991 1993 1995
Allen, Carol M.	Washington, Knox	D	1983 1985 1987 1989

Maine House, continued

Name	City, County	Party	Legislative Year
Allen, Katharine C.	Hampden, Penobscot	R	1925
Aloupis, Angela Z.	Bangor, Penobscot	R	1977 1979 1981
Attean, Priscilla A.	Old Town, Penobscot	Pen	1985* 1987 1989 1991 1993 1995
Ault, Wendy L.	Wayne, Kennebec	R	1989 1991 1993 1995
Backrach, Anne J.	Brunswick, Cumberland	D	1975 1977 1979
Baker, Ethel B.	Orrington, Penobscot	R	1959 1961 1965 1967 1969 1971 1973
Baker, Reta E.	E. Winthrop, Androscoggin	R	1965 1967
Bangs, Jean Lois	Brunswick, Cumberland	R	1941 1943
Beam, Joline Landry	Lewiston, Androscoggin	D	1993
Beaulieu, Edith S.	Portland, Cumberland	D	1977 1979 1981 1983 1985
Begley, Jeanne F.	Waldoboro, Lincoln	R	1985 1987 1989
Bell, Susan Jane	S. Paris, Oxford	R	1981 1983 1985
Beniot, Sharon B.	S. Portland, Cumberland	D	1977 1979 1981 1983
Berry, Glenys W.	Madison, Somerset	R	1971 1973 1975
Berube, Georgette B.	Lewiston, Androscoggin	D	1971 1973 1975 1977 1979 1981
Birney, Brenda	Paris, Oxford	R	1995
Boudreau, Anne M.	Portland, Cumberland	D	1967 1969 1971 1973 1975 1977
Brown, Ada K.	S. Windham, Cumberland	D	1979 1981 1983 1985 1987
Brown, Karen Lee	Bethel, Oxford	R	1977 1979 1981 1983
Brown, Marion Fuller *see Fuller*	York, York	R	1969 1971
Burke, Christine F.	Vassalboro, Kennebec	D	1989
Burnham, Mabel W.	York, York	R	1957
Byers, Charlotte Z.	Newcastle, Lincoln	R	1975 1977
Cahill, Mary F.	Mattawamkeag, Penobscot	D	1991
Cahill, Pamela Leedall	Woolwich, Sagadahoc	R	1981 1983 1985
Carswell, Catherine Hendricks *see Hendricks*	Portland, Cumberland	D	1963 1965 1967
Carter, Bessie M.	Fairfield, Somerset	D	1931 1933
Cathcart, Mary R.	Orono, Penobscot	D	1989 1991 1993
Chaney, Mabelle P.	Lisbon, Androscoggin	D	1927
Chase, Gail M.	North Vassalboro, Kennebec	D	1993 1995
Chizmar, Nancy L.	Lisbon, Androscoggin	D	1995
Chonko, Lorraine N.	Pejepscot, Sagadahoc	D	1973 1975 1977 1979 1981 1983 1985 1987 1989 1991 1993

Christie, Augusta K.	Presque Isle, Aroostook	R	1953 1955 1957 1959
Church, Grace N.	Stockton Springs, Waldo	R	1937
Clark, Margaret Pruitt	Brunswick, Cumberland	D	1987 1989 1991
Clark, Nancy Randall	Freeport, Cumberland	D	1973 1975 1977
Clough, Ruth Thorndike	Bangor, Penobscot	R	1939 1941 1943
Coffey, Barbara J.	Topsham, Sagadahoc	D	1969
Constantine, Virginia	Bar Harbor, Hancock	D	1989 1991 1993
Cormier, Lucia M.	Bangor, Penobscot	D	1947 1949 1953 1955 1957 1959
Cornell, Thelma B.	Orono, Penobscot	R	1967
Cote, Constance D.	Auburn, Androscoggin	D	1983 1985 1987 1989 1991 1993
Cummings, Minnette H.	Newport, Penobscot	R	1969 1971
Currier, Marion	Bangor, Penobscot	R	1935 1937
Curtis, Judith H.	Mildbridge, Washington	D	1979
Daggett, Ada M.	Ashland, Aroostook	R	1951
Daggett, Beverly C.	Augusta, Kennebec	D	1989 1991 1993 1995
Damren, Catharine L.	Belgrade, Kennebec	R	1979 1981 1995
Day, Lena M.	Gorham, Cumberland	R	1929 1931
Dean, R. Blanche	Buxton, York	R	1959
Deering, Elizabeth	Bath, Lincoln	R	1941 1943 1945
Dellert, Jean T.	Gardiner, Kennebec	R	1985 1987 1989
Desmond, Mabel J.	Mapleton, Aroostook	D	1995
Dore, Susan E.	Auburn, Androscoggin	D	1987 1989 1991 1993 1995
Downing, Eleanor F.	N. Kennebunkport, York	R	1953
Doyle, Dorothy	Bangor, Penobscot	D	1971
Duplessis, Susan Dubay	Stillwater, Penobscot	R	1991
Durgin, Lena C.	Kittery, York	R	1975 1977
Ellingwood, Ruth A.	Rockland, Knox	R	1945
Erwin, Phyllis R.	Rumford, Oxford	D	1981 1983 1985 1987 1989 1991 1993
Farnsworth, Susan	Hallowell, Kennebec	D	1989 1991 1993
Fay, Marguerite R.	Portland, Cumberland	R	1949 1951
Files, Florence C.	Portland, Cumberland	R	1955
Folsom, Blanche E.	Norridgewock, Somerset	R	1927 1929
Forbes, Sarah Hughes	Dover-Foxcroft, Piscataquis	D	1935
Foss, Judith C.	Yarmouth, Cumberland	R	1985 1987 1989 1991 1993
Foster, Ruth S.	Blue Hill, Hancock	R	1981 1983 1985 1987 1989
Fowles, Neota A. *see* *Grandy*	Whitefield, Lincoln	R	1939
Fuller, Marion *see* *Brown*	York, York	R	1967
Gavett, Katharine J.	Orono, Penobscot	R	1979 1981
Gay, Maude Clark	Waldoboro, Lincoln	R	1927 1929
Gill, Barbara A.	S. Portland, Cumberland	R	1977
Giroux, Naomi L.	Waterville, Kennebec	D	1967 1969
Goodridge, Tracy R.	Pittsfield, Somerset	D	1991

Maine House, continued

Name	City, County	Party	Legislative Year
Goodwin, Kathleen Watson *see Watson*	Bath, Lincoln	D	1971 1973 1975 1977
Gowen, Marian E.	Sargentville, Hancock	R	1979 1981
Grandy, Neota Fowles *see Fowles*	Whitefield, Lincoln	R	1941
Gray, Glenith C.	Sargentville, Hancock	D	1991 1993
Green, Bonnie	Monmouth, Kennebec	D	1995
Hale, Mona Walker	Sanford, York	D	1985 1987 1989 1991 1993 1995
Hanson, Bernice B.	E. Lebanon, York	R	1951 1959 1961 1965 1967
Harper, Betty J.	Lincoln, Penobscot	R	1985 1987
Harriman, Hallie M.	Lovell, Oxford	R	1957
Harrington, Ida M.	Patten, Penobscot	R	1957 1959 1961
Harvey, Alice M.	Windham, Cumberland	D	1965
Hatch, Edith V.	W. Minot, Androscoggin	R	1947 1957
Hatch, Pamela H.	Skowhegan, Somerset	D	1993 1995
Hendricks, Catherine I. *see Carswell*	Portland, Cumberland	D	1957 1959 1961
Hoglund, Annette M.	Portland, Cumberland	D	1985 1987 1989 1991 1993
Holloway, Muriel D.	N. Edgecomb, Lincoln	R	1981 1983 1985 1987
Holt, Maria Glen	Bath, Lincoln	D	1987 1989 1991 1993
Huber, Sherry F.	Falmouth, Cumberland	R	1977 1979 1981
Hutchings, Marjorie C.	Lincolnville, Waldo	R	1975 1977 1979 1981
Ingraham, Gennette Macnair	Houlton, Aroostook	R	1981 1983 1985 1987
Joseph, Ruth	Waterville, Kennebec	D	1983 1985 1987 1989 1991 1993 1995
Kane, Mary E.	Waterville, Kennebec	R	1977
Kany, Judy C.	Waterville, Kennebec	D	1975 1977 1979 1981
Kelley, Dorothy B.	Machias, Washington	R	1973 1975
Ketover, Harriet A.	Portland, Cumberland	D	1981 1983 1987 1989 1991
Kilkelly, Marjorie L.	Wiscasset, Lincoln	D	1987 1989 1991 1993 1995
Kilroy, Jane Cullan	S. Portland, Cumberland	D	1935 1959 1961 1963 1965 1967 1969 1971 1973
Knapp, Minnie E.C.	Yarmouth, Cumberland	R	1957 1959 1961*
Knight, Patricia S.	Scarborough, Cumberland	R	1973
Kontos, Carol A.	Windham, Cumberland	D	1991 1993 1995
Labrecque, Janice E.	Gorham, Cumberland	R	1995
Lacroix, Elaine	Oakland, Kennebec	D	1985 1987
Lane, Priscilla	Enfield, Penobscot	R	1995
Laplante, Sharon A.	Sabattus, Androscoggin	D	1983
Lapointe, Jo Anne D.	Auburn, Androscoggin	D	1987 1989 1991

Larrivee, Anne M.	Gorham, Cumberland	D	1989 1991 1993
Latno, Florence M.	Old Town, Penobscot	D	1935 1937 1939
Laughlin, Gail	Portland, Cumberland	R	1927 1929 1933
Laverty, Dorothy	Millinocket, Penobscot	R	1975
Lawry, Dorothy G.	Rockland, Knox	R	1953 1955
Lebowitz, Catharine Koch	Bangor, Penobscot	R	1983 1985 1987 1989 1991
Leidy, Ella A.	Fort Kent, Aroostook	R	1943
Lemaire, Patricia	Lewiston, Androscoggin	D	1995
Lewis, Joyce	Auburn, Androscoggin	R	1973 1975 1977 1979 1981 1983
Lincoln, E. Louise	Bethel, Oxford	R	1961 1963 1965 1967 1969 1971
Locke, Stephainie	Dover-Foxcroft, Piscataquis	D	1977 1979 1981 1983
Longstaff, Marion Lee	Crystal, Aroostook	R	1943 1945 1947 1949
Look, Theone F.	Jonesboro, Washington	R	1987 1989 1991 1993 1995
Lord, Hazel C.	S. Portland, Cumberland	R	1945 1953
Lovett, Glenys P.	Scarborough, Cumberland	R	1995
Lumbra, Lisa	Bangor, Penobscot	R	1995
Lund, Sylvia V.	Augusta, Kennebec	R	1979 1981
Luther, M. Ida	Mexico, Oxford	D	1989 1991 1995
MacBride, Mary H.	Presque Isle, Aroostook	R	1979* 1981 1983 1985 1987 1989 1991 1993
Mahany, Carolyne T.	Easton, Aroostook	D	1987 1989 1991
Mann, Bessie L.	Paris, Oxford	R	1955 1957
Martin, Antoinette C.	Brunswick, Cumberland	D	1975 1977 1979 1981 1983
Martin, Hilda C.	Van Buren, Aroostook	D	1981 1983 1985 1987 1989 1991 1993
Martin, Marion E.	Bangor, Penobscot	R	1931 1933
Marvin, Jean Ginn	Cape Elizabeth, Cumberland	R	1995
Massey, Vivian F.	Bangor, Penobscot	Pen	1973*
Masterton, Nancy N.	Cape Elizabeth, Cumberland	R	1977 1979 1981 1983
Maybury, Mary-Ellen	Brewer, Penobscot	R	1983
McCormick, Dorothy	Union, Knox	R	1971 1973
Melendy, Rita B.	Rockland, Knox	D	1983 1985 1987 1989 1991 1993
Meres, June C.	Norridgewock, Somerset	D	1995
Merrill, Kathryn D.	Dover-Foxcroft, Piscataquis	R	1989 1991
Michaud, Rita C.	Madawaska, Aroostook	R	1955
Miskavage, Margaret Brown	Augusta, Kennebec	R	1975
Mitchell, Elizabeth H.	Vassalboro, Kennebec	D	1975 1977 1979 1981 1983 1991 1993 1995

Maine House, continued

Name	City, County	Party	Legislative Year
Mitchell, J. Elizabeth	Portland, Cumberland	D	1995
Moffatt, Elizabeth D.	Bath, Lincoln	R	1951
Morey, Maude E.	Lewiston, Androscoggin	D	1931
Morgan, Johanna	S. Portland, Cumberland	D	1969
Morin, Leatrice	Old Orchard Beach, York	D	1973 1975
Murchison, Edna M.	Mattawamkeag, Penobscot	R	1971* 1973
Murphy, Belinda A.	Auburn, Androscoggin	D	1995
Murphy, Eleanor M.	Berwick, York	R	1985 1987 1989 1991 1993 1995
Najarian, Mary	Portland, Cumberland	D	1973 1975 1977
Nelson, Merle	Portland, Cumberland	D	1977 1979 1981 1983 1985
Oakes, Alma H.	Portland, Cumberland	R	1963
Paradis, Judy A.	Frenchville, Aroostook	D	1987 1989 1991
Payne, Nancy H.	Portland, Cumberland	R	1979
Payson, Mary W.	Falmouth, Cumberland	R	1967* 1969 1971
Peavey, Judith B.	Woolwich, Sagadahoc	R	1995
Pendexter, Joan M.	Scarborough, Cumberland	R	1991 1993
Pendleton, Peggy A.	Scarborough, Cumberland	R	1989 1991 1993
Pfeiffer, Sophia D.	Brunswick, Cumberland	D	1991 1993
Pines, Susan J.	Limestone, Aroostook	R	1983 1985 1987 1989 1991
Pinette, Elizabeth	Fort Kent, Aroostook	D	1993
Pinkham, Dora	Fort Kent, Aroostook	R	1923
Plowman, Debra D.	Hampden, Penobscot	R	1993 1995
Post, Bonnie	Owl's Head, Knox	D	1975 1977 1979 1981
Prescott, Sandra K.	Bangor, Penobscot	D	1977 1979 1981
Quint, Brenda Birney	Paris, Oxford	R	1993
Rand, Anne M.	Portland, Cumberland	D	1987 1989 1991 1993
Reeves, Polly R.	Gardiner, Kennebec	D	1979 1981 1983 1985 1987
Rice, Sally	Stonington, Hancock	R	1985 1987
Robbins, Dorothy P.	Harrison, Cumberland	R	1941*
Roberts, Cora D.	Westbrook, Cumberland	R	1943 1945
Roberts, Phyllis J.	Buxton, York	D	1981 1983
Robichaud, Julie Maire	Caribou, Aroostook	R	1993 1995
Robinson, Etta W.	S. Portland, Cumberland	R	1939
Rotondi, Dorothy A.	Athens, Somerset	D	1983 1985 1987 1989 1991 1993 1995
Ruby, Christine L.	Bangor, Penobscot	D	1965
Rydell, Charlene B.	Brunswick, Cumberland	D	1985 1987 1989 1991 1993
Saunders, Emily C.	Bethel, Oxford	D	1975
Savage, Christine R.	Union, Knox	R	1995
Sawyer, Mary E.	Brunswick, Cumberland	D	1967*
Saxl, Jane W.	Bangor, Penobscot	D	1993 1995
Sewall, Charlotte Zahn	Newcastle, Lincoln	R	1977 1979

Shaw, Esther L.	Chelsea, Kennebec	R	1961 1963
Shepard, Natalie A.	Stonington, Hancock	R	1959* 1961
Small, Mary E.	Bath, Lincoln	R	1979 1981 1983 1985 1987 1989 1991 1993
Smith, Marguerite H.	Falmouth, Cumberland	R	1957 1959 1961 1963
Smith, Mildred E.	Van Buren, Aroostook	D	1935 1937
Snowe, Olympia J.	Auburn, Androscoggin	R	1973* 1975
Soctomah, Madonna M.	Princeton, Washington	Pas	1991* 1993
Sproul, Margaret	Bristol, Lincoln	R	1961
St. Onge, Vivian	Greene, Androscoggin	D	1991 1993
Steeves, Louise E.	Lincoln, Penobscot	R	1953
Stevens, Kathleen	Orono, Penobscot	D	1993 1995
Stevens, Patricia M.	Bangor, Penobscot	D	1983 1985 1987 1989 1991
Stevenson, Madeline D.	Unity, Waldo	R	1989 1991
Stickney, Isabel H.	Brownfield, Oxford	R	1935
Strout, Barbara E.	Windham, Cumberland	R	1987 1989
Sullivan, Mary E.	Bangor, Penobscot	D	1993
Tarr, Gail H.	Bridgton, Cumberland	R	1975 1977
Taylor, Priscilla G.	Camden, Knox	R	1985 1987
Thomas, Ellen E.	Anson, Somerset	R	1955
Thompson, Agnes Mavourneen	S. Portland, Cumberland	D	1981 1983
Thurston, Florence H.	Bethel, Oxford	D	1937
Townsend, Elizabeth	Portland, Cumberland	D	1993 1995
Townsend, Louise	Canaan, Somerset	D	1993
Trafton, Barbara M.	Auburn, Androscoggin	D	1977
Treat, Sharon	Gardiner, Kennebec	D	1991 1993 1995
Tupper, Helen M.	Orrington, Penobscot	R	1987 1989 1991
Vaughn, Mary S.	Peru, Oxford	R	1961 1963
Walker, Ellen W.	Blue Hill, Hancock	D	1993
Watson, Elizabeth	Farmingdale, Kennebec	D	1995
Watson, Kathleen D. see *Goodwin*	Bath, Lincoln	D	1969
Webster, Mary Clark	Cape Elizabeth, Cumberland	R	1985 1987 1989
Weed, Alma R.	Monticello, Aroostook	R	1937
Wentworth, Alberta M.	Wells, York	R	1979 1981 1983 1985 1987 1989
Wheeler, Mildred F.	Portland, Cumberland	D	1965 1967 1969 1971 1973
White, Charlotte H.	Guilford, Piscataquis	R	1963 1965 1967 1969 1971 1973
Winn, Julie	Bangor, Penobscot	D	1993 1995
Wood, Marie W.	Castine, Hancock	R	1971

*Notes:
Attean, Priscilla A.—Penobscot Nation Representative
Carter, Claire S.—Appointed 1928 (Carter)
Knapp, Minnie E. C.—Resigned June 23, 1961

Maine, continued

MacBride, Mary H.—Appointed (Booth)
Massey, Vivian F.—Penobscot Nation Representative
Murchison, Edna M.—Appointed Jan. 24, 1972
Payson, Mary W.—Appointed Jan. 9, 1968
Robbins, Dorothy P.—Appointed (Robbins)
Sawyer, Mary E.—Appointed April 17, 1967 (Sawyer)
Shepard, Natalie A.—Appointed Jan. 19, 1960 (Shepard)
Snowe, Olympia J.—Appointed Jan. 11, 1973 (Snowe)
Soctomah, Madonna M.—Passamaquoddy Tribe Representative

MARYLAND (1922–1995)

Maryland women gained suffrage on August 26, 1920. In the first state elections after suffrage, in November 1921, Mary E. W. Risteau (D–Forest Hill) was elected to the House.

Before 1923, Maryland elected senators and delegates to the House every two years in the odd years. Since 1926, after a transitional three year term election in 1923, delegates and senators have been elected every four years in the even years for four year terms. Between 1960 and 1966, the Senate increased from 29 to 43 members, and the House from 110 to 142 members. The last state elections were in 1994. Vacancies are filled by governor's appointment.

Women as Percentage of Maryland Legislators

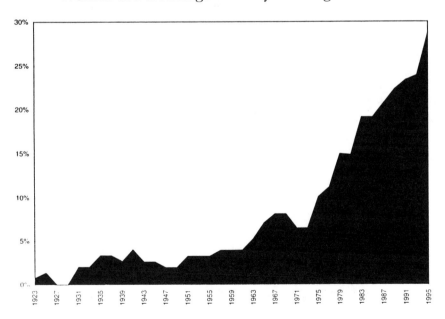

146 women have served in the Maryland General Assembly:
25 in the Senate
140 in the House
(19 in the House and Senate)

Senate
4 Year Terms (Before 1927, 2 Year Terms)

Name	City, County	Party	Legislative Year
Abrams, Rosalie S.	Baltimore, Baltimore	D	1971 1973 1975 1977 1979 1981 1983*
Boergers, Mary H.	Kensington, Montgomery	D	1991 1993
Conroy, Mary A.	Bowie, Prince Georges	D	1981*
Crothers, Margaret J.	Elkton, Cecil	D	1953*
Cushwa, Patricia	Hagerstown, Washington	D	1989*
Forehand, Jennie M.	Rockville, Montgomery	D	1995
Garrott, Idamae T.	Wheaton, Montgomery	D	1987 1989 1991 1993
Gore, Louise	Rockville, Montgomery	R	1967 1969
Hoffman, Barbara A.	Baltimore, Baltimore	D	1983* 1985 1987 1989 1991 1993 1995
Hollinger, Paula Colodny	Baltimore, Baltimore	D	1987 1989 1991 1993 1995
Hornberger, Sharon	Westminster, Carroll	R	1989*
Kelley, Delores G.	Baltimore, Baltimore	D	1995
Lawlah, Gloria	Hillcrest Heights, Prince Georges	D	1991 1993 1995
Murphy, Louise G.	Baltimore, Baltimore	D	1981*
Murphy, Nancy L.	Baltimore, Baltimore	D	1989* 1991 1993
Nock, Mary L.	Salisbury, Wilcomico	D	1955 1957 1959 1961 1963 1965 1967 1969 1971 1973
Piccinini, Janice	Cockeysville, Baltimore	D	1991 1993
Riley, Catherine I.	Bel Air, Harford	D	1983 1985 1987 1989
Risteau, Mary E. W.	Forest Hill, Harford	D	1935 1937
Roesser, Jean W.	Potomac, Montgomery	R	1995
Ruben, Ida G.	Silver Spring, Montgomery	D	1987 1989 1991 1993 1995
Schweinhaut, Margaret C.	Kensington, Montgomery	D	1961* 1967 1969 1971 1973 1975 1977 1979 1981 1983 1985 1987 1989
Sher, Patricia R.	Silver Spring, Montgomery	D	1991 1993
Tignor, Beatrice	Mitchellville, Prince Georges	D	1993*
Welcome, Verda F.	Baltimore, Baltimore	D	1963 1965 1967 1969 1971 1973 1975 1977 1979 1981

House
4 Year Terms (3 Year Term in 1927; Before 1924, 2 Year Terms)

Name	City, County	Party	Legislative Year
Abrams, Rosalie S.	Baltimore, Baltimore	D	1967 1969
Adams, Mary B.	Baltimore, Baltimore	D	1983 1985
Adams, Victorine Q.	Baltimore, Baltimore	D	1967*
Aiken, Patricia O.	Annapolis, Anne Arundel	D	1975 1977
Baker, Anne E.	Ellicott City, Howard	D	1979 1981
Barber, Elsie B.	Davidsonville, Anne Arundel	D	1924 1926*
Benson, Joanne C.	Landover, Prince Georges	D	1991 1993 1995
Bienen, Kay G.	Laurel, Prince Georges	D	1975 1977 1979 1981
Billings, Patricia H.	Silver Spring, Montgomery	D	1989* 1991*
Blumenthal, Rosa Lee	Oxon Hill, Prince Georges	D	1987 1989 1991 1993
Bobo, Elizabeth	Columbia, Howard	D	1995
Boergers, Mary H.	Kensington, Montgomery	D	1981* 1983 1985 1987 1989
Bonsack, Rose Mary Hatem	Aberdeen, Harford	D	1991 1993 1995
Booth, Bert	Lutherville, Baltimore	R	1975 1977 1979; I 1981
Boswell, Hildagardeis	Baltimore, Baltimore	D	1971 1973
Boucher, Lulu W.	Barton, Allegany	R	1931 1933 1935 1937 1939 1941 1943 1945
Brinsfield, Lottie R.	Rhodesdale, Dorchester	D	1953* 1955 1957
Burkheimer, Nancy Ann Brown	Colora, Cecil	D	1963 1965 1967 1969
Buswell, Susan R.	Elridge, Howard	D	1983 1985 1987 1989*
Cadden, Joan	Brooklyn Park, Anne Arundel	D	1991 1993 1995
Cary, Vesta M.	Baltimore, Baltimore	D	1939 1941
Cassady, Helen B.	Baltimore, Baltimore	D	1965* 1967 1969
Clagett, Virginia P.	West River, Anne Arundel	D	1995
Collins, Mayne A.	Crisfield, Sommerset	D	1935 1937
Conroy, Mary A.	Bowie, Prince Georges	D	1985* 1987 1989 1991 1993 1995
Cook, Edna P.	Silver Spring, Montgomery	D	1959 1961 1963 1965 1967 1969
Cryor, Jean	Potomac, Montgomery	R	1995
DeCarlo, Diane	Baltimore, Baltimore	D	1995
Dejuliis, Connie C. Galiazzo	Baltimore, Baltimore	D	1991 1993
Dixon, Irma G.	Baltimore, Baltimore	D	1959 1961 1963 1965*
Doory, Ann Marie	Baltimore, Baltimore	D	1987 1989 1991 1993 1995
Doub, Elizabeth Boys	Cumberland, Allegany	R	1939 1941

Name	Location	Party	Years
Eckardt, Adelaide C.	Cambridge, Dorcester	R	1995
Engle, Lavinia	Forest Glen, Montgomery	D	1931 1933
Faulkner, Patricia Anne	Silver Spring, Montgomery	R	1995
Felling, Donna M.	Baltimore, Baltimore	D	1987 1989
Forehand, Jennie M.	Rockville, Montgomery	D	1979 1981 1983 1985 1987 1989 1991 1993
Frush, Barbara	Calverton, Prince Georges	D	1995
Garrott, Idamae T.	Wheaton, Montgomery	D	1979 1981 1983 1985
Glotfelty, Martha I.	Accident, Garrett	R	1963 1965
Goldwater, Marilyn	Bethesda, Montgomery	D	1975 1977 1979 1981 1983 1985 1995
Gore, Louise	Rockville, Montgomery	R	1963 1965
Greenip, Janet	Crofton, Anne Arundel	R	1995
Grosfeld, Sharon	Silver Spring, Montgomery	D	1995
Harkness, Mildred	Hyattsville, Prince Georges	D	1977*
Harrison, Hattie N.	Baltimore, Baltimore	D	1973* 1975 1977 1979 1981 1983 1985 1987 1989 1991 1993 1995
Healey, Anne	Hyattsville, Prince Georges	D	1991 1993 1995
Hecht, Sue		D	1995
Hixson, Sheila Ellis	Silver Spring, Montgomery	D	1975* 1977 1979 1981 1983 1985 1987 1989 1991 1993 1995
Hollinger, Paula Colodny	Baltimore, Baltimore	D	1979 1981 1983 1985
Holub, Frances	Baltimore, Baltimore	D	1959 1961 1963 1965*
Hostetler, Alice W.	Kensington, Montgomery	D	1961*
Howard, Carolyn J. B.	Mitchellville, Prince Georges	D	1987* 1989 1991* 1993 1995
Hughes, Brenda B.	Capitol Heights, Prince Georges	D	1993* 1995
Hull, Ann R.	Tacoma Park, Prince Georges	D	1967 1969 1971 1973 1975 1977
Hutchinson, Leslie	Baltimore, Baltimore	D	1991 1993
Huyett, Mildred C.	Clear Spring, Washington	D	1965*
Jackson, Dorothy T.	Towson, Baltimore	D	1951 1953 1955 1957
Jacobs, Nancy	Edgewood, Harford	R	1995
Joffe, Mary	Bowie, Prince Georges	D	1945*
Johnson, M. Theresa O'Hare	Hyattsville, Prince Georges	D	1989*
Jones, Christine Miller	Hillcrest Heights, Prince Georges	D	1981* 1983 1985 1987 1989 1991 1993
Kagan, Cheryl C.	Rockville, Montgomery	D	1995
Kelley, Delores G.	Baltimore, Baltimore	D	1991 1993
Kirchenbauer, Diane	Silver Spring, Montgomery	D	1983 1985
Kirk, Ruth M.	Baltimore, Baltimore	D	1983 1985 1987 1989 1991 1993 1995

Maryland House, continued

Name	City, County	Party	Legislative Year
Klausmeier, Katherine	Baltimore, Baltimore	D	1995
Klima, Martha S.	Lutherville, Baltimore	R	1983 1985 1987 1989 1991 1993 1995
Koonce, Sarah Ada	Prince Georges County	D	1963* 1965
Kopp, Nancy K.	Bethesda, Montgomery	D	1975 1977 1979 1981 1983 1985 1987 1989 1991 1993 1995
Koss, Helen L.	Wheaton, Montgomery	D	1971 1973 1975 1977 1979 1981 1983 1985
Kreamer, Barbara Osburn	Aberdeen, Harford	D	1983 1985 1987 1989
Krysiak, Carolyn	Baltimore, Baltimore	D	1991 1993 1995
Lady, Elaine	Chevy Chase, Montgomery	R	1967 1969
Lawlah, Gloria	Hillcrest Heights, Prince Georges	D	1987 1989
Lawlor, Kathryn J.	Chevy Chase, Montgomery	D	1953*
Lee, Lena K.	Baltimore, Baltimore	D	1967 1969 1971 1973 1975 1977 1979 1981
Long, Paula A.	Baltimore, Baltimore	D	1983*
Loose, Katherine	Baltimore, Baltimore	R	1957*
Love, Mary Ann	Glen Burnie, Anne Arundel	D	1993* 1995
Mackie, Josephine A.	Elkton, Cecil	D	1941* 1943 1945
MacKinnon, Anne	Riverdale, Prince Georges	D	1987 1989*
Mandel, Adrienne	Silver Spring, Montgomery	D	1995
Marriott, Salima	Baltimore, Baltimore	D	1991 1993 1995
Maurer, Lucille S.	Silver Spring, Montgomery	D	1969* 1971 1973 1975 1977 1979 1981 1983 1985
McCurdy, Jacqueline	Towson, Baltimore	D	1963 1965
McIntosh, Maggie	Baltimore, Baltimore	D	1993* 1995
Meloy, Frances	Upper Marlboro, Prince Georges	D	1965*
Menes, Pauline H.	College Park, Prince Georges	D	1967 1969 1971 1973 1975 1977 1979 1981 1983 1985 1987 1989 1991 1993 1995
Miller, Juanita D.	Suitland, Prince Georges	D	1987 1989

Morella, Constance A.	Bethesda, Montgomery	R	1979 1981 1983 1985
Moss, Elizabeth Dorsey	Annapolis, Anne Arundel	D	1949*
Murphy, Margaret A.	Baltimore, Baltimore	D	1963* 1965 1967 1969
			1971 1973
Murphy, Margaret H.	Baltimore, Baltimore	D	1977* 19791981 1983
			1985 1987 1989
			1991 1993 1 995
Murphy, Nancy L.	Baltimore, Baltimore	D	1983 1985 1987
			1989*
Murphy, Rose Marie	Elkton, Cecil	D	1947 1949
Murray, Ethel Ann	Elkton, Cecil	D	1983 1985 1987 1989
			1991 1993
Nathan-Pullman,			
Shirley	Baltimore, Baltimore	D	1995
Nimmerrichter,			
Loretta W.	Waldorf, Charles	R	1967 1969 1971 1973
Nock, Mary L.	Salisbury, Wilcomico	D	1947 1949 1951 1953
Parker, Joan N.	Baltimore, Baltimore	D	1995
Patterson, Marian L.	Temple Hills, Prince		
	Georges	D	1983 1985
Pendergrass, Shane	Columbia, Howard	D	1995
Perkins, Anne Scarlett	Baltimore, Baltimore	D	1979 1981 1983 1985
			1987 1989 1991*
Perry, Jerry E.	Upper Marlboro, Prince		
	Georges	D	1983* 1985
Perry, Marsha G.	Crofton, Anne Arundel	D	1987 1989 1991 1993
			1995
Petzold, Carol Stoker	Rockville, Montgomery	D	1987 1989 1991 1993
			1995
Phillips, E. Blanche	Baltimore, Baltimore	D	1935 1937*
Pilchard, Shirley W.	Pocomote, Worcester	D	1989*
Pippen, Dorothy S.	Baltimore, Baltimore	D	1939 1941*
Pitkin, Joan Breslin	Bowie, Prince Georges	D	1979 1981 1983 1985
			1987 1989 1991
			1993 1995
Polk, Myrtle A.	Pocomoke, Worcester	D	1951 1953 1955
			1957*
Preis, Mary Louise	Bel Air, Harford	D	1991 1993 1995
Rehrmann, Eileen M.	Bel Air, Harford	D	1983 1985 1987 1989
Riley, Catherine I.	Bel Air, Harford	D	1975 1977 1979 1981
Risteau, Mary E. W.	Forest Hill, Harford	D	1922 1924 1926* 1931
			1933 1951 1953
Roesser, Jean W.	Potomac, Montgomery	R	1987 1989 1991 1993
Ruben, Ida G.	Silver Spring, Mont-	D	1975 1977 1979 1981
	gomery		1983 1985
Rush, Leona M.	Chevy Chase, Mont-		
	gomery	R	1947 1949 1951
Rutkowski, Madeline A.	Baltimore, Baltimore	D	1975* 1977
Sauerbrey, Ellen R.	Baldwin, Montgomery	R	1979 1981 1983 1985
			1987 1989 1991
			1993

Maryland House, continued

Name	City, County	Party	Legislative Year
Schade, Victoria L.	Passadena, Anne Arundel	R	1995
Schweinhaut, Margaret C.	Kensington, Montgomery	D	1955 1957 1959 1961*
Sheehan, Lorraine M.	Suitland, Prince Georges	D	1975 1977 1979 1981 1983*
Sher, Patricia R.	Silver Spring, Montgomery	D	1979 1981 1983 1985 1987 1989
Shoemaker, Ruth E.	Bethesda, Montgomery	D	1935 1937 1939 1941
Smith, Elizabeth S.	Davidsonville, Anne Arundel	R	1975 1977 1979 1981 1983 1985 1987 1989 1991 1993
Snodgrass, Louise V.	Middletown, Frederick	R	1995
Stocksdale, Nancy Reter	Westminster, Carroll	R	1995
Stup, J. Anita	Frederick, Frederick	R	1991 1993 1995
Thomas, Virginia M.	Columbia, Howard	D	1983 1985 1987 1989 1991 1993
Tignor, Beatrice	Mitchellville, Prince Georges	D	1991 1993*
Tingley, Helen C.	Baltimore, Baltimore	D	1943*
Toth, Judith C.	Cabin John, Montgomery	D	1975 1977 1979 1981 1983 1985 1987 1989
Walkup, Mary Roe	Worton, Kent	R	1995
Welcome, Verda F.	Baltimore, Baltimore	D	1959 1961
Wells, Genevieve H.	Silver Spring, Montgomery	D	1943 1945
Wilkinson, Mabel	Hyattsville, Prince Georges	D	1981*
Wood, E. Sharon	Baltimore, Baltimore	R	1977*
Workman, Betty	Lavale, Allegany	D	1987 1989 1991 1993 1995

*Notes:

Abrams, Rosalie S. — Resigned Oct. 1, 1983 (Hoffman)[F]
Adams, Victorine Q. — Resigned Oct. 1, 1967 (Randolph)
Barber, Elsie B. — Elected 1923 (3 year term)
Billings, Patricia H. — Appointed Jan. 10, 1989 (Robertson), died Dec. 29, 1990 (Billings)
Boergers, Mary H. — Appointed July 1, 1981 (Sculll)
Brinsfield, Lottie R. — Appointed March 1953 (Brinsfield)
Buswell, Susan R. — Resigned Nov. 1989
Cassady, Helen B. — Appointed Aug. 29, 1965 (Holub)[F]
Conroy, Mary A. — Appointed Feb. 1982 (Conroy). Appointed May 27, 1986 (Devlin)
Crothers, Margaret J. — Appointed 1954 (Crothers)
Cushwa, Patricia — Appointed June 20, 1990 (Cushwa)
Dixon, Irma G. — Died June 30, 1965
Harkness, Mildred — Appointed 1978 (Garrity)

Harrison, Hattie N.—Appointed Aug. 2, 1973 (Scott)
Hixson, Sheila Ellis—Appointed Aug. 24, 1976 (Becker)
Hoffman, Barbara A.—Appointed Oct. 1983 (Abrams)[F]
Holub, Frances—Died Aug. 29, 1965 (Cassady)[F]
Hornberger, Sharon—Appointed Dec. 1989
Hostetler, Alice W.—Appointed Nov. 7, 1961 (Schweinhaut)[F]
Howard, Carolyn J. B.—Appointed Aug. 2, 1988 (Santangelo). Appointed March 6, 1991
    (Wood)
Hughes, Brenda B.—Appointed Feb. 4, 1993 (Tignor)[F]
Huyett, Mildred C.—Appointed Dec. 31, 1964 (Huyett)
Joffe, Mary—Appointed 1945 (Joffe)
Johnson, M. Theresa O'Hare—Appointed July 19, 1990 (McKinnon)
Jones, Christine Miller—Appointed Jan. 13, 1982
Koonce, Sarah Ada—Resigned Dec. 1964 (Meloy)[F]
Lawlor, Kathryn J.—Appointed 1953
Long, Paula A.—Died April 15, 1983
Loose, Katherine—Appointed 1957 (Loose)
Love, Mary Ann—Appointed June 25, 1993 (Scannelo)
Mackie, Josephine A.—Appointed 1941 (Johnson)
MacKinnon, Anne—Resigned June 12, 1990
Maurer, Lucille S.—Appointed Jan. 15, 1969 (Crawford)
McCurdy, Jacqueline—Appointed March 10, 1964 (Boone)
McIntosh, Maggie—Appointed Nov. 2, 1992 (Perkins)[F]
Meloy, Frances—Appointed Jan. 1965 (Koonce)[F]
Moss, Elizabeth Dorsey—Appointed Dec. 17, 1949 (Stromeyer)
Murphy, Louise G.—Appointed Feb. 26, 1982 (Byrnes)
Murphy, Margaret A.—Appointed May 17, 1963 (Myers)
Murphy, Margaret H.—Appointed July 24, 1978 (Murphy)
Murphy, Nancy L.—Resigned June 1, 1989, appointed to Senate
Perkins, Anne Scarlett—Resigned Oct. 27, 1992 (McIntosh)[F]
Perry, Jerry E.—Appointed 1982 (Sheehan)[F]
Phillips, E. Blanche—Resigned 1937
Pilchard, Shirley W.—Appointed May 11, 1989 (Pilchard)
Pippen, Dorothy S.—Appointed 1940
Polk, Myrtle A.—Resigned Feb. 1958 (Polk)
Risteau, Mary E. W.—Elected 1921 (2 year term), 1923 (3 year term), 1930 (4 year term)
Rutkowski, Madeline A.—Appointed July 24, 1975 (Rutowski)
Schweinhaut, Margaret C.—Resigned, (Hostetler)[F], appointed Nov. 7, 1961 (Northrop) to
    Senate
Sheehan, Lorraine M.—Resigned Nov. 1982 (J.Perry)[F], appointed Secretary of State
Tignor, Beatrice—Resigned Jan.7, 1993 (Hughes)[F], appointed to Senate (Wynn)
Tingley, Helen C.—Resigned March 1943 (O'Malley)
Wilkinson, Mabel—Appointed Aug. 1982 (Palumbo)
Wood, E. Sharon—Appointed 1978 (Linton)

MASSACHUSETTS (1923–1995)

Massachusetts women gained school and tax and bond suffrage in 1879 and full
suffrage on August 26, 1920. Even though women ran for state offices on minor
party tickets as early as the turn of the century, the Massachusetts Attorney
General ruled that the Nineteenth Amendment did not guarantee women rights

to run for office. The legislature amended the statutes to allow women to run for state offices on May 21, 1921. Representative M. Sylvia Donaldson (R–Brockton) and Susan Walker Fitzgerald (D–Jamaica Plains) were elected to the House in 1922.

In 1978, the House decreased from 240 to 160 representatives who are elected every two years with 40 senators for two year terms. State legislative service is limited to four consecutive terms during a nine year period. Vacancies are filled by special election.

123 women have served in the Massachusetts General Court:
    19 in the Senate
    110 in the House
    (6 in the House and Senate)

Women as Percentage of Massachusetts Legislators

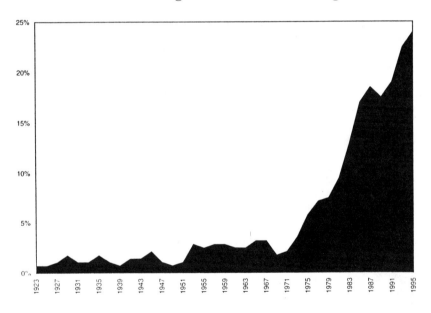

Senate
2 Year Terms

Name	City, County	Party	Legislative Year
Amick, Carol C.	Bedford, Middlesex	D	1977 1979 1981 1983 1985 1987 1989*

Buckley, Anna P.	Brockton, Plymouth	D	1973 1975 1977 1979 1981 1983 1985 1987
Cutler, Leslie Bradley	Needham, Norfolk	R	1949 1951 1953 1955 1957 1959 1961 1963 1965 1967
Fonseca, Mary L.	Fall River, Bristol	D	1953 1955 1957 1959 1961 1963 1965 1967 1969 1971 1973 1975 1977 1979 1981 1983
Hicks, Lucile P.	Wayland, Middlesex	R	1989* 1991 1993 1995
Holmes, Sybil H.	Brookline, Norfolk	R	1937
Jacques, Cheryl A.	Needham, Norfolk	D	1993 1995
McGovern, Patricia	Lawrence, Essex	D	1981 1983 1985 1987 1989 1991
Melconian, Linda J.	Springfield, Hampden	D	1983 1985 1987 1989 1991 1993 1995
Murray, Therese	Plymouth, Plymouth	D	1993 1995
O'Brien, Shannon P.	East Hampton, Hampshire	D	1993
Padula, Mary L.	Lenenburg, Worcester	R	1983 1985 1987 1989 1991
Pines, Lois G.	Newton, Middlesex	D	1987 1989 1991 1993 1995
Pollard, Sharon Margaret	Methuen, Essex	D	1977 1979 1981 1983*
Stanton, Elizabeth A.	Fitchburg, Worcester	D	1953 1955 1957 1959 1961
Sullivan, Nancy Achin	Lowell, Middlesex	R	1991
Swift, Jane Maria	North Adams, Berkshire	R	1991 1993 1995
Walsh, Marian	Boston, Suffolk	D	1993 1995
Wilkerson, Diane	Boston, Suffolk	D	1993 1995

House
2 Year Terms

Name	City, County	Party	Legislative Year
Alexander, Frances F.	Beverly, Essex	D	1983 1985 1987 1989
Amick, Carol C.	Bedford, Middlesex	D	1975
Barrows, Mary Livermore	Melrose, Middlesex	R	1929 1931 1933 1935 1937
Barsom, Valerie	Wilbraham, Hampden	R	1993 1995
Brenton, Marianne W.	Burlington, Middlesex	R	1991 1993 1995
Brigham, Emma E.	Springfield, Hampden	R	1929 1931 1933 1935
Brooks, Martha N.	Gloucester, Essex	R	1927 1929
Buell, Carmen D.	Greenfield, Franklin	D	1985 1987 1989 1991 1993 1995

Massachusetts House, continued

Name	City, County	Party	Legislative Year
Bump, Suzanne M.	Braintree, Norfolk	D	1985 1987 1989 1991
Bunte, Doris	Boston, Suffolk	D	1973 1975 1977 1979 1981 1983 1985
Burrows, Marion Cowan	Lynn, Essex	R	1929 1931
Buzzel, Fannie M.	Hudson, Middlesex	R	1945 1947
Campobasso, Eleanor M.	Arlington, Middlesex	D	1965 1967 1969 1971 1973 1975 1977
Canavan, Ellen M.	Needham, Norfolk	R	1981 1983 1985 1987
Carnavan, Christine E.	Brockton, Plymouth	D	1993 1995
Chandler, Harriette	Brockton, Plymouth	D	1995
Chesky, Evelyn G.	Holyoke, Hampden	D	1993 1995
Clapprood, Majorie A.	Sharon, Norfolk	D	1985 1987 1989
Cleven, Carol C.	Chelmsford, Middlesex	R	1987 1989 1991 1993 1995
Cochran, Deborah R.	Dedham, Norfolk	R	1979 1981
Cook, Florence E.	Roxbury, Suffolk	D	1943 1945
Corliss, Beatrice Keene	Gloucester, Essex	R	1961 1963
Counihan, Genevra R.	Concord, Middlesex	D	1975 1977
Crockett, Gladys G.	Upton, Worcester	R	1953
Cuomo, Donna F.	North Andover, Essex	R	1993* 1995
Cutler, Leslie Bradley	Needham, Norfolk	R	1939 1941 1943 1945 1947
Donaldson, M. Sylvia	Brockton, Plymouth	R	1923 1925 1927 1929
Donovan, Carol A.	Woburn, Middlesex	D	1991 1993 1995
Donovan, Susan K.	E. Boston, Suffolk	D	1939 1941
Dorman, Allison R.	Bedford, Middlesex	R	1953
Evans, Nancy	Wayland, Middlesex	R	1991 1993 1995
Falvey, Catherine E.	Somerville, Middlesex	D	1941 1943
Fantasia, Mary E.	Somerville, Middlesex	D	1971 1973 1975 1977
Fiero, Patricia G.	Gloucester, Essex	D	1985 1987 1989
Fitzgerald, Susan W.	Jamaica Plain, Suffolk	D	1923
Flavin, Nancy A.	Easthampton, Hampshire	D	1993 1995
Foley, Katherine A.	Lawrence, Essex	D	1935 1937
Fox, Gloria L.	Boston, Suffolk	D	1985 1987 1989 1991 1993 1995
Gannett, Ann Cole	Wayland, Middlesex	R	1969 1971 1973 1975 1977 1979
Gardner, Barbara	Holliston, Middlesex	D	1987 1989 1991 1993 1995
Garrison, Althea	Boston, Suffolk	R	1993
Garrt, Colleen M.	Dracut, Middlesex	D	1995
Gibson, Mary Jane	Belmont, Middlesex	D	1979 1981 1983 1985 1987 1989 1991
Gilligan, Julie	Lynn, Essex	D	1959 1961 1963 1965 1967
Goldman, Roberta A.	Shrewsbury, Worcester	D	1985
Gomes, Shirley	Harwich, Barnstable	R	1995

Goode, Mary H.	Boston, Suffolk	D	1975 1977
Graham, Saundra M.	Cambridge, Middlesex	D	1977 1979 1981 1983 1985 1987
Gray, Barbara E.	Framingham, Middlesex	R	1973 1975 1977 1979 1981 1983 1985 1987 1989 1991 1993 1995
Hahn, Cele	Westfield, Hampden	R	1995
Harkins, Lida Eisen-stadt	Needham, Norfolk	D	1989 1991 1993 1995
Hart, Harriet Russel	West Lynn, Essex	R	1925
Hicks, Lucile P.	Wayland, Middlesex	R	1981 1983 1985 1987 1989*
Hildt, Barbara A.	Amesbury, Essex	D	1985 1987 1989 1991
Holland, Iris K.	Springfield, Hampden	R	1973 1975 1977 1979 1981 1983 1985 1987 1989 1991*
Hornblower, Augusta	Groton, Middlesex	R	1985 1987 1989 1991 1993
Howe, Marie E.	Somerville, Middlesex	D	1965 1967 1969 1971 1973 1975 1977 1979 1981 1983 1985 1987
Hyland, Barbara C.	Foxborough, Norfolk	R	1991* 1993 1995
Jehlen, Patricia D.	Somerville, Middlesex	D	1991 1993 1995
Kane, Katherine D.	Boston, Suffolk	D	1965 1967
Kaprielian, Rachel	Watertown, Middlesex	D	1995
Kehoe, Marie-Louise	Dedham, Norfolk	D	1983 1985 1987 1989 1991 1993
Kerans, Sally P.	Danvers, Essex	D	1991 1993 1995
Khan, Kay	Newton, Middlesex	D	1995
Koplow, Fredya P.	Brookline, Norfolk	R	1955 1957 1959 1961 1963 1965 1967
Lewis, Jacqueline	Bridgewater, Plymouth	R	1985 1987 1989 1991 1993 1995
Lewis, Maryanne	Dedham, Norfolk	D	1995
McKenna, Mary Jane	Holden, Worcester	R	1983 1985 1987 1989 1991 1993*
Menard, Joan M.	Somerset, Bristol	D	1979 1981 1983 1985 1987 1989 1991 1993 1995
Metayer, Elizabeth N.	Braintree, Norfolk	D	1975 1977 1979 1981 1983
Murray, Bessie I.	Northborough, Worcester	R	1957
Murray, Mary Jeanette	Cohasset, Plymouth	R	1977 1979 1981 1983 1985 1987 1989 1991 1993 1995
Myerson, Eleanor	Brookline, Norfolk	D	1983 1985 1987 1989
Newman, Mary B.	Cambridge, Middlesex	R	1953 1957* 1959 1961 1963 1965 1967 1969

Massachusetts House, continued

Name	City, County	Party	Legislative Year
Noble, Elaine	Boston, Suffolk	D	1975 1977
O'Brien, Janet W.	Hanover, Plymouth	D	1991 1993 1995
O'Brien, Shannon P.	East Hampton, Hampshire	D	1987 1989 1991
O'Donnell, Karen	Waltham, Middlesex	D	1993
Owens-Hicks, Shirley	Boston, Suffolk	D	1987 1989 1991 1993 1995
Parente, Marie J.	Milford, Worcester	I	1981; D 1983 1985 1987 1989 1991 1993 1995
Parker, Katherine V.	S. Lancaster, Worcester	R	1935
Paulsen, Anne M.	Belmont, Middlesex	D	1993 1995
Pines, Lois G.	Newton, Middlesex	D	1973 1975 1977
Pitaro, Mimie B.	Boston, Suffolk	D	1971
Platt, Marsha R.	Crafton, Worcester	D	1993
Resor, Pamela P.	Acton, Middlesex	D	1991 1993 1995
Richie, Charlotte Golar	Boston, Suffolk	D	1995
Rogeness, Mary S.	Longmeadow, Hampden	R	1991* 1993 1995
Rourke, Susan F.	Lowell, Middlesex	D	1983* 1985 1987 1989 1991
Schlapp, Alyce L.	Methuen, Essex	R	1943 1945
Schur, Susan D.	Newton, Middlesex	D	1981 1983 1985 1987 1989 1991 1993
Simmons, Mary Jane	Leominster, Worcester	D	1993 1995
Slocomb, Florence S.	Worcester, Worcester	R	1927
Spear, Margaret L.	Newton, Middlesex	R	1941 1945 1945 1947 1949
Sprague, Jo Ann	Walpole, Norfolk	R	1993 1995
Stanley, Harriet	Merrimac, Essex	D	1995
Starr, Janet Kirkland	Belmont, Middlesex	R	1963 1965 1967
Story, Ellen	Amherst, Hampshire	D	1991* 1993 1995
Stouffer, Caroline J.	Hingham, Plymouth	D	1977
Swanson, Karen J.	Brockton, Plymouth	D	1975 1977
Sweetser, Mollie A.	Reading, Middlesex	R	1933 1935
Teagan, Linda	Plymouth, Plymouth	R	1995
Telford, Edna B.	Plainville, Norfolk	R	1955* 1957 1959
Thresher, Irene K.	Newton, Middlesex	R	1951 1953 1955 1957 1959
Tracy, Susan	Boston, Suffolk	D	1991 1993
Travinski, Marilyn L.	Southbridge, Worcester	D	1983 1985 1987 1989
Tucker, Susan C.	Andover, Essex	D	1983 1985 1987 1989
Walrath, Patricia A.	Stow, Middlesex	D	1985 1987 1989 1991 1993 1995
Walsh, Marian C.	Boston, Suffolk	D	1989 1991
Ware, Martha	Abington, Plymouth	R	1951 1953 1955

*Notes:
Amick, Carol C. — Resigned Nov. 7, 1989 (L. Hicks)[F]
Cuomo, Donna F. — Elected Sept. 14, 1993 (Herman)
Hicks, Lucile P. — Resigned, elected May 1, 1990 to Senate (Amick)[F]
Holland, Iris K. — Resigned April 2, 1991 (Rogeness)[F]
Hyland, Barbara C. — Elected April 7, 1992
McKenna, Mary Jane — Resigned Jan. 15, 1993
Newman, Mary B. — Appointed April 1957 (Lindstrom)
Pollard, Sharon Margaret — Resigned Jan. 6, 1983
Rogeness, Mary S. — Elected Oct. 24, 1991 (Holland)[F]
Rourke, Susan F. — Elected 1983 (Rourke)
Story, Ellen — Elected March 17, 1992
Telford, Edna B. — Elected March 8, 1955 (Telford)

MICHIGAN (1921–1995)

Michigan women gained school suffrage in 1875, tax and bond suffrage in 1908, presidential suffrage by legislative enactment in 1917 and state suffrage by constitutional amendment in 1918. Women first voted in state elections in 1920 and elected Eva McCall Hamilton (R–Grand Rapids, Kent) to the senate.

Women as Percentage of Michigan Legislators

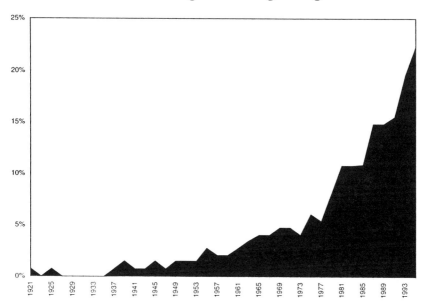

State elections are held every two years and all legislators were elected for two year terms until 1966 when four year staggered terms were implemented for the senate. There are 38 senators and 110 representatives. State legislative service is limited for the house to three terms and for the senate to two terms. Vacancies are filled by governor's appointment or special election.

78 women have served in the Michigan Legislature:
    10 in the Senate
    72 in the House
    (4 in the House and Senate)

Senate
4 Year Terms (Before 1966, 2 Year Terms)

Name	City, County	Party	Legislative Year
Beebe, N. Lorraine	Dearborn, Wayne	R	1967 1969
Binsfeld, Connie Berube	Maple City, Leelanau	R	1983 1985 1987 1989
Brown, Cora M.	Detroit, Wayne	D	1953 1955
Byrum, Dianne	Holt, Ingham	D	1995
Emmons, Joanne G.	Big Rapids, Mecosta	R	1991 1993 1995
Hamilton, Eva McCall	Grand Rapids, Kent	R	1921
Holmes, Patricia Ann	Detroit, Wayne	D	1993*
Pollack, Lana	Ann Arbor, Washtenaw	D	1983 1985 1987 1989 1991 1993
Stabenow, Debbie	Lansing, Ingham	D	1991 1993
Wheeler-Smith, Alma	South Lyon, Livingston	D	1995

House
2 Year Terms

Name	City, County	Party	Legislative Year
Anderson, Cora Belle Reynolds	L'Anse, Baraga	R	1925
Baird, Laura	Okemos, Ingham	D	1995
Ballantine, Mary Keith	Jackson, Jackson	R	1979 1981
Bankes, Lyn R.	Livonia, Wayne	R	1985 1987 1989 1991 1993 1995
Barns, Justine	Westland, Wayne	D	1983 1985 1987 1989 1991 1993
Belen, Elizabeth Lehman	Lansing, Ingham	D	1937
Berman, Maxine L.	Southfield, Oakland	D	1983 1985 1987 1989 1991 1993 1995

Name	Location	Party	Years
Binsfeld, Connie Berube	Maple City, Leelanau	R	1975 1977 1979 1981
Bodem, Beverly A.	Alpena, Alpena	R	1991 1993 1995
Brater, Liz	Ann Arbor, Vanburen	D	1995
Brown, Mary C.	Kalamazoo, Kalamazoo	D	1977 1979 1981 1983 1985 1987 1989 1991 1993
Byrum, Dianne	Holt, Ingham	D	1991 1993
Cherry, Deborah	Burton, Genesee	D	1995
Collins, Barbara Rose	Detroit, Wayne	D	1975 1977 1979 1981
Crandall, Nancy	Muskegon, Muskegon	R	1989
Crissman, Penny M.	Rochester, Oakland	R	1993 1995
Curtis, Candace A.	Swartz Creek, Genesee	D	1993 1995
Dalman, Jessie F.	Holland, Ottawa	R	1991 1993 1995
Dehart, Eileen	Westland, Wayne	D	1995
Dobb, Barbara J.	Union Lake, Oakland	R	1991 1993 1995
Dobronski, Agnes M.	Dearborn, Wayne	D	1987 1991 1993 1995
Dolan, Jan C.	Farmington Hills, Oakland	R	1989 1991 1993 1995
Edwards, Norma Dee	Detroit, Wayne	D	1949
Elliott, Daisy	Detroit, Wayne	D	1963 1965 1967 1969 1971 1973 1975 1977 1981
Emmons, Joanne G.	Big Rapids, Mecosta	R	1987 1989
Engler, Colleen House see House	Mt. Pleasant, Isabella	R	1975 1983 1985
Farhat, Debbie	Muskegon, Muskegon	D	1987
Ferguson, Rosetta	Detroit, Wayne	D	1965 1967 1969 1971 1973 1975 1977
Gire, Sharon L.	Mt. Clemens, Macomb	D	1987 1989 1991 1993 1995
Goss, Georgina	Northville Township, Wayne	R	1991*
Griffiths, Martha W.	Detroit, Wayne	D	1949 1951
Hager, Marie L.	Lansing, Ingham	R	1961 1963
Hammerstrom, Beverly	Temperence, Monroe	R	1993 1995
Hart, Kay M.	Swartz Creek, Genesee	D	1987 1989
Hill, Sandra J.	Montrose, Genesee	R	1993 1995
House, Colleen see Engler	Bay City, Bay	R	1973*
Hunsinger, Josephine D.	Troy, Wayne	D	1955 1957 1959 1961 1963 1965 1967 1969 1971 1973 1975
Hunter, Teola P.	Detroit, Wayne	D	1981 1983 1985 1987 1989 1991*
Johnson, Shirley	Royal Oak, Oakland	R	1981 1983 1985 1987 1989 1991 1993 1995
Kilpatrick, Carolyn Cheeks	Detroit, Wayne	D	1979 1981 1983 1985 1987 1989 1991 1993 1995

Michigan House, continued

Name	City, County	Party	Legislative Year
Lipsey, Triette E.	Detroit, Wayne	D	1991*
Martinez, Lynne	Lansing, Ingham	D	1993* 1995
McCollough, Lucille H.	Dearborn, Wayne	D	1955 1957 1959 1961 1963 1965 1967 1969 1971 1973 1975 1977 1979 1981
McManus, Michelle A.	Traverse City, Grand Traverse	R	1993 1995
McNamee, Ruth B.	Birmingham, Oakland	R	1975 1977 1979 1981 1983
Miller, Judith	Birmingham, Oakland	R	1985 1987 1989
Munsell, Susan Grimes	Fowlerville, Livingston	R	1987 1989 1991 1993 1995
Nowak, Evelyn M.	Detroit, Wayne	D	1945
O'Connor, Margaret	Ann Arbor, Washtenaw	R	1983 1985 1987 1989 1991
Parks, Mary Lou	Detroit, Wayne	D	1993* 1995
Parrott, Mary Ellen	Utica, Macomb	D	1983
Rivers, Lynn Nancy	Ann Arbor, Washtenaw	D	1993
Rocca, Sue	Sterling Heights, Macomb	R	1995
Saunders, Nelis J.	Detroit, Wayne	D	1969 1971
Schroer, Mary B.	Ann Arbor, Washtenaw	D	1993 1995
Scott, Martha	Highland Park, Wayne	D	1995
Skrel, Sylvia M.	Livonia, Wayne	R	1979* 1981
Stabenow, Debbie	Lansing, Ingham	D	1979 1981 1983 1985 1987 1989
Stallworth, Alma G.	Detroit, Wayne	D	1971 1973 1983 1985 1987 1989 1991 1993 1995
Stockman, Dora H.	East Lansing, Ingham	R	1939 1941 1943 1945
Symons, Joyce	Allen Park, Wayne	D	1965 1967 1969 1971 1973 1975 1977 1979 1981
Terrell, Ethel	Highland Park, Wayne	D	1979 1981 1983 1985 1987 1989
Thompson, Ruth	Muskegon, Muskegon	R	1939
Tomboulian, Alice	Lake Orion, Oakland	D	1979
Varga, Ilona	Detroit, Wayne	D	1987 1989 1991 1993 1995
Watkins, Juanita	Detroit, Wayne	D	1979 1981 1983 1985 1987 1989
Watson, Bernice M.	Flint, Genesee	R	1947
White, Charline	Detroit, Wayne	D	1951 1953 1955 1957 1959*
Whyman, Deborah	Canton, Wayne	R	1993 1995
Willard, Karen	Fair Haven, St. Clair	D	1993 1995

Willoughby, L. Jean	Bloomfield Hills, Oakland	R	1981
Yokich, Tracey A.	St. Clair Shores, Macomb	D	1991 1993 1995
Young, Maxcine	Detroit, Wayne	D	1961 1963 1965

*Notes:

Goss, Georgina—Elected 1991
Holmes, Patricia Ann—Elected Nov. 8, 1994—Dec. 31, 1994
House, Colleen—Elected July 1974
Hunter, Teola P.—Resigned Jan. 12, 1992 (Lipsey)[F]
Lipsey, Triette E.—Appointed Nov. 18, 1992–Jan. 1, 1993 (Hunter)[F]
Martinez, Lynne—Elected April 1, 1994 (Hollister)
Parks, Mary Lou—Elected June 29, 1993
Skrel, Sylvia M.—Elected March 25, 1980 (Law)
White, Charline—Died Sept. 9, 1959

MINNESOTA (1923–1995)

Minnesota women gained school suffrage in 1875, presidential suffrage by legislative enactment in 1919 and state suffrage on August 26, 1920. Women

Women as Percentage of Minnesota Legislators

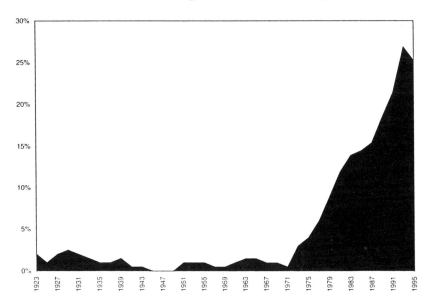

first voted in state elections in 1920. Women first ran for the state legislature in the 1922 nonpartisan state elections. Four won house seats: Myrtle Cain (DFL–Minneapolis, Hennepin), Sue Metzger Dickey Hough (R–Friberg, Otter Tail), Hannah Jensen Kempfer (I–Minneapolis, Hennepin) and Mabeth Hurd Paige (R–Minneapolis, Hennepin).

State elections are held every two years for 134 representatives who serve two year terms and 67 senators who serve four year terms. Senators are all elected every fourth year, i.e., 1992, 1996. Candidates ran in nonpartisan elections until 1972. All legislators are listed in the roster as nonpartisan until 1972 when the Minnesota Democrat Farmer Labor party (which is aligned with the Democratic national party) and the Minnesota Independent Republican party (which is aligned with the Republican national party) became designated party labels on state ballots. Vacancies are filled by special election.

110 women have served in the Minnesota Legislature:
   30 in the Senate
   85 in the House
   (5 in the House and Senate)

Senate
4 Year Terms

Name	City, County	Party	Legislative Year
Adkins, Betty	St. Michael, Hennepin	DFL	1983 1985 1987 1989 1991 1993
Anderson, Ellen	St. Paul, Ramsey	DFL	1993 1995
Benson, Joanne E.	St. Cloud, Benton	IR	1991 1993 1995*
Berglin, Linda	Minneapolis, Hennepin	DFL	1981 1983 1985 1987 1989 1991 1993 1995
Brataas, Nancy Osborn	Rochester, Olmsted	IR	1975* 1977 1979 1981 1983 1985 1987 1989 1991
Flynn, Carol	Minneapolis, Hennepin	DFL	1989* 1991 1993 1995
Hanson, Paula E.	Hoyt Lakes, St. Louis	DFL	1993 1995
Johnson, Janet	North Branch, Chisago	DFL	1991 1993 1995
Johnston, Terry	Prior Lake, Scott	IR	1991 1993 1995
Kiscaden, Sheila	Rochester, Olmsted	IR	1993 1995
Knaak, Dee	White Bear, Ramsey	IR	1977* 1979
Krentz, Jane	Marine on St. Cloud, Washington	DFL	1993 1995
Kronebusch, Patricia Louise	Rollingtone, Winona	IR	1981 1983 1985
Lantry, Marilyn M.	St. Paul, Ramsey	DFL	1981 1983 1985 1987 1989
Lesewski, Arlene J.	Marshall, Lyon	IR	1993 1995

McQuaid, Phyllis W.	St. Louis, Hennepin	IR	1983 1985 1987 1989
Naplin, Laura E. Johnson	Thief River, Pennington	Np	1927 1929 1931 1933
Olson, Gen	Minnetrista, Hennepin	IR	1983 1985 1987 1989 1991 1993 1995
Pappas, Sandy	St. Paul, Ramsey	DFL	1991 1993 1995
Pariseau, Patricia	Farmington, Dakota	IR	1989* 1991 1993 1995
Peterson, Donna C.	Detroit, Hennepin	DFL	1983 1985 1987 1989*
Piper, Pat	Austin, Mower	DFL	1987 1989 1991 1993 1995
Ranum, Jane	Minneapolis, Hennepin	DFL	1991 1993 1995
Reichgott, Ember	New Hope, Hennepin	DFL	1983 1985 1987 1989 1991 1993 1995
Robertson, Martha	Minnetonka, Hennepin	IR	1993 1995
Runbeck, Linda	Circle Pine, Anoka	IR	1993 1995
Staples, Emily Anne	Wayzata, Hennepin	DFL	1977 1979
Stokowski, Anne K.	Minneapolis, Hennepin	DFL	1979* 1981
Traub, Judy	Minnetonka, Hennepin	DFL	1991
Wiener, Deanna	Eagan, Dakota	DFL	1993 1995

House
2 Year Terms

Name	City, County	Party	Legislative Year
Berglin, Linda	Minneapolis, Hennepin	DFL	1973 1975 1977 1979
Betterman, Hilda	Brandon, Douglas	IR	1991 1993 1995
Blatz, Kathleen A.	Bloomington, Hennepin	IR	1979 1981 1983 1985 1987 1989 1991 1993*
Boudreau, Lynda	Faribault, Rice	IR	1995
Broecker, Sherry	Vadnais Heights, Ramsey	IR	1995
Brown, Kay	Northfield, Rice	DFL	1993
Burchett, Constance	Coon Rapid, Anoka	Np	1963 1965
Byrne, Peggy	St. Paul, Ramsey	DFL	1975 1977 1979 1981
Cain, Myrtle	Minneapolis, Hennepin	Np	1923
Christianson, Donna	Halsted, Polk	Np	1969*
Clark, Janet	Minneapolis, Hennepin	DFL	1975 1977 1979 1981 1983
Clark, Karen	Minneapolis, Hennepin	DFL	1981 1983 1985 1987 1989 1991 1993 1995
Coleman, Sharon L.	Spring Lake, Anoka	DFL	1983
Daggett, Roxann	Frazee, Becker	IR	1995
Dyke, Carol	Worthington, Nobles	IR	1985
Evans, Geri	New Brighton, Ramsey	DFL	1993
Fieldman, Esther Fox	Park Rapid, Hubbard	Np	1961
Forsythe, Mary M.	Edina, Hennepin	IR	1973 1975 1977 1979 1981 1983 1985 1987 1989

Minnesota House, continued

Name	City, County	Party	Legislative Year
Garcia, Edwina	Richfield, Hennepin	DFL	1991 1993 1995
Greiling, Mindy	Roseville, Ramsey	DFL	1993 1995
Growe, Joan R.	Minnetonka, Hennepin	DFL	1973
Hansen, Bertha Lee Smith	Tyler, Lincoln	Np	1939
Harder, Elaine	Jackson, Jackson	IR	1995
Hasskamp, Kris	Crosby, Crow Wing	DFL	1989 1991 1993 1995
Hausman, Alice	St. Paul, Ramsey	DFL	1989* 1991 1993 1995
Henry, Joyce	Bloomington, Hennepin	IR	1989 1991
Hokanson, Shirley Ann	Richfield, Hennepin	DFL	1975 1977 1979 1981
Hokr, Dorothy	New Hope, Hennepin	IR	1981 1983
Hough, Sue Metzger Dickey	Minneapolis, Hennepin	Np	1923
Johnson, Alice M.	Spring Lake, Anoka	DFL	1987 1989 1991 1993 1995
Kahn, Phyllis	Minneapolis, Hennepin	DFL	1973 1975 1977 1979 1981 1983 1985 1987 1989 1991 1993 1995
Kelso, Becky	Shakopee, Scott	DFL	1987 1989 1991 1993 1995
Kempfer, Hannah Jensen	Friberg, Otter Tail	Np	1923 1925 1927 1929 1933 1935 1937 1939
Klinzing, Stephanie	Elk River, Sherburne	DFL	1993
Knutson, Cornelia "Coya"	Oklee, Red Lake	Np	1951 1953
Larsen, Peg	Lakeland, Washington	IR	1995
Lehto, Arlene I.	Duluth, St. Louis	DFL	1977 1979 1981
Leppik, Peggy	Golden Valley, Hennepin	IR	1991 1993 1995
Levi, Connie M.	Delwood, Washington	IR	1979 1981 1983 1985
Long, Dee	Minneapolis, Hennepin	DFL	1979 1981 1983 1985 1987 1989 1991 1993 1995
Lourey, Becky	Kerrick, Pine	DFL	1991 1993 1995
Luknic, Marnie J.	Faribault, Rice	IR	1979 1981
Lund, Joyce Treton	Wasbasha, Wasbasha	Np	1955
Luther, Darlene	Minneapolis, Hennepin	DFL	1993 1995
Luther, Sara Lee	Minneapolis, Hennepin	Np	1951 1953 1955 1957 1959 1961
Lynch, Teresa	Andover, Anoka	IR	1989 1991 1993 1995
Marko, Sharon	Newport, Washington	DFL	1995
McArthur, Ernee	Brooklyn Center, Hennepin	IR	1973
McCollum, Betty	North St. Paul, Ramsey	DFL	1993 1995
McGuire, Mary Jo	Falcon Heights, Ramsey	DFL	1989 1991 1993 1995
McMillan, Helen E.	Austin, Mower	Np	1963 1965 1967 1969 1971; IR 1973

McPherson, Harriet A.	Stillwater, Washington	IR	1985 1987 1989 1991
Meier, Claudia	Rice, Benton	DFL	1975
Minne, Lona A.	Hibbing, St. Louis	DFL	1979 1981 1983 1985 1987
Molnau, Carol	Chaska, Carver	IR	1993 1995
Morrison, Connie	Burnsville, Dakota	IR	1987 1989 1991 1993
Murphy, Mary	Hermantown, St. Louis	DFL	1977 1979 1981 1983 1985 1987 1989 1991 1993 1995
Neary, Pamela	Afton, Washington	DFL	1993
Olsen, Sally	St. Louis, Hennepin	IR	1979 1981 1983 1985 1987 1989 1991
Olson, Katy	Sherburn, Martin	DFL	1987 1989 1991 1993
Paige, Mabeth Hurd	Minneapolis, Hennepin	Np	1923 1925 1927 1929 1931 1933 1935 1937 1939 1941 1943
Pappas, Sandy	St. Paul, Ramsey	DFL	1985 1987 1989
Pauly, Sidney J.	Eden Prairie, Hennepin	IR	1983 1985 1987 1989 1991 1993
Payne, Rosanna C. Stark	Deer River, Itasca	Np	1927 1929 1931
Peterson, Donna C.	Minneapolis, Hennepin	DFL	1979* 1981
Piper, Pat	Austin, Mower	DFL	1983 1985
Rest, Ann H.	New Hope, Hennepin	DFL	1985 1987 1989 1991 1993 1995
Rodriguez, Carolyn	Apple Valley, Dakota	DFL	1981 1983
Runbeck, Linda	Circle Pine, Anoka	IR	1989* 1991
Scheid, Linda J.	Brooklyn, Hennepin	DFL	1977 1983 1985 1987 1989 1991
Schumacher, Leslie	Princeton, Millelacs	DFL	1995
Seagren, Alice	Bloomington, Hennepin	IR	1993 1995
Segal, Gloria M.	St. Louis, Hennepin	DFL	1983 1985 1987 1989 1991 1993*
Sekhon, Kathleen	Anoka, Anoka	DFL	1993
Smaby, Alpha	Minneapolis, Hennepin	Np	1965 1967
Sykora, Barbara	Excelsior, Hennepin	IR	1995
Tompkins, Eileen	Apple Valley, Dakota	IR	1985 1987 1989 1991 1993 1995
Torgerson, Virginia	Winona, Winona	Np	1963
Vellenga, Kathleen	St. Paul, Ramsey	DFL	1981 1983 1985 1987 1989 1991 1993
Vickerman, Barbara	Redwood Falls, Red Wood	IR	1993 1995
Wagenius, Jean	Minneapolis, Hennepin	DFL	1987 1989 1991 1993 1995
Weeks, Harriet Hil-dreth	Detroit Lake, Becker	Np	1929 1931
Wejcman, Linda	Minneapolis, Hennepin	DFL	1991 1993 1995
Williams, Diane Wray	St. Paul, Ramsey	DFL	1989
Wynia, Ann J.	St. Paul, Ramsey	DFL	1977 1979 1981 1983 1985 1987 1989*

Minnesota, continued

*Notes:
Benson, Joanne E.—Resigned 1994, elected Lt. Governor
Blatz, Kathleen A.—Resigned Dec. 1993
Brataas, Nancy Osborn—Elected Feb. 1, 1975 (Krieger)
Christianson, Donna—Elected April 8, 1969 (Christianson)
Flynn, Carol—Elected Feb. 10, 1990 (Peterson)[F]
Hausman, Alice—Elected Nov. 7, 1989 (Wynia)[F]
Knaak, Dee—Elected Dec. 3, 1977 (Milton)
Pariseau, Patricia—Elected Nov. 8, 1988 (Wegscheid)
Peterson, Donna C.—Elected Jan. 17, 1980 (Enebo), resigned Jan. 16, 1990 (Flynn)[F]
    from Senate
Runbeck, Linda—Elected 1989 (Pellow)
Segal, Gloria M.—Resigned after re-election Dec. 1992 (Rhodes)
Stokowski, Anne K.—Elected Oct. 17, 1979 (Stokowski)
Wynia, Ann J.—resigned Nov. 1989 (Hausman)[F]

MISSISSIPPI (1924–1995)

Mississippi women gained suffrage on August 26, 1920, but were not allowed to vote in the 1920 federal elections because the state would not waive the poll tax requirement. Women first voted in state elections in 1923 and elected

Women as Percentage of Mississippi Legislators

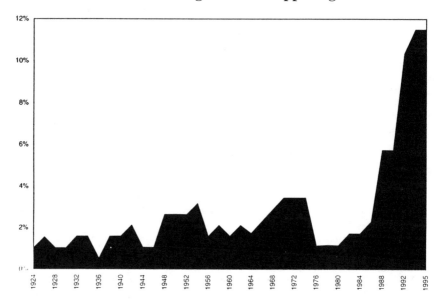

Carrie Belle Kearney (D–Flora, Madison) to the Senate and Nellie Nugent Somerville (D–Greenville, Washington) to the House.

Legislative elections are held every four years in the odd years for 52 senators and 122 representatives who serve four year terms. The last regular election was held in 1991, but due to reapportionment, a special election was held in 1992. The next regular election is scheduled for 1995. Vacancies are filled by special election.

68 women served in the Mississippi Legislature:
  12 in the Senate
  59 in the House
  (3 in the House and Senate)

Senate
4 Year Terms

Name	City, County	Party	Legislative Year
Blackmon, Barbara	Canton, Madison	D	1992* 1994
Blanton, Barbara	Brandon, Rankin	R	1988 1990
Cobb, Kay	Oxford, Lafayette	R	1992 1994
Farese, Orene	Ashland, Benton	D	1956 1958
Godbold, Mary Lou	Oxford, Lafayette	D	1956* 1958
Harden, Alice	Jackson, Hinds	D	1988 1990 1992 1994
Kearney, Carrie Belle	Flora, Madison	D	1924 1926
Muirhead, Jean	Jackson, Hinds	D	1968 1970
Powell, Amy Tuck	Starkville, Oktibbeha	D	1990* 1992 1994
Tate, Margaret	Picayune, Hancock	D	1988 1990
White, Berta Lee	Bailey, Lauderdale	D	1968 1970 1972 1974
Yancy, Barbara	Jackson, Hinds	D	1970*

House
4 Year Terms

Name	City, County	Party	Legislative Year
Alexander, Mildred	Jasper, Jasper	D	1940 1942
Allen, Margaret	Amory, Monroe	D	1970* 1972 1974
Barclift, Anne Virginia	Vicksburg, Warren	D	1948 1950
Baxter, Thelma W. Farr *see Farr*	Prentiss, Jefferson Davis	D	1952 1954
Bennett, Georgia R. Mauldin	Louisville, Winston	D	1940* 1942
Bonds, Anne H.	Holly Springs, Marshall	D	1952* 1954
Bourdeaux, Norma	Meridian, Lauderdale	D	1992 1994

Mississippi House, continued

Name	City, County	Party	Legislative Year
Bruce, Mabel	Greenwood, Carroll	D	1944 1946
Clark, Matilda F. Tann	Dekalb, Kemper	D	1940 1942
Clark, Pauline Alston	Clarksdale, Coahoma	D	1928 1930
Clarke, Alyce Griffin	Jackson, Hinds	D	1984* 1986 1988
			1990 1992 1994
Cole, Dorothy	Richton, Perry	D	1988 1990
Coleman, Linda	Mound Bayou, Bolivar	D	1992 1994
Coleman, Mary H.	Jackson, Hinds	D	1994*
Dickson, Reecy L.	Macon, Noxubee	D	1992 1994
Dunaway, Willie Mae	Columbia, Marion	D	1950*
Farese, Orene	Ashland, Benton	D	1952 1954
Farr, Thelma W. *see*			
Baxter	Prentiss, Jefferson Davis	D	1950*
Fredericks, Frances	Gulfport, Harrison	D	1990* 1992 1994
Fugler, Madge Quin	McComb, Pike	D	1932 1934
Gandy, Edythe Evelyn	Hattiesburg, Forrest	D	1948 1950
Gore, Lovie Landrum	Sturgis, Oktibbeha	D	1952 1954 1956 1958
Green, Tomie T.	Jackson, Hinds	D	1992 1994
Hammond, Otelia	Morgantown, Marion	D	1960* 1962
Harris, Ella Duke	Water Valley, Yalobusha	D	1930*
Holden, Reta	Grenada, Grenada	D	1992 1994
Howorth, Lucy R.			
Somerville	Jackson, Hinds	D	1932 1934
Long, Betty Jane	Meridian, Lauderdale	D	1956 1958 1960 1962
			1964 1966 1968
			1970 1972 1974
			1976 1978 1980
			1982
Mansell, Zilpha Ellis	Madison, Madison	D	1940* 1942
Martinson, Rita	Madison, Madison	R	1992 1994
McDade, Helen Jacobs	Dekalb, Kemper	D	1968 1970 1972 1974
			1976 1978
McGehee, Mary			
Magruder	Woodville, Wilkinson	D	1948 1950
Miller, Pat	Walls, Desoto	D	1992 1994
Nail, Mary Mildred			
Jeffries	Senatobia, Desoto	D	1928 1930
O'Fallon, Kathleen			
Michael	Lesley, Wilkinson	D	1960 1962
Peranich, Diane C.	Pass Christian, Harrison	D	1988 1990 1992 1994
Phillips, Alice C. Snyder	Macon, Noxubee	D	1964* 1966
Price, Zelma W.	Greenville, Washington	D	1944 1946 1948 1950
			1952*
Reese, Jessie Lee	Tupelo, Lee	D	1952 1954
Robinson, Minnie Lou	Madison, Madison	D	1936 1938
Savage, Frances Martha	Brandon, Rankin	D	1984 1986 1988 1990
Scott, Eloise	Tupelo, Lee	D	1988 1990 1992 1994
Scott, Omeria McDonald	Laurel, Jones	D	1992 1994

Simmons, Miriam	Columbia, Marion	D	1988 1990 1992 1994
Slayden, Gladys Miller	Holly Springs, Marshall	D	1960 1962 1964 1966 1968 1970 1972 1974
Sledge, Wilma B.	Sunflower, Sunflower	D	1952* 1954
Somerville, Nellie Nugent	Greenville, Washington	D	1924 1926
Stansel, Dorie Pearl High	Ruleville, Sunflower	D	1936* 1938 1940 1942
Steadman, Louise	Louisville, Winston	D	1966*
Stevens, Mary Ann	West, Attala	D	1980* 1982 1984 1986 1988 1990 1992 1994
Tate, Margaret	Picayune, Hancock	D	1984 1986
Terry, Mary Frances	Vicksburg, Claiborne	R	1978*
Topp, Mildred Spurrier	Greenwood, Leflore	D	1932 1934
Vaiden, Mynelle McClurg	Vaiden, Chickasaw	D	1948 1950
Wells, Carmel	Pascagoula, Jackson	R	1992 1994
White, Berta Lee	Bailey, Lauderdale	D	1964 1966
White, Martha Carole	Baldwyn, Prentiss	D	1972 1974
Williamson, Julia Faye	Louisville, Winston	D	1980 1982
Winn, Neita McCargo	Horn Lake, Desoto	D	1946*
Woodward, Ellen Sullivan	Louisville, Winston	D	1926*

*Notes:
Allen, Margaret—Elected June 29, 1971
Bennett, Georgia R. Mauldin—Elected Sept. 23, 1941 (Miller)
Blackmon, Barbara—Elected March 16, 1992
Bonds, Anne H.—Elected March 3, 1953 (Bonds)
Clarke, Alyce Griffin—Elected March 19, 1985
Coleman, Mary H.—Elected Jan. 25, 1994
Dunaway, Willie Mae—Elected 1951 (Dunaway)
Farr, Thelma W.—Elected Nov. 7, 1950 (Farr)
Fredericks, Frances—Elected June 18, 1990 (Fredericks)
Godbold, Mary Lou—Elected May 30, 1957 (Godbold)
Hammond, Otelia—Elected Jan. 10, 1961 (Hammond)
Harris, Ella Duke—Elected 1931 (Harris)
Mansell, Zilpha Ellis—Elected 1939 (Mansell)
Phillips, Alice C. Snyder—Elected June 29, 1965 (Phillips)
Powell, Amy Tuck—Elected Dec. 29, 1990
Price, Zelma W.—Resigned 1953
Sledge, Wilma B.—Elected May 1, 1953 (Baston)
Stansel, Dorie Pearl High—Elected Sept. 14, 1936 (Stansel)
Steadman, Louise—Elected June 7, 1966 (Steadman)
Stevens, Mary Ann—Elected Feb. 2, 1981 (Pierce)
Terry, Mary Frances—Elected Jan. 27, 1979 (Rogers)
Winn, Neita McCargo—Elected Nov. 5, 1946 (Winn)
Woodward, Ellen Sullivan—Elected 1925 (Woodward)
Yancy, Barbara—Elected Nov. 3, 1970 (Yancy)

MISSOURI (1925–1995)

Missouri women gained presidential suffrage by legislative enactment in 1919 and full suffrage on August 26, 1920 but had to wait for a state constitutional amendment to allow them to run for the state legislature. The constitutional amendment passed on August 2, 1921 even though the city of St.Louis narrowly defeated it. The next year, in 1922, Mellcene T. Smith (D–University City, St. Louis) and Sarah Lucille Turner (D–Kansas City, Jackson) became the first women legislators when they were elected to the House.

State elections are held every two years for 163 representatives who serve two year terms and 34 senators who serve four year terms. Legislative service is limited to eight years in the same house and a total of sixteen years. Vacancies are filled by special election.

113 women served in the Missouri General Assembly:
  8 in the Senate
  107 in the House
  (2 in the House and Senate)

Women as Percentage of Missouri Legislators

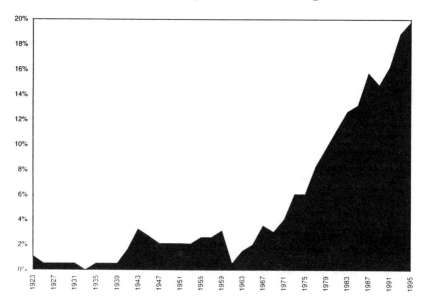

Senate
4 Year Terms

Name	City, County	Party	Legislative Year
Bentley, Roseann	Springfield, Greene	R	1995
Danner, Pat	Smithville, Jackson	D	1983 1985 1987 1989 1991 1993*
Gant, Mary L.	Independence, Jackson	D	1973 1975 1977 1979
Giles, Gwen B.	St. Charles, St. Charles	D	1977* 1979 1981*
Renneu, Margaret	Kansas City, Jackson	D	1993*
Sims, Betty	St. Louis, St. Louis	R	1995
Treppler, Irene E.	St. Louis, St. Louis	R	1985 1987 1989 1991 1993 1995
Woods, Harriett	University City, St. Louis	D	1977 1979 1981 1983

House
2 Year Terms

Name	City, County	Party	Legislative Year
Aeschliman, Mabel	Lancaster, Schuyler	R	1943
Backer, Gracia Yancey	New Bloomfield, Callaway	D	1983 1985 1987 1989 1991 1993 1995
Bartelsmeyer, Linda	Aurora, Lawrence	R	1995
Benson, Karen *see* McCarthy	Kansas City, Jackson	D	1977 1979 1981 1983
Bland, Mary Groves	Kansas City, Jackson	D	1981 1983 1985 1987 1989 1991 1993 1995
Bowlin, Zania May	Harrisonville, Cass	D	1949
Boykins, Billie	St. Louis, St. Louis	D	1979 1981
Bray, Joan	St. Louis, St. Louis	D	1993 1995
Brown, Harriet	Wentzville, Marion	R	1993 1995
Burbes, Earlene M.	St. Louis, St. Louis	R	1981*
Burns, Lulu White	Appleton City, St. Clair	R	1941 1943 1945 1947
Burns, Reba	Huntsville, Randolph	R	1957*
Cairns, Marion G.	Webster Groves, St. Louis	R	1977 1979 1981 1983 1985 1987 1989
Calloway, Deverne Lee	St. Louis, St. Louis	D	1963 1965 1967 1969 1971 1973 1975 1977 1979 1981
Carter, Paula J.	St. Louis, St. Louis	D	1987 1989 1991 1993 1995
Champion, Norma	Springfield, Greene	R	1993 1995
Chinn, Jennie	Shelbyville, Shelby	D	1953 1955 1957 1959 1961 1963
Cierpiot, Connie	Independence, Jackson	R	1995
Coleman, Donna	St. Louis, St. Louis	R	1981 1983
Cooper, Bonnie Sue	Kansas City, Jackson	R	1983 1985 1987 1989 1991 1993 1995

Missouri House, continued

Name	City, County	Party	Legislative Year
Davis, Dorathea	St. Louis, St. Louis	D	1993* 1995
Days, Rita D.	St. Louis, St. Louis	D	1993* 1995
Dixon, Jeanette T.	Springfield, Greene	R	1989
Doll, Dotty	Kansas City, Jackson	D	1975 1977 1979
Donovan, Lorita	Florissant, St. Louis	R	1983 1985 1987 1989 1991 1993 1995
Eads, Edna	Bonne Terre, St. Francois	R	1967 1969 1971 1973
Edwards, Marilyn A.	House Springs, Jefferson	R	1993* 1995
Enz, Catherine	St. Louis, St. Louis	R	1995
Farmer, Nancy	St. Louis, St. Louis	D	1993 1995
Gant, Mary L.	Independence, Jackson	D	1967 1969 1971
Gault, Sue Nelle	Gainsville, Ozark	R	1965
Hadley, Della M.	Kansas City, Jackson	D	1975 1977 1979
Hagan-Harrell, Mary M.	Ferguson, St. Louis	D	1987 1989 1991 1993 1995
Hardy, Helen Coleman	Belle, Maries	D	1955 1959 1963 1965
Hartzler, Vicky	Harrisonville, Cass	R	1995
Hearnes, Betty Cooper	Charleston, Mississippi	D	1979* 1981 1983 1985 1987
Hill, Elsa D.	St. Louis, St. Louis	D	1967
Huffman, Mildred P.	Chesterfield, St. Louis	R	1973 1975
Humphreys, Mildred M.	St. Joseph, Buchanan	D	1985* 1987 1989 1991 1993
Immken, Caroline Mary	St. Louis, St. Louis	D	1945*
Irvine, Georgia Daniel	Vandalia, Audrain	D	1943 1945 1947
Jarman, Martha	Excelsior Springs, Clay	D	1983 1985 1987 1989 1991
Jordan, Orchid Irene	Kansas City, Jackson	D	1971 1973 1975 1977 1979 1981 1983 1985
Karll, Jo Ann	Fenton, Jefferson	D	1991 1993
Kasten, Mary C.	Cape Girardeau, Cape Girardeau	R	1983 1985 1987 1989 1991 1993 1995
Kauffmann, Sandra	Kansas City, Jackson	R	1987 1989 1991 1993 1995
Kelly, Glenda	St. Joseph, Buchannan	D	1995
Kennedy, Jewell	Raytown, Jackson	R	1967 1969 1971 1973 1977
Knell, Emma R.	Carthage, Jasper	R	1925 1927 1931
Langsdorf, Elsie H.	St. Louis, St. Louis	D	1943
Long, Beth	Lebanon, Laclede	R	1989* 1991 1993 1995
Lumpe, Sheila	University City, St. Louis	D	1981 1983 1985 1987 1989 1991 1993 1995
Maness, Macye Jones	Ripley County	D	1941

Marriott, Gladys	Kansas City, Jackson	D	1967 1969 1971 1973 1975 1977 1979 1981 1983 1985 1987
Martinette, Janne	Grandview, Jackson	R	1985 1987 1989
Mathews, Jean H.	Florissant, St. Louis	R	1981 1983 1985 1987 1989
Mays, Carol Jean	Independence, Jackson	D	1989 1991 1993 1995
McReynolds, Ruby M.	La Belle, Knox	R	1929
McCann, Eileen M.	St. Louis, St. Louis	D	1981
McCarthy, Karen		D	1985 1987 1989 1991
Benson *see Benson*	Kansas City, Jackson		1993
McCaskill, Claire	Kansas City, Jackson	D	1983 1985 1987
McClelland, Emmy M.	Webster Groves, St. Louis	R	1991 1993 1995
McGee, Jacqueline Townes	Kansas City, Jackson	D	1987 1989 1991 1993
McKaughan, Edna M.	Kansas City, Jackson	D	1945
McQuire, Olive Hedger	Amoret, Bates	D	1959
Meagher, Dorothy E.	St. Louis, St. Louis	D	1967 1969 1971
Miller, Margaret	Marshfield, Webster	R	1973 1975
Montgomery, Jean	St. Louis, St. Louis	R	1985*
Moore, Agnes	St. Genevieve, St. Genevieve	D	1957 1959
Morgan, Annette Noble	Kansas City, Jackson	D	1981 1983 1985 1987 1989 1991 1993 1995
Murray, Dana	St. Louis, St. Louis	D	1995
Neel, Anne E.	Huntsville, Randolph	D	1949 1951
Nunn, Beulah C.	Nevada, Vernon	D	1933*
O'Connor, Judith	Bridgeton, St. Louis	D	1971* 1973 1975 1977 1979 1981 1983 1985 1987 1989 1991
Ordower, Ilene	St. Louis, St. Louis	D	1993
Osbourn, Lois M.	Monroe City, Monroe	D	1985* 1987
Ostmann, Cindy	St. Peters, Monroe	R	1993 1995
Park, Carole Roper	Sugar Creek, Jackson	D	1977 1979 1981 1983 1985 1987 1989 1991 1993
Parks, Opal W.	Caruthersville, Pemiscott	D	1987 1989 1991
Patterson, Margot Truman	Columbia, Boone	D	1965*
Polizzi, Jan	St. Louis, St. Louis	D	1993
Pope, Icie Mae	Marshfield, Webster	R	1951 1953 1955 1957
Quinn, Doris	Independence, Jackson	D	1975
Reeves, Sandra Lee	Kansas City, Jackson	D	1979 1981 1983 1985 1987 1989 1991
Ridgeway, Luann	Smithville, Jackson	R	1993 1995

Missouri House, continued

Name	City, County	Party	Legislative Year
Sallee, Mary Lou	Ava, Phelps	R	1993 1995
Scheve, May	St. Louis, St. Louis	D	1991 1993 1995
Secrest, Patricia	Manchester, St. Louis	R	1991 1993 1995
Shear, S. Sue	Clayton, Jackson	D	1973 1975 1977 1979 1981 1983 1985 1987 1989 1991 1993 1995
Smith, Mellcene T.	University City, St. Louis	D	1923
Speer, Clara Aiken	Kansas City, Jackson	R	1947 1949 1951 1953 1955 1957
Steele, Katie	Kirksville, Adair	D	1989 1991 1993
Steinmetz, Kaye	Florissant, St. Louis	D	1977 1979 1981 1983 1985 1987 1989 1991 1993
Stewart, Gladys Berger	Ava, Douglas	R	1935 1937 1939 1941 1943
Stokan, Lana	Florissant, St. Louis	D	1995
Stone, Evelyn G.	St. Louis, St. Louis	D	1957 1959
Tanner, Alice J.	Kansas City, Jackson	R	1947
Tobin, Joan T.	Lake St. Louis, St. Charles	R	1985
Treppler, Irene E.	St. Louis, St. Louis	R	1973 1975 1977 1979 1981 1983
Turner, Sarah Lucille	Kansas City, Jackson	D	1923
Underwood, Marguerite	Everton, Dade	R	1943
Walsh, Jennie Spindler	St. Louis, St. Louis	D	1945 1949 1951 1953 1955
Weber, Gloria	St. Louis, St. Louis	D	1993
Weber, Winnifred P.	House Springs, Jefferson	D	1971 1973 1977 1979 1981 1983 1985 1987
Wheeler, Beth M.	Trenton, Grundy	D	1987 1989 1991
Wible, Connie	Springfield, Greene	R	1991 1993 1995
Williams, Deleta	Warrensburg, Lafayette	D	1993 1995
Williams, Marilyn Taylor	Dudley, Cape	D	1991* 1993 1995

*Notes:

Burbes, Earlene M. — Elected May 26, 1981 (Amelung)
Burns, Reba — Elected Aug. 6, 1957 (Burns)
Danner, Pat — Resigned Nov. 1992, elected US Congress
Davis, Dorathea — Elected Aug. 3, 1993 (White)
Days, Rita D. — Elected Nov. 2, 1993 (Molloy)
Edwards, Marilyn A. — Elected Nov. 2, 1993 (Karll)[F]
Giles, Gwen B. — Elected Dec. 1977, resigned July 31, 1981
Hearnes, Betty Cooper — Elected Feb. 27, 1979 (Defield)
Humphreys, Mildred M. — Elected 1985 (Humphreys)

Immken, Caroline Mary—Replaced deceased nominee (Immken)
Long, Beth—Elected Feb. 1990 (Page)
Montgomery, Jean—Elected Aug. 6, 1985 (Fowler)
Nunn, Beulah C.—Elected Oct. 9, 1933 (Phelps)
O'Connor, Judith—Elected June 29, 1971 (O'Connor)
Osbourn, Lois M.—Elected Aug. 6, 1985 (Osburn)
Patterson, Margot Truman—Elected April 22, 1965 (Patterson)
Renneu, Margaret—Elected Nov.2, 1993 (Johnson)
Williams, Marilyn Taylor—Elected Feb. 19, 1991

MONTANA (1917–1995)

Montana women gained school suffrage in 1889 and full suffrage by constitutional amendment in 1914. Women first voted in state elections in 1916 and
elected Margaret Smith Hathaway (D–Stevensville, Ravalli) and Emma S.
Ingalls (R–Kalispell, Flat Head) to the house. The first woman to serve in the
U.S. Congress, Jeanette Rankin (R–Missoula), also won election in 1916.

State elections are held every two years for 100 representatives who serve two
years and 50 senators who serve four year terms. State legislative service is

Women as Percentage of Montana Legislators

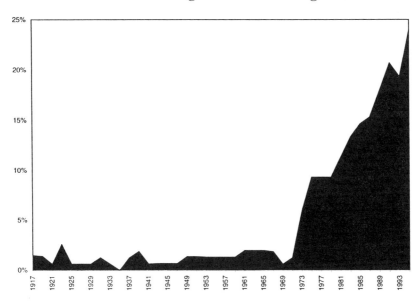

limited for the house to six years in a twelve year period and for the senate to eight years in a sixteen year period. Vacancies are filled by governor's appointment.

122 women have served in the Montana Legislature:
25 in the Senate
103 in the House
(6 in the House and Senate)

Senate
4 Year Terms

Name	City, County	Party	Legislative Year
Anderson, Helen F.	Wilbaux, Wilbaux	R	1963 1965
Bartlett, Sue	Helena, Lewis & Clark	D	1993 1995
Baumgartner, Augusta A.	Ronan, Lake	R	1955
Bengtson, Esther G.	Shepherd, Yellowstone	D	1985 1987 1989 1991
Bridenstine, Ellenore	Terry, Prairie	R	1945 1947
Brooke, Vivian M.	Missoula, Missoula	D	1995
Bruski, Betty	Wilbaux, Wilbaux	D	1991 1993
Eck, Dorothy	Bozeman, Gallatin	D	1981 1983 1985 1987 1989 1991 1993 1995
Estrada, Sharon	Billings, Yellowstone	R	1995
Franklin, Eve	Great Falls, Cascade	D	1991 1993 1995
Hager, Connye	Billings, Yellowstone	R	1993*
Hall, Frances M.	Great Falls, Cascade	D	1973
Harding, Ethel M.	Polson, Lake	R	1985 1987 1989 1991 1993 1995
Howe, Ramona E.	Lodge Grass, Big Horn	D	1993*
Jacobson, Judy H.	Butte, Silver Bow	D	1981* 1983 1985 1987 1989 1991 1993 1995
Johnson, Jan *see Wolfe*	Missoula, Missoula	R	1981
Nelson, Linda J.	Medicine Lake, Sheridan	D	1995
Phillips, Ruth Clara T.	Landusky, Phillips	D	1949 1951
Regan, Ann K.	Billings, Yellowstone	D	1975 1977 1979 1981 1983 1985 1987 1989
Rosell, Antoinette Fraser *see Fraser*	Billings, Yellowstone	R	1967 1969 1971 1973 1975
Seibel, Ann M.	Bozeman, Gallatin	D	1975
Streeter, Bertha E.	Lake, Lake	R	1957 1959
Vaughn, Eleanor L.	Libby, Lincoln	D	1987 1989 1991 1993
Warden, Margaret S.	Great Falls, Cascade	D	1975 1977
Waterman, Mignon	Helena, Lewis & Clark	D	1991 1993 1995
Wolfe, Jan Johnson *see Johnson*	Missoula, Missoula	R	1983

House
2 Year Terms

Name	City, County	Party	Legislative Year
Ahner, Chris	Helena, Lewis & Clark	R	1995
Arnold, Adeline	Rosebud, Rosebud	R	1953
Arnott, Peggy	Billings, Yellowstone	R	1995
Babcock, Betty L.	Helena, Lewis & Clark	R	1975
Barnhart, Beverly	Bozeman, Gallatin	D	1991 1993 1995
Beadle, Minnie Huser	Silver Bow, Silver Bow	D	1939
Becker, Arlene	Billings, Yellowstone	D	1991
Bengtson, Esther G.	Shepherd, Yellowstone	D	1975 1977 1979 1981 1983
Bennetts, Barbara K.	Helena, Lewis & Clark	D	1973
Bergene, Toni	Great Falls, Cascade	R	1981 1983 1985
Bergman, Ellen	Miles City, Custer	R	1993 1995
Bird, Joann T.	Superior, Mineral	D	1993
Bradley, Dorothy	Bozeman, Gallatin	D	1971 1973 1975 1977 1985 1987 1989 1991
Brooke, Vivian M.	Missoula, Missoula	D	1989 1991 1993
Brown, Jan	Helena, Lewis & Clark	D	1983 1985 1987 1989 1991
Castles, Ruth B.	Helena, Lewis & Clark	R	1973
Cocchiarella, Vicki	Missoula, Missoula	D	1989 1991 1993 1995
Cody, Dorothy A.	Wolf Point, Roosevelt	D	1985 1987 1989 1991
Conn, Alison R.	Kalispell, Flathead	R	1981
Connelly, Mary Ellen	Kalispell, Flathead	D	1983 1985 1987 1989 1991
Cox, Edith E.	Livingston, Park	R	1977
Cruickshank, Mabel	Gallatin, Gallatin	D	1937
Curran, Lucy A.	Roosevelt, Roosevelt	R	1927 1929 1931
Curtiss, Aubyn A.	Fortine, Lincoln	R	1977 1979 1981 1983 1995
Cusker, Dolly	Roosevelt, Roosevelt	D	1933
Darko, Paula A.	Libby, Lincoln	D	1983 1985 1987 1989 1991
Debruycker, Jane	Dutton, Teton	D	1991
Dougherty, Eleanor M.	Great Falls, Cascade	D	1967
Dussault, Ann Mary	Missoula, Missoula	D	1975 1977 1979 1981
Estenson, Jo Ellen	Helena, Lewis & Clark	D	1977
Facey, Florence Kerr	Malta, Phillips	R	1923
Farris, Carol	Great Falls, Cascade	D	1983
Fisher, Marjorie I.	Whitefish, Flathead	R	1993 1995
Forbes, Rose	Great Falls, Cascade	R	1995
Fraser, Antoinette *see* Rosell	Billings, Yellowstone	R	1957
Gesek, Patricia E.	Whitefish, Flathead	D	1979
Good, M. Susan	Great Falls, Cascade	R	1989
Gunderson, Edna A.	Havre, Hill	D	1977

Montana House, continued

Name	City, County	Party	Legislative Year
Hagener, Antoinette R.	Havre, Hill	D	1995
Halvorson, Ora J.	Kalispell, Flathead	D	1973 1975 1977
Hamilton, Wilhelmtina Williams	Dodson, Phillips	D	1923 1931 1937
Hansen, Stella Jean	Missoula, Missoula	D	1983 1985 1987 1989 1991 1993
Hanson, Marian W.	Ashland, Rosebud	R	1983 1985 1987 1989 1991 1993 1995
Hart, Margorie	Glendive, Dawson	D	1981 1983 1985
Hathaway, Margaret Smith	Stevensville, Ravalli	D	1917 1919 1921
Hayne, Harriet	Dupuyer, Pondera	R	1979 1985 1987 1989 1991 1993 1995
Hemstad, Andrea	Great Falls, Cascade	R	1979 1981 1983
Herlevi, Martha S.	Red Lodge, Carbon	D	1975
Holliday, Gay	Roundup, Musselshell	D	1981 1983 1985 1987
Holmes, Polly	Billings, Yellowstone	D	1973 1975 1977 1979
Howe, Ramona E.	Lodge Grass, Big Horn	D	1983 1985
Hurdle, Joan	Billings, Yellowstone	D	1995
Ingalls, Emma S.	Kalispell, Flathead	R	1917 1919
James, Isabel	Grant, Beaverhead	R	1965 1967
Johnson, Helen	Bozeman, Gallatin	R	1961
Johnson, Vicki	Columbus, Stilwater	D	1979
Kasten, Betty Lou	Brockway, McCone	R	1989 1991 1993 1995
Keenan, Nancy A.	Anaconda, Deer Lodge	D	1983 1985 1987
Kottel, Deb	Great Falls, Cascade	D	1995
Martin, Clara E.	Lewiston, Fergus	D	1939 1941
Martinez, Bonnie	Billings, Yellowstone	R	1995
Masolo, Gay Ann	Townsend, Broadwater	R	1995
McBride, Kathleen	Butte, Silver Bow	D	1979 1981 1983
McCarty, Catherine C.	Glendive, Dawson	D	1923 1925
McCarthy, Bea	Anaconda, Deer Lodge	D	1991 1993
McCarthy, June	Butte, Silver Bow	D	1949
McCulloch, Linda	Missoula, Missoula	D	1995
McDonough, Mary	Billings, Yellowstone	D	1989
McKee, Jeanette S.	Hamilton, Ravalli	R	1995
McLane, V. Jean	Laurel, Yellowstone	R	1977 1981
Melin, Marion A.	Park, Park	D	1939
Messmore, Charlotte K.	Great Falls, Cascade	R	1991
Miles, Joan	Helena, Lewis & Clark	D	1985 1987
Moore, Janet	Condon, Missoula	D	1985 1987 1989
Nash, Joy I.	Townsend, Broadwater	R	1963
Nelson, Linda J.	Medicine Lake, Sheridan	D	1989 1991 1993
O'Connell, Helen G.	Great Falls, Cascade	D	1975 1977 1979 1981 1983 1985 1987 1989
Page, Dolly M.	Phillipsburg, Granite	D	1959
Peterson, Margaret L.	Missoula, Missoula	D	1943

Peterson, Mary Lou	Eureka, Lincoln	R	1985 1987 1989 1991 1993
Reed, Dallas Bess	Missoula, Missoula	R	1951 1953 1955 1961
Regan, Ann K.	Billings, Yellowstone	D	1973
Reichert, Arlyne	Great Falls, Cascade	D	1979
Rice, Sheila	Great Falls, Cascade	D	1991 1993
Rice-Murdock, Judy	Lodge Grass, Big Horn	R	1995
Roscow, Jessie	Butte, Silver Bow	D	1923
Rosell, Antoinette Fraser *see Fraser*	Billings, Yellowstone	R	1961 1963
Roth, Audrey	Big Sandy, Chouteau	R	1977 1979 1981
Russell, Angela	Lodge Grass, Big Horn	D	1987 1989 1991 1993
Scherf, Margaret	Kalispell, Flathead	D	1965
Shea, Debbie	Butte, Silver Bow	D	1993* 1995
Smith, Liz	Deer Lodge, Powell	R	1993 1995
Smith, Susan L.	Kalispell, Flathead	R	1995
Spilker, Barbara J.	Helena, Lewis & Clark	R	1979 1981
Squires, Carolyn M.	Missoula, Missoula	D	1987 1989 1991 1993 1995
Stickney, Jessica	Miles City, Custer	D	1989 1991
Stoltz, Gail	Valier, Pondera	D	1973 1975
Stratford, Tonia	Miles City, Custer	R	1987
Swanson, Emily	Bozeman, Gallatin	D	1993 1995
Taylor, Lila V.	Busby, Big Horn	R	1995
Travis, Geraldine W.	Great Falls, Cascade	D	1975
Tuss, Carley	Black Eagle, Cascade	D	1993 1995
Winslow, Karyl	Billings, Yellowstone	R	1993
Wyatt, Diana E.	Great Falls, Cascade	D	1989 1991 1993 1995

*Notes:
Hager, Connye—Appointed May 10, 1993 (Hager)
Howe, Ramona E.—Appointed Jan. 1994 (Yellowtail)
Jacobson, Judy H.—Appointed 1981 (Peterson)
Shea, Debbie—Appointed Oct. 20, 1993 (Brown)

NEBRASKA (1925-1995)

Nebraska women gained school suffrage in 1883, presidential suffrage by legislative enactment in 1917 and state suffrage on August 26, 1920. Women first voted in state elections in 1920 and had the unique opportunity to vote on a state constitutional amendment for women suffrage on the ballot—it passed.

Mabel A. Gillespie (D–Gretna, Sarpy), Clara C. Humphrey (R–Mullen, Hooker) and Sarah T. Muir (R–Lincoln, Lancaster) were elected to the house in 1924.

The Nebraska Legislature was composed of two chambers with state elections held every two years for 33 senators and 100 representatives who served two year terms until a constitutional amendment was adopted on November 6, 1934. Since 1936, the Nebraska Legislature has been unicameral with nonpartisan state elections. From 1936 to 1964, 43 senators were elected every two years for two year terms. In 1964 the senate terms were increased to four years with one half the senate elected every two years. Due to reapportionment, a special election was held in 1992 for all senators and the next regular election was in 1994. State legislative serivce is limited to two consecutive terms. Vacancies are filled by governor's appointment.

46 women have served in the Nebraska Legislature:
     37 in the Senate
     9 the House

Women as Percentage of Nebraska Legislators

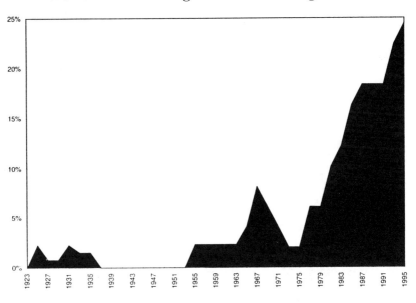

Senate
4 Year Terms (Before 1964, 2 Year Terms)

Name	City, County	Party	Legislative Year
Apking, Shari	Hebron, Thayer	Np	1981*
Beck, Sharon K.	Omaha, Douglas	Np	1989

Bohlke, Ardyce L.	Hastings, Adams	Np	1993 1995
Britt, Fay O.	Lincoln, Lancaster	Np	1953*
Brown, Pam	Omaha, Douglas	Np	1995
Campbell, Helen	Columbus, Platte	Np	1989*
Craft, Ellen E.	North Platte, Lincoln	Np	1965* 1967 1969 1971
Crosby, Lavon K.	Lincoln, Lancaster	Np	1991 1993 1995
Day, Connie J.	Norfolk, Madison	Np	1993 1995
Foote, Kathleen	Axtell, Kearney	Np	1955 1957
Higgins, Marge	Omaha, Douglas	Np	1981* 1983 1985 1987
Hillman, Joyce	Gering, Scotts Bluff	Np	1991 1993 1995
Hudkins, Carol I.	Malcolm, Lancaster	Np	1993 1995
Hughes, Calista C.	Humbolt, Richardson	Np	1965 1967
Johanns, Stephanie A.	Lincoln, Lancaster	Np	1987*
Kilgarin, Karen	Omaha, Douglas	Np	1981 1983*
Krause, Nell	Albion, Boone	Np	1945*
Labedz, Bernice Kozoil	Omaha, Douglas	Np	1975* 1977 1979 1981 1983 1985 1987 1989 1991
Langford, Lorraine	Kearney, Kearney	Np	1987 1989
Marsh, Shirley	Lincoln, Lancaster	Np	1973 1975 1977 1979 1981 1983 1985 1987
Maxey, Jo Ann	Lincoln, Lancaster	Np	1977*
McKenzie, Janis	Harvard, Clay	Np	1993* 1995
Morehead, Patricia S.	Beatrice, Gage	Np	1983 1985 1987
Moylan, Margaret E.	Omaha, Douglas	Np	1979*
Nelson, Arlene B.	Grand Island, Hale	Np	1985 1987 1989 1991
Orme, Fern Hubbard	Lincoln, Lancaster	Np	1959 1961 1963 1965 1967 1969 1971
Parks, Shirley A.	Ogallala, Keith	Np	1977*
Pirsch, Carol McBride	Omaha, Douglas	Np	1979 1981 1983 1985 1987 1989 1991 1993 1995
Rasmussen, Jessie K.	Omaha, Douglas	Np	1991 1993
Reynolds, Florence B.	Omaha, Douglas	Np	1967 1969
Robak, Jennie	Columbus, Platte	Np	1989 1991 1993 1995
Schimek, Dianna R.	Lincoln, Lancaster	Np	1989 1991 1993 1995
Scofield, Sandra K.	Chadron, Dawes	Np	1983* 1985 1987 1989 1991*
Smith, Jacklyn J.	Hastings, Adams	Np	1985 1987 1989 1991
Stuhr, Elaine	Bradshaw,	Np	1995
Witeck, Kate	Omaha, Douglas	Np	1993 1995
Wylie, Fannie B.	Elgin, Antelope	Np	1963*

House
2 Year Terms

Name	City, County	Party	Legislative Year
Beckman, Edith	Omaha, Douglas	D	1935*
Byers, Effie Marie	Hastings, Adams	D	1935*

Nebraska House, continued

Name	City, County	Party	Legislative Year
Cushing, Ruth Odell	Work Ord, Valley	R	1935*
Gillespie, Mabel A.	Gretna, Sarpy	D	1925 1927 1929 1931 1933
Humphrey, Clara C.	Mullen, Hooker	R	1925
Muir, Sarah T.	Lincoln, Lancaster	R	1925 1933
Musser, Myrtle E.	Rushville, Sheridan	D	1931
Owens, Claire E.	Exeter, Fillmore	D	1931 1935
Stark, Marjorie	Norfolk, Madison	D	1935

*Notes:

Apking, Shari—Appointed June 8, 1981 (Maresh)
Beckman, Edith—Appointed Oct. 1935 (Rohlff)
Britt, Fay O.—Appointed April 7, 1954 (Britt)
Byers, Effie Marie—Appointed Oct. 1935 (Turbyfill)
Campbell, Helen—Appointed 1988
Craft, Ellen E.—Appointed March 18, 1966 (Craft)
Cushing, Ruth Odell Work—Appointed 1935 (Cushing)
Higgins, Marge—Appointed Dec. 1, 1980(Powers)
Johanns, Stephanie A.—Appointed 1987
Kilgarin, Karen—Resigned 1984
Krause, Nell—Appointed 1946 (Rakow)
Labedz, Bernice Kozoil—Appointed July 22, 1976 (Mahoney)
Maxey, Jo Ann—Appointed Jan. 1, 1977 (Simpson)
McKenzie, Janis—Appointed Dec. 1992 (Johnson)
Moylan, Margaret E.—Appointed Nov. 1978 (Moylan)
Parks, Shirley A.—Appointed 1978 (Mills)
Scofield, Sandra K.—Appointed 1983, resigned Jan. 10, 1991 (Wickersham)
Wylie, Fannie B.—Appointed March 19, 1964 (Wylie)

NEVADA (1919–1995)

Nevada women gained suffrage by constitutional amendment in 1914. Women first voted and ran for state office in 1916. Sadie D. Hurst (R–Reno, Washoe) was the first woman to serve in the legislature after she won an assembly seat in 1918. Assemblywoman Gene Wines Segerblom is the third generation in her family to serve in the Nevada Legislature. She follows her mother, Hazel Bell Wines who served in 1935-36, and her maternal grandfather, who served in the 1906–1914.

State elections are held every two years for 42 assembly members who serve two year terms and 21 senators who serve four year terms. State legislative service is limited for the assembly to twelve years or six terms and for the senate to twelve years or three terms. Vacancies are filled by governor's appointment and special election.

87 women have served in the Nevada Legislature:
    16 in the Senate
    78 in the Assembly
    (7 in the Assembly and Senate)

Women as Percentage of Nevada Legislators

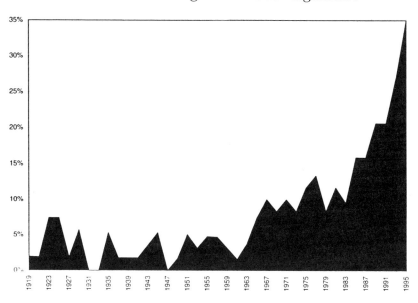

Senate
4 Year Terms

Name	City, County	Party	Legislative Year
Augustine, Kathy Marie	Las Vegas, Clark	R	1995
Foley, Helen A.	Las Vegas, Clark	D	1983 1985
Foote, Margie	Sparks, Sparks	D	1975 1977
Ford, Jean E.	Las Vegas, Clark	D	1979 1981
Friedhoff, Frances	Yerington, Lyon	D	1935*
Glomb, Diana	Reno, Washoe	D	1991 1993
Gojack, Mary L.	Reno, Washoe	D	1975 1977
Herr, Helen K.	Las Vegas, Clark	D	1967* 1969 1971 1973 1975

Nevada Senate, continued

Name	City, County	Party	Legislative Year
Lipman-Brown, Lori	Las Vegas, Clark	D	1993
Lowden, Sue	Las Vegas, Clark	R	1993 1995
Martin-Mathews, Bernice	Sparks, Washoe	D	1995
O'Connell, Ann	Las Vegas, Clark	R	1985* 1987 1989 1991 1993 1995
O'Neill, Margaret E.	Reno, Washoe	D	1989*
Titus, Constandina	Las Vegas, Clark	D	1989 1991 1993 1995
Tyler, Stephanie	Sparks, Washoe	R	1991*
Wagner, Sue	Reno, Washoe	R	1981 1983 1985 1987 1989 1991*

Assembly
2 Year Terms

Name	City, County	Party	Legislative Year
Allen, Daisy	Fallon, Churchill	D	1925
Augustine, Kathy Marie	Las Vegas, Clark	R	1993
Averill, Ruth	Tonopah, Nye	R	1921
Berkley, Shelly L.	Las Vegas, Clark	D	1983
Braunlin, Deanna	Las Vegas, Clark	R	1995
Brookman, Eileen B.	Las Vegas, Clark	D	1967 1969 1971 1973 1975 1977 1987 1989
Brower, Maureen E.	Las Vegas, Clark	R	1995
Buckley, Barbara E.	Las Vegas, Clark	D	1995
Cafferata, Patty D.	Reno, Washoe	R	1981
Castle, Fronica E.	Elko, Elko	R	1953*
Cavnar, Peggy	Las Vegas, Clark	R	1979
Chowning, Vonne Stout	N. Las Vegas, Clark	D	1989 1993 1995
Collins, Rita	Ely, White Pine	D	1957*
De Braga, Marcia D.	Fallon, Churchill	D	1993 1995
Deimel, Lois	Pahrump, Nye	D	1937
Denton, Hazel B.	Caliente, Lincoln	D	1953 1955
Diamond, Renee L.	Las Vegas, Clark	D	1989
Drumm, Luella K.	Churchill, Churchill	D	1939
Dungan, Flora	Las Vegas, Clark	D	1963 1967
Evans, Jan	Sparks, Washoe	D	1987 1989 1991 1993 1995
Foley, Helen A.	Las Vegas, Clark	D	1981
Foote, Margie	Sparks, Sparks	D	1967 1969 1971 1973
Ford, Jean E.	Las Vegas, Clark	R	1973 1975
Frazier, Maude	Las Vegas, Clark	D	1951 1953 1955 1957 1959 1961*
Frazzini, Mary	Reno, Washoe	R	1965 1967 1969 1971
Freeman, Vivian L.	Reno, Washoe	D	1987 1989 1991 1993 1995

Gibbons, Dawn	Reno, Washoe	R	1991*
Giunchigliani, Chris-			
tina R.	Las Vegas, Clark	D	1991 1993 1995
Gojack, Mary L.	Reno, Washoe	D	1973
Gomes, Nancy A.	Reno, Washoe	D	1977
Gosse, Marguerite H.	Reno, Washoe	R	1923
Grier, Glenn E.	Ely, White Pine	D	1935
Ham, Jane F.	Las Vegas, Clark	R	1981 1983 1985
Hawkins, Frances	Hawthorne, Mineral	D	1971
Hayes, Karen Wood	Las Vegas, Clark	D	1975 1977 1979 1981
Hays, Louise M.	Tonopah, Nye	R	1923
Herr, Helen K.	Las Vegas, Clark	D	1957 1959 1963 1965
Howard, Marian	Winnemucca, Humbolt	R	1977*
Hurst, Sadie D.	Reno, Washoe	R	1919
Isbell, Mabel C.	Reno, Washoe	D	1955 1957
Jameson, Courtenay C.			
see Swain	Reno, Washoe	D	1983
Kenny, Erin	Las Vegas, Clark	D	1993
Krenzer, Saundra	Las Vegas, Clark	D	1991 1995
Lambert, Joan A.	Reno, Washoe	R	1985 1987 1989 1991
			1993 1995
Little, Patricia L.	N. Las Vegas, Clark	D	1985 1991
McGuire, Ethel	Tonopah, Nye	D	1927 1929
McKeough, Edna J.	Hawthorne, Mineral	D	1945
Millar, Marguerita D.	Hawthorne, Mineral	D	1923
Monaghan, Jan F.	N. Las Vegas, Clark	R	1995
Ohrenschall, Genie	Las Vegas, Clark	D	1995
Olson, Pauline L.	Ely, White Pine	D	1951
Parsons, Jewel E.	Coaldale, Esmeralda	D	1965
Pinger, Lillian V.	Fallon, Churchill	R	1929
Rose, Mary G.	Winnemucca, Humboldt	D	1925
Schweble, Mayme	Tonopah, Nye	R	1925
Segerblom, Gene Wines	Boulder City, Clark	D	1993 1995
Sharp, Mary	Currant, Nye	D	1943
Smith, Louise Aloys	Lovelock, Pershing	D	1949 1951
Smith, Stephanie	Boulder City, Clark	D	1993
Spriggs, Gaylyn J.	Hawthorne, Mineral	R	1985 1987 1989 1991
Steel, Dianne	Las Vegas, Clark	R	1995
Stroth, Jeannine	Las Vegas, Clark	R	1995
Swain, Courtenay C.			
see Jameson	Reno, Washoe	D	1985 1987 1989
Swasey, Florence B.	Pahrump, Nye	R	1925
Tiffany, Sandra	Henderson, Clark	R	1993 1995
Towle, Alice S.	Fallon, Churchill	R	1923
Tripple, Patricia A.	Reno, Washoe	R	1995
Tyson, Geraldine B.	Las Vegas, Clark	D	1963* 1965 1967
			1969*
Wagner, Sue	Reno, Washoe	R	1975 1977 1979
Waters, Neva	Hawthorne, Mineral	R	1929
Westall, Peggy B.	Sparks, Washoe	D	1977 1979 1981
White, Juanita Greer	Boulder City, Clark	R	1971

Nevada Assembly, continued

Name	City, County	Party	Legislative Year
Williams, Helen DuPont	Hot Creek, Nye	D	1941
Williams, Myrna T.	Las Vegas, Clark	D	1985 1987 1989 1991 1993
Wines, Hazel Bell	Winnemucca, Humboldt	D	1935
Wisdom, Jane A.	Las Vegas, Clark	D	1987 1989
Woods, Josie Alma	Eureka, Eureka	R	1943 1945
Woolridge, Martha C.	Tonopah, Nye	R	1945*
Zimmer, Barbara A.	Las Vegas, Clark	R	1983 1985

*Notes:

Castle, Fronica E.—Appointed Jan. 1954 (Castle)
Collins, Rita—Appointed June 30, 1958 (Hose)
Frazier, Maude—Resigned July 1962, appointed Lt. Governor
Friedhoff, Frances—Appointed March 16, 1935 (Friedhoff)
Gibbons, Dawn—Appointed Jan. 17, resigned April 16, 1991
Herr, Helen K.—Elected reapportionment election Nov. 1966, two year term
Howard, Marian—Appointed April 1977 (Howard)
O'Neill, Margaret E.—Appointed Nov. 1989 (Mello)
Tyler, Stephanie—Appointed Jan. 21, 1991 (Wagner)[F]
Tyson, Geraldine B.—Appointed Sept. 21, 1963 (Tyson), resigned Dec. 1970
Wagner, Sue—Resigned Jan. 21, 1991(Tyler)[F], elected Lt. Governor
Woolridge, Martha C.—Appointed Feb. 7, 1945 (Terrell)

NEW HAMPSHIRE (1921–1995)

New Hampshire women property owners gained school and tax and bond suffrage in 1878. Full suffrage came for all women on August 26, 1920. Women first voted in state elections in 1920 and elected Jessie Doe (R–Rollinsford) and Dr. Mary L. R. Farnum (D–Boscawen) on write-in ballots.

State elections are held every two years for 24 senators and 400 representatives who serve two year terms. The New Hampshire House of Representatives is the one of the largest democratically elected bodies in the world. Vacancies are filled by special election.

786 women have served in the New Hampshire General Court:
43 in the Senate
777 in the House
(34 in the Senate and House)

Women as Percentage of
New Hampshire Legislators

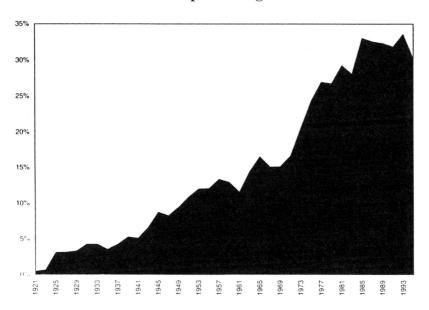

Senate
2 Year Terms

Name	City, County	Party	Legislative Year
Baldizar, Barbara J.	Nashua, Hillsborough	D	1993
Bourque, Ann J.	Manchester, Hillsborough	D	1993
Caron, Marye Walsh	Manchester, Hillsborough	D	1945 1949 1951 1953 1955 1957 1959 1961
Carswell, Minnie F.	Merrimack, Hillsborough	R	1983
Charbonneau, Rhona M.	Hudson, Hillsborough	R	1983* 1985 1987 1989
DeLude, Margaret B.	Unity, Sullivan	R	1957 1963
Ferguson, Edgar Maude	Bristol, Grafton	R	1931
Foley, Eileen	Portsmouth, Rockingham	D	1965 1967 1969 1971 1973 1975 1977
Gardner, Edith B.	Gilford, Belknap	R	1961 1963 1965 1967 1969 1971 1973 1975 1977 1979
Graves, Margery W.	Brentwood, Rockingham	R	1951 1953

New Hampshire Senate, continued

Name	City, County	Party	Legislative Year
Green, Dorothy	Manchester, Hillsborough	R	1965
Greene, Marjorie M.	Concord, Merrimack	R	1953
Griffin, Ruth L.	Portsmouth, Rockingham	R	1985
Hancock, Mary Louise	Concord, Merrimack	D	1977 1979*
Hollingworth, Beverly	Hampton, Rockingham	D	1991 1993
Holmes, Nelle L.	Amherst, Hillsborough	R	1957 1959 1961 1963
Horner, Ida M.	Thornton, Grafton	R	1957
Jackson, Katharine G.	Dublin, Cheshire	R	1953
Keeney, Phyllis M.	Hudson, Hillsborough	R	1977
Krasker, Elaine S.	Portsmouth, Rockingham	D	1987 1989
Lamirande, Carole A.	Berlin, Coos	D	1993
Landers, Irene Weed	Keene, Cheshire	R	1955
Larsen, Sylvia B.	Concord, Merrimack	D	1995
Loizeaux, Suzanne	Plymouth, Grafton	R	1951
Martin, Eda C.	Littleton, Grafton	R	1959 1965
McLane, Susan Neidlinger	Concord, Merrimack	R	1979* 1983 1985 1987 1989 1991 1993
Morris, Lula J.A.	Lancaster, Coos	R	1937
Nelson, Mary S.	Nashua, Hillsborough	D	1987 1989 1991
O'Gara, Molly	Dover, Strafford	R	1965*
Otis, Sara E.	Concord, Merrimack	R	1949 1951
Phillips, Marion L.	Claremont, Sullivan	R	1961
Pignatelli, Debora B.	Nashua, Hillsborough	D	1993 1995
Podles, Eleanor P.	Manchester, Hillsborough	R	1981 1983 1985 1987 1989 1991 1993 1995
Poulsen, Greta I.	Littleton, Grafton	R	1981* 1983
Pressly, Barbara B.	Nashua, Hillsborough	D	1987 1991
Read, Lena A.	Plainfield, Sullivan	R	1951
Roberge, Sheila	Bedford, Hillsborough	R	1985 1987 1989 1991 1993 1995
Rodeschin, Beverly T.	Newport, Sullivan	R	1995
Roy, Vesta M.	Salem, Rockingham	R	1979 1981 1983 1985
Shaheen, Jeanne C.	Madbury, Strafford	D	1991 1993 1995
Spollett, Doris M.	Hampstead, Rockingham	R	1947 1949
White, Jean T.	Rindge, Cheshire	R	1983 1985 1987
Wild, Winifred G.	Jackson, Carroll	R	1951

House
2 Year Terms

Name	City, County	Party	Legislative Year
Abbott, Clara A.	Brentwood, Rockingham	R	1927
Abbott, Frances J.	Manchester, Hillsborough	R	1971

Abbott, Helen S.	Concord, Merrimack	R	1929
Abrams, Holly	Goffstown, Hillsborough	D	1981 1983
Adams, Alice E.	Charlestown, Sullivan	R	1963 1965
Adams, Ferne P. *see*			
Prescott	Derry, Rockingham	R	1969 1971
Aeschilman, Lea H.	Portsmouth, Rockingham	D	1977 1979 1981
Ahern, Debora A.	Nashua, Hillsborough	D	1981 1983
Ahlgren, Madelyn T.	Manchester, Hillsborough	D	1993
Ainley, Greta M.	Manchester, Hillsborough	R	1957 1959 1961 1963 1965 1967 1971 1973 1975 1977 1979 1981
Aksten, Cheryl	Nashua, Hillsborough	R	1995
Allard, Nanci A.	Conway, Carroll	R	1987 1989 1991 1993
Amidon, Eleanor H.	Hancock, Hillsborough	R	1989 1991 1993 1995
Anderson, Eleanor M.	Epsom, Merrimack	R	1983 1985 1987 1989 1991
Appel, Melissa A.	Rye, Rockingham	R	1975 1977
Aranda, Kathryn	Derry, Rockingham	R	1993 1995
Arndt, Janet S.	Windham, Rockingham	R	1993 1995
Arnesen, Deborah A.	Orford, Grafton	D	1985 1987 1989 1991
Arnold, Barbara E.	Manchester, Hillsborough	R	1983 1985 1987 1991 1993
Arnold, Jo-Ann M.	Nashua, Hillsborough	D	1981
Arsenault, Mary E.	Randolph, Coos	R	1963
Asplund, Bronwyn L.	West Franklin, Merrimack	R	1987 1989 1991
Atkins, Edith P.	Hanover, Grafton	R	1949 1951 1953 1955*
Atwood, Betha Hayes	Barrington, Strafford	R	1937 1939
Atwood, Marion H.	Sanbornton, Belknap	R	1945 1949 1951 1953 1955 1957 1959
Austin, Edith J.	Franklin, Merrimack	R	1987
Ayer, Mary R.	Pittsfield, Merrimack	R	1955 1957 1959
Ayre, Ellis J.	Laconia, Belknap	R	1959 1961 1963
Bagley, Amy L.	Milford, Hillsborough	D	1993
Bailey, Elsie Cora	Newport, Sullivan	D	1935 1941 1943 1945 1951 1955 1959 1961 1963 1965
Baker, Bessie H.	Roxbury, Cheshire	R	1947
Baldizar, Barbara J.	Nashua, Hillsborough	D	1987 1989 1991
Balomenos, Sandra			
Jean *see Keans*	Rochester, Strafford	R	1967 1971
Banfield, Edith D.	Moultonborough, Carroll	R	1937 1939 1941 1943 1945 1947 1949
Bangs, Geraldine S.	Derry, Rockingham	R	1983 1985
Banks, Virginia M.	Milton, Strafford	D	1983
Barden, Margaret H.	Berlin, Coos	D	1925 1927 1929 1931 1933 1935 1937 1939
Bardsley, Elizabeth S.	Andover, Merrimack	R	1983 1985 1987 1989
Barker, Helen A.	Nashua, Hillsborough	R	1965 1967 1969
Barnard, Mary C.	Dunbarton, Merrimack	D	1927

New Hampshire House, continued

Name	City, County	Party	Legislative Year
Barnes, Bernice B.	Hampton Falls, Rockham	R	1965 1967
Barrett, Katherine K.	Keene, Cheshire	R	1973*
Barry, Janet Gail	Manchester, Hillsborough	R	1985 1989 1995
Barry, Vivian	Milford, Hillsborough	R	1989
Bartlett, Emma L.	Raymond, Rockingham	D	1923
Bartlett, Ruth Grace	Kingston, Rockingham	R	1929 1931
Batchelder, Grace F.	Hanover, Grafton	R	1939 1943 1945
Batchelder, Leifa H.	Ellsworth, Grafton	R	1927
Battenfeld, Barbara B.	Keene, Cheshire	D	1969
Battles, Marjorie H.	Brentwood, Rockingham	R	1993 1995
Baybutt, Nancy E.	Keene, Cheshire	R	1979 1981
Beach, Mildred A.	Wolfeboro, Carroll	R	1991 1993 1995
Bean, Mary E.	Webster, Merrimack	R	1955
Bean, Pamela B.	Lebanon, Grafton	R	1985 1987 1989 1991 1993 1995
Beaton, Nancy C.	Bradford, Merrimack	D	1987 1989
Bell, Helen D. W.	Hollis, Hillsborough	R	1945 1953*
Bell, Juanita L.	Portsmouth, Rockingham	D	1989 1991 1993
Belzil, Gloria	Nashua, Hillsborough	D	1971
Bennett, Shirley M.	Plymouth, Grafton	R	1989
Bennette, Jennie B.	Richmond, Cheshire	R	1963 1967 1969 1971
Bernard, Mary Elizabeth	Dover, Strafford	D	1967 1969 1971 1973 1975 1981 1983 1985 1987 1989 1991*
Bernier, Suzanne T.	Manchester, Hillsborough	D	1985
Berry, Dorothy B.	Barrington, Strafford	R	1957 1959 1961 1963 1965 1967
Bickford, Drucilla	Rochester, Strafford	R	1981 1989 1991
Bickford, Laura Y.	Epsom, Merrimack	R	1945 1947
Biondi, Christine A.	Manchester, Hillsborough	R	1989
Birch, Clara K.	Lyman, Grafton	R	1943 1945
Bishop, Beverly A.	Nashua, Hillsborough	D	1975
Bixby, Esther C.	Berlin, Coos	D	1933 1935 1937 1939 1941 1943 1945
Blanchard, Mary Ann N.	Portsmouth, Rockingham	D	1983 1985 1987 1989
Blanchette, Alice F.	Dover, Strafford	D	1957 1959 1961 1963 1965 1967 1971
Blanchette, Patricia Jennings	Newmarket, Rockingham	D	1975 1977 1979 1981 1983 1985 1987
Bonneau, Sarah K.	Westmoreland, Cheshire	D	1993
Bourdon, Germaine Y.	Nashua, Hillsborough	R	1985
Bourn, Helen D.	Exeter, Rockingham	R	1939 1941 1943 1945
Bourque, Ann J.	Manchester, Hillsborough	D	1985 1987 1989 1991
Boutain, Claire	Northumberland, Coos	R	1953
Bowers, Dorothy C.	Bedford, Hillsborough	R	1987 1989 1991 1993

Bowler, Barbara B.	Tilton, Belknap	R	1973* 1975 1977 1979 1981 1983 1985 1987
Brack, Rita M.	Manchester, Hillsborough	D	1977 1979 1981 1983
Bradley, Paula E.	Randolph, Coos	D	1993 1995
Brady, Bonnie B. *see*			
Packard	Suncook, Merrimack	R	1981
Brady, Carolyn L.	Suncook, Hillsborough	R	1989
Braiterman, Thea G.	Henniker, Merrimack	D	1989 1991 1993
Brennan, Madalyn	Rochester, Strafford	D	1967
Bridgewater, Nancy E.	Manchester, Hillsborough	R	1981 1985
Brock, Lillian R.	Atkinson, Rockingham	R	1953
Brody, Sharon E.	Nashua, Hillsborough	D	1977
Brooks, Clara P.	Claremont, Sullivan	R	1943 1947 1951
Brown, Edith L.	South Hampton, Rock- ingham	R	1945
Brown, Elsie M.	Durham, Strafford	R	1957
Brown, Julie M.	Rochester, Strafford	R	1989 1991 1993 1995
Brown, Mary	Pittsfield, Merrimack	R	1995
Brown, Mary Senior	Sandwich, Carroll	R	1959 1961 1963
Brown, Patricia B.	Enfield, Grafton	R	1991 1993
Brungot, Catherine M.V.	Berlin, Coos	R	1979 1981 1985 1987 1989 1991
Brungot, Hilda C.F.	Berlin, Coos	R	1931 1933 1935 1937 1941 1943 1945 1947 1949 1951 1953 1955 1957 1959 1965 1967 1969 1971 1973
Bryant, Beverly B.	Madbury, Strafford	D	1985
Buckley, Eula H.	Dover, Strafford	R	1929
Buckley, Gertrude M.	Mt. Vernon, Hillsborough	R	1961*
Bucklin, Gertrude M.	Bridgewater, Grafton	R	1957
Buessing, Marjorie B.	Concord, Merrimack	R	1993 1995
Burke, M. Virginia	Bedford, Hillsborough	R	1993 1995
Burley, Helen C.	Chesterfield, Cheshire	R	1985
Burns, A. Leslie	Bedford, Hillsborough	R	1983 1985 1987
Butler, Gertrude I.	Fremont, Rockingham	R	1979 1981 1983 1985 1987
Cailler, Lee Ann	Concord, Merrimack	R	1985
Caldwell, Gertrude M.	Portsmouth, Rockingham	D	1923
Campbell, Eunice C.	Derry, Rockingham	R	1987 1989 1991*
Campbell, Marilyn R.	Salem, Rockingham	R	1973 1975 1977 1979 1981 1983 1985 1987 1989 1991 1993
Canney, Ethel M.	Rochester, Strafford	R	1975 1977
Caron, Marye Walsh	Manchester, Hillsborough	D	1939 1941 1943
Carpenito, Eleanor F.	Salem, Rockingham	D	1979 1981 1983
Carpenter, Karen A.	Milford, Hillsborough	R	1991*
Carragher, Audrey A.	Nashua, Hillsborough	R	1981 1983 1985

New Hampshire House, continued

Name	City, County	Party	Legislative Year
Carrier, Maria L.	Manchester, Hillsborough	D	1969
Carrier, Terese C.	Dover, Strafford	D	1947
Carroll, Maura	Concord, Merrimack	D	1977 1979 1981
Carswell, Minnie F.	Merrimack, Hillsborough	R	1973 1975 1977 1979 1981
Carter, Susan D.	Sow, Merrimack	R	1989 1991 1993*
Cary, Beatrice B.	Manchester, Hillsborough	D	1955 1957 1959 1961
Case, Margaret A.	Raymond, Rockingham	D	1983 1985 1993*; R 1995
Castaldo, Margaret H.	Concord, Merrimack	D	1975
Cepaitis, Elizabeth A.	Nashua, Hillsborough	R	1993 1995
Chagnon-Boisver, Yvette L.	Nashua, Hillsborough	R	1977* 1979 1981 1985
Chambers, Mary P.	Hanover, Grafton	D	1973 1975 1977 1979 1981 1983 1985 1987 1989 1991
Champagne, Joce-lyne D.	Manchester, Hillsborough	D	1985 1987
Champagne, Norma Greer	Manchester, Hillsborough	R	1995
Chapman, Marie G.	Berlin, Coos	R	1925
Charbonneau, Rhona M.	Hudson, Hillsborough	R	1983*
Chardon, Phoebe A.	Jefferson, Coos	R	1981 1983 1985
Charois, Bernadette E.	Greenville, Hillsborough	D	1931 1933 1935 1937 1939 1941 1943 1945
Charpentier, Mary	Nashua, Hillsborough	R	1981
Chase, Lila S.	Concord, Merrimack	R	1959 1969
Chesley, Ruby A.	Farmington, Strafford	R	1943
Christiansen, Marie A.	Berlin, Coos	R	1939 1941 1943 1945 1947 1949 1953 1955 1957 1959
Cid, Irene Birch	Hillsborough, Merrimack	R	1987
Clark, Cynthia M.	Plymouth, Grafton	D	1975
Clark, Martha Fuller	Portsmouth, Rockingham	D	1991 1993 1995
Clark, Shirley M.	Lee, Strafford	R	1961 1963 1965 1967 1969 1971 1975
Clark, Vivian R.	Hampstead, Rockingham	R	1993 1995
Clay, Alberta Z.	Portsmouth, Rockingham	R	1985
Clements, Hannah C.	New London, Merrimack	R	1979
Clemons, Jane A.	Nashua, Hillsborough	D	1991 1993 1995
Coes, Betsy A.	Newfields, Rockingham	D	1993 1995
Cogswell, Charlotte P.	Dover, Strafford	R	1971* 1973
Colburn, Marjorie D.	New Boston, Hillsborough	R	1965 1967 1971 1973
Cole, Martha	Nashua, Hillsborough	R	1959 1961 1963
Collyer, Rita	Lisbon, Grafton	R	1955 1957 1959 1961

Colson, Dorothy Foss	Hollis, Hillsborough	R	1975 1977
Conroy, Janet M.	Derry, Rockingham	R	1985 1987 1989 1991
			1993 1995
Cook, Valerie S.	Manchester, Hillsborough	R	1991
Cooke, Annette M.	Salem, Rockingham	R	1987 1989 1991
Cooke, Muriel K.	Keene, Cheshire	R	1973*1975
Cooper, Mabel		R	1937 1939 1941 1945
Thompson	Nashua, Hillsborough		1947 1949 1951
			1953 1957 1959
			1961 1963
Copenhaver,		D	1973 1975 1977 1979
Marion L.	Hanover, Grafton		1981 1983 1985
			1987 1989 1991
			1993 1995
Corliss, Marion B.	Manchester, Hillsborough	R	1949 1951 1953
Cote, Margaret Sulli-		D	1969 1971 1973 1975
van	Nashua, Hillsborough		1977
Cote, Patricia L.	Danville, Rockingham	R	1979 1981 1989 1991
			1993 1995
Cotton, Mary Eliza-		D	1973 1975 1977 1979
beth	Portsmouth, Rockingham		1981 1983
Coughlin, Anne E.	Concord, Merrimack	D	1993* 1995
Coulombe, Yvonne	Berlin, Coos	D	1983 1985 1987
			1995
Cox, Gladys M.	Hollis, Hillsborough	R	1985 1987 1989
Cox, Grace N.	Conway, Carroll	R	1969 1971 1973
Cressy, Ellen M.	South Hampton, Rock-		
	ingham	D	1975 1983 1987
Croft, Shirley	Portsmouth, Rockingham	D	1969 1971
Crory, Elizabeth Ann		D	1977 1979 1981 1983
Lupien	Hanover, Grafton		1985 1993 1995
Crosby, Toni	Concord, Merrimack	D	1995
Cross, Amelia Thomp-			
son H.	Portsmouth, Rockingham	R	1959 1961
Currie, Rhoda Parker	Bedford, Hillsborough	R	1927
Currier, Norma Stud-			
ley *see Studley*	Rochester, Strafford	R	1957
Cushman, Kathryn M.	Canterbury, Merrimack	D	1973 1975
Cutting, Mable G.	Claremont, Sullivan	R	1979 1981 1987
Danforth, Bonnie L.	Fremont, Rockingham	R	1975 1977
Danforth, Florence J.	Manchester, Hillsborough	R	1947
Daniels, Blancha L.	Plainfield, Sullivan	R	1927
Davis, Alice	Concord, Merrimack	R	1955 1957 1959 1961
			1965 1967 1969
			1971 1973 1975
Davis, Dagmar	Woodstock, Grafton	R	1959
Davis, Dorothy W.	Moultonborough, Carroll	R	1965 1967 1969 1971
			1973
Davis, Esther M.	Conway, Carroll	R	1961 1963 1965 1967
			1969 1971 1973
			1981

New Hampshire House, continued

Name	City, County	Party	Legislative Year
Dawson, Ruth H.	Milton, Strafford	R	1957 1963 1965 1967 1969 1973
Day, Catherine Ann	Manchester, Hillsborough	D	1975 1977 1979
De Cesare, Grace L.	Salem, Rockingham	D	1973 1975 1977*
Dean, Evelyn S.	Concord, Merrimack	R	1981 1983
Dearborn, Ann G.	Laconia, Belknap	D	1965 1967 1969
Dechane, Marlene M.	Barrington, Strafford	D	1995
Decker, Minnie C.	Claremont, Sullivan	D	1941
Degnan, Kathleen A.	Concord, Merrimack	D	1981 1983*
DeLude, Margaret B.	Unity, Sullivan	R	1953 1955 1959 1961 1965
Demers, Mary E.	Lebanon, Grafton	D	1961 1963 1965
Demers, Sharon	Rochester, Strafford	D	1979
Denafio, Phyllis S.	Dover, Strafford	D	1979* 1981
Denafio, Teresa L.	Dover, Strafford	D	1979 1981
Derosier, Ann M.	Nashua, Hillsborough	D	1987 1989*
Desmarais, Vivian J.	Manchester, Hillsborough	R	1995
Dion, Arline L.	Manchester, Hillsborough	D	1977
Dion, L. Penny	Nashua, Hillsborough	D	1977 1979
Dipietro, Carmela M.	Exeter, Rockingham	R	1991 1993
Dodge, Emma M.	Merrimack, Hillsborough	R	1989 1991 1993 1995
Doe, Jessie A.	Rollinsford, Strafford	R	1921 1931
Dokmo, Cynthia. J.	Amherst, Hillsborough	R	1995
Domaingue, Jacquelyn	Manchester, Hillsborough	R	1987 1989 1991 1993*
Domini, Irene C.	Charlestown, Sullivan	R	1985 1987 1989 1991 1993
Donahue, Katherine	Livermore, Grafton	D	1925
Dondero, Mary C.	Portsmouth, Rockingham	D	1935 1937 1941 1943 1945 1949 1951 1955 1957 1959
Donnelly, Helene R.	Dover, Strafford	D	1965 1973 1975 1977 1979 1981 1983 1985
Donovan, Patricia Janelle	Nashua, Hillsborough	D	1985
Doon, Helen C.	Henniker, Merrimack	D	1963*
Dorley, Anna C.	Portsmouth, Rockingham	D	1969
Douville, Anna H.	Manchester, Hillsborough	D	1957
Dowd, Sandra K.	Derry, Rockingham	R	1991 1993 1995
Dowling, Patricia A.	Derry, Rockingham	R	1991 1993 1995
Downing, Mabel M.	Littleton, Grafton	R	1941 1943 1945 1947
Drabinowicz, Alice Rose Theresa	Nashua, Hillsborough	D	1967 1969 1971 1989 1991 1993 1995
Drewniak, Dorothy J.	Manchester, Hillsborough	D	1973*1975 1977 1979 1981 1983*
Drouin, Florence G.	Laconia, Belknap	D	1971
Dube, Ellen C.	Merrimack, Hillsborough	D	1987 1989

Ducharme, Doris R.	Hudson, Hillsborough	R	1985 1987
Dudley, Dudley W.	Durham, Strafford	D	1973 1975
Dudley, Frances B.	Lebanon, Grafton	R	1969 1971
Duffett, Jean H.	Bedford, Hillsborough	R	1981 1983
Dugas, Alfonsine M.B.	Berlin, Coos	D	1935 1937 1941 1943 1945
Dulac, Lucina A.	Lebanon, Grafton	D	1967
Dunbar, Dorothea	Enfield, Grafton	R	1949
Dunham, Janet W.	Keene, Cheshire	R	1969 1971 1973
Dunham, Vivian L.	Londonderry, Rockingham	R	1995
Dunlap, Patricia C.	Rochester, Strafford	R	1993 1995
Dunn, Miriam D.	Concord, Merrimack	D	1989 1991 1993 1995
Duperron, Aurore M.	Manchester, Hillsborough	R	1985
Dupont, Beverly A.	Manchester, Hillsborough	D	1979
Dupont, Helene R.	Manchester, Hillsborough	D	1983
Durham, Susan B.	Hollis, Hillsborough	R	1991 1993 1995
Dustin, Margaret E.	Rochester, Strafford	D	1943 1945 1949 1951 1955
Dwyer, Patricia R.	Manchester, Hillsborough	D	1987 1989 1991 1993
Dykstra, Leona	Manchester, Hillsborough	D	1985 1987 1989 1993 1995
Eaton, Stephanie	Littleton, Grafton	R	1993 1995
Ellis, Etta L.	Manchester, Hillsborough	D	1951
Emerson, Bessie	Windham, Rockingham	R	1933 1935
Emons, Imogene V.	Wilmot, Merrimack	R	1925
Espinola, Joan E.	Salem, Rockingham	R	1981
Fair, Patricia A.	Pembroke, Merrimack	D	1989 1991
Farnum, Mary L. R.	Boscawen, Merrimack	D	1921
Faulkner, Ellen	Keene, Cheshire	R	1957 1959 1961 1963 1965
Ferguson, Edgar Maude	Bristol, Grafton	R	1927 1929
Fiske, Marguerite B.	Hampton Falls, Rockingham	R	1969 1971
Flanagan, Natalie S.	Atkinson, Rockingham	R	1975 1977 1979 1981 1983 1985 1987 1989 1991 1993 1995
Fleisher, Hilda W.	Manchester, Hillsborough	R	1975
Flood, Jacqueline J.	Merrimack, Hillsborough	D	1989*
Flynn, Anita A.	Somersworth, Strafford	D	1981 1983 1985 1987 1989
Fogg, Edna D.	Milan, Coos	R	1963 1965
Fontaine, Jennie G.	Berlin, Coos	D	1947 1949 1951 1953 1955 1957 1961 1963 1965
Forbes, Roxie A.	Marlow, Cheshire	R	1945 1949 1959 1963 1965 1967 1969 1971

New Hampshire House, continued

Name	City, County	Party	Legislative Year
Ford, Nancy M.	Nashua, Hillsborough	R	1981* 1983 1985 1987 1989 1991
Fortier, Jennie	Berlin, Coos	D	1925
Foss, Patricia H.	Ctr. Strafford, Strafford	R	1985 1987 1989 1991
Foster, Katherine D.	Keene, Cheshire	D	1987 1989 1991 1993
Foster, Linda T.	Mt. Vernon, Hillsborough	D	1993 1995
Found, M.Susan	Conway, Carroll	R	1977
Fournier, Eulalie L.	Nashua, Hillsborough	D	1939
Frank, Nancy G.	Merrimack, Hillsborough	D	1987 1989
Franks, Suzan L. R.	Nashua, Hillsborough	R	1993 1995
Fraser, Marilyn Anne	Concord, Merrimack	D	1995
French, Barbara C.	Henniker, Merrimack	D	1993
Frew, Patricia A.	Dover, Strafford	D	1985 1987
Fried, Barbara A.	Greenville, Hillsborough	R	1983* 1985
Frizzell, Martha H. McDonalds	Charlestown, Sullivan	R	1951 1953 1955 1957 1959 1961 1963 1965 1967 1969 1971 1973 1975 1977
Fuller, Bertha J.	Clarksville, Coos	R	1947
Funkhouser, Helen C.	Durham, Strafford	R	1953 1955
Gage, Beverly A.	Salem, Rockingham	R	1975 1977 1979 1981 1983 1985 1987 1989 1991 1993 1995
Gage, Ruth E.	Goffstown, Hillsborough	D	1987 1991 1993
Gagne, Marie A.	Berlin, Coos	D	1929 1931
Gagnon, Gabrielle V.	Nashua, Hillsborough	D	1975 1977 1979 1981 1983 1985 1987 1989 1991*
Gagnon, Nancy R.	Merrimack, Hillsborough	R	1975* 1977 1979
Gagnon, Rebecca A.	Berlin, Coos	D	1939 1941 1947 1949 1955 1957 1959 1961 1963 1965 1967 1969 1971 1973 1975
Ganley, Barbara T.	Exeter, Rockingham	D	1975 1977
Gardner, Edith B.	Springfield, Sullivan	R	1943 1945 1949 1953 1955
Gelt, Jeanette	Salem, Rockingham	R	1965 1967 1969 1971
George, Olie M.	Gorham, Coos	R	1933
Gerber, Fannie	Portsmouth, Rockingham	D	1967
Gilmartin, Medora	Manchester, Hillsborough	D	1941 1943 1945
Girouard, Shirley A.	West Lebanon, Grafton	D	1983
Goff, Elizabeth E.	Salem, Rockingham	D	1973 1975 1977
Goodrich, Vera E.	Epping, Rockingham	R	1967 1969 1971 1973 1975

New Hampshire House, continued

Name	City, County	Party	Legislative Year
Harlan, Susan N.	Nashua, Hillsborough	R	1989
Harland, Jane A.	Claremont, Sullivan	D	1989 1991
Harriman, Katherine J.	Concord, Merrimack	D	1973 1975
Harrington, Marian R.	Hancock, Hillsborough	R	1983 1985 1987
Hartford, Margaret M.	New Castle, Rockingham	R	1977 1979
Hartigan, Winifred E.	Rochester, Strafford	D	1959 1963 1965 1967
Hashem, Elaine M.	Barrington, Strafford	D	1991 1993
Hawkinson, Marie C.	Berlin, Coos	D	1991 1993 1995
Hayden, Margretta M.	Ossipee, Carroll	R	1955
Hayes, Eleanor R.	Northumberland, Coos	R	1953
Hayes, Margaret M.	Portsmouth, Rockingham	R	1957
Hayner, Helen D.	Laconia, Belknap	R	1963 1965
Hayward, Elizabeth W.	Hanover, Grafton	R	1953 1955 1957 1959 1961 1963
Head, Joanne C.	Amherst, Hillsborough	R	1977 1979 1981 1983
Head, Mary H.	Hooksett, Merrimack	R	1931*
Hendrick, Nancy C.	Manchester, Hillsborough	D	1979 1981 1983 1985
Herchek, Dianne L.	Dover, Strafford	D	1977 1979
Herrick, Mary Rosa-mond	Deering, Hillsborough	R	1955 1959
Hess, Judith Ann	Hooksett, Merrimack	R	1975 1977
Hickey, Delina R.	Nashua, Hillsborough	D	1981 1983
Hickey, Everol M.	Dover, Strafford	D	1965*
Hickey, Janet E.	Nashua, Hillsborough	R	1991*
Hill, Addie C.	Belmont, Belknap	R	1927
Hill, Nettie M.	Conway, Carroll	R	1957 1959
Hilton, Marcia F.	Andover, Merrimack	R	1925
Hoelzel, Kathleen M.	Raymond, Rockingham	R	1989 1991
Holden, Carol H.	Amherst, Hillsborough	R	1985 1987 1989 1991 1993 1995
Holden, Mary B.	Deering, Hillsborough	R	1929
Holl, Ann C.	Claremont, Sullivan	D	1993
Holley, Sylvia A.	Nashua, Hillsborough	R	1993 1995
Holliday, Jane	Warner, Merrimack	D	1979
Hollingworth, Beverly	Hampton, Rockingham	D	1981 1983 1985 1987 1989
Holmes, Mary C.	Penacook, Merrimack	R	1981 1983 1985 1987 1989 1991 1993 1995
Holmes, Nelle L.	Amherst, Hillsborough	R	1951 1953 1955
Horner, Ida M.	Thornton, Grafton	R	1947 1951 1953
Howard, Donalda K.	Bartlett, Carroll	R	1963 1965 1967 1969 1971 1973 1975 1977 1979 1981 1983*
Howison, Gertrude N.	Milford, Hillsborough	R	1929 1931 1933 1935
Hoyt, Florence Ward	Lebanon, Grafton	R	1933 1935 1937 1939

Hundley, Hilda	Portsmouth, Rockingham	D	1953 1955
Hunter, Margaret E.	Tuftonboro, Carroll	R	1933
Hurlbert, Celia G.	Errol, Coos	D	1947 1955
Hurst, Sharleene Page	Hampton, Rockingham	R	1991 1993 1995
Hussey, Mary E.	Manchester, Hillsborough	D	1995
Hutchinson, Ann L.	Milford, Hillsborough	R	1957*
Hutchinson, Karen Keegan	Londonderry, Rockingham	R	1991 1993 1995
Hynes, Carolyn E.	Portsmouth, Rockingham	D	1987 1989 1991
Ingram, Mildred S.	Acworth, Sullivan	R	1977 1981 1983 1985 1987
Irwin, Virginia O'Brien	Newport, Sullivan	D	1983
Jackson, Katharine G.	Dublin, Cheshire	R	1951
Jackson, Selma R.	Kingston, Rockingham	R	1979 1981
Jean, Claudette R.	Nashua, Hillsborough	D	1991* 1993 1995
Jenkins, Mary	Manchester, Hillsborough	D	1989
Johnson, Joyce May	Tilton, Belknap	D	1991 1993
Johnson, Katherine G.	Monroe, Grafton	R	1959 1965
Johnson, Polly B.	Concord, Merrimack	R	1977
Joncas, Grace Lucille	Rollinsford, Strafford	D	1969 1971 1973 1975 1977
Jones, Helen Gwendo-lyn	Concord, Merrimack	R	1973 1975
Jones, Mabel M.	New Ipswich, Hills-borough	R	1929
Jones, Myra J.	New Durham, Strafford	D	1933
Jordan, Mary H.	Nashua, Hillsborough	D	1991
Joslyn, Lynn	Salem, Rockingham	R	1983 1985
Joyce, Susan M.	Epping, Rockingham	D	1983* 1987
Kane, Cecelia D.	Portsmouth, Rockingham	D	1989 1991 1993 1995
Kane, Joan S.	Claremont, Sullivan	D	1993
Kane, Laura A.	Nashua, Hillsborough	D	1995
Kashulines, Juanita E.	Windham, Rockingham	R	1973 1975 1977 1979 1981 1983
Katsakiores, Phyllis M.	Derry, Rockingham	R	1985 1987 1989 1991* 1993 1995
Katsiaficas, Chry-soula A.	Nashua, Hillsborough	D	1981 1983
Keans, Sandra Balo-menos *see Balo-menos*	Rochester, Strafford	R	1985 1987 1989 1991 1993 1995
Keefe, Mary E.	Portsmouth, Rockingham	R	1969 1971
Keeney, Phyllis M.	Hudson, Hillsborough	R	1967 1969 1971
Keith, Brenda E.	Derry, Rockingham	R	1991
Kelley, Jane	Hampton, Rockingham	D	1975 1995
Kelley, Ruth G.	Middleton, Strafford	D	1927
Kelly, Donna C.	Goffstown, Hillsborough	D	1987
Kendall, Elizabeth E.	Epping, Rockingham	R	1951
Kenison, Linda	Concord, Merrimack	R	1975
Kersting, Constance	Pembroke, Merrimack	R	1967

New Hampshire House, continued

Name	City, County	Party	Legislative Year
Kidder, Barbara Ann	Laconia, Belknap	R	1975
Kimball, Phyllis A.	Jefferson, Coos	R	1959 1961
King, Evelyn A.	Manchester, Hillsborough	D	1983
Kinghorn, Meda L.	Piermont, Grafton	D	1959 1961
Kinney, Paula J.	Dover, Strafford	R	1987 1989 1991
Knight, Alice Tirrell	Goffstown, Hillsborough	R	1967 1969 1971 1973 1977 1981 1983 1985 1987 1989
Krasker, Elaine S.	Portsmouth, Rockingham	D	1975 1977 1979 1981 1983 1985
Kress, Gloria W.	Manchester, Hillsborough	R	1989
La Bonte, Claire A.	Somersworth, Strafford	D	1937
Lacaillade, Margaret M.	Manchester, Hillsborough	D	1979
Lagassie, Lucille M.	Manchester, Hillsborough	R	1969*
Ladd, Elizabeth R.	Winchester, Cheshire	R	1973 1975 1977 1979
Lake, Nellie G.	Brentwood, Rockingham	R	1931
Lampere, Martha E.	Lyme, Grafton	R	1943 1945
Lamy, Catherine G.	Manchester, Hillsborough	D	1971 1973 1975 1977 1979 1981 1983 1985
Landers, Irene Weed	Keene, Cheshire	R	1949 1951 1953
Langley, Jane S.	Rye Beach, Rockingham	R	1995
Langlois, Victoria M.	Nashua, Hillsborough	D	1925
Lareau, Amelia	Manchester, Hillsborough	D	1949 1951 1953 1955
Lawless, Mary E.	Eaton, Carroll	R	1931
Lawrence, Eva M.	Pelham, Hillsborough	R	1991
Lawrence, Susan J.	Claremont, Sullivan	D	1983
Laycock, Beatrice N.	Salem, Rockingham	D	1977 1979
Lazure, Clara A.	Berlin, Coos	D	1941 1943 1945 1947 1949
Lebel, Lorraine F.	Nashua, Hillsborough	D	1973 1975*
Lee, Rebecca E.	Derry, Rockingham	R	1993 1995
Legasse, Dorothy L.	Portsmouth, Rockingham	R	1963
Lemay, Mary S.	Salem, Rockingham	R	1973
Leslie, Anne	Salem, Rockingham	D	1979 1981 1983
Letendre, Evelyn S.	Bedford, Hillsborough	R	1995
Lewis, Mary Ann	Contoocook, Merrimack	R	1981 1983 1985 1987 1989 1991
Lint, Janis R.	Merrimack, Hillsborough	D	1973
Loder, Suzanne K.	Durham, Strafford	D	1993 1995
Loizeaux, Suzanne	Plymouth, Grafton	R	1949 1953 1957 1959 1961
Long, Linda D.	Nashua, Hillsborough	D	1987 1989
Long, Martha A.	Kingston, Rockingham	R	1959
Lord, Marion M.	Gilford, Belknap	R	1957 1959 1961
Lovejoy, Marian E.	Raymond, Rockingham	R	1993 1995

Lovejoy, Virginia K.	Derry, Rockingham	R	1977 1979 1981 1983 1985 1987 1989 1991
Lown, Elizabeth D.	Amherst, Hillsborough	R	1985 1987 1989 1991 1993
Lozeau, Donnalee M.	Nashua, Hillsborough	R	1985 1987 1989 1991 1993 1995
Lucy, Irene M.	Conway, Carroll	R	1949
Lunderville, Virginia P.	Berlin, Coos	D	1925
Lyman, L. Randy	Ossipee, Carroll	R	1993 1995
Lynch, Doris T.	Merrimack, Hillsborough	D	1971 1973 1975
Lynch, Margaret A.	Keene, Cheshire	D	1979 1981 1991 1993 1995
Lyons, Elaine T.	Merrimack, Hillsborough	R	1971 1973 1975 1977 1979
Lyons, Patricia M.	Nashua, Hillsborough	D	1983
MacDonald, Irene S.	Kingston, Rockingham	R	1953
Mace, Ada L.	Windham, Rockingham	R	1981 1983 1985 1987 1989
MacIntyre, Doris R.	Merrimack, Hillsborough	R	1995
MacIvor, Donna T.	Penacook, Merrimack	R	1977
MacKinnon, Nancy W.	East Derry, Rockingham	R	1989 1991
MacPhee, Gladys E.	Andover, Merrimack	R	1939
Mahoney, Victoria E.	Concord, Merrimack	R	1953 1955 1957
Maloomian, Helen	Somersworth, Strafford	D	1971 1973 1975 1977
Martel, Albina S.	Manchester, Hillsborough	D	1963 1965 1967 1969*
Martin, Eda C.	Littleton, Grafton	R	1951 1953 1955 1957 1961 1963
Martin, Josephine Coster	Amherst, Hillsborough	R	1975 1977
Martin, Mary Ellen	Nashua, Hillsborough	D	1991 1993 1995
Marx, Eleanor F.	Langdon, Sullivan	R	1963 1965
Mason, Elisabeth H.	Berlin, Coos	D	1933 1935 1937 1939 1941 1943 1945 1947 1949
Mayhew, Josephine	Groveton, Coos	D	1981 1985 1987 1989 1991 1993 1995
Maynard, Pauline Hanson *see Hanson, see Miller*	Fitzwilliam, Cheshire	R	1953
McAvoy, Rita C.	Littleton, Grafton	R	1977 1979 1983 1985 1987
McCann, Bonnie Lou	Nashua, Hillsborough	D	1987 1989 1991 1993*
McCullough, Mary E.	Middleton, Strafford	D	1947
McDonough, Kathleen B.	Newcastle, Rockingham	R	1963 1965 1967
McEachern, Donna J.	Portsmouth, Rockingham	D	1977
McGee, Edna B.	Lincoln, Grafton	D	1967 1969 1971
McGlynn, Margaret L.	Nashua, Hillsborough	D	1973 1975 1977 1981 1983 1985 1987

New Hampshire House, continued

Name	City, County	Party	Legislative Year
McGovern, Cynthia Ann	Portsmouth, Rockingham	D	1987 1989 1991 1993 1995
McIlwaine, Deborah P.	Sugar Hill, Grafton	D	1991 1993
McKee, Cynthia W.	Claremont, Sullivan	R	1985 1987
McKinney, Betsy	Londonderry, Rockingham	R	1985 1987 1989 1991 1993 1995
McLane, Susan B. R.	Portsmouth, Rockingham	D	1983
McLane, Susan Neidlinger	Concord, Merrimack	R	1969 1971 1973 1975 1977 1979*
McNamara, Wanda G.	W. Chesterfield, Cheshire	R	1993 1995
McNicols, Bernadette	Bow, Merrimack	R	1975 1977
McPhail, Isabell C.	Manchester, Hillsborough	D	1949
McRae, Karen K.	Goffstown, Hillsborough	R	1987 1989 1991 1993 1995
Mehegan, Constance M.	Sunapee, Sullivan	R	1983* 1985
Merrill, Amanda A.	Durham, Strafford	D	1989 1991 1993 1995
Merrill, Shirley Kimball	Lebanon, Grafton	R	1967 1969 1971 1973
Merritt, Deborah F.	Durham, Strafford	D	1993 1995
Messier, Irene M.	Manchester, Hillsborough	R	1981 1985 1987 1989 1991 1993 1995
Messina, Lois K.	Goffstown, Hillsborough	R	1973*
Metzger, Katherine H.	Fitzwilliam, Cheshire	R	1989 1991 1993 1995
Micklon, Stephanie R.	Salem, Rockingham	R	1989
Millar, Julia H.	Claremont, Sullivan	R	1951 1953 1955
Millard, Elizabeth Sanford	Boscawen, Merrimack	R	1975 1985 1987 1989 1991
Miller, Pauline Hanson see Hanson, see Maynard	Fitzwilliam, Cheshire	R	1947 1949 1951
Milligan, Ida V.C.	Newbury, Merrimack	R	1965
Miner, Ruth Fay	Meredith, Belknap	R	1955 1957
Mitchell, Eleanor	Concord, Merrimack	R	1977* 1979
Molner, Mary E.	Henniker, Merrimack	D	1991
Moore, Carol	Concord, Merrimack	D	1993 1995
Moore, Elizabeth A.	New Boston, Hillsborough	R	1985 1987 1989 1991 1993
Morey, Florence P.	Hart's Location, Carroll	R	1929 1951 1953
Moriarty, Mary M.	Merrimack, Hillsborough	D	1965
Morin, Anna M.	Somersworth, Strafford	D	1933
Morradian, Jody E.	Durham, Strafford	D	1981
Morrill, Olive B.	West Franklin, Merrimack	R	1995
Morrill, Ruth T.	Albany, Carroll	R	1957
Morris, Debbie L.	Windham, Rockingham	R	1995
Morris, Lula J.A.	Lancaster, Coos	R	1931 1933 1935 1941 1943

Name	Town, County	Party	Years
Morrison, Bessie Matilda	Salem, Rockingham	R	1963 1965 1967 1969 1971
Morrison, Gail C.	Hudson, Hillsborough	R	1977 1979
Morse, Ellen D.	Concord, Merrimack	D	1981
Morse, Joann T.	Spofford, Cheshire	R	1983 1985 1987 1989 1991
Moulton, Idanelle T.	New Durham, Strafford	R	1957 1959 1963 1965 1967
Mourgenos, Nicolette	Dover, Strafford	D	1979*
Mousseau, Ann L.	Pittsfield, Merrimack	R	1967 1969
Murphy, Elizabeth D.	Kearsarge, Carroll	D	1983
Myler, Letitia Jane	Berlin, Coos	D	1931 1933 1935 1937
Nagel, Carol Ann	Salem, Rockingham	R	1983 1985 1987
Nardi, Theodora P.	Manchester, Hillsborough	D	1973 1975 1977 1979 1981 1989 1991 1993
Neale, Genevieve S.	Hanover, Grafton	D	1959 1961
Nelson, Mary S.	Nashua, Hillsborough	D	1983 1985
Nemzoff-Berman, Ruth	Nashua, Hillsborough	D	1977 1979 1981
Nevins, Carole M.	Auburn, Rockingham	R	1981 1983
Nichols, Avis B.	Warner, Merrimack	R	1979 1981 1983 1985 1987 1989 1991 1993 1995
Nighswander, Esther R.	Gilford, Belknap	R	1969 1971 1973 1975 1977 1979 1983
Nixon, Leslier C.	Goffstown, Hillsborough	R	1987
Nordgren, Sharon L.	Hanover, Grafton	D	1989 1991 1993 1995
Normandin, Margaret Ealashie	Laconia, Belknap	D	1963 1965 1967 1969
Noyes, Anna M.	Salem, Rockingham	R	1953 1955
Nutter, Eleanora C.	Epsom, Merrimack	R	1953; D 1955 1957
O'Brien, Catherine	Dover, Strafford	D	1985
O'Hearn, Jane E.	Nashua, Hillsborough	R	1993* 1995
O'Keefe, Patricia M.	Seabrook, Rockingham	D	1993
O'Neil, Dorthea M.	Manchester, Hillsborough	D	1973 1975 1977
O'Neill, Christina	Laconia, Belknap	R	1981
O'Rourke, Joanne A.	Manchester, Hillsborough	D	1983 1985 1987 1989 1991 1993 1995
Olimpio, J. Lisbeth	Sanbornville, Carroll	D	1985 1987 1989
Orcutt, Jo Ellen	Goffstown, Hillsborough	D	1973* 1975 1977
Ordway, Norma T.	Berlin, Coos	D	1935
Otis, Sara E.	Concord, Merrimack	R	1941 1943 1945 1947 1953
Ottolini, Lucille A.	Berlin, Coos	D	1985
Packard, Bonnie Brady *see Brady*	New Ipswich, Hillsborough	R	1985 1987 1989 1991 1993 1995
Page, Nellie J.	Atkinson, Rockingham	R	1925
Palmer, Lorraine R.	Claremont, Sullivan	D	1993 1995
Palmer, Mildred L.	Plaistow, Rockingham	R	1955 1957 1959 1961 1963 1965 1967 1969 1971

New Hampshire House, continued

Name	City, County	Party	Legislative Year
Pantelakos, Laura C.	Portsmouth, Rockingham	R	1979 1981 1983 1985 1987 1989 1991 1993 1995
Papadopoulos, Christofily	Nashua, Hillsborough	D	1979* 1981
Pappas, Toni	Manchester, Hillsborough	R	1985 1987 1989
Pardy, Nancy	Concord, Merrimack	D	1977*
Pariseau, Judy L.	Manchester, Hillsborough	R	1981 1985 1987
Park, Hazel I.	Lyme, Grafton	R	1963 1965 1967 1969
Parmenter, Ann M.	Nashua, Hillsborough	D	1983 1985
Parr, Ednapearl Flores	Hampton, Rockingham	R	1973 1975 1977 1979 1981 1983 1985 1987 1989 1991
Pastor, Selma R.	Nashua, Hillsborough	D	1979 1981
Patenaude, Amy	Henniker, Merrimack	R	1995
Patten, Betsey L.	Center Harbor, Carroll	R	1995
Patten, Lois Lyman	Nashua, Hillsborough	R	1927
Payette, Lise Labelle	Portsmouth, Rockingham	D	1949 1953 1955 1957
Peabody, Nina E.	Franconia, Grafton	R	1953 1957
Pearson, Gertrude B.	Keene, Cheshire	R	1989 1991 1993
Pelletier, Marsha L.	Dover, Strafford	D	1993
Pelley, Janet R.	Gonic, Strafford	D	1983 1985 1987 1989 1991
Pelton, Frances E.	Langdon, Sullivan	R	1945
Pelton, Susan W.	Henniker, Merrimack	D	1977
Perry, Lenna Wilson see *Wilson*	Jaffrey, Cheshire	R	1955
Peters, Marjorie Y.	Bedford, Hillsborough	R	1975 1977 1979 1981 1983
Pevear, Roberta C.	Hampton Falls, Rockingham	R	1979 1981 1983 1985 1987
Phelan, Grace M.	Stark, Coos	R	1945 1949 1955
Philbrook, Paula L.	Nashua, Hillsborough	D	1993 1995
Phillips, Marion L.	Claremont, Sullivan	R	1959
Phinney, Mary E.	Manchester, Hillsborough	R	1927 1929 1933
Pierce, Carol J.	Laconia, Belknap	R	1973
Pignatelli, Debora B.	Nashua, Hillsborough	D	1987 1989 1991
Pillsbury, Augusta	Manchester, Hillsborough	R	1925 1927
Pitman, Mary Ellen	Pembroke, Merrimack	R	1995
Plomaritis, Claire	Pelham, Hillsborough	D	1977 1979 1981
Podles, Eleanor P.	Manchester, Hillsborough	R	1977 1979
Poehlman, Barbara S.	Goffstown, Hillsborough	D	1969 1971
Popov, Elizabeth M.	Newmarket, Rockingham	D	1983 1985 1987 1989
Potter, Natalie M.	Northumberland, Coos	R	1961 1963
Powers, Phoebe Downing	Ellsworth, Grafton	R	1961*
Pratt, Irene A.	Winchester, Cheshire	D	1989 1991 1993 1995
Pratt, Katheran	Hampton, Rockingham	R	1993 1995

Prescott, Ferne *see* Adams	Brentwood, Rockingham	R	1957 1959
Pressly, Barbara B.	Nashua, Hillsborough	D	1983 1985
Price, Dolores R.	Nashua, Hillsborough	D	1987
Proctor, Nancy J.	Keene, Cheshire	D	1975 1977 1979 1981
Proulx, Sarah A.	Manchester, Hillsborough	D	1979
Pucci, Phyllis Jeanne	Salem, Rockingham	D	1977 1979
Putnam, Rose S.	Lebanon, Grafton	D	1965 1967
Racicot, Rachel I.	Manchester, Hillsborough	R	1989
Raiche, Denise	Manchester, Hillsborough	D	1981
Raiche, Maureen E.	Manchester, Hillsborough	D	1981 1983 1985
Ralph, Katharine J.	Franklin, Merrimack	D	1975 1977 1979
Ramsdell, Alice L.	Nashua, Hillsborough	R	1943 1945 1947 1949 1951 1953 1955 1957
Ramsey, Margaret Russell	Swanzey, Cheshire	D	1977 1979 1981 1983 1985 1987
Randlett, Dorothy V.	Laconia, Belknap	R	1969 1971 1973
Randlett, Gloria M.	Boscawen, Merrimack	R	1979
Read, Lena A.	Plainfield, Sullivan	R	1943 1945 1947 1949
Reardon, Judy E.	Manchester, Hillsborough	D	1985 1987
Record, Alice B.	Nashua, Hillsborough	R	1989 1991 1993
Record, Clara M.	Nashua, Hillsborough	R	1943 1947 1951 1957
Reed, Irene L.	Henniker, Merrimack	R	1969
Reese, Delight H.	Hampstead, Rockingham	R	1975 1979
Remick, Barbara R.	Hampton, Rockingham	R	1989
Reney, Doris C.	Grantham, Sullivan	R	1955 1957
Rheault, Lillian I.	Manchester, Hillsborough	R	1989 1991 1993
Rice, Edith S.	Hooksett, Merrimack	R	1973
Rich, Marcia Tefft	Littleton, Grafton	R	1965 1967 1969 1971
Richards, Maude B.	Exeter, Rockingham	R	1945 1947 1949 1951 1953
Richardson, Barbara Hull	Fitzwilliam, Cheshire	D	1993 1995
Richardson, Harriett W.B.	Dover, Strafford	R	1959 1961 1963 1967 1969 1971 1973
Richardson, Mabel Lowe	Randolph, Coos	R	1947 1969 1971 1973 1975 1977 1979
Riley, Doris J.	Hooksett, Merrimack	R	1971; D 1975 1977 1979 1981 1983 1985 1987
Riley, Frances L.	Manchester, Hillsborough	R	1985 1989 1991 1993 1995
Rix, Maude G.	Shelburne, Coos	R	1937 1947
Roberts, Louise Petit	Suncook, Merrimack	D	1983
Roberts, Margaret D.	Franklin, Merrimack	R	1981 1985
Robertson, Abbie H.	Hinsdale, Cheshire	R	1937 1939 1941 1943 1945 1947
Robinson, Ellen-Ann	Litchfield, Hillsborough	R	1983 1985 1987 1989 1991

New Hampshire House, continued

Name	City, County	Party	Legislative Year
Rodeschin, Beverly T.	Newport, Sullivan	R	1985 1987 1989 1991 1993
Roe, Glayds D.	Newport, Sullivan	R	1953 1955
Rogers, Katherine D.	Concord, Merrimack	D	1993 1995
Rogers, Myrtle B.	Newton, Rockingham	R	1973 1975 1977 1979 1981
Rogers, Rose Marie	Rochester, Strafford	D	1993
Rossley, Eileen G.	Portsmouth, Rockingham	D	1965 1967
Rouillard, Marilee	Keene, Cheshire	D	1981
Roulston, Majorie L.	Salem, Rockingham	R	1959 1961
Rounds, Ruth M.	Hill, Merrimack	R	1941 1943
Rowell, Ruth T.	Barrington, Strafford	R	1973 1975
Roy, Antoinette B.	Manchester, Hillsborough	R	1969
Roy, Mary R.	Claremont, Sullivan	D	1973
Roy, Vesta M.	Salem, Rockingham	R	1973
Rubins, Glenna H.	Rochester, Strafford	D	1963 1965 1967
Russell, Elva B.	Concord, Merrimack	R	1933
Russell, Gertrude M.	Harrisville, Cheshire	R	1931
Russell, Margaret A.	Keene, Cheshire	D	1963 1965
Russell, Patricia T.	Keene, Cheshire	D	1975 1977 1979 1981 1985
Sabella, Norma A.	Derry, Rockingham	R	1995
Saddler, Ann A.	Portsmouth, Rockingham	D	1953 1955 1957 1963 1965 1967
Saltmarsh, Gertrude E.	Concord, Merrimack	R	1951 1953 1955
Sanders, Jane F.	Alton, Belknap	R	1977 1979 1981 1983
Sanderson, Patricia O.	Portsmouth, Rockingham	R	1985 1987 1989*
Sawyer, Ida T.	Woodstock, Grafton	D	1951
Schneiderat, Catherine A.	Manchester, Hillsborough	R	1987 1989 1991
Schreiber, Joan M.	Dover, Strafford	D	1977 1979 1981 1983
Schwaner, Annie Mae	Plaistow, Rockingham	R	1963 1965 1967 1969 1971 1973 1975 1977 1979 1981 1983 1985 1987
Schwartz, Susan *see* Spear	Keene, Cheshire	D	1985 1987
Scott-Craig, Mary M.	Hanover, Grafton	D	1965 1967
Scranton, Andrea A.	Keene, Cheshire	R	1973 1975 1977 1979 1981 1983 1985
Senter, Merilyn P.	Plaistow, Rockingham	R	1989 1991 1993 1995
Shea, Barbara F.	Manchester, Hillsborough	D	1973 1975
Shea, Roberta T.	Keene, Cheshire	R	1963 1965
Shepard, Irene James	Concord, Merrimack	R	1975 1977 1979 1983 1985
Shields, Lena M.	Berlin, Coos	D	1951
Shriver, Mary L.	Bedford, Hillsborough	R	1985 1987
Simard, Constance L.	Plaistow, Rockingham	R	1975

Skinner, Patricia M.	Windham, Rockingham	R	1973 1975 1977 1979 1981 1983 1985 1987 1989 1991 1993
Sliney, Mabel	Lebanon, Grafton	D	1937
Smith, Alfreda A.	Salem, Rockingham	D	1977 1979
Smith, Elsie Linn	New Hampton, Belknap	R	1937
Smith, Florence B.	Hebron, Grafton	R	1939
Smith, Linda Ann	Laconia, Belknap	R	1993 1995
Snyder, Clair A.	Somersworth, Strafford	D	1993 1995
Soldati, Jennifer G.	Concord, Merrimack	D	1989 1991 1993*
Solomon, Jane A.	Nashua, Hillsborough	D	1975*
Soper, Ada Agnes	Littleton, Grafton	R	1937 1939
Soucy, Donna M.	Manchester, Hillsborough	D	1991 1993 1995
Soucy, Lillian E.	Manchester, Hillsborough	D	1987 1989
Spaulding, Roma Alma	Claremont, Sullivan	R	1967 1969 1971 1973 1975 1977 1979 1981 1985 1987
Spear, Barbara L.	Farmington, Strafford	R	1993 1995
Spear, Susan Schwartz see *Schwartz*	Keene, Cheshire	D	1989 1991*
Spollett, Doris M.	Hampstead, Rockingham	R	1941 1943 1945 1953 1955 1957 1959 1961 1963 1965 1967 1969 1971 1973
St. George, Judith	Nashua, Hillsborough	D	1977
St. John, Eda	Barnstead, Belknap	D	1965
St. Pierre, Angeline M.	Rochester, Strafford	D	1949 1951 1953 1955 1957 1959 1961 1963 1965 1967
Stachowske, Vicki Lynn	Londonderry, Rocking- ham	R	1985 1989
Stafford, Deloria L.	Laconia, Belknap	R	1953
Stahl, Judith M.	Nashua, Hillsborough	R	1977 1979
Stamatakis, Carol M.	Newport, Sullivan	D	1989 1991 1993
Stark, Eleanor H.	Concord, Merrimack	R	1979* 1981 1983
Steiner, Lee Anne S.	Manchester, Hillsborough	R	1979 1981 1983 1985 1987 1989 1991
Stettenheim, Sandra	Lebanon, Grafton	D	1995
Stiles, Bessie G.	Dummer, Coos	R	1935 1939
Stomberg, Carol	Canaan, Grafton	D	1977
Story, Ann	Manchester, Hillsborough	R	1929 1931
Straw, Zatae L.	Manchester, Hillsborough	R	1925 1927
Streeter, Janice B.	Nashua, Hillsborough	R	1995
Studley, Norma M. see *Currier*	Rochester, Strafford	R	1949 1951 1953 1955
Sukeforth, Alice W.	Portsmouth, Rockingham	R	1951
Sullens, Joan C.	Nashua, Hillsborough	R	1993* 1995
Sullivan, Mary J.	Manchester, Hillsborough	D	1973 1975 1981 1983 1985 1987

New Hampshire House, continued

Name	City, County	Party	Legislative Year
Swasey, E. Christine	Brentwood, Rockingham	R	1933
Symons, Joanne L.	Lebanon, Grafton	D	1973* 1975
Sysyn, Olga	Manchester, Hillsborough	R	1971*
Sytek, Donna P.	Salem, Rockingham	R	1977* 1979 1981 1983 1985 1987 1989 1991 1993 1995
Taffe, Betty Jo	Rumney, Grafton	R	1977 1979 1981 1983 1985
Tamposi, R. Betty	Nashua, Hillsborough	R	1979* 1981 1983 1985
Tarpley, Nancy L.	Amherst, Hillsborough	R	1987 1989 1991
Tarrant, Harriet B.	Pittsfield, Merrimack	R	1961 1963
Tate, Joan C.	Hudson, Hillsborough	R	1991 1993
Taylor, Ada C.	Whitefield, Coos	R	1947 1949 1951 1953 1955 1957 1959 1961 1963 1965 1967*
Taylor, Virginia F.	Effingham, Carroll	R	1963
Terninko, Maggie Boyle	Nottingham, Rockingham	D	1991 1993*
Terry, Joan E.	Keene, Cheshire	D	1977
Thompson, Barbara Cooper	Rochester, Strafford	R	1969 1971 1973 1975
Thompson, Doris L.	Northfield, Merrimack	R	1961 1963 1965 1967 1971 1973 1975 1977
Thompson, Marianne H.	Pelham, Hillsborough	D	1981
Thomson, Glyneta B.	Orford, Grafton	R	1977 1979 1981
Tibbetts, Thelma P.	Rochester, Strafford	R	1973 1975
Tilton, Elmira F.	Salem, Rockingham	D	1987
Tolman, Janet	Nelson, Cheshire	R	1957
Toomey, Kathryn W.	Nashua, Hillsborough	D	1993 1995
Torr, Ann M.	Dover, Strafford	R	1985 1987 1989 1991 1993 1995
Torrey, Janet B.	Dover, Strafford	R	1975 1977
Townsend, Madeline G.	Lebanon, Grafton	R	1973 1977
Townsend, Sara M.	Plainfield, Sullivan	R	1971 1973 1975 1977 1979 1981 1983 1985 1987
Travis, Elizabeth L.	Portsmouth, Rockingham	R	1955
Trottier, Georgianna L.	Berlin, Coos	R	1939 1943 1947*
Turner, Virginia W.	East Sullivan, Cheshire	R	1973 1975
Ulschoeffer, Esther A.	Berlin, Coos	R	1931
Underwood, Barbara J.	Concord, Merrimack	R	1971 1973* 1975 1979 1981 1983
Upton, Barbara Allen	Bedford, Hillsborough	R	1989 1991 1993
Vachon, Rose C.	Manchester, Hillsborough	D	1975 1979 1981 1983
Valley, Iris	Dover, Strafford	R	1977 1979
Valliere, Blanche E.	Rollinsford, Strafford	D	1957

Van Loan, Anna S.	Bedford, Hillsborough	R	1963 1965 1969 1971 1973 1975 1977 1979 1981 1983 1985
Vartanian, Elsie	Salem, Rockingham	R	1979 1981 1983 1985 1987 1989
Vey, Mary T.	Brentwood, Rockingham	R	1961 1963 1971 1973
Voll, Sarah P.	Durham, Strafford	R	1977
Vrakatitsis, Zoe	Keene, Cheshire	R	1977 1979
Wadsworth, Karen O.	Lebanon, Grafton	R	1985 1987 1989 1991 1993 1995
Wagner, Joan A.	Hudson, Hillsborough	D	1985 1987
Waldron, Hermine	Portsmouth, Rockingham	D	1983
Walker, E.Jane	Hampton, Rockingham	R	1983 1985 1987
Wall, Janet G.	Madbury, Strafford	D	1987 1989 1991 1993 1995
Wallin, Jean Rogers	Nashua, Hillsborough	D	1967 1969 1975* 1977 1979
Wallner, Mary Jane	Concord, Merrimack	D	1981 1983 1985 1987 1989 1991 1993 1995
Walter, Lorine M.	Lebanon, Grafton	R	1979 1981 1983 1985 1987
Ward, Kathleen W.	Littleton, Grafton	R	1975 1977 1979 1981 1983 1985 1987 1989 1991 1993
Ware, Marietta A.	Sullivan, Cheshire	R	1929
Wastcoat, Mary W.	Candia, Rockingham	R	1951 1953
Watson, Geraldine G.	Merrimack, Hillsborough	R	1977 1983 1985 1987
Webb, Martha G.	Dover, Strafford	R	1955 1957
Webber, Sadie C.	Dover, Strafford	D	1969 1971
Weber, Margaret L.	Croydon, Sullivan	R	1961 1963
Webster, Margaret T.	Keene, Cheshire	D	1967
Webster, T.Anne	Ossipee, Carroll	R	1971 1973
Weeks, Edna Batchelder	Greenland, Rockingham	R	1959 1961 1963 1965 1967 1969 1971 1973
Weeks, Lena D.	Gilford, Belknap	R	1949 1951
Weergang, Alida	Hudson, Hillsborough	R	1993
Welch, Bernice M.	Manchester, Hillsborough	D	1979 1981
Welch, Shirley B.	Concord, Merrimack	R	1969* 1971
Wendelboe, Francine	New Hampton, Belknap	R	1995
Wentworth, Dorothy L.	Madbury, Strafford	R	1955
Weston, Lucie	Concord, Merrimack	R	1947
Wheeler, Emma B.	Milford, Hillsborough	R	1977 1979 1981 1983 1985 1987
Wheeler, Glenn L.	Bristol, Grafton	R	1945 1947 1949
Wheeler, Katherine Wells	Durham, Strafford	D	1989 1991 1993 1995
Whipple, Gladys L.	Lebanon, Grafton	R	1957 1959 1961 1963 1965 1967

New Hampshire House, continued

Name	City, County	Party	Legislative Year
White, Edna K.	Portsmouth, Rockingham	R	1959 1961
White, Jean T.	Rindge, Cheshire	R	1979 1981
White, Julia Humphrey	Portsmouth, Rockingham	R	1959 1961 1963 1965 1967 1969
White, Shirley J.	Somersworth, Strafford	D	1975* 1977
Whitehead, Mary E.	Somersworth, Strafford	D	1979 1981
Whittemore, Eleanor H.	Hollis, Hillsborough	R	1983
Wihby, Linda S.	Manchester, Hillsborough	R	1989 1991
Wild, Winifred G.	Jackson, Carroll	R	1945 1949
Wilkinson, Nana	Tilton, Belknap	R	1971
Williams, Elsie F.	Grafton, Grafton	R	1949 1951 1953 1957
Wilson, Helen Francis	Candia, Rockingham	R	1971 1973 1975 1977 1979
Wilson, Lenna G. *see* Perry	Sharon, Hillsborough	R	1927
Winkley, Noreen D.	Rochester, Strafford	D	1965 1967 1973 1975 1979 1981
Winn, Cecelia L.	Nashua, Hillsborough	D	1973 1975 1977 1979 1981 1983 1985 1987
Winters, Barbara	Rochester, Strafford	R	1951
Wiswell, Marguerite H.	Colebrook, Coos	R	1975 1977 1979 1981
Wood, Lucille T.	Nashua, Hillsborough	R	1983 1985 1987
Woodbury, Marjorie S.	Manchester, Hillsborough	R	1939
Woodman, Louisa K.	Hampton, Rockingham	R	1979 1981
Woodruff, Marian D.	Nashua, Hillsborough	D	1973 1975
Woods, Deborah L.	Stratham, Rockingham	R	1991 1993
Woods, Phyllis L.	Dover, Strafford	D	1975
Woodward, Neila P.	Groveton, Coos	D	1977 1979*
Woodward, Sarah J.	Waterville, Grafton	R	1951 1953
Worcester, Georgie E.	Dover, Strafford	R	1925 1929
Worthen, Dorothy M.	Manchester, Hillsborough	R	1995
Wuelper, Marion	Belmont, Belknap	R	1969 1971 1973
Yantis, Effie E.	Manchester, Hillsborough	R	1923 1925
Yennaco, Carol A.	Windham, Rockingham	R	1993 1995
Young, Helen J.	Easton, Grafton	D	1925
Zabarsky, Joyce R.	Portsmouth, Rockingham	D	1977
Zechausen, Barbara	Laconia, Belknap	R	1981 1983 1985
Zechel, Caroline N.	Nashua, Hillsborough	R	1973 1975
Ziegra, Alice S.	Alton, Belknap	R	1989 1991 1993 1995

*Notes:

Atkins, Edith P.—Died May 1955
Barrett, Katherine K.—Resigned Feb. 16, 1973 (Cooke)[F]
Bell, Helen D. W.—Resigned Dec. 12, 1952 (Goodwin)[F]
Bernard, Mary E.—Died Decv. 10, 1991 (Knowles)

Bowler, Barbara B. — Elected March 13, 1973 (Dodge)
Buckley, Gertrude M. — Elected 1962 (Buckley)
Campbell, Eunice C. — Resigned May 17, 1991 (Katsakiores)[F]
Carter, Susan D. — Resigned July 1, 1994
Carpenter, Karen A. — Elected Oct. 31, 1991 (Perham)
Case, Margaret — Elected Nov. 11, 1993 (Terninko)[F]
Chagnon-Boisver, Yvette L. — Elected Sept. 16, 1977 (Sing)
Charbonneau, Rhona M. — Resigned 1984, elected to Senate (Champange)
Cogswell, Charlotte P. — Elected Dec. 1971 (Mudgett)
Cooke, Muriel K. — Elected Jan. 2, 1974 (Barrett)[F]
Coughlin, Anne E. — Elected Feb. 8, 1994 (Hill)
De Cesare, Grace L. — Resigned June 6, 1977 (Sytek)[F]
Degnan, Kathleen A. — Elected Feb. 2, 1983
Denafio, Phyllis S. — Elected Dec. 6, 1979 (Mourgenos)[F]
Derosier, Ann M. — Resigned Dec. 12, 1989
Domaingue, Jacquelyn — Resigned March 1, 1994
Doon, Helen C. — Elected April 1963 (Carpenter)
Drewniak, Dorothy J. — Elected Nov. 14, 1973 (Messina)[F]. Died Dec. 21, 1983
Flood, Jacqueline J. — Elected April 26, 1989 (Granger)
Ford, Nancy M. — Elected Nov. 17, 1981
Fried, Barbara A. — Elected May 17, 1983 (Bartlett)
Gagnon, Gabrielle V. — Died Nov. 17, 1991
Gagnon, Nancy R. — Elected Oct. 2, 1975 (Geiger)
Goodwin, Ann J. — Elected Jan. 1953 (Bell)[F]
Gross, Caroline L. — Died Dec. 5, 1993 (Hager)[F]
Hancock, Mary Louise — Resigned July 13, 1979 (S.N.McLane)[F]
Head, Mary H. — Elected Jan. 1931 (Gilbert)
Hickey, Everol M. — Elected with a tie vote, seated with one-half vote
Hickey, Janet E. — Resigned April 3, 1991
Howard, Donalda K. — Died Feb. 19, 1983 (Chandler)
Hutchinson, Ann L. — Elected Feb. 1957 (Wadlegh)
Jean, Claudette R. — Elected April 8, 1992
Joyce, Susan M. — Elected Oct. 25, 1983 (Blake)
Katsakiores, Phyllis M. — Elected Sept. 9, 1991 (Campbell)([F]
Lagassie, Lucille M. — Elected March 1970 (Rousseau)
Lebel, Lorraine F. — Resigned Feb. 27, 1975 (Madigan)
Martel, Albina S. — Died March 1969 (Joseph Martle)
McCann, Bonnie Lou — Resigned July 21, 1993 (Sullen)[F]
McLane, Susan Neidlinger — Resigned (Stark)[F], elected to Senate Nov. 29, 1979 (Hancock)[F]
Mehegan, Constance M. — Elected June 29, 1983 (Quinlan)
Messina, Lois K. — Resigned Summer 1973 (Drewniak)[F]
Mitchell, Eleanor — Elected Sept. 13, 1977 (Pratt)
Mourgenos, Nicolette — Resigned May 2, 1979 (P. Denafio)[F]
O'Gara, Molly — Elected March 1965 (Karkavelas)
O'Hearn, Jane E. — Elected Feb. 9, 1994 (Ackerman)
Orcutt, Jo Ellen — Elected Sept. 26, 1973 (Fletcher)
Papadopoulos, Christofily — Elected March 1980
Pardy, Nancy — Elected May 9, 1977 (Shapiro)
Poulsen, Greta I. — Elected June 1981 (Poulsen)
Powers, Phoebe Downing — Resigned Jan. 1961 (Avery)
Sanderson, Patricia O. — Died May 1, 1990
Soldati, Jennifer G. — Resigned Sept. 17, 1993 (Mitchell)
Solomon, Jane A. — Resigned Dec. 1, 1975
Spear, Susan Schwartz — Resigned Oct. 1, 1991 (Mohr)
Stark, Eleanor H. — Elected Feb. 1980 (S.N.McLane)[F]
Sullens, Joan C. — Elected Nov. 8, 1993 (McCann)[F]
Symons, Joanne L. — Elected Nov. 14, 1973 (Merrill)

New Hampshire, continued

Sysyn, Olga—Elected March 16, 1971 (R. Martel)
Sytek, Donna P.—Elected Sept. 13, 1977 (De Cesare)[F]
Tamposi, R. Betty—Elected Feb. 1980
Taylor, Ada C.—Died June 1967
Terninko, Maggie Boyle—Died July 18, 1993 (Case)[F]
Trottier, Georgianna L.—Died April 1947
Underwood, Barbara J.—Elected 1973 (Filides)
Wallin, Jean Rogers—Elected Oct. 2, 1975 (Gramling)
Welch, Shirley B.—Elected March 1970 (Welch)
White, Shirley J.—Elected Nov. 3, 1975 (Dumais)
Woodward, Neila P.—Resigned Jan. 16, 1979 (R. Mayhew)

NEW JERSEY (1921–1995)

New Jersey women, the first women to have suffrage in the United States, voted until 1807 when the legislature revoked the privilege. They regained full suffrage in 1919 and voted in state elections in 1920 to elect Margaret B. Laird (R–Newark, Essex) and Jennie Van Ness (R–East Orange, Essex) to the Assembly.

Women as Percentage of
New Jersey Legislators, 1921–1947

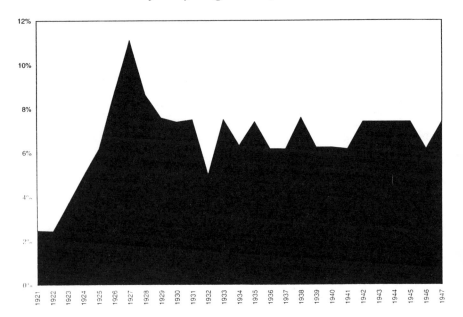

Women as Percentage of
New Jersey Legislators, 1948–1995

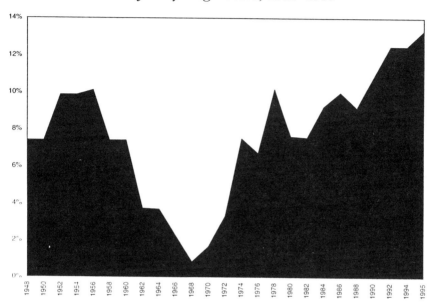

Until 1947, legislative elections were held annually for one year terms in the Assembly and three year terms in the Senate. Since 1947 elections were held in odd years for 60 representatives who served two year terms and 21 senators who served four year staggered terms. A special reapportionment election was held in 1965 with two year terms for the senate. In 1967 the Senate was increased to 40 and the General Assembly to 80 members. Senators serve two-four-four year terms commencing the year after the decennial census. Vacancies are filled by special election.

118 women have served in the New Jersey Legislature:
  7 in the Senate
  114 in the General Assembly
  (3 in the General Assembly and Senate)

Senate
2-4-4 Year Terms (Before 1947, 3 Year Terms)

Name	City, County	Party	Legislative Year
Ammond, Alene S.	Cherry Hill, Camden	D	1974 1976
Brown, Leann	Florham Park, Morris	R	1984 1986 1988 1990 1992*

New Jersey Senate, continued

Name	City, County	Party	Legislative Year
Costa, Catherine A.	Burlington, Burlington	D	1984 1986 1988 1990*
English, Jerry F.	Union, Union	D	1970*
Hughes, Mildred Barry	Union, Union	D	1966
Lipman, Wynona M.	Newark, Essex	D	1972 1974 1976 1978 1980 1982 1984 1986 1988 1990 1992 1994
Martindell, Anne C.	Princeton, Mercer	D	1974 1976*

Assembly
2 Year Terms (Before 1948, 1 Year Terms)

Name	City, County	Party	Legislative Year
Anderson, Priscilla B.	Delran, Burlington	R	1992
Barlow, Florence A.	Paterson, Passaic	R	1930 1931
Berger, Ellen M.	Nutley, Essex	R	1954
Berman, Barbara	Cherry Hill, Camden	D	1978
Berman, Gertrude	Longbranch, Monmouth	D	1974
Bivona, Clara K.	Rutherford, Bergen	R	1956* 1958
Brady, Eileen G.	East Orange, Essex	D	1937
Brown, Irene	Jersey City, Hudson	D	1956 1958 1960
Brown, Katherine W.	Jersey City, Hudson	D	1922 1923
Brown, Leann	Florham Park, Morris	R	1980* 1982
Buono, Barbara	N. Brunswick, Middlesex	D	1994*
Burgio, Jane	North Caldwell, Essex	R	1974 1976 1978 1980
Bush, Esther B.	Montclair, Essex	R	1956
Bush, Stephanie R.	East Orange, Essex	D	1988 1990 1992*
Carroll, Rosemary	Newark, Essex	D	1932
Carty, May Margaret	Jersey City, Hudson	D	1924 1925 1926 1927 1928 1929 1930
Cooper, Delores G.	Atlantic City, Atlantic	R	1982* 1984 1986 1988 1990
Costa, Catherine A.	Burlington, Burlington	D	1982
Cox, Elizabeth L.	Union, Union	R	1970*
Crecco, Marion	Bloomfield, Essex	R	1986 1988 1990 1992 1994
Croce, Mary Keating	Pennsauken, Camden	D	1974 1976 1978
Cruc-Perez, Nilsa	Camden, Camden	D	1994*
Curran, Barbara A.	Summit, Union	R	1974 1976 1978 1980*
Derman, Harriet	Edison, Middlesex	R	1992 1994*
Dilger, Esther	Paterson, Passaic	R	1948
Donohue, Nan V.	Paterson, Passaic	D	1937
Donovan, Kathleen A.	Rutherford, Bergen	R	1986

NEW JERSEY (1921–1995) 215

Doremus, Mattie S.	Paterson, Passaic	R	1939 1940 1941 1942 1943 1944 1945 1946 1947
Dwyer, Florence Price	Elizabeth, Union	R	1950 1952 1954 1956*
Ebert, Madge Irene	Newark, Essex	R	1925 1926
Farragher, Clare M.	Freehold, Monmouth	R	1986* 1988 1990 1992 1994
Fenwick, Millicent	Bernardsville, Somerset	R	1970 1972*
Finn, Catherine M.	West Hoboken, Hudson	D	1924 1925 1926 1927 1928
Ford, Marlene Lynch	Toms River, Ocean	D	1984 1990
Fort, Margretta	West Orange, Essex	R	1924
Francisco, Pamela J.	Ridgewood, Bergen	R	1927
Freeman, Grace	East Orange, Essex	R	1947 1948 1950
Garvin, Mildred Barry	East Orange, Essex	D	1978 1980 1982 1984 1986
Gill, Nia H.	Montclair, Essex	D	1994
Gilmore, Anna	Paterson, Passaic	D	1934 1935
Gluck, Hazel S.	Lakewood, Ocean	R	1980
Greenbaum, Minna P.	Newark, Essex	R	1945 1946 1947 1948
Gregory-Scocchi, Joanna	N. Brunswick, Middlesex	R	1994*
Griffin, Irene T.	Westfield, Union	R	1945
Haines, Florence L.	Newark, Essex	R	1927 1928 1929 1930 1931
Haines, Margaret D.	Newark, Essex	R	1950 1952
Haines, Virginia	Newark, Ocean	R	1992 1994*
Hand, Constance W.	Orange, Essex	R	1935 1936 1938 1939 1940 1941
Hardester, Mildred V.	East Orange, Essex	R	1943 1944 1945 1946
Heck, Rose	Ridgefield Park, Bergen	R	1990* 1992 1994
Higgins, Marion West	Hillsdale, Bergen	R	1960 1962 1964
Hughes, Mildred Barry	Union, Union	D	1958 1960 1962 1964
Jones, Agnes C.	South Orange, Essex	R	1926 1927 1928 1929 1930 1931
Kalik, Barbara Faith	Edgewater Park, Burlington	D	1978 1980 1982 1984 1986 1988 1990
Kiernan, Greta	Harrington Park, Bergen	D	1978
Klein, Ann	Morristown, Morris	D	1972
Kordja, Betty McNamara	Paterson, Passaic	D	1958 1960 1962 1964 1966
Laird, Margaret B.	Newark, Essex	R	1921 1922
MacCarthy, Gloanna W.	Maplewood, Essex	R	1942 1943 1944
Maebert, Marie F.	South Orange, Essex	R	1952 1954 1956
Maloney, Teresa A.	Jersey City, Hudson	D	1931 1932 1933 1934 1935 1936 1937 1938 1939 1940
Margetts, Josephine S.	New Vernon, Morris	R	1968 1970 1972

New Jersey House, continued

Name	City, County	Party	Legislative Year
Marggraff, Wilma	Westwood, Bergen	R	1948 1950 1952 1954*
Mathis, Lillian A.	Hackensack, Bergen	R	1942 1943 1944 1945 1946 1947
McConnell, Barbara	Flemington, Hunterdon	D	1978 1980
Miszkiewicz, Alina	Jersey City, Hudson	D	1976
Muhler, Marie A.	Marlboro, Monmouth	R	1976 1978 1980 1982 1984 1986*
Mullen, Ann A.	Blackwood, Gloucester	D	1990
Murphy, Carol J.	Lake Valhalla, Morris	R	1992* 1994
Murphy, Jessie	Jersey City, Hudson	D	1952 1954
Mutchler, Julia C.	Dover, Morris	R	1932 1933
Newton, Emma E.	Packanack Lake, Passaic	R	1952 1954 1956
North, Mable C.	Verona, Essex	R	1923
Ogden, Maureen B.	Milburn, Essex	R	1982 1984 1986 1988 1990 1992 1994
Pearce, Remay	Newark, Essex	D	1978*
Perfette, Ruby V.	East Orange, Essex	R	1954 1956
Perun, Angela L.	Plainfield, Union	D	1982; R 1984
Peters, Emma	Rutherford, Bergen	R	1929 1930 1931 1932 1933
Pilch, Jenniee W.	Madison, Morris	R	1937 1938
Pilger, Ruth A.	Verona, Essex	R	1950 1952
Preen, Mildred A.	Oldwick, Hunterdon	D	1942 1943 1944*
Quigley, Joan M.	Jersey City, Hudson	D	1994
Randall, Elizabeth	Westwood, Bergen	R	1984* 1986 1988 1990*
Reinert, Isabella C.	Collingwood, Camden	R	1933 1934 1935
Sanford, Olive C.	Nutley, Essex	R	1935 1936 1938 1939 1940 1941 1942
Savage, Lettie E.	Lakewood, Ocean	R	1941 1942 1943 1944 1945 1946 1947 1948 1950 1952 1954 1956 1958
Scanlon, Marye M.	Newark, Essex	D	1978
Schermerhorn, Agnes A.	East Orange, Essex	R	1923
Shelton, Mary P.	Leonia, Bergen	R	1935
Smith, Elizabeth Van D.	Paterson, Passic	R	1936 1938
Smith, Joann H.	Matawan, Middlesex	R	1986 1988 1990 1992 1994
Smith, Mary Mac G.	West Wood, Bergen	R	1936 1937 1938 1939 1940 1941
Stelle, Ida M.	Newark, Essex	R	1927 1928 1929 1930 1931
Stiles, Beatrice J.	Bloomfield, Essex	R	1960
Summers, Isabelle M.	Paterson, Passaic	R	1926 1927 1928 1929

Szabo, Helen Chiarello	Trenton, Mercer	D	1976* 1978*
Talmadge, Quilla E.	East Orange, Essex	D	1992*
Thompson, Lila W.	New Egypt, Ocean	R	1924 1925
Thropp, May A.	Trenton, Mercer	R	1925 1926 1927
Totaro, Rosemarie	Denville, Morris	D	1974 1978
Trube, Myrtle M.	South Orange, Essex	R	1933 1934
Turner, Shirley K.	Lawrenceville, Mercer	D	1994
Urbanski, Eugenia M.V. Courtney	Jersey City, Hudson	D	1947 1948
Urbanski, Marian	Jersey City, Hudson	D	1926 1927 1928
Van Ness, Jennie C.	East Orange, Essex	R	1921
Vandervalk, Charlotte	Westwood, Bergen	R	1990* 1992 1994
Walker, Jacqueline	Aberdeen, Monmouth	D	1984
Weber, Mary Virginia	Glassboro, Gloucester	R	1992
Weinberg, Loretta	Teaneck, Bergen	D	1992* 1994
Williams, Madeline A.	East Orange, Essex	D	1958 1960*
Wilson, Betty	Berkeley Heights, Union	D	1974
Wright, Barbara	Hamilton, Middlesex	R	1992 1994
Wright, Joan M.	Woodcliff Lake, Bergen	R	1980 1982*
Yuill, Mary L.	Newark, Essex	R	1933 1934

*Notes:

Bivona, Clara K. — Elected Nov. 1956 (Fields)
Brown, Leann — Elected Nov. 6, 1980 (Curran)[F], resigned July 1983
Buono, Barbara — Elected Nov. 7, 1994 (Gregory)[F]
Bush, Stephanie R. — Resigned Sept. 15, 1992 (Talmadge)[F]
Cooper, Delores G. — Elected Nov. 2, 1982 (Gormley)
Costa, Catherine A. — Resigned Nov. 19, 1990 (Foy)
Cox, Elizabeth L. — Appointed Nov. 1971 (Heilman)–Jan. 1972
Cruc-Perez, Nilsa — Appointed Feb. 23, 1995 (Bryan)
Curran, Barbara A. — Resigned June 23, 1980 (L.Brown)[F]
Derman, Harriet — Resigned Jan. 1994 (Gregory)[F]
Dwyer, Florence Price — Resigned Nov. 6, 1956, elected US Congress
English, Jerry F. — Appointed Nov. 1971 (Lacorte)–Jan. 1972
Farragher, Clare M. — Elected Feb. 3, 1987 (Muhler)
Fenwick, Millicent — Resigned Dec. 14, 1972 (Rizzolo)
Gregory-Scocchi, Joanna — Appointed March 1994 (Derman)[F]
Haines, Virginia — Resigned 1994
Heck, Rose — Appointed Jan. 5, 1991 (Schuber)
Marggraff, Wilma — Resigned 1954
Martindell, Anne C. — Resigned 1977
Muhler, Marie A. — Resigned Oct. 29, 1986 (Farrager)[F]
Murphy, Carol J. — Elected 1993 (Martin)
Pearce, Remay — Elected Nov. 1979 (Shapiro)
Preen, Mildred A. — Resigned 1944
Randall, Elizabeth — Elected March 26, 1985, resigned Jan. 31, 1991 (Vandervalk)[F]
Szabo, Helen Chiarello — Elected Nov. 2, 1976 (Woodson), resigned 1978 (Stockman)
Talmadge, Quilla E. — Appointed Oct. 9, 1992 (Bush)[F]
Vandervalk, Charlotte — Appointed Feb. 9, 1991 (Randall)[F]
Weinberg, Loretta — Appointed March 12, 1992 (Mazur)
Williams, Madeline A. — Resigned 1960
Wright, Joan M. — Resigned March 1983 (Rooney)

NEW MEXICO (1923–1995)

New Mexico women gained school suffrage in 1910 statehood constitution as well as the right to run for school offices. Full suffrage came with the passage of the Nineteenth Amendment to the U.S. constitution in August 1920 and women voted in the November 1920 elections. A state constitutional amendment was required for women to run for state offices and was placed on the ballot in a special election on September 20, 1921 with several other constitutional amendments. Women voted and helped to pass Amendment No. 1 to allow women to run for state offices. In the next state election, in 1922, Bertha M. Paxton (D–Las Cruces, Dona Ana County) won a seat in the House.

State elections are held every two years for 70 representatives who serve two year terms and 42 senators who serve four year terms. All senators are elected at the same time; there was a senate election in 1996. Vacancies are filled by governor's appointment.

94 women have served in the New Mexico Legislature:
    15 in the Senate
    79 in the House

Women as Percentage of New Mexico Legislators

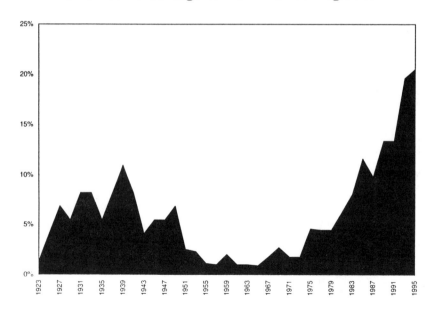

Senate
4 Year Terms

Name	City, County	Party	Legislative Year
Brubaker, Lucy Keys	Belen, Valencia	D	1981* 1983
Coe, Louise Holland	Carrizozo, Lincoln	D	1925 1927 1929 1931 1933 1935 1937 1939
Donisthorpe, Christine A.	Bloomfield, San Juan	R	1979* 1981 1983 1985 1987 1989 1991 1993 1995
Duran, Dianna J.	Alamogordo, Otero	R	1993 1995
Garcia, Mary Jane M.	Dona Ana, Dona Ana	D	1989 1991 1993 1995
Hall, Lois R.	Albuquerque, Bernalillo	R	1981 1983
Hansen, Gladys	Las Cruces, Dona Ana	D	1973 1975 1977 1979
Howes, Gloria	Gallup, McKinley	D	1989 1991 1993 1995
Kitzes, Consuelo Jaramillo	Santa Fe, Santa Fe	D	1971* 1973 1975
Nava, Cynthia	Mesquite, Dona Ana	D	1993 1995
Paster, Janice D.	Albuquerque, Bernalillo	D	1989 1991 1993 1995
Riley, Ann J.	Albuquerque, Bernalillo	D	1993 1995
Steele, Ellen L.	Organ, Dona Ana	R	1985 1987
Stefanics, Elizabeth T.	Santa Fe, Santa Fe	D	1993 1995
Vesely, Edith Huff	Silver City, Grant	D	1965* 1967 1969

House
2 Year Terms

Name	City, County	Party	Legislative Year
Appelman, Ruby V.	Albuquerque, Bernalillo	R	1975 1977 1979
Armijo, Frances P.	Albuquerque, Bernalillo	D	1987 1989
Baca, E. Shirley	Las Cruces, Dona Ana	D	1993 1995
Baca, Patricia V.	Albuquerque, Bernalillo	R	1985 1987 1989 1991 1993
Bell, Blanche Alice	Las Cruces, Dona Ana	R	1953
Blancett, Treciafaye W.	Aztec, San Juan	R	1985
Bryan, Susie R.	Albuquerque, Bernalillo	D	1925
Casey, Barbara A. Perea	Roswell, Chaves	D	1985 1987 1989 1991 1993 1995
Cavanaugh, Maria	Fort Stanton, Lincoln	D	1929 1931 1933
Chacon, Soledad Chavez	Albuquerque, Bernalillo	D	1935*
Chavez, Susie	Las Vegas, San Miguel	R	1933 1935
Cinelli, Adele P. see Hundley	Albuquerque, Bernalillo	D	1975 1977
Cosper, Jane Hyde	Blue Water, Valencia	D	1959
Crook, Anna Marie	Clovis, Curry	R	1995

New Mexico House, continued

Name	City, County	Party	Legislative Year
Dickinson, Ollibel C.	Lovington, Lea	D	1945
Dominquez, Patricia P.	Las Cruces, Dona Ana	R	1985
Dowden, Claire	Gallup, McKinley	R	1927
Dyche, Carmen Cornell R.	Albuquerque, Bernalillo	D	1939
Eisenstadt, Pauline B.	Corrales, Sandoval	D	1985 1987 1989 1991
Evans, Ernestine D.	Canjilon, Rio Arriba	D	1941
Eylar, Calla K. *see* Wolfe	La Mesa, Dona Ana	D	1941 1943
Foraker, Minerva	Albuquerque, Bernalillo	R	1929
Gallegos, Fedelina Lucero	Wagon Mound, Mora	R	1931
Green, Toots	Alamogordo, Otero	R	1985 1987 1989
Gubbels, Pauline K.	Albuquerque, Bernalillo	R	1995
Heth, Pat I.	Belen, Valencia	R	1977
Hoffman, Violet	Santa Fe, Santa Fe	D	1937
Hogrefe, Margaret	Albuquerque, Bernalillo	D	1931 1933
Honeyfield, Hilda	Las Vegas, San Miguel	D	1939
Hood, Norma P.	Albuquerque, Bernalillo	R	1983 1985
Hoover, Louise W.	Santa Fe, Santa Fe	R	1947 1949
Hundley, Adele Cinelli *see Cinelli*	Albuquerque, Bernalillo	D	1979 1981
Johnson, Elizabeth C.	Cuba, Sandoval	D	1979*
Kittell, Virginia A.	Bloomfield, San Juan	R	1947 1949
Lambert, Martha L.	Albuquerque, Bernalillo	R	1981 1983 1985 1987 1989 1991 1993
Lane, Nancy	Santa Fe, Santa Fe	D	1933
Larkin, Anna S.	East Las Vegas, San Miguel	R	1927*
Linard, Sharlyn	Las Cruces, Dona Ana	D	1975 1977
Love, Ida Viola	Raton, Colfax	D	1937 1939 1941 1943
Lovejoy, Lynda Morgan *see Morgan*	Crownpoint, McKinley	D	1995
Lyon, Mary Lou	Los Alamos, Los Alamos	D	1955
Mann, Irene	Albuquerque, Bernalillo	R	1957
Masters, Cecilia R. Rosale *see Rosale*	Gallup, McKinley	R	1981
McDowell, Susan	Clovis, Curry	R	1985
McGaffey-Brown, Luella	Roswell, Chaves	D	1927 1933 1935 1937 1939
McNeill, Muriel	Hobbs, Lea	D	1971
Morgan, Lynda M. *see Lovejoy*	Crownpoint, McKinley	D	1989 1991 1993
Neal, Margaret	Santa Fe, Santa Fe	D	1939
Ortiz Y. Pino, Concha De	Galisteo, Santa Fe	D	1937 1939 1941
Palmer, Charlotte	Taos, Taos	R	1925
Paxton, Bertha M.	Las Cruces, Dona Ana	D	1923

Perez, Angie Vigil	Santa Fe, Santa Fe	D	1987 1989 1991 1993
Picraux, Danice R.	Albuquerque, Bernalillo	D	1991 1993 1995
Portwood, Mabel Upton	Deming, Luna	D	1927 1939
Pratt, Judith A.	Albuquerque, Bernalillo	D	1979 1981 1983
Reynolds, Viola K.	Raton, Colfax	D	1945 1947 1949
Ringler, Louise A.	Albuquerque, Bernalillo	D	1937
Roberts, Earlene	Lovington, Lea	R	1989 1991 1993 1995
Rodella, Debbie A.	San Juan Pueblo, Rio Arriba	D	1993 1995
Rogers, Mary B.	Albuquerque, Bernalillo	D	1941 1943 1945
Rosales, Cecilia R.	Gallup, McKinley	R	1979
Saiz, Porfirria Hidalgo	Mangas, Catron	D	1931
Scott, Deloma A.	Alamogordo, Otero	D	1965* 1967 1969
Soper, Ruth	Deming, Luna	D	1941
Stewart, Mimi	Albuquerque, Bernalillo	D	1995
Strong, Clara F.	Albuquerque, Bernalillo	R	1927
Taichert, Ruth	Santa Fe, Santa Fe	D	1951
Thompson, Lillian B.	Gallup, McKinley	D	1949 1951 1953
Thompson, Mary L.	Las Cruces, Dona Ana	R	1981 1983 1985 1987 1989
Tinker, Carol W.	Las Vegas, San Miguel	R	1969 1971
Townsend, Sandra L.	Aztec, San Juan	R	1995
Trigg, Blanch S.	Fort Sumner, De Baca	D	1929 1931
Trujillo, Patsy G.	Santa Fe, Santa Fe	D	1995
Tucker, Mary	Las Cruces, Dona Ana	D	1983
Tytler, Linda J.	Albuquerque, Bernalillo	R	1983 1985 1987 1989 1991 1993
Vaughn, Gloria	Alamogordo, Otero	R	1995
Wallace, Jeannette O.	Los Alamos, Los Alamos	R	1991 1993 1995
Wells, Helen G.	Mountainair, Torrance	D	1959 1961 1963
Wells, Ima L.	Las Cruces, Dona Ana	D	1993
Whitney-Welles, Darla	Aztec, San Juan	D	1991 1993
Williams, Sheryl M.	Albuquerque, Bernalillo	D	1995
Wolfe, Calla K. Eylar *see Eylar*	La Mesa, Dona Ana	D	1945 1947 1949
Wright, Delores C.	Chaparral, Dona Ana	D	1993 1995

*Notes:

Brubaker, Lucy Keys — Appointed June 4, 1982 (Chavez)
Chacon, Soledad Chavez — Died August 1936
Donisthorpe, Christine A. — Appointed Aug. 1979 (Sitta)
Johnson, Elizabeth C. — Appointed Aug. 20, 1979 (Kloeppel)
Kitzes, Consuelo Jaramillo — Appointed July 25, 1972 (Dilgado)
Larkin, Anna S. — Unseated Feb. 3, 1925 (Gallegos, Democrat seated)
Scott, Deloma A. — Appointed April 1965 (Scott)
Vesely, Edith Huff — Appointed March 1, 1965 (Vesely)

NEW YORK (1919-1995)

New York women gained school suffrage in 1880 and tax and bond suffrage in 1901. A constitutional amendment in 1917 granted women full suffrage. Women first voted in state elections in 1918 and elected Mary M. Lilly (D–New York) and Ida B. Sammis (R–Huntington, Suffolk) to the Assembly.

The New York Legislature held annual state elections to elect 150 assembly members who served one year terms and 51 senators who served two year terms until 1937. Since 1938, all legislators are elected in even years for two year terms. Vacancies are filled by special election.

94 women have served in the New York Legislature:
    20 in the Senate
    79 in the Assembly
    (5 in the Assembly and Senate)

Women as Percentage of New York Legislators

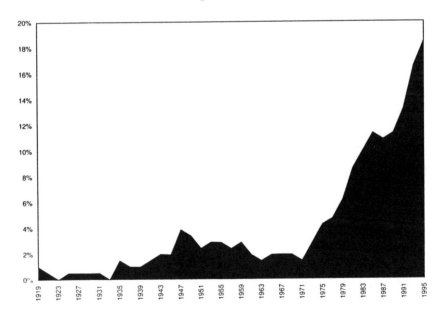

Senate
2 Year Terms

Name	City, County	Party	Legislative Year
Abate, Catherine M.	New York, New York	D	1995
Bellamy, Carol	Brooklyn, Kings	D	1973 1975 1977*
Berman, Carol	Lawrence, Nassau	D	1979 1981 1983
Burstein, Karen S.	Woodmere, Nassau	D	1973 1975 1977
Goodhue, Mary B.	Mt. Kisco, Westchester	R	1979 1981 1983 1985 1987 1989 1991
Gordon, Janet Hill	Norwich, Chenango	R	1959 1961
Graves, Rhoda Fox	Gouverneur, St. Lawrence	R	1935 1937 1939 1941 1943 1945 1947
Hoffmann, Nancy Larraine	Syracuse, Onondaga	D	1985 1987 1989 1991 1993 1995
Jefferson, Anna V.	Brooklyn, Kings	D	1983
Jones, Mary E.	Rochester, Monroe	D	1993 1995
Krupsak, Mary Anne	Amsterdam, Montgomery	D	1973*
Mendez, Olga A.	New York, New York	D	1977* 1979 1981 1983 1985 1987 1989 1991 1993 1995
Montgomery, Velmanette	Brooklyn, Kings	D	1985 1987 1989 1991 1993 1995
Motley, Constance B.	New York, New York	D	1963* 1965*
Oppenheimer, Suzi	Mamaroneck, Westchester	D	1985 1987 1989 1991 1993 1995
Rath, Mary Lou	Amherst, Niagara	R	1995
Santiago, Nellie	Brooklyn, Kings	D	1993 1995
Smith, Ada L.	Brooklyn, Kings	D	1989 1991 1993 1995
Strong, Genesta Mitchell	Plandome, Nassau	R	1959*
Winikow, Linda	Spring Valley, Rockland	D	1975 1977 1979 1981 1983*

House
2 Year Terms (Before 1938, 1 Year Terms)

Name	City, County	Party	Legislative Year
Acampora, Patricia	Riverhead, Suffolk	R	1995
Amatucci, Jean	White Lake, Orange	D	1975 1977
Arroyo, Carmen	Bronx, Bronx	D	1995
Banks, Gladys	Bronx, Bronx	R	1945 1947 1949 1953
Buchanan, Bessie A.	New York, New York	D	1955 1957 1959 1961
Byrne, Doris I.	Bronx, Bronx	D	1934 1935 1936
Calhoun, Nancy	Washingtonville, Orange	R	1991 1993 1995
Cheney, Edith C.	Corning, Steuben	R	1939* 1941 1943

New York House, continued

Name	City, County	Party	Legislative Year
Chisholm, Shirley	Brooklyn, Kings	D	1965 1967
Christensen, Joan	Syracuse, Onondaga	D	1991 1993 1995
Clark, Barbara M.	Queens Village, Queens	D	1987 1989 1991 1993 1995
Connelly, Elizabeth A.	Staten Island, Richmond	D	1973* 1975 1977 1979 1981 1983 1985 1987 1989 1991 1993 1995
Cook, Constance E.	Ithaca, Tompkins	R	1963 1965 1967 1969 1971 1973
Cook, Vivian E.	Jamaica, Queens	D	1991 1993 1995
Cooke, Audre T.	Rochester, Monroe	R	1977* 1979 1981 1983 1985 1987 1989
Daniels, Geraldine L.	New York, New York	D	1981 1983 1985 1987 1989 1991
Davis, Gloria	Bronx, Bronx	D	1981 1983 1985 1987 1989 1991 1993 1995
Destito, Roann M.	Rome, Oneida	D	1993 1995
Diggs, Estella B.	Bronx, Bronx	D	1973 1975 1977 1979
Dugan, Eileen C.	Brooklyn, Kings	D	1981 1983 1985 1987 1989 1991 1993 1995
Ferrara, Donna	Hempstead, Nassau	R	1993 1995
Gadson, Jeannette	Brownsville, Kings	D	1975*
Galef, Sandra R.	Ossining, Westchester	D	1993 1995
Gillen, Mary A.	New York, Kings	D	1941* 1943 1945 1947 1949 1951 1953 1955
Gillette, Elizabeth Van R.	Schenectady, Schenectady	D	1920
Glick, Deborah	New York, New York	D	1991 1993 1995
Goodhue, Mary B.	Mt. Kisco, Westchester	R	1975 1977
Gordon, Janet Hill	Norwich, Chenango	R	1947 1949 1951 1953 1955 1957
Graves, Rhoda Fox	Gouverneur, St. Lawrence	R	1925 1926 1927 1928 1929 1931 1932
Greene, Aurelia	Bronx, Bronx	D	1981* 1985 1987 1989 1991 1993 1995
Gunning, Rosemary R.	Ridgewood, Queens	R	1969 1971 1973 1975
Hague, Joan B.	Glens Falls, Warren	R	1979 1981
Hanniford, Elizabeth	Bronx, Bronx	R	1947 1949
Harrison, Julia	Flushing, Queens	D	1983* 1985*
Hellenbrand, Gail	Brooklyn, Kings	D	1967 1969
Hickey, Eileen M.	Rhinebeck, Duchess	D	1993
Hill, Earlene H.	Hempstead, Nassau	D	1987* 1989 1991 1993 1995
Hochberg, Audrey G.	Scarsdale, Westchester	D	1993 1995

Hoffman, Elizabeth C.	N. Tonawanda, Niagara	R	1993 1995
Jacobs, Rhoda S.	Brooklyn, Kings	D	1979 1981 1983 1985 1987 1989 1991 1993 1995
Jenkins, Cynthia	Jamaica, Queens	D	1983 1985 1987 1989 1991 1993
John, Susan V.	Rochester, Monroe	D	1991 1993 1995
Katz, Melinda	Forest Hills, Queens	D	1995
Krupsak, Mary Anne	Amsterdam, Montgomery	D	1969 1971
Lawrence, Dorothy Bell	New York, New York	R	1959 1961 1963*
Lilly, Mary M.	New York, New York	D	1919
Lipschutz, Gerdi E.	Queens, Queens	D	1975* 1977 1979 1981 1983 1985
Marlatt, Frances K.	Mt. Vernon, Westchester	R	1953* 1955 1957 1959
Marshall, Helen M.	East Elmhurst, Queens	D	1983 1985 1987 1989 1991
Matusow, Naomi C.	Bedford, Westchester	D	1993 1995
Mayersohn, Nettie	Flushing, Queens	D	1983 1985 1987 1989 1991 1993 1995
Mazzarelli, Debra J.	Long Island, Nassau	R	1995
McGee, Mary Rose	Huntington, Suffolk	D	1977
McGee, Patricia K.	Franklinville, Cattaraugus	R	1987* 1989 1991 1993 1995
McPhillips, Mary M.	Middletown, Orange	D	1983 1985 1987 1989
Newburger, May W.	Great Neck, Nassau	D	1979 1981 1983 1985
Nolan, Catherine T.	Ridgewood, Queens	D	1985 1987 1989 1991 1993 1995
O'Neil, Chloe Ann	Hopkinton, St. Lawrence	R	1993* 1995
Patton, Barbara A.	Freeport, Nassau	D	1983 1985 1987*
Pheffer, Audrey I.	Far Rockway, Queens	D	1987* 1989 1991 1993 1995
Rettaliata, Antonia P.	Huntington, Suffolk	R	1979 1981 1983 1985 1987*
Rose, Dorothy H.	Angola, Erie	D	1965 1967
Runyon, Marie M.	New York, New York	D	1975
Ryan, Aileen B.	Bronx, Bronx	D	1959 1961 1963 1965
Sammis, Ida B.	Huntington, Suffolk	R	1919
Shaffer, Gail S.	North Blenheim, Schoharie	D	1981
Singer, Cecile A.	Yonkers, Westchester	R	1989 1991 1993
Siwek, Carol A.	Buffalo, Erie	R	1981
Slaughter, Louise M.	Fairport, Monroe	D	1983 1985
Smith, Marguerite L.	New York, New York	R	1920 1921
Strong, Genesta Mitchell	Plandome, Nassau	R	1945 1947 1949 1951 1953 1955 1957
Sullivan, Florence M.	Brooklyn, Kings	R	1979 1981
Sullivan, Frances I.	Fulton, Oswego	R	1991 1993 1995
Taylor, Mildred Frick	Lyons, Wayne	R	1947 1949 1951 1953 1955 1957 1959
Ten Eyck, Maude E.	New York, New York	R	1947 1949 1951 1953

New York House, continued

Name	City, County	Party	Legislative Year
Todd, Jane Hedges	Tarrytown, Westchester	R	1935 1936 1937 1939 1941 1943
Weinstein, Helene E.	Brooklyn, Kings	D	1981 1983 1985 1987 1989 1991 1993 1995
Wirth, Sandra Lee	Buffalo, Erie	R	1995
Yoswine, Joni	Brooklyn, Kings	D	1991*

*Notes:
Bellamy, Carol — Resigned 1978
Cheney, Edith C. — Elected 1940 (Cheney)
Connelly, Elizabeth A. — Elected Nov. 4, 1973
Cooke, Audre T. — Elected Feb. 14, 1978
Gadson, Jeannette — Elected 1975, resigned 1976
Gillen, Mary A. — Elected March 1942 (Gillen)
Greene, Aurelia — Elected April 1, 1982 (Johnson)
Harrison, Julia — Elected May 23, 1983 (Stavisky), resigned Nov. 1986
Hill, Earlene H. — Elected March 15, 1988 (Patton)[F]
Krupsak, Mary Anne — Resigned Nov. 1974
Lawrence, Dorothy Bell — Resigned 1963
Lipschutz, Gerdi E. — Elected Feb. 19, 1976
Marlatt, Frances K. — Elected 1953
McGee, Patricia K. — Elected June 14, 1987 (Walsh)
Mendez, Olga A. — Elected April 11, 1978
Motley, Constance B. — Elected 1964, resigned Feb. 24, 1965
O'Neil, Chloe Ann — Elected Feb. 1993 (O'Neil)
Patton, Barbara A. — Resigned March 15, 1988 (Hill)[F]
Pheffer, Audrey I. — Elected April 28, 1987
Rettaliata, Antonia P. — Resigned Nov., 1987
Strong, Genesta Mitchell — Resigned due to illness Dec. 1958
Winiklow, Linda — Resigned 1984
Yoswine, Jonie — Elected Feb. 1992 (Miller)

NORTH CAROLINA (1921-1995)

North Carolina women gained suffrage on August 26, 1920. Women first voted in state elections in 1920. In the June state party primaries of 1920, the Buncombe County Democratic party allowed Lillian E. Clement (D–Black Mountain) to run before she could vote. She beat two male candidates and went on to win the November general election to become the first women lawmaker in her state and in the south.

State elections are every two years for 50 senators and 120 representatives for two year terms. Vacancies are filled by governor's appointment.

100 women have served in the North Carolina General Assembly:
  25 in the Senate
  85 in the House
  (10 in the House and Senate)

Women as Percentage
of North Carolina Legislators

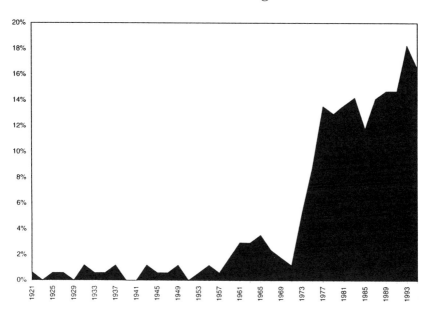

Senate
2 Year Terms

Name	City, County	Party	Legislative Year
Bagnal, Anne	Winston-Salem, Forsyth	R	1979
Brumby, Mary Faye	Murphy, Cherokee	D	1967
Cochrane, Betsy Lane	Advance, Davie	R	1989 1991 1993 1995
Evans, Martha W.	Charlotte, Mecklenburg	D	1965 1967 1969
Ferguson, Sue R.	Taylorsville, Alexander	D	1947
Foxx, Virginia	Banner Elk, Watauga	R	1995
Gray, Rachel Gillean	High Point, Guilford	D	1977 1979 1981 1983
Gunter, Linda	Cary, Wake	D	1993
Hunt, Wanda H.	Chapel Hill, Orange	D	1983 1985 1987 1989*
Little, Teena S.	Southern Pines, Moore	R	1995
Lucas, Jeanne Hopkins	Durham, Durham	D	1993* 1995

North Carolina Senate, continued

Name	City, County	Party	Legislative Year
Marshall, Elaine	Lillington, Harnett	D	1993
Marvin, Helen Rhyne	Gastonia, Gaston	D	1977 1979 1981 1983 1985 1987 1989 1991
Mathis, Carolyn Williamson	Charlotte, Mecklenburg	D	1977 1979 1981
McKee, Gertrude Dills	Sylva, Jackson	D	1931 1937 1943*
Nielson, Geraldine R.	Winston-Salem, Forsyth	R	1967 1969
Odom, Mary Horne	Wagram, Scotland	D	1975
Perdue, Beverly M.	New Bern, Craven	D	1991 1993 1995
Sebo, Katherine Ann Hagen	Greensboro, Guilford	D	1975 1977 1979
Seymour, Mary Powell	Greensboro, Guilford	D	1987 1991 1993
Tally, Lura Self	Fayetteville, Cumberland	D	1983 1985 1987 1989 1991 1993
Wilkie, Elizabeth Anne	Fletcher, Henderson	R	1973
Wilson, Constance K.	Charlotte, Mecklenburg	R	1989*
Winner, Leslie	Charlotte, Mecklenburg	D	1993 1995
Woodard, Wilma Cummings	Garner, Wake	D	1983 1985

House
2 Year Terms

Name	City, County	Party	Legislative Year
Adams, Alma S.	Greensboro, Guilford	D	1993* 1995
Alexander, Julia M.	Charlotte, Mecklenburg	D	1925
Alexander, Martha Bedell	Charlotte, Mecklenburg	D	1993 1995
Barnes, Anne Craig	Chapel Hill, Orange	D	1981* 1983 1985 1987 1989 1991 1993 1995
Berry, Cherie Killan	Newton, Catawba	R	1993 1995
Bissell, Marilyn R.	Charlotte, Mecklenburg	R	1973 1975 1977 1979
Bowie, Joanne W.	Greensboro, Guilford	R	1989 1991 1993 1995
Boyd-McIntyre, Flossie	Jameston, Guilford	D	1995
Brennan, Louise S.	Charlotte, Mecklenburg	D	1977 1979 1981 1983
Brumby, Mary Faye	Murphy, Cherokee	D	1965
Burnley, Dorothy R.	High Point, Guilford	R	1981 1983
Chase, Nancy	Eureka, Wayne	D	1963 1965 1967 1969 1971 1973 1975 1977

Clary, Debbie A.	Shelby, Cleveland	R	1995
Clement, Lillian E.	Black Mountian, Buncombe	D	1921
Cochrane, Betsy Lane	Advance, Davie	R	1981 1983 1985 1987
Colton, Marie W.	Asheville, Buncombe	D	1979 1981 1983 1985 1987 1989 1991 1993
Cook, Elinor C.	Franklin, Macon	R	1961
Cook, Ruth E.	Raleigh, Wake	D	1975 1977 1979 1981 1983
Cover, Lillian M.	Andrews, Cherokee	D	1943 1945 1959
Craven, Jennie G.E.	Charlotte, Mecklenburg	D	1949
Cummings, Frances M.	Lumberton, Robeson	D	1993 1995
Davis, Rachael Darden	Kinston, Lenoir	D	1959 1961 1963
Duncan, Ann Q.	Winston-Salem, Forsyth	R	1985 1987 1989*
Earle, Beverly	Charlotte, Mecklenburg	D	1995
Easterling, Ruth M.	Charlotte, Mecklenburg	D	1977 1979 1981 1983 1985 1987 1989 1991 1993 1995
Ervin, Susan G.	Charlotte, Mecklenburg	D	1949
Esposito, Theresa H.	Winston-Salem, Forsyth	R	1985 1987 1989 1991 1993 1995
Evans, Martha W.	Charlotte, Mecklenburg	D	1963
Fenner, Jeanne	Wilson, Wilson	D	1979* 1981 1983
Fisher, Thelma R.	Brevard, Transylvania	R	1955*
Fletcher, Tressie P.	Taylorsville, Alexander	R	1961
Foster, Jo Graham	Charlotte, Mecklenburg	D	1973 1975 1977 1979 1981 1983 1985 1987 1989 1991
Gardner, Charlotte A.	Salisbury, Rowan	R	1985 1987 1989 1991 1993 1995
Gottovi, Karen	Wilmington, New Hanover	D	1991 1993
Griffin, Pat O.	Durham, Durham	D	1975 1977
Hargett, Iona T.	Trenton, Jones	D	1963* 1965
Hayden, Margaret	Sparta, Alleghany	D	1981* 1983
Holt, Bertha Merrill	Burlington, Alamance	D	1975* 1977 1979 1981 1983 1985 1987 1989 1991 1993
Howard, Julia Craven	Mocksville, Davie	R	1989 1991 1993 1995
Huffman, Doris R.	Newton, Catawba	R	1985 1987 1989 1991
Hunt, Judy Frances	Blowing Rock, Watauga	D	1987 1989 1991 1993*
Hunt, Particia Stanford	Chapel Hill, Orange	D	1973 1975 1977 1979 1981
Hurst, Wilda H.	Hubert, Onslow	D	1975 1977
Hutchins, Effie	Burnsville, Yancey	D	1935 1937
Jarrell, Mary Long	High Point, Guilford	D	1983 1987 1991 1993
Jeffus, Margaret P. *see* Keesee	Greensboro, Guilford	D	1991 1993
Keesee, Margaret P. *see Jeffus*	Greensboro, Guilford	R	1973 1979 1981 1983 1985 1987

North Carolina House, continued

Name	City, County	Party	Legislative Year
Kennedy, Annie Brown	Winston-Salem, Forsyth	D	1979* 1981 1983 1985 1987 1989 1991 1993
Kuczmarski, Erin J.	Raleigh, Wake	D	1993
Lail, Doris L.	Lincolnton, Lincoln	R	1989
Lutz, Edith Ledford	Lawndale, Cleveland	D	1975* 1977 1979 1981 1983 1985 1987 1989 1991 1993
Mathis, Carolyn Williamson	Charlotte, Mecklenburg	R	1973 1975
McAllister, Mary	Fayetteville, Cumberland	D	1991 1993 1995
McLean, Carrie L.	Charlotte, Mecklenburg	D	1927
Mebane, Lillie M.	Spray, Rockingham	D	1931 1933
Mosley, Jane H.	Cary, Wake	D	1993*
Nesbitt, Mary C.	Asheville, Buncombe	D	1975 1977 1979*
Odom, Mary Horne	Wagram, Scotland	D	1971
Pegg, Mary N.	Winston-Salem, Forsyth	R	1979 1981*
Perdue, Beverly M.	New Bern, Craven	D	1987 1989
Phelps, Caredwyn T.	Creswell, Washington	D	1961*
Pickler, Janet W.	New London, Stanley	D	1975* 1977
Preston, Jean Rouse	Emerald Isle, Cateret	R	1993 1995
Pulley, Arlene	Raleigh, Wake	R	1995
Ramsey, Frances C.	Walnut, Madison	R	1965
Roderbough, Grace Taylor	Walnut Cove, Stokes	D	1953 1955 1957 1959 1961 1963 1965
Russell, Carolyn	Goldsboro, Wayne	R	1991 1993 1995
Setzer, Frances E.	Newton, Catawba	D	1975 1977
Seymour, Mary Powell	Greensboro, Guilford	D	1977 1979 1981 1983
Sharpe, Joanne	Greensboro, Guilford	R	1995
Sherrill, Wilma	Asheville, Buncombe	R	1995
Shubert, Fern Haywood	Marshville, Union	R	1995
Stamey, Margaret	Raleigh, Wake	D	1983 1985 1987 1989 1991 1993*
Tally, Lura Self	Fayetteville, Cumberland	D	1973 1975 1977 1979 1981
Tennille, Margaret	Winston-Salem, Forsyth	D	1975 1977 1979 1981 1983
Thomas, Betty Dorton	Concord, Cabarrus	D	1975* 1977 1979 1981 1983
Thompson, Sharon A.	Durham, Durham	D	1987 1989
Tomlin, Frances F.	Concord, Cabarrus	R	1973
Walker, Lois S.	Statesville, Iredell	R	1985 1987 1989
Watson, Cynthia	Rose Hill, Duplin	R	1995
Wilson, Constance K.	Charlotte, Mecklenburg	R	1993 1995
Wilson, Peggy Ann	Madison, Madison	R	1989 1991 1993*
Wiseman, Myrtle Lura Belle	Spruce Pine, Avery	D	1975 1977

Wiser, Betty H.   Raleigh, Wake   D   1985 1987 1989
Woodard, Wilma C.   Garner, Wake   D   1977* 1979 1981

*Notes:
Adams, Alma S.—Appointed April 7, 1994 (Gist)
Barnes, Anne Craig—Appointed Dec. 11, 1981 (P.Hunt)[F]
Duncan, Ann Q.—Resigned Sept. 29, 1989
Fenner, Jeanne—Appointed May 20, 1980
Fisher, Thelma R.—Appointed April 26, 1955 (Fisher)
Hargett, Iona T.—Dec. 18, 1962 (Hargett)
Holt, Bertha Merrill—Appointed Aug. 16, 1975 (Long)
Hunt, Judy Frances—Resigned July 26, 1993 (Cromer)
Hunt, Wanda—Resigned Jan. 31, 1990
Kennedy, Annie Brown—Appointed Oct. 19, 1979
Lucas, Jeanne Hopkins—Appointed July 30, 1993 (R. Hunt)
Lutz, Edith Ledford—Appointed May 3, 1976 (Hunt)
McKee, Gertrude Dills—Resigned April 1943, elected and died Nov. 1948
Mosley, Jane H.—Appointed Aug. 31, 1993 (Stamey)[F]
Nesbitt, Mary C.—Died Aug. 1, 1979 (Nesbitt, Son)
Pegg, Mary N.—Resigned Aug. 14, 1981
Phelps, Caredwyn T.—Appointed March 30, 1961 (Phelps)
Pickler, Janet W.—Appointed Feb. 25, 1976 (Brown)
Stamey, Margaret—Resigned July 25, 1993 (Mosley)[F]
Thomas, Betty Dorton—Appointed Oct. 21, 1975 (Thomas)
Wilson, Constance K.—Appointed Sept. 1, 1989 (Cobb)
Wilson, Peggy Ann—Resigned July 11, 1993 (Sexton)
Woodard, Wilma C.—Appointed Jan. 13, 1978 (Farmer)

NORTH DAKOTA (1923–1995)

North Dakota women gained school suffrage in 1889 and three years later in 1892 elected the first woman to a state wide office in the United States, State Superintendent of Education Laura J. Eisenhuth, a Democrat. Women won presidential suffrage by legislative enactment in 1917 but had to wait until August 26, 1920 for state suffrage.

Minnie D. Craig (R–Esmond, Benson) and Nellie Dougherty (D–Minot, Ward) became the first women legislators in the 1922 election. Representative Mable Lindgren's daughter, Audrey Lindgren Gruger (D–Seattle, King) served in the Washington House of Representatives 1977–1981.

State elections are held every two years for 98 representatives who serve two year terms and 49 senators who serve four year terms. All party designations for the Non Partisan Voters League and the Independent Voters Association are counted as Independent until 1936 when identification with the national Republican party and the national Democratic party became clear. Vacancies are filled by special election.

90 women have served in the North Dakota Legislative Assembly:
    18 in the Senate
    78 in the House
    (6 in the House and Senate)

Women as Percentage of North Dakota Legislators

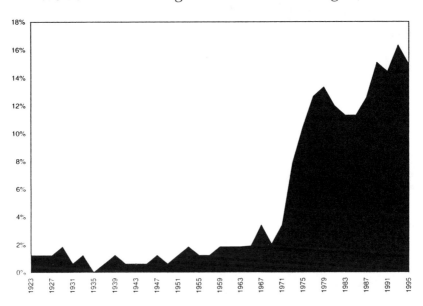

Senate
4 Year Terms

Name	City, County	Party	Legislative Year
Demers, Judy L.	Grand Forks, Grand Forks	D	1993 1995
Evanson, Barbara	Bismarck, Burleigh	R	1991 1993
Fritzell, Stella H.	Grand Forks, Grand Forks	R	1973 1975 1977 1979 1981 1983
Geelan, Agnes Kjorlie	Enderlin, Ransom	R	1951 1953
Heinrich, Bonnie L. Miller *see Miller*	Bismarck, Burleigh	D	1979 1983 1985 1987 1989 1991 1993 1995
Holland, Pamela Krisida	Fargo, Cass	D	1975
Kelly, Particia	Fargo, Cass	D	1991 1993
Krebsbach, Karen K.	Minot, Ward	R	1989 1991 1993 1995

Lee, Judy West	Fargo, Cass	R	1995
Lee, Shirley W.	Turtle Lake, Mclean	R	1973 1975 1977 1979 1981 1983
Meyer, Jerry	Berthold, Ward	D	1983 1985 1987 1989
Miller, Bonnie L. *see* *Heinrich*	Bismarck, Burleigh	D	1977
Mushik, Corliss	Mandan, Morton	D	1985 1987 1989 1991 1993 1995
Nalewaja, Donna	Fargo, Cass	R	1987 1989 1991 1993 1995
Nelson, Carolyn C.	Fargo, Cass	D	1995
O'Brien, Rosamund	Park River, Walsh	D	1953 1955 1957 1959
Scherber, Catherine	Fargo, Cass	D	1993 1995
Tierney, Marie	Bismarck, Burleigh	R	1981
Watne, Darlene	Minot, Ward	R	1995

House
2 Year Terms

Name	City, County	Party	Legislative Year
Allmaras, Lorraine	New Rockford, Eddy	D	1993
Amsberry, Lavina	Wheelock, Williams	NPL	1929
Backlin, Lugale	Bismarck, Burleigh	R	1973
Beauclair, Sister Mary	Carrington, Foster	D	1977
Benedict, Pauline M.	Berthold, Ward	D	1977 1979
Bjornson, Florenz	West Fargo, Cass	R	1979
Black, Rosie	Grand Forks, Grand Forks	R	1977 1979 1981 1983
Brodshaug, Jackie	West Fargo, Cass	D	1993
Cann, Kay	Fargo, Cass	D	1975
Carlson, Sarah A.	Grand Forks, Grand Forks	D	1989 1991
Christenson, Linda	Grand Forks, Grand Forks	D	1995
Christopherson, Chris	Fargo, Cass	R	1993 1995
Cleary, Audrey	Bismarck, Burleigh	D	1991 1993
Cleveland, Connie L.	Grand Forks, Grand Forks	R	1985 1987
Craig, Minnie D.	Esmond, Benson	NPL	1923 1925 1927 1929 1931 1933
Delmore, Lois	Grand Forks, Grand Forks	D	1995
Demers, Judy L.	Grand Forks, Grand Forks	D	1983 1985 1987 1989 1991
Demers, Patricia	Dunseith, Rolette	D	1987 1989
Dietz, Dayle	Wahpeton, Richland	R	1979 1981
Dougherty, Nellie	Minot, Ward	IVA	1923
Eagles, Aloha Taylor	Fargo, Cass	R	1967 1969 1971 1973 1975 1977 1979 1981 1983
Ellingson, Nettie E.	Rugby, Pierce	R	1947
Enget, June Y.	Powers Lake, Burke	D	1985 1987 1989 1991
Ferguson, Helen Carrie	Rugby, Pierce	R	1967

North Dakota House, continued

Name	City, County	Party	Legislative Year
Froeschle, Frances	Fargo, Cass	R	1965
Gilmore, Kathy	Bottineau, Bottineau	D	1989 1991
Gulleson, Pam	Rutland, Sargent	D	1993 1995
Gunter, F. Jane	Towner, Ward	R	1995
Haugland, Brynhild	Minot, Ward	R	1939 1941 1943 1945 1947 1949 1951 1953 1955 1957 1959 1961 1963 1965 1967 1969 1971 1973 1975 1977 1979 1981 1983 1985 1987 1989
Hendrickson, Elynor	Grand Forks, Grand Forks	R	1973
Herman, Jean E.	Fargo, Cass	R	1977 1979
Hill, Julie A.	Roseglen, Mclean	D	1983 1985 1987
Holm, Ruth E.	Fargo, Cass	R	1993 1995
Houmann, Carolyn	Westhope, Bottineau	R	1979 1981
Irving, Terry Kathryn	Grand Forks, Grand Forks	D	1973* 1975
Ista, Susie Jane	Walcott, Richland	R	1939
Jensen, Roxanne	Grand Forks, Grand Forks	R	1989 1991
Kelly, Particia	Fargo, Cass	D	1975 1977 1979 1981 1983 1985 1987 1989
Kelly, Sybil Baker	Devils Lake, Ramsey	R	1959 1961 1963
Kelsch, Rae Ann	Mandan, Morton	R	1991 1993 1995
Kermott, Marjorie L.	Minot, Ward	R	1973 1975 1977 1979
Kliniske, Amy N.	Grand Forks, Grand Forks	R	1995
Lagrave, Violette	Mandan, Morton	R	1973
Larson, Diane	Bismarck, Burleigh	R	1989
Lee, Fern E.	Towner, McHenry	R	1967 1971 1973 1975 1977 1979
Lindgren, Mabel	Minot, Ward	NPL	1929
McCaffrey, Joann Wilkinson	Grand Forks, Grand Forks	D	1977
McGinnis, Mary	Jamestown, Stutsman	NPL	1927
Meiers, Ruth	Ross, Mountrail	D	1975 1977 1979 1981 1983
Miller, Alice	Towner, Mchenry	R	1991
Moum, Dorothy	Ayr, Cass	R	1981
Mushik, Corliss	Mandan, Morton	D	1971 1975 1977 1979 1981 1983
Myrdal, Rosemarie	Edinburg, Walsh	R	1985 1987 1989 1991
Nalewaja, Donna	Fargo, Cass	R	1983 1985
Nelson, Carolyn C.	Fargo, Cass	D	1987 1993
Ness, Diane	Underwood, Mclean	D	1989 1993
Olsen, Dagne B.	Manvel, Grand Forks	R	1981 1983 1985 1987 1989 1991 1993*

Olson, Alice A.	Cavalier, Pembina	R	1973 1975 1977 1979 1981 1983 1985 1987 1989 1991 1993 1995
Olson, Nellie C.	Wilton, Mclean	R	1937
Powers, Anna Bertha Josephine	Leonard, Cass	D	1961 1963 1965 1975 1977
Price, Clara Sue	Minot, Ward	R	1991 1993 1995
Pyle, Barbara	West Fargo, Cass	D	1991 1993
Rathbun, Mary	Crystal, Pembina	IVA	1933
Rayl, Jean	West Fargo, Cass	D	1983
Reed, Burness	Grand Forks, Grand Forks	R	1977 1979 1981
Reiten, Gayle	Grand Forks, Grand Forks	R	1981
Ring, Jennifer E.	Grand Forks, Grand Forks	D	1989 1991 1993
Rydell, Catherine M.	Bismarck, Burleigh	R	1985 1987 1989 1991 1993 1995
Sanderson, Laura	Lamoure, Lamoure	IVA	1925
Sandvig, Sally	Fargo, Cass	D	1995
Sauter, Mary Kay	Grand Forks, Grand Forks	D	1985
Scherber, Catherine	Fargo, Cass	D	1987 1989 1991
Smette, Beth	Newburg, Bottineau	R	1985 1987 1989
Stone, J. Grace	Grand Forks, Grand Forks	R	1967 1969 1971 1973
Vig, Elaine	Grand Forks, Grand Forks	R	1979 1981
Watkins, Cheryl	Fargo, Cass	R	1973 1975
Wentz, Janet Marie	Minot, Ward	R	1975 1977 1979 1981 1983 1985 1987 1989 1991 1993 1995
Williams, Adella J.	Lidgerwood, Richland	D	1983 1985 1987 1989

*Notes:

Irving, Terry Kathryn—Elected Dec. 1973
Olsen, Dagne B.—Died Aug. 20, 1994 (Whide)

**Party Affiliation Before 1936:

Amsberry, Lavina—NPL(R)
Craig, Minnie D.—NPL(R)
Dougherty, Nellie—NPL(D)
Lindgren, Mabel—NPL(R)
McGinnis, Mary—NPL(R)
Rathbun, Mary—IVA(D)
Sanderson, Laura—IVA(R)

NORTHERN MARIANA ISLANDS, Territory of (1977–1995)

Representatives Serafina King (D–Tinian) and Felicidad Ogumoro (R–Saipan) were the first women elected to the Northern Mariana Islands Territorial Legislature.

The Northern Mariana Islands Territorial Legislature has nine senators who are elected for four year terms and fifteen representatives elected for two year terms.

4 women have served in the Northern Mariana Island Territorial Legislature:
   0 in the Senate
   4 in the House

Women as Percentage of Northern Marianas Territorial Legislators

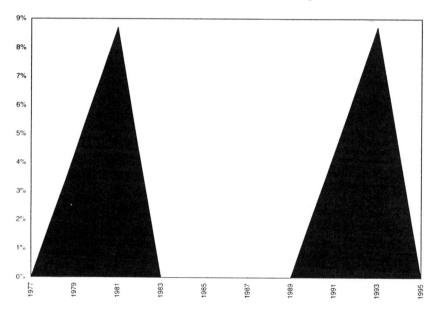

House
2 Year Terms

Name	City, County	Party	Legislative Year
King, Serafina	Tinian	D	1979
Ogumoro, Felicidad	Saipan	R	1979 1981
Peter, Maira T.	Saipan	R	1993
Teregeyo, Ana S.	Saipan	R	1991 1993

OHIO (1923–1995)

Ohio women gained school suffrage in 1891, presidential suffrage by legislative enactment in 1919 and state suffrage on August 26, 1920. In 1922, five women

Women as Percentage of Ohio Legislators

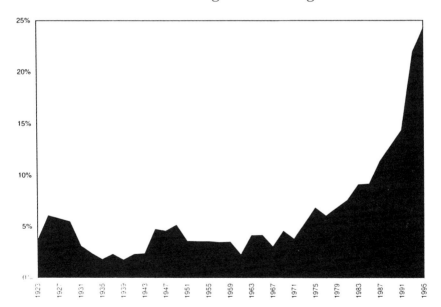

were elected to the Ohio General Assembly. Nettie B. Loughead (R–Cincinnati, Hamilton) and Maude C. Waitt (R–Cleveland, Cuyahoga) were elected to the Senate; Nettie M. Clapp (R–Cleveland, Cuyahoga), Lulu T. Gleason (R–Toledo, Lucas), Adelaide Ott (R–Youngstown, Mahoning) and May M. Van Wye (R–Clifton, Hamilton) were elected to the House.

Ohio elected 137 members to the House and 33 members to the Senate every two years until 1958 when the Senate terms were increased to four years. In 1966 the Ohio House was reduced to the present 99 representatives who serve two year terms. Senators with odd-numbered districts were elected in 1994, and those with even numbered districts were elected in 1996. State legislative service is limited for the House to four consecutive terms and for the Senate to two consecutive terms. Terms are consecutive unless there is a four year break. Vacancies are filled by governor's appointment.

104 served in the Ohio General Assembly:
  18 in the Senate
  94 in the House
  (8 in the House and Senate)

Senate
4 Year Terms (Before 1958, 2 Year Terms)

Name	City, County	Party	Legislative Year
Dix, Nancy Chiles	Hebron, Licking	R	1993* 1995
Dobbs, Catherine R.	Barberton, Summit	D	1949
Drake, Grace L.	Solon, Cuyahoga	R	1985 1987 1989 1991 1993 1995
Furney, Linda J.	Toledo, Lucas	D	1987 1989 1991 1993 1995
Gillmor, Karen L.	Old Fort, Seneca	R	1993 1995
Gorman, Elizabeth F.	Cleveland, Cuyahoga	D	1951 1953 1955
Howard, Janet C.	Forest Park, Hamilton	R	1995
Johnson, Anice W.	Aurora, Portage	R	1973 1975
Kearns, Merle	Springfield, Clark	R	1991* 1993 1995
Loughead, Nettie B.	Cincinnati, Hamilton	R	1923 1925 1927
Mahoney, Margaret A.	Cleveland, Cuyahoga	D	1943 1945 1947 1949
McLlin, Rhine L.	Dayton, Montgomery	D	1995
Montgomery, Betty D.	Perryburg, Lucas	R	1989 1991 1993 1995*
Sheerer, Judy B.	Shaker Heights, Cuyahoga	D	1993* 1995
Valiquette, Marigene	Toledo, Lucas	D	1969 1971 1973 1975 1977 1979 1981 1983 1985
Van Wye, May M.	Clifton, Hamilton	R	1929
Waitt, Maude C.	Lakewood, Cuyahoga	R	1923 1925 1927 1929
Weisenborn, Clara E.	Dayton, Montgomery	R	1967 1969 1971 1973
Wells, Florence	Toledo, Lucas	R	1927

House
2 Year Terms

Name	City, County	Party	Legislative Year
Abel, Mary	Athens, Athens	D	1991 1993 1995
Aveni, Virginia	Lyndhurst, Cuyahoga	D	1975 1977
Babka, Marie	Cleveland, Cuyahoga	D	1949
Barkley, Margaret E.	Cleveland, Cuyahoga	R	1947
Benjamin, Ann Wormer	Aurora, Portage	R	1995
Bergansky, Suzanne M.	Bedford Heights, Cuya-hoga	D	1989 1991
Boster, Jolynn	Gallipolis, Gallia	D	1983 1985 1987 1989
Bowman, Marguerite E.	Elyria, Lorain	R	1981
Boyd, Barbara	Cleveland Heights, Cuya-hoga	D	1993 1995
Boyle, Mary O.	Cleveland Heights, Cuya-hoga	D	1979 1981 1983
Cain, Madeline A.	Lakewood, Cuyahoga	D	1989 1991 1993 1995
Campbell, Jane Louise	Cleveland, Cuyahoga	D	1985 1987 1989 1991 1993 1995
Carr, Judy	Alliance, Stark	D	1993*
Clapp, Nettie M.	Cleveland, Cuyahoga	R	1923 1925 1927 1929
Cramer, Emma M.	Portsmouth, Scioto	R	1929 1931
Cronin, Ila Marshall	E. Liverpool, Columbiana	R	1933
Davidson, Jo Ann	Reynoldsburg, Franklin	R	1981 1983 1985 1987 1989 1991 1993 1995
Davis, Rachel	Sharon, Trumbull	D	1945
Deffler, Edna	Cuyahoga County	R	1981*
Dennison, Margaret	Warren, Trumbull	R	1963 1965 1967
Derr, Clara W.	Cleveland, Cuyahoga	R	1925 1927 1929
Donnelly, Anne M.	Cleveland, Cuyahoga	D	1957 1959 1961 1963 1965
Doty, Karen M.	Akron, Summit	D	1993 1995
Douglass, Joan M.	Mansfield, Richland	R	1973
Edmonston, Golda May	Columbus, Franklin	R	1945 1947 1953 1955 1957
Fisher, Sue J.	New Richmond, Clermont	R	1983
Fix, Helen H.	Cincinnati, Hamilton	R	1975 1977 1979 1981
Ford, Grace V.	Warren, Trumbull	R	1933 1939
Fuller, Eva	Warren, Trumbull	D	1937
Gleason, Lulu T.	Toledo, Lucas	R	1923
Gorman, Elizabeth F.	Cleveland, Cuyahoga	D	1943 1945 1947 1949
Grendell, Diane V.	Chesterland, Geaugu	R	1993 1995
Hanna, Myrna B.	Bowling Green, Wood	R	1929 1931
Harding, Virginia B.	Cheshire, Gallia	D	1927 1931
Hardy, Esther	Fremont, Sandusky	R	1949 1951
Harter, Sophia E.	Akron, Summit	D	1947 1949
Hower, Blanche E.	Akron, Summit	R	1935
Huston, Bertha M.	Napoleon, Henry	R	1943 1945 1947 1949

Ohio House, continued

Name	City, County	Party	Legislative Year
Hyre, Sarah E.	Cleveland, Cuyahoga	R	1929 1931
Johnson, Anice W.	Aurora, Portage	R	1969
Jones, Doris J.	Columbus, Franklin	R	1969 1971
Karmol, Irma L.	Toledo, Lucas	R	1975 1977 1979
Keplinger, Bernice K. *see MacKenzie*	Canton, Stark	D	1941
Kreuzer, June April	Parma, Cuyahoga	D	1983 1985
Lawrence, Joan W.	Galena, Delaware	R	1983 1985 1987 1989 1991 1993 1995
Lloyd, Ruth	Portsmouth, Scioto	D	1935 1937
Lucas, June H.	Mineral Ridge, Trumbull	D	1987 1989 1991 1993 1995
MacKenzie, Bernice Keplinger *see Keplinger*	Canton, Stark	D	1959 1961 1963 1965
Mahoney, Margaret A.	Cleveland, Cuyahoga	D	1939 1941
Makepeace, Grace	Cleveland, Cuyahoga	R	1925
Mayer, Edith P.	Cincinnati, Hamilton	R	1977* 1979 1981
Mayne, Ruth D.	Dayton, Montgomery	R	1951
McLlin, Rhine L.	Dayton, Montgomery	D	1989* 1991 1993
McGovern, Frances	Akron, Summit	D	1955 1957 1959
McGowan, Mary E.	Akron, Summit	D	1963 1965
Mead, Priscilla	Columbus, Franklin	R	1993 1995
Mundy, Opal J.	Toledo, Lucas	R	1945 1947 1951 1953
O'Brien, Jacquelyn K.	Cincinnati, Hamilton	R	1985* 1987 1989 1991 1993 1995
O'Neil, Anna F.	Akron, Summit	D	1933 1937 1939 1941 1943 1945 1947 1949 1951 1953
Ott, Adelaide	Youngstown, Mahoning	R	1923 1925 1927
Padgett, Joy	Coschocton, Coschocton	R	1993 1995
Panehal, Francine M.	Cleveland, Cuyahoga	D	1975 1977 1979 1981 1983 1985 1987
Penny, Osa	Montgomery, Montgomery	R	1925 1927
Perz, Sally	Toledo, Lucas	R	1993 1995
Polcar, Gertrude E.	Parma, Cuyahoga	R	1969 1971
Pope, Donna	Parma, Cuyahoga	R	1971* 1973 1975 1977 1979 1981
Prentiss, Carolyn J.	Cleveland, Cuyahoga	D	1991* 1993 I 1995
Pringle, Barbara C.	Cleveland, Cuyahoga	D	1983 1985 1987 1989 1991 1993 1995
Rankin, Helen	Cincinnati, Hamilton	D	1977* 1979 1981 1983 1985 1987 1989 1991 1993
Reid, Marilyn J.	Beavercreek, Greene	R	1993 1995
Roman, Twyla	Akron, Summit	R	1995
Romans, Viola D.	Columbus, Franklin	R	1925 1927

Ryan, Ann	Canton, Stark	D	1941 1949
Salerno, Amy	Columbus, Franklin	R	1995
Sheerer, Judy B.	Shaker Heights, Cuyahoga	D	1983 1985 1987 1989 1991 1993*
Singer, Arlene	Toledo, Lucas	D	1987
Slagle, Della M.	Youngstown, Mahoning	R	1929 1931 1933
Smart, Irene Balogh	Canton, Stark	D	1973 1975 1977
Smith, Alma	Parma, Cuyahoga	D	1935 1937
Smith, Elizabeth T.	Barbeton, Summit	D	1959
Sotak, Mary K.	Cleveland, Cuyahoga	D	1945
Sutton, Betty Williams see *Williams*	Barberton, Summit	D	1995
Swanbeck, Ethel G.	Huron, Huron	R	1955 1957 1959 1961 1963 1965 1967 1969 1971 1973 1975
Tansey, Marie	Vermillion, Erie	R	1977 1979 1981 1983 1985 1987
Tavares, Charletta B.	Columbus, Franklin	D	1993* 1995
Valentine, Emma P.	Columbus, Franklin	R	1929
Valiquette, Marigene	Toledo, Lucas	D	1963 1965 1967
Van Wye, May M.	Clifton, Hamilton	R	1923 1925 1927
Vesper, Rose	New Richmond, Clermont	R	1993 1995
Walsh, Katherine H.	Oberlin, Lorain	D	1989 1991 1993
Weisenborn, Clara E.	Dayton, Montgomery	R	1953 1955 1957 1959 1961 1963 1965
Wells, Florence	Toledo, Lucas	R	1925
Whalen, Vermel M.	Cleveland, Cuyahoga	D	1987 1989 1991 1993 1995
Williams, Betty see *Sutton*	Barberton, Summit	D	1993
Winkler, Cheryl J.	Cincinnati, Hamilton	R	1991 1993 1995
Woods, Loretta Cooper	Portsmouth, Scioto	R	1951 1953 1955 1957

*Notes:
Carr, Judy—Appointed May 4, 1993 (Carr)
Deffler, Edna—Appointed 1981
Dix, Nancy—Appointed Jan. 4, 1994 (Williams)
Kearns, Merle—Appointed Jan. 7, 1991 (Mottl)
Mayer, Edith P.—Appointed April 1977
McLin, Rhine L.—Appointed 1989 (McLin)
Montgomery, Betty D.—Resigned Nov. 1994, elected Attorney General
O'Brien, Jacquelyn K.—Appointed
Pope, Donna—Appointed 1972
Prentiss, Carolyn J.—Appointed
Rankin, Helen—Appointed (Rankin)
Sheerer, Judy—Resigned Nov. 1992, appointed to Senate (Fingernut)
Tavarres, Charlotte—Appointed July 1, 1993 (Miller)

OKLAHOMA (1921–1995)

Oklahoma women gained school suffrage in 1890 and full suffrage by constitutional amendment in 1918. Women first voted in state elections in 1920 and elected Lamar Looney (D–Hollis, Harmon) to the Senate and Bessie S. McColgin (R–Rankin, Roger Mills) to the House.

State elections are held every two years to elect 99 representatives who serve two year terms and 48 senators who serve four year staggered terms. State legislative service is limited to twelve years. Vacancies are filled by special election.

58 women have served in the Oklahoma Legislature:
   12 in the Senate
   49 in the House
   (3 in the House and Senate)

Women as Percentage of Oklahoma Legislators

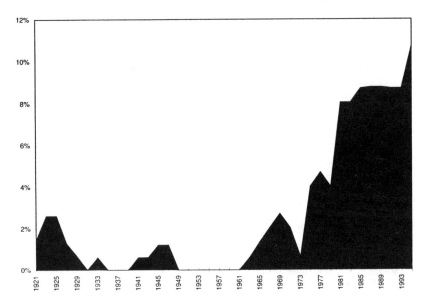

Senate
4 Year Terms

Name	City, County	Party	Legislative Year
Cole, Helen G.	Moore, Cleveland	R	1985 1987 1993 1995
Dudley, Evelyn Kay	Oklahoma City, Oklahoma	R	1987 1989
Floyd, Billie Jean	Ada, Ponotoc	D	1985 1987
Helm, Mary Alnita	Oklahoma City, Oklahoma	R	1975 1977
Horner, Maxine	Tulsa, Tulsa	D	1987 1989 1991 1993 1995
Looney, Lamar	Hollis, Harmon	D	1921 1923 1925 1927
Martin, Carol	Comanche, Stephens	R	1995
Miles-Lagrange, Vicki	Oklahoma City, Oklahoma	D	1987 1989 1991 1993*
Monson, Angela	Oklahoma City, Oklahoma	D	1993* 1995
Shedrick, Mary Bernice	Stillwater, Payne	D	1981 1983 1985 1987 1989 1991 1993 1995
Weedn, Trish Throck-morton	Purcell, Cleveland	D	1989 1991 1993 1995
Williams, Penny Baldwin	Tulsa, Tulsa	D	1989 1991 1993 1995

House
2 Year Terms

Name	City, County	Party	Legislative Year
Anderson, Lulu D.	Drumright, Creek	D	1923
Arnold, Helen T.	Tulsa, Tulsa	R	1977 1979 1981
Askins, Jari	Duncan, Stephens	D	1995
Atkins, Hannah Diggs	Oklahoma City, Oklahoma	D	1969 1971 1973 1975 1977 1979
Baker, Arlene Britton	Oklahoma City, Oklahoma	D	1981 1983
Blackburn, Debbie	Oklahoma City, Oklahoma	D	1995
Boyd, Betty	Tulsa, Tulsa	D	1991 1993 1995
Boyd, Laura W.	Norman, Cleveland	D	1993 1995
Cole, Helen G.	Moore, Cleveland	R	1979 1981 1983
Coleman, Carolyn S.	Moore, Cleveland	R	1991 1993 1995
Collins, Elna Jan	Oklahoma City, Oklahoma	R	1985
Conaghan, Dorothy Dell	Tonkawa, Kay	R	1973* 1975 1977 1979 1981 1983 1985
Dank, Odilia	Oklahoma City, Oklahoma	R	1995
Davis, Ella D.	Norman, Cleveland	D	1933*
Deatherage, Cleta Beth	Norman, Cleveland	D	1977 1979 1981 1983
Eylar, Elma R.	Oklahoma City, Oklahoma	R	1929
Fallin, Mary	Oklahoma City, Oklahoma	R	1991 1993
Gray, Twyla Mason see Mason	Tulsa, Tulsa	D	1983

244   OKLAHOMA (1921–1995)

Oklahoma House, continued

Name	City, County	Party	Legislative Year
Greenwood, Joan	Moore, Cleveland	R	1989 1991 1993 1995
Hamilton, Rebecca	Oklahoma City, Oklahoma	D	1981 1983 1985
Hastings, Joan King	Tulsa, Tulsa	R	1975 1977 1979 1981 1983
Hatchett, Texanna L.	Oklahoma City, Oklahoma	R	1967 1969 1971
Henry, Claudette	Oklahoma City, Oklahoma	R	1987
Hibon, Mina Mae	Norman, Cleveland	R	1973* 1975
Huff, Ila	Oklahoma City, Oklahoma	D	1941 1943
Kincheloe, Maxine Carol	Oklahoma City, Oklahoma	R	1981 1983 1985
Larason, Linda H.	Oklahoma City, Oklahoma	D	1985 1987 1989 1991 1993
Laskey, Anna	Oklahoma City, Oklahoma	D	1923 1925 1927
Mason, Twyla *see* Gray	Tulsa, Tulsa	D	1981
McColgin, Bessie S.	Rankin, Roger Mills	R	1921
Milton, Sue	Midwest City, Oklahoma	R	1985
Mitchell, Edith	Yale, Payne	D	1923
Mitchelson, Grace	Commerce, Payne	D	1945 1947
Monson, Angela	Oklahoma City, Oklahoma	D	1991 1993*
Musser, Alice	Oklahoma City, Oklahoma	D	1989
Patterson, Ruth M.	Guthrie, Logan	R	1965 1967
Peltier, Wanda Jo	Oklahoma City, Oklahoma	D	1987 1989 1991 1993 1995
Robertson, Ida L.	Drumright, Creek	D	1925
Russell, Mona Jean	Picher, Ottawa	D	1945 1947
Staggs, Barbara	Muskogee, Muskogee	D	1995
Swinton, Judy Ann	Oklahoma City, Oklahoma	D	1975 1977
Tabor, Pauline	Durant, Bryan	D	1963 1965 1967 1969
Thompson, Carolyn Ann	Norman, Cleveland	D	1985 1987 1989 1991
Turner, Jan F.	Edmond, Edmond	R	1973
Virtue, Nancy Starr	Norman, Cleveland	D	1983 1985
White, Vickie H.	Norman, Cleveland	D	1987 1989
Whittett, Gladys	McCloud, Pottawatomie	D	1925
Wiedemann, Anna Belle	Piedmont, Canadian	D	1969 1971
Williams, Freddye Harper	Oklahoma City, Oklahoma	D	1981 1983 1985 1987 1989
Williams, Penny Baldwin	Tulsa, Tulsa	D	1981 1983 1985 1987

*Notes:
Conaghan, Dorothy Dell — Elected May 29, 1973 (Conaghan)
Davis, Ella D. — Elected Feb. 22, 1933 (Davis)
Hibon, Mina Mae — Elected Oct. 2, 1973 (Cate)
Miles-Lagrange, Vicki — Resigned Nov. 21, 1993 (Monson)[F]
Monson, Angela — Resigned Nov. 21, 1993 (Toure), elected to Senate (Miles-Lagrange)[F]

OREGON (1915–1995)

Oregon women gained school suffrage in 1878 and full suffrage by a constitutional amendment approved in 1912. Women first voted in state elections in 1914 and elected Marian B. Towne (D–Phoenix, Jackson County) to the House. Following the elections, in December 1912, Governor West appointed Kathryn Clarke (R–Glendale, Douglas County) to fill a Senate vacancy but the legislature refused to accept the appointment. Clarke ran against two male candidates in a special election January 20, 1915 and won.

State elections are held every two years for 60 representatives who serve two year terms and 30 senators who serve four year terms. State legislative service is limited to twelve years. Vacancies are filled by governor's appointment and special election.

102 women have served in the Oregon Legislative Assembly:
  26 in the Senate
  92 in the House
  (16 in the House and Senate)

Women as Percentage of Oregon Legislators

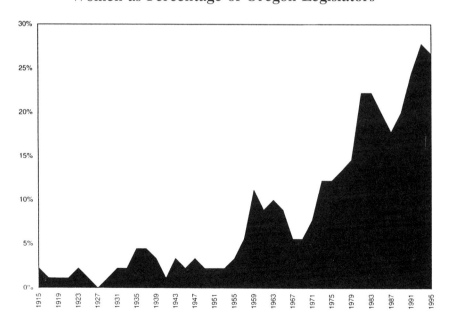

Senate
4 Year Terms

Name	City, County	Party	Legislative Year
Browne, Elizabeth W.	Eugene, Lane	D	1971 1973 1975 1977*
Carnahan, Judy	Portland, Klamath	D	1983*
Cease, Jane	Portland, Multnomah	D	1985 1987 1989 1991*
Clarke, Kathryn	Glendale, Douglas	R	1915*
Cohen, Joyce	Lake Oswego, Clackamas	D	1983 1985 1987 1989 1991 1993
Corbett, Alice	Portland, Multnomah	D	1957* 1959 1961 1963 1965
Dukes, Joan	Astoria, Clatsop	D	1987 1989 1991 1993 1995
Frazier, Marie	Creswell, Lane	D	1987*
Gold, Shirley	Portland, Multnomah	D	1989 1991 1993 1995
Hamby, Jeannette	Hillsboro, Washington	R	1983 1985 1987 1989 1991 1993 1995
Hendriksen, Margie	Eugene, Lane	D	1983 1985
Honeyman, Nanny Wood	Portland, Multnomah	D	1941*
Jolin, Peggy	Cottage Grove, Lane	D	1989 1991 1993*
Karnopp, Lura B.	Portland, Multnomah	R	1943*
Kinney, Mary Strong	Astoria, Clatsop	R	1923 1925
Lee, Dorothy McCullough	Portland, Multnomah	R	1933 1935 1939 1941 1943*
Lewis, Jean L.	Portland, Multnomah	D	1957 1959 1961
McFarland, Ruth	Gresham, Multnomah	D	1981 1983
Roberts, Betty R.	Portland, Multnomah	D	1969 1971 1973 1975 1977*
Roberts, Mary L.	Portland, Multnomah	D	1975 1977
Ryles, Nancy	Portland, Washington	R	1983 1985 1987*
Smith, Trica	Salem, Marion	D	1991 1993
Stull, Shirley	Salem, Marion	R	1995
Webber, Catherine	Salem, Marion	D	1993*
Wilcox, Marie	Grants Pass, Josephine	R	1949 1951
Yih, Mae	Albany, Benton	D	1983 1985 1987 1989 1991 1993 1995

House
2 Year Terms

Name	City, County	Party	Legislative Year
Banzer, Cindy	Portland, Multnomah	D	1985
Bauman, Judith G.	Portland, Multnomah	D	1987 1989 1991*
Bell, Marie	Eugene, Lane	R	1991
Bevans, Daisy B.	Milwaukie, Clackamas	D	1937

Brown, Katherine	Portland, Multnomah	D	1991* 1993 1995
Browne, Elizabeth W.	Eugene, Lane	D	1969
Burrows, Mary		R	1973 1975 1977 1979
McCauley	Eugene, Lane		1981 1983 1985
Carter, Margaret	Portland, Multnomah	D	1985 1987 1989 1991
			1993 1995
Cease, Jane	Portland, Multnomah	D	1979 1981 1983
Chuinard, Fritzi	Portland, Multnomah	R	1961 1963 1965 1967
			1969 1971
Clarno, Beverly A.	Bend, Jefferson	R	1989 1991 1993 1995
Cohen, Joyce	Lake Oswego, Clackamas	D	1979 1981
Cutlip, Stella A.	North Bend, Coos	R	1943
Deboer, Rebecca	Medford, Jackson	R	1981 1983
Dell, Marilyn	Mcminnville, Yamhill	D	1993
Dereli, Margaret			
Ulricka	Salem, Marion	D	1973 1975 1977
Ellis, Anna M.	Garibaldi, Tillamook	R	1943 1945 1947
Fadeley, Nancie		D	1971 1973 1975 1977
Peacocke	Eugene, Lane		1979
Farmer, Annette	Portland, Multnomah	D	1979* 1981 1983
Field, Shirley A.	Portland, Multnomah	R	1957 1959 1963 1965
Ford, Mary Alice	Portland, Washington	R	1979* 1981 1983 1985
			1987 1989 1991
			1993
Gold, Shirley	Portland, Multnomah	D	1981 1983 1985 1987
Gordly, Avel	Portland, Multnomah	D	1991* 1993 1995
Graham, Marva	Portland, Washington	R	1967
Hamby, Jeannette	Hillsboro, Washington	R	1981
Hammerstad, Judi	Lake Oswego, Clackamas	D	1987*
Hand, Beulah J.	Milwaukie, Clackamas	D	1957* 1959 1961 1963
			1965
Hendriksen, Margie	Eugene, Lane	D	1981
Honeyman, Nanny			
Wood	Portland, Multnomah	D	1935
Hooley, Darlene	West Linn, Clackamas	D	1981 1983 1985
			1987*
Jolin, Peggy	Cottage Grove, Lane	D	1981 1983 1985 1987
Jones, Delna	Aloha, Washington	R	1983 1985 1987 1989
			1991 1993
Kafoury, Gretchen	Portland, Multnomah	D	1977 1979 1981
Katz, Vera	Portland, Multnomah	D	1973 1975 1977 1979
			1981 1983 1985
			1987 1989 1991
Kelsay, Elizabeth D.	Roseburg, Douglas	D	1963*
Kinney, Mary Strong	Astoria, Clatsop	R	1921
Kirkpatrick, Nancy	Lebanon, Linn	D	1959 1961 1963
Lee, Dorothy McCul-			
lough	Portland, Multnomah	R	1929 1931
Lewis, Jean L.	Portland, Multnomah	D	1955
Lewis, Leslie	Newberg, Yamhill	R	1995
Lindquist, Robin	Gladstone, Clackamas	D	1983 1985

Oregon House, continued

Name	City, County	Party	Legislative Year
Lokan, Jane	Milwaukie, Clackamas	R	1995
Magruder, Caroline	Clatskanie, Columbia	D	1977* 1979 1981
Magruder, Grace Kent	Clatskanie, Columbia	D	1935 1937
Martin, Hannah K.	Salem, Marion	R	1933 1935 1937 1939
McCready, Connie	Portland, Multnomah	R	1967 1969
Meriwether, Kayne	Salem, Marion	D	1955
Miller, Lois	Portland, Multnomah	R	1977*
Milne, Patricia R.	Woodburn, Marion	R	1993 1995
Munroe, Christina	Hood River, Hood River	D	1937 1939
Musa, Katherine	The Dalles, Wasco	D	1955 1957 1959 1961 1963 1965
Naito, Lisa H.	Portland, Multnomah	D	1991 1993 1995
Neuberger, Maurine B.	Portland, Multnomah	D	1951 1953
Nye, Evelyn	Medford, Jackson	R	1959
Oakley, Carolyn	Albany, Benton	R	1989 1991 1993 1995
Orr, Juanita N.	Lake Grove, Clackamas	D	1959 1961 1963 1965
Paulus, Norma	Salem, Marion	R	1971 1973 1975
Peck, Grace Oliver	Portland, Multnomah	D	1949 1957 1959 1961 1963 1965 1967 1969 1971 1973 1975
Peterson, Nancy	Ashland, Jackson	D	1985 1987 1989 1993
Piercy, Kitty	Eugene, Lane	D	1995
Pisha, Susan C.	Portland, Multnomah	D	1979
Poole, Rose M.	Kalmath Falls, Kalmath	R	1945 1947
Qutub, Elleen	Portland, Multnomah	R	1995
Rasmussen, Anitra	Portland, Multnomah	D	1995
Richards, Sandra L.	Portland, Multnomah	D	1977 1979*
Rieke, Mary W.	Portland, Multnomah	R	1971 1973 1975 1977*
Rijken, Hedy L.	Newport, Benton	D	1989 1991 1993
Roberts, Barbara	Portland, Multnomah	D	1981 1983
Roberts, Betty R.	Portland, Multnomah	D	1965 1967
Roberts, Mary L.	Portland, Multnomah	D	1973
Ross, Barbara	Corvallis, Clatsop	D	1995
Ryles, Nancy	Portland, Washington	R	1979 1981
Shaw, Wickes Sarah A.	Eugene, Lane	D	1959
Shibley, Gail	Portland, Multnomah	D	1991* 1993 1995
Simmons, Effie C.	Portland, Multnomah	R	1923
Simpson, Josephine H.	Portland, Multnomah	R	1979
Smith, Lotta C.	Salem, Marion	R	1931*
Snodgrass, Lynn	Portland, Multnomah	R	1995
Stein, Beverly	Portland, Multnomah	D	1989 1991 1993*
Taylor, Jackie	Astoria, Clatsop	D	1991
Thompson, Sylvia Alexander	The Dalles, Wasco	D	1917 1919
Towne, Marian B.	Phoenix, Jackson	D	1915
Uherbelau, Judy	Ashland, Jackson	D	1995

Vanleeuwen, Liz	Halsay, Linn	R	1981 1983 1985 1987 1989 1991 1993 1995
Wallace, Dorothy	Portland, Multnomah	R	1953
Whiting, Pat	Tigard, Washington	D	1973 1975 1977
Wilcox, Marie	Grants Pass, Josephine	R	1947
Wilmot, Veola Petersen	Eugene, Lane	D	1963*
Wooten, Cynthia	Eugene, Lane	D	1993 1995
Wylie, Sharon	Gresham, Clackamas	D	1993 1995
Yih, Mae	Albany, Benton	D	1977 1979 1981
Zajonc, Donna	Salem, Marion	R	1979 1981 1983

*Notes:
Bauman, Judith G.—Resigned Nov. 1, 1991 (Brown)[F]
Brown, Katherine—Appointed Dec. 1991 (Bauman)[F]
Browne, Elizabeth W.—Resigned July 5, 1977 (Kulongoski)
Carnahan, Judy—Appointed Aug. 18, 1983 (Heard)
Cease, Jane—Resigned July 31, 1991 (Cease)
Clarke, Kathryn—Elected Jan. 20, 1915 (Neuner)
Corbett, Alice—Elected Nov. 1956
Farmer, Annette—Appointed Aug. 1980 (Richards)[F]
Ford, Mary Alice—Appointed 1979 (Ragsdale)
Frazier, Marie—Appointed Aug. 22, 1988 (Frye)
Gordly, Avel—Appointed Sept. 19, 1991 (Cease)
Hammerstad, Judi—Appointed April 28, 1987 (Hooley)[F]
Hand, Beulah J.—Appointed Oct. 25, 1957
Honeyman, Nanny Wood—Appointed July 1941, resigned Oct. 1941
Hooley, Darlene—Resigned April 27, 1987 (Hammestad)[F]
Jolin, Peggy—Resigned March 8, 1993 (Rasmussen)
Karnopp, Lura B.—Appointed Sept. 8, 1943 (Lee)[F]
Kelsay, Elizabeth D.—Appointed Oct. 22, 1963 (Kelsay)
Lee, Dorothy McCullough—Resigned Sept. 9, 1943 (Karnopp)[F]
Magruder, Caroline—Appointed July 18, 1978 (Magruder)
Miller, Lois—Appointed 1978 (Rieke)[F]
Richards, Sandra L.—Resigned Aug. 1980 (Farmer)[F]
Rieke, Mary W.—Died 1978 (Miller)[F]
Roberts, Betty R.—Resigned Sept. 1, 1977
Ryles, Nancy—Resigned May 15, 1987 (Bloom)
Shibley, Gail—Appointed Jan. 16, 1991 (Keisling)
Smith, Lotta C.—Appointed Jan. 2, 1931 (Mott)
Stein, Beverly—Resigned May 1993
Webber, Catherine—Appointed Dec. 1992 (Hill)
Wilmot, Veola Petersen—Elected Jan. 2, 1963

PENNSYLVANIA (1923–1995)

Pennsylvania women gained suffrage on August 26, 1920. Eight women were elected to the Pennsylvania General Assembly in 1922. Alice M. Bentley (R–Meadville, Crawford County), Rosa S. DeYoung (R–Philadelphia, Philadelphia

County), Sarah McCune Gallaher (R–Ebensburg, Cambia County), Helen Grimes (R–Pittsburgh, Allegheny County), Sarah Gertrude MacKinney (R–Chicora, Butler County), Lillie H. Pitts (R–Philadelphia, Philadelphia County), Martha S. Speiser (R–Philadelphia, Philadelphia County), and Martha G. Thomas (R–Whitford, Chester County).

State elections are held every two years for 203 representatives who serve two year terms and 50 senators who serve four year terms. Vacancies are filled by special election.

100 women have served in the Pennsylvania General Assembly:
    6 in the Senate
    95 in the House
    (1 in the House and Senate)

Women as Percentage of Pennsylvania Legislators

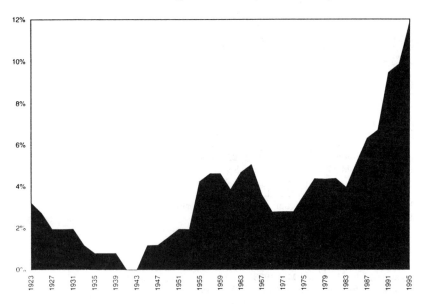

Senate
4 Year Terms

Name	City, County	Party	Legislative Year
Hart, Melissa A.	Allison Park, Allegheny	R	1991 1993 1995
Jones, Roxanne H.	Philadelphia, Philadelphia	D	1985 1987 1989 1991 1993 1995

Reibman, Jeanette F.	Easton, North Hampton	D	1967 1969 1971 1973 1975 1977 1979 1981 1983 1985 1987 1989 1991 1993
Schwartz, Allyson Y.	Philadelphia, Philadelphia	D	1991 1993 1995
Tartaglione, Tina	Philadelphia, Philadelphia	D	1995
Vare, Flora M.	Philadelphia, Philadelphia	R	1925*

House
2 Year Terms

Name	City, County	Party	Legislative Year
Adams, Ella C.	Georges, Fayette	R	1927 1929
Alexander, Jane M.	Dillsburg, York	D	1965 1967
Anderson, Sarah A.	Philadelphia, Philadelphia	D	1955 1957 1959 1961 1963 1965 1967 1969 1971
Arty, Mary Ann	Springfield, Delaware	R	1979 1981 1983 1985 1987
Bard, Ellen	Jenkintown, Montgomery	R	1995
Bebko-Jones, Linda	Erie, Erie	D	1993 1995
Bentley, Alice M.	Meadville, Crawford	R	1923 1925 1927
Bishop, Louise Williams	Philadelphia, Philadelphia	D	1989 1991 1993 1995
Boscola, Lisa	Bethlehem, Northhampton	D	1995
Brancato, Anna M.	Philadelphia, Philadelphia	D	1933 1935 1937 1939 1945
Brown, Teresa E.	Cambridge Springs, Crawford	R	1991 1993 1995
Brugger, Jeanne D.	Wayne, Montgomery	R	1965
Burns, Barbara A.	Pittsburg, Allegheny	D	1993*
Carone, Patricia Ann	Harmony, Butler	D	1991 1993; R 1995
Clark, Rita	Johnstown, Cambria	R	1979
Cohen, Lita Indzel	Merion, Montgomery	R	1993 1995
Coyle, Josephine C.	Philadelphia, Philadelphia	D	1945 1951 1953
Crawford, Patricia A.	Devon, Chester	R	1969 1971 1973 1975
De Young, Rosa S.	Philadelphia, Philadelphia	R	1923
Denman, Mary T.	Labrobe, Westmoreland	R	1931
Donahue, Ruth S.	Lock Haven, Centre	R	1955 1957 1959
Duffy, Mary Alice	Philadelphia, Philadelphia	D	1957
Durham, Kathryn-ann W.	Glen Mills, Delaware	R	1979 1981 1983 1985 1987 1989 1991 1993 1995
Dye, Jeanette M.	Sandy Lake, Mercer	R	1945 1947 1949
Farmer, Elaine F.	Pittsburg, Allegheny	R	1987 1989 1991 1993 1995
Fauset, Crystal Bird	Philadelphia, Philadelphia	D	1939*

Pennsylvania House, continued

Name	City, County	Party	Legislative Year
Fawcett, Charlotte D.	Huntingdon Valley, Montgomery	R	1971 1973 1975
Gallaher, Sarah McCune	Ebensburg, Cambria	R	1923
George, Lourene Walker	Carlisle, Cumberland	R	1963* 1965 1967 1969
George, Margaret H.	Carlisle, Cumberland	D	1977 1979
Gillette, Helen D.	Natrona Heights, Allegheny	D	1967 1969 1971 1973 1975 1977
Grimes, Helen	Pittsburgh, Allegheny	R	1923 1925 1927 1929
Hagarty, Lois Sherman	Bala Cynwyd, Montgomery	R	1979* 1981 1983 1985 1987 1989 1991
Harhart, Julie	North Catsaqua, North Hampton	R	1995
Harley, Ellen A.	Villanova, Montgomery	R	1991 1993
Harper, Ruth B.	Philadelphia, Philadelphia	D	1977 1979 1981 1983 1985 1987 1989 1991
Heiser, Lorraine	Pittsburgh, Allegheny	R	1981
Henzel, Evelyn Glazier	Glenside, Montgomery	R	1955 1957 1959 1961
Honaman, June N.	Landisville, Lancaster	R	1977 1979 1981 1983 1985 1987
Horting, Ruth Grigg	Lancaster, Lancaster	D	1937
Jones, Frances R.	Philadelphia, Philadelphia	D	1959* 1961 1963 1965
Josephs, Babette	Philadelphia, Philadelphia	D	1985 1987 1989 1991 1993 1995
Kelly, Anita Palermo	Philadelphia, Philadelphia	D	1963* 1965 1967 1969 1971 1973 1975 1977
Kernaghan, Mae W.	Yeadon, Delaware	R	1957 1959 1961 1963 1965 1967 1969
Kernick, Phyllis T.	Pittsburgh, Allegheny	D	1975 1977 1979
Kirkbride, Mabelle M.	Norristown, Montgomery	R	1929 1931
Kooker, Margarette S.	Quakertown, Bucks	R	1955 1957 1959 1961 1963 1965
Langtry, Alice S.	Pittsburgh, Allegheny	R	1985 1987 1989 1991
Laughlin, Susan	Conway, Beaver	D	1989 1991 1993 1995
Lederer, Marie A.	Philadelphia, Philadelphia	D	1993 1995
Leiby, Mary E.	Allentown, Lehigh	D	1955
Lewis, Marilyn S.	Schwenksville, Montgomery	R	1979 1981
MacKinney, Sarah Gertrude	Chicora, Butler	R	1923
Maine, Connie G.	Meadville, Crawford	D	1987 1989
Major, Sandra	New Milford, Montgomery	R	1995
Manderino, Kathy M.	Philadelphia, Philadelphia	D	1993 1995

Markley, Marian E.	Macungie, Lehigh	R	1951 1953 1955 1957 1959 1961 1963 1965 1967
McCosker, Henrietta C.	Philadelphia, Philadelphia	R	1947
McHale, Katherine Pecka	Lehigh County, Leghigh	D	1991*
McHugh, Connie	Philadelphia, Philadelphia	R	1991
Miller, Beatrice Z.	Philadelphia, Philadelphia	R	1957 1959
Miller, Sheila M.	Womelsdorf, Berks	R	1993 1995
Monroe, Susie	Philadelphia, Philadelphia	D	1949 1951 1953 1955 1957 1959 1961 1963 1965 1967
Mundy, Phyllis	Kingston, Luzerne	D	1991 1993 1995
Munley, Marion L.	Archbald, Lackawanna	D	1947* 1949 1951 1953 1955 1957 1959 1961 1963
Odorisio, Helen	Wayne, Montgomery	R	1967*
Pashley, Kathryn Graham	Philadelphia, Philadelphia	D	1955 1957 1959 1961 1963 1965
Pennock, Martha M.	Philadelphia, Philadelphia	R	1925 1927 1929 1931 1933
Pitts, Lillie H.	Philadelphia, Philadelphia	R	1923 1925 1927 1929 1931
Reibman, Jeanette F.	Easton, North Hampton	D	1955 1959 1961 1963 1965
Ritter, Karen A.	Allentown, Lehigh	D	1987 1989 1991 1993
Rubley, Carole A.	Wayne, Chester	R	1993 1995
Rudy, Ruth Corman	Centre Hall, Centre	D	1983 1985 1987 1989 1991 1993 1995
Scanlon, Agnes M.	Philadelphia, Philadelphia	D	1977
Sheenan, Colleen	Wayne, Montgomery	R	1995
Sirianni, Carmel A.	Hop Bottom, Susquehanna	R	1975 1977 1979 1981 1983 1985 1987
Speiser, Martha S.	Philadelphia, Philadelphia	R	1923
Steelman, Sara Gerling	Indiana, Indiana	D	1991 1993 1995
Taylor, Elinor Z.	Westchester, Chester	R	1977 1979 1981 1983 1985 1987 1989 1991 1993 1995
Telek, Leona Lee	Johnstown, Cambria	R	1989 1991
Thomas, Martha G.	Whitford, Chester	R	1923 1925
Toll, Rose	Philadelphia, Philadelphia	D	1971 1973 1975
Trescher, Maud B.	Hempfiled, Westmoreland	R	1925*
True, Katie	Lancaster, Lancaster	R	1993 1995
Vance, Patricia H.	Mechanicsburg, Cumberland	R	1991 1993 1995
Varallo, Mary A.	Philadelphia, Philadelphia	D	1947 1949 1951 1953 1955 1957 1959*
Washington, Leanna M.	Philadelphia, Philadelphia	D	1993* 1995

Pennsylvania House, continued

Name	City, County	Party	Legislative Year
Weston, Frances	Philadelphia, Philadelphia	R	1981 1983 1985 1987 1989
Whittlesey, Faith Ryan	Haverford, Delaware	R	1973 1975
Wilson, Jean T.	Warminster, Berks	R	1989 1991
Wilson, Lilith M.	Reading, Berks	Soc	1931 1933 1935
Winter, Elizabeth A.	Philadelphia, Philadelphia	R	1963
Wise, Dr. Helen D.	State College, Centre	D	1977
Wynd, Elisabeth S.	Tunkhannock, Wyoming	R	1961* 1963 1965
Youngblood, Rosita C.	Philadelphia, Philadelphia	D	1993* 1995

*Notes:
Burns, Barbara A.—Elected Feb. 15, 1994 (Murphy)
Fauset, Crystal Bird—Resigned Nov. 1939
Vare, Flora M.—Elected Nov. 1924 (Vare)
George, Lourene Walker—Elected 1962
Hagarty, Lois Sherman—Elected March 11, 1980 (Scirica)
Jones, Frances R.—Elected May 18, 1959 (Jones)
Kelly, Anita Palermo—Elected Nov. 5, 1963 (Kelly)
McHale, Katherine Pecka—Elected May 21, 1991 (McHale)
Munley, Marion L.—Elected Sept. 9, 1947
Odorisio, Helen—Elected 1967 (Odorisio)
Trescher, Maud B.—Only 1925
Varallo, Mary A.—Resigned Jan.4, 1960
Vare, Flora A.—Elected 1925 (Vare)
Washington, Leanna M.—Elected Nov. 22, 1993 (Linton)
Wynd, Elisabeth S.—Elected May 16, 1961 (Wynd)
Youngblood, Rosita C.—Elected March 8, 1994 (O'Donnell)

PUERTO RICO, Territory of (1933–1995)

Puerto Rican women gained suffrage on April 16, 1929 by legislative enactment of the Territorial Legislative Assembly. Women first voted and ran for office in the next territorial elections in 1932. Maria Luisa Arcelay de la Rosa (Union Republicana—Mayaguez) was the first woman elected to the Puerto Rico Legislative Assembly in 1932.

From 1932 to 1965, 32 senators and 65 representatives were elected for four year terms in even years. Since 1968, 27 senators and 51 (or slightly more for party representation) house members are elected for four year terms. The last election was in 1992. Vacancies are filled by governor's appointment. There are no counties in Puerto Rico.

38 women have served in the Puerto Rico Legislative Assembly:
21 in the Senate
17 in the House

Women as Percentage of
Puerto Rican Territorial Legislators

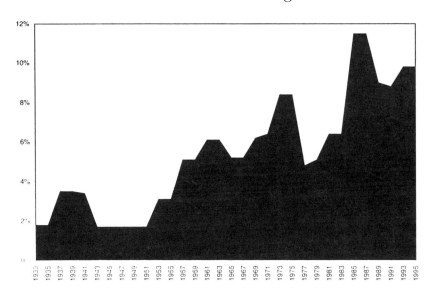

Senate
4 Year Terms

Name	City	Party	Legislative Year
Acevedo De Galarza, Gladys Rosario	Arecibo	PPD	1981 1983 1985 1987
Arroyo De Colon, Maria	Rio Piedras	PPD	1969 1971 1973 1975
Benitez Rivera, Celeste	Cabarra Heights	PPD	1977 1979
Cabassa Vda. De Fajardo, Antonia	Mayaguez	ER	1953 1955 1957 1959 1961 1963
Cabrera De Ibarra, Palmira	Vega Alta	PPD	1957 1959 1961 1963
Calderon De Hernandez, Elsie	Trujillo Alta	PPD	1985 1987 1989 1991
Carranza, Norma L.	Arecibo	PPD	1993 1995
Fernandez, Ruth	Cabarra Heights	PPD	1973 1975 1977 1979

Puerto Rican Territorial Senate, continued

Name	City	Party	Legislative Year
Gonzales Garcia, Velda	Cayey	PPD	1981 1983 1985 1987 1989 1991 1993 1995
Goyco Graziani, Ana Nisi	Ponce	PPD	1981 1983 1985 1987 1989 1991
Lebron Burgos, Luisa	Trujillo Alta	PNP	1993 1995
Martinez De Perez Almiroty, Maria	Humacao	Lib	1937 1939
Mendoza Tio, Angeles	Mayaguez	PNP	1969 1971 1973 1975
Munoz Mendoza, Victoria	Trujillo Alta	PPD	1985 1987 1989 1991
Nazario De Ferrer, Sila	Rio Piedras	PNP	1969 1971 1973 1975
Ojeda De Battle, Josefina	Santurce	PPD	1965 1967
Otero De Ramos, Mercedes	Rio Piedras	PPD	1993 1995
Rivera De Vivaldi, Albita	San Juan	PNP	1985 1987
Rodriguez Mundo, Juana	Rio Piedras	PPD	1953 1955 1957 1959 1961 1963
Santiago De Hernandez, Edma	Aguadilla	PPD	1969 1971 1973 1975
Torres De Perez, Mercedes	Rio Piedras	PNP	1977 1979 1981 1983

House
4 Year Terms

Name	City	Party	Legislative Year
Amadeo, Myrna Passalacqua	San Juan	PNP	1993 1995
Arce De Franklin, Julia	San Juan	ER	1961 1963
Arcelay De La Rosa, Maria Luisa	Mayaguez	URS	1933 1935 1937 1939
Colberg De Rodriquez, Blanca E	Cabo Rojo	PPD	1965 1967
Couto Octaviani, Milagros	Aguadilla	PNP	1985 1987 1989 1991
Cruz De Nigaglioni, Olga	Rio Piedras	PPD	1967 1969 1973 1975 1969 1971
Echevarria, Brunilda Soto	Trujillo Alta	PNP	1993 1995
Gomez Garriga, Maria Libertad	Utuado	PPD	1941 1943 1945 1947 1949 1951 1953 1955
Gonzalez Chapel, Milagros	Arasco	PPD	1957 1959 1961 1963 1965 1967
Hidalgo Diaz, Antonia	Carolina, Carolina	PNP	1973 1975
Llovet Diaz, Josefina	El Comandante	ER	1965 1967*

Marin Vda. Munoz Rivera, Amali	Mayaguez	Pop	1941*
Monrozeau Martinez, Celia C.	Hatillo	PNP	1977 1979
Sola De Pereira, Carmen	Ponce	PPD	1957 1959 1961 1963 1965 1967
Torres, Lisette Diaz	Naranjito	PNP	1993 1995
Torres, Zaida Hernandez	San Juan	PNP	1985 1987 1989 1991 1993 1995
Velez De Acevedo, Mabel	Aguadilla	PPD	1981 1983 1985 1987 1989 1991

Political Parties:
ER: Republican Statehood; Partido Estadista Republicano
Lib: Liberal; Partido Liberal
PNP: New Progressive (R); Partido Nuevo Progresista
Pop: Popular; Partido Popular
PPD: Popular Democrat (D); Partido Popular Democratico
URS: Republican socialist Union; Union Republicana-Socialista

*Notes:
Marin Vda. Munoz Rivera, Amali—Appointed 1942 (Garcia), resigned 1943 (Laboy)
Llovet Diaz, Josefina—Died April 25, 1967

RHODE ISLAND (1923–1995)

Rhode Island women gained presidential suffrage by legislative enactment in 1917 and state suffrage on August 26, 1920. Women first voted and ran for state offices in 1920. Isabella Ahearn O'Neill (D–Providence, Providence) became the first woman legislator in 1922 when she won a House seat.

State elections are held every two years for 100 representatives who serve two year terms and 50 senators who serve four year terms. Reapportionment elections were held for the Senate in June 1983. Vacancies are filled by special election.

93 women have served in the Rhode Island General Assembly:
    31 in the Senate
    68 in the House
    (6 in the House and Senate)

Women as Percentage of Rhode Island Legislators

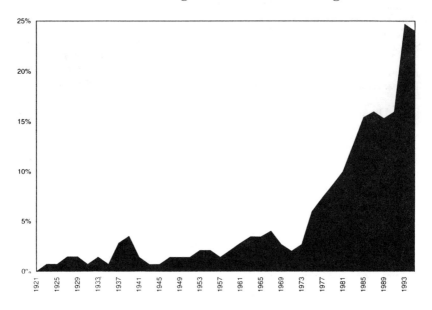

Senate
2 Year Terms

Name	City, County	Party	Legislative Year
Brightman, Gladys M.	Bristol, Bristol	D	1957 1959 1961
Cesario, Elizabeth M.	Woonsocket, Providence	R	1983*
Day, Jennie D.	Coventry, Kent	D	1985 1987 1989 1991 1993 1995
Fleck, Gloria Kennedy	Warwick, Kent	D	1977 1979 1981 1983*
Foster, Millicent S.	N. Kingstown, Washington	R	1967* 1969
Gencarelli, Jane B.	New Shoreham, Washington	R	1983* 1985 1987
Gibbs, June N.	Middletown, Newport	R	1985 1987 1989 1991 1993 1995
Goodwin, Maryellen	Providence, Providence	D	1987 1989 1991 1993 1995
Graziano, Catherine E.	Providence, Providence	D	1993 1995
Grimes, Ruth	Providence, Providence	D	1975 1977
Hanaway, Sandra K.	Cumberland, Providence	D	1991* 1993 1995
Hanson, Ann H.	Barrington, Bristol	R	1983* 1985 1987 1989 1991
Lederberg, Victoria	Providence, Providence	D	1985 1987 1989

Logee, Edith C.	Burrillville, Providence	R	1939
Mathieu, Helen M.	Portsmouth, Newport	D	1987 1989 1991 1993 1995
Misek, Rita K.	Cumberland, Providence	R	1983*
Murray, Florence K.	Newport, Newport	D	1949 1951 1953 1955
O'Neill, Isabella Ahearn	Providence, Providence	D	1931 1933*
Paiva-Weed, M. Teresa	Newport, Newport	D	1993 1995
Parella, Mary A.	Bristol, Bristol	R	1993 1995
Perry, Rhoda E.	Providence, Providence	D	1991 1993 1995
Sapinsley, Lila M.	Providence, Providence	R	1973 1975 1977 1979 1981 1983
Sasso, Eleanor C.	Cranston, Providence	D	1979 1981 1983 1985 1987 1989 1991 1993 1995
Schlesinger, Lulu Mowry	Charlestown, Washington	R	1929
Shannon, Marilyn	Pawtucket, Providence	D	1981 1983
Slater, Eleanor Frances	Warwick, Kent	D	1967
Smith, Irene P.	Burrillville, Providence	D	1977 1979 1981 1983
Stewart, Bonnie W.	Warwick, Kent	R	1983* 1985 1987 1989
Wiesner, Joan R.	Harrisville, Providence	R	1983* 1985 1987 1989
York, Myrth	Providence, Providence	D	1991 1993
Zanni, Vilma	Johnston, Providence	R	1983*

House
2 Year Terms

Name	City, County	Party	Legislative Year
Ajello, Edith J.	Providence, Providence	D	1993 1995
Anderson, Mabel M.	Pawtucket, Providence	D	1983 1985 1987 1989 1991 1993 1995
Barone, Sandra M.	Barrington, Bristol	D	1991 1993 1995
Benoit, Nancy L.	Woonsocket, Providence	D	1985 1987 1989 1991 1993 1995
Benson, Melvoid A.	N. Kingstown, Washington	D	1991 1993 1995
Borden, Nancy H.	N. Scituate, Providence	R	1983
Brightman, Gladys M.	Bristol, Bristol	D	1945 1947 1949 1951 1953 1955
Bucci, Elaine T.	N. Providence, Providence	D	1985 1987 1989 1991
Bumpus, Marguerite	Richmond, Providence	D	1995
Burlingame, Barbara C.	Woonsocket, Providence	D	1987*1989 1991 1993 1995
Callahan, Christine H.	Middletown, Newport	R	1987 1989 1991 1993 1995
Cambio, Bambilyn Breece	N. Providence, Providence	D	1993 1995

Rhode Island House, continued

Name	City, County	Party	Legislative Year
Campbell, Sandra J.	Foster, Providence	R	1991 1993 1995
Carpenter, Marsha E.	Foster, Providence	D	1995
Champagne, Jennifer A.	Johnston, Providence	D	1993
Coderre, Elaine A.	Pawtucket, Providence	D	1985 1987 1989 1991 1993 1995
D'Attore, Harriet J.	E. Greenwich, Kent	R	1959* 1961 1963 1965 1967 1969 1971
Deveney, Susan B.	Cranston, Providence	R	1993
Dinsmore, Helen B.	Warwick, Kent	R	1967
Donnelly, Marion G.	Warwick, Kent	D	1979 1981 1983 1985 1987
Edwards, Dorothy B.	Portsmouth, Newport	R	1967 1969 1971 1973 1975 1977 1979
Fagan, Veronica Barrett	Burrillville, Providence	D	1955*
Giannini, Joanne M.	Providence, Providence	D	1995
Hanson, Ann H.	Barrington, Bristol	R	1981 1983*
Healy, Theresa M.	Pawtucket, Providence	D	1977
Henseler, Suzanne M.	N. Kingstown, Washington	D	1983 1985 1987 1989 1991 1993 1995
Hetherington, Nancy	Cranston, Providence	D	1995
Hewett, Anna D.	N. Providence, Providence	D	1933
Iannitelli, Susan	Greenville, Providence	R	1993 1995
Kane, Lorraine L.	Warwick, Kent	R	1977 1979; D 1981 1983 1985
Kelley, Leona A.	Peace Dale, Washington	R	1985 1987 1989 1991 1993 1995
Kellner, Ellen A.	Glocester, Providence	D	1993 1995
Kilmarx, Mary N.	Barrington, Bristol	D	1975 1977 1979
Kiven, Arline R.	Providence, Providence	D	1961 1963 1965
Kushner, Linda J.	Providence, Providence	D	1983 1985 1987 1989 1991 1993
Lafond, Alice E.	N. Smithfield, Providence	D	1935
Lamb, Susan V.	W. Warwick, Kent	D	1937 1939
Lanzi, Beatrice A.	Cranston, Providence	D	1993 1995
Lederberg, Victoria	Providence, Providence	D	1975 1977 1979 1981
Levesque, Mary E.	Jamestown, Newport	D	1989 1991 1993 1995
Lima, Charlene	Providence, Providence	D	1993 1995
Lopes, Maria J.	Adamsville, Newport	D	1989 1991 1993 1995
Love, Lucille A.	Little Compton, Newport	R	1963 1965 1967 1969 1971 1973 1975
Lynch, Gertrude D.	Providence, Providence	D	1953 1955
Maigret, Marueen E.	Warwick, Kent	D	1975 1977 1979 1981 1983
McDermott, Helena E.	Warwick, Kent	D	1977 1979 1981 1983 1985 1987 1989
McMahon, Mary F.	Pawtucket, Providence	D	1981 1983 1985 1987 1989

Melvin, Theresa J.	Cumberland, Providence	R	1983 1985
Migliaccio, Helen	Cranston, Providence	D	1975
Morancy, Elizabeth	Providence, Providence	D	1979 1981 1983 1985 1987
Naughton, Eileen Slattery	Warwick, Kent	D	1993 1995
Nicholson, Barbara W.	Warwick, Kent	R	1967
Nicols, Helen I.	Woonsocket, Providence	D	1983
O'Neill, Isabella Ahearn	Providence, Providence	D	1923 1925 1927 1929
O'Rouke, Jeanne N.	Newport, Newport	D	1977* 1979 1981
Quick, Joan B.	Little Compton, Newport	R	1991 1993 1995
Ross, Mary C.	Providence, Providence	R	1993
Saucier, Emily M.	Providence, Providence	D	1963* 1965
Schlesinger, Lulu Mowry	Charlestown, Washington	R	1927
Shunney, Katherine T.	Woonsocket, Providence	D	1935* 1937 1939 1941 1943 1947
Slater, Eleanor Frances	Warwick, Kent	D	1959 1961 1963 1965
Smith, Clara A.	Newport, Newport	R	1937 1939
Stoddard, E. Louise	Providence, Providence	R	1957 1959
Tootell, Lucy Rawlings	Charlestown, Washington	R	1973 1975
Walter, Mary Lou	Westerly, Washington	R	1985 1987 1989 1991 1993 1995
Williams, Anastasia P.	Providence, Providence	D	1993 1995
Willis, Norma B.	Jamestown, Newport	R	1981 1983 1985 1987
Yatman, Marion F.	Providence, Providence	R	1937 1939 1941

*Notes:

Burlingame, Barbara C. — Elected Nov. 3, 1987 (Brien)
Cesario, Elizabeth M. — Elected reapportionment June 21, 1983
D'Attore, Harriet J. — Elected January, 1960 (D'Attore)
Fagan, Veronica Barrett — Elected February 10, 1956 (Fagan)
Foster, Millicent S. — Elected September 1967 (Percy)
Gencarelli, Jane B. — Elected reapportionment June 21, 1983
Hanaway, Sandra K. — Elected July 9, 1991
Hanson, Ann H. — Resigned, elected reapportionment June 21, 1983 to Senate
Misek, Rita K. — Elected reapportionment June 21, 1983
O'Neill, Isabella Ahearn — Resigned September 1933
O'Rouke, Jeanne N. — Elected May, 1977 (O'Rouke)
Saucier, Emily M. — Elected 1962 (father, Thomas D.)
Shunney, Katherine T. — Elected March, 1936 (brother, Frank D.)
Stewart, Bonnie — Elected reapportionment June 21, 1983
Wiesner, Joan R. — Elected reapportionment June 21, 1983
Zanni, Vilma — Elected reapportionment June 21, 1983

SOUTH CAROLINA (1929–1995)

South Carolina women gained suffrage on August 26, 1920. Women voted but were not allowed to run for the state legislature in November 1920. The General Assembly passed a law March 7, 1921 entitling women to serve in the legislature. The first woman legislator in South Carolina was Senator Mary G. Ellis (D–Coosawhatchie, Jasper County) who was elected in 1928.

State elections are held every two years for 124 representatives who serve two year terms and 46 senators who serve four year terms. Senators are elected at the same time. Senate elections were held in 1996. Vacancies are filled by special election.

54 women have served in the South Carolina General Assembly:
    9 in the Senate
    49 in the House
    (4 in the House and Senate)

Women as Percentage of
South Carolina Legislators

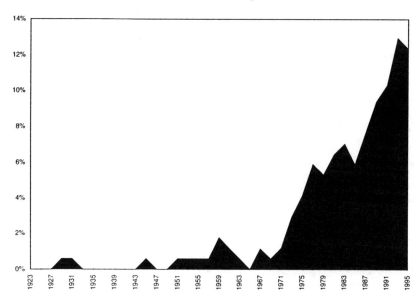

Senate
4 Year Terms

Name	City, County	Party	Legislative Year
Cork, Holly A.	Hilton Head Island, Beaufort	R	1991* 1993 1995
Ellis, Mary Gordon	Coosawhatchie, Jasper	D	1929 1931
Glover, Maggie Wallace	Florence, Florence	D	1993 1995
Martschink, Sherry Shealy *see Shealy*	Mt. Pleasant, Charleston	R	1987* 1989 1991
Mason, Thomasine Grayson	Summerton, Clarendon	D	1967*
Patterson, Elizabeth Johnston	Spartanburg, Spartanburg	D	1979* 1981 1983 1985 1987*
Russell, Norma Caldwell	Columbia, Richland	R	1981 1983
Short, Linda H.	Chester, Chester	D	1993 1995
Smith, Nell Whiteley	Easley, Pickens	D	1981* 1983 1985 1987 1989 1991

House
2 Year Terms

Name	City, County	Party	Legislative Year
Allison, Merita Ann	Lyman, Spartanburg	R	1993 1995
Baskin, Jewel Senn	Columbia, Richland	R	1973 1975
Burch, Kimberly	Chester, Chester	D	1991*
Byrd, Dr. Alma W.	Columbia, Richland	D	1991* 1993 1995
Cobb-Hunter, Gilda Yvette	Orangeburg, Orangeburg	D	1993 1995
Cork, Holly A.	Hilton Head Island, Beaufort	R	1989* 1991*
Council, Brenda	Orangeburg, Orangeburg	R	1991*
Crocker, Virginia L.	Clinton, Laurens	D	1977* 1979 1981 1983
Dreyfus, Sylvia K.	Greenville, Greenville	D	1977
Eargle, M. Lois	Conway, Horry	D	1977 1979 1981 1983
Fitzgerald, Martha Thomas	Columbia, Richland	D	1951 1953 1955 1957 1959 1961
Frederick, Carolyn E.	Greenville, Greenville	R	1967 1969 1971 1973 1975
Gamble, Margaret J.	W. Columbia, Lexington	R	1993 1995
Glover, Maggie Wallace	Florence, Florence	D	1989 1991
Goggins, Juanita W.	Rock Hill, York	D	1975 1977 1979*
Gourdin, Virginia	Charleston, Charleston	D	1959 1961

South Carolina House, continued

Name	City, County	Party	Legislative Year
Harris, Jean Laney	Cheraw, Chesterfield	D	1979 1981 1983 1985 1987 1989 1991 1993 1995
Hearn, Joyce C.	Columbia, Richland	R	1975* 1977 1979 1981 1983 1985 1987 1989
Johnson, Harriet F.	Rock Hill, York	D	1945*
Kempe, Kathleen G.	Inman, Spartanburg	D	1991
Keyserling, Harriet H.	Beaufort, Beaufort	D	1977 1979 1981 1983 1985 1987 1989 1991
Manly, Sarah Gillespie	Greenville, Greenville	D	1989* 1991
McDermott, Emma Jane	Rock Hill, York	D	1953*
Meacham, Rebecca D.	Fort Mill, York	R	1989* 1991 1993 1995
Meyers, Jean B.	Myrtle Beach, Horry	D	1977 1979 1981
Miles, Mary P.	St. Matthews, Calhoun	D	1983
Moody-Lawrence, Bessie	Rock Hill, York	D	1993 1995
Moss, Donna A.	Gaffney, Cherokee	D	1985 1987 1989
Neilson, Denny Woodall	Darlington, Darlington	D	1983* 1985 1987 1989 1991 1993 1995
Rudnick, Irene Krugman	Aiken, Aiken	D	1973 1975 1977 1981 1983 1987 1989 1991 1993
Russell, Norma Caldwell	Columbia, Richland	R	1973 1975 1977 1979
Seithel, Lynn	Charleston, Charleston	R	1995
Shealy, Sherry *see* Martschink	Cayce, Lexington	R	1971 1973
Shelton, Sara V.	Greenville, Greenville	D	1985 1987
Shissias, June Strother	Columbia, Richland	R	1991* 1993 1995
Spearman, Molly Mitchell	Saluda, Saluda	D	1993 1995
Stevenson, Nancy B.	Charleston, Charleston	D	1975 1977
Stuart, Elsie Rast	Pelion, Lexington	R	1993 1995
Taylor, Levola S.	Columbia, Richland	D	1991*
Thomas, Paula H.	Pawleys Island, Georgetown	R	1993 1995
Toal, Jean Hoefer	Columbia, Richland	D	1975 1977 1979 1981 1983 1985 1987
Waites, Candy Y.	Columbia, Richland	D	1987* 1989 1991 1993
Wells, Carole C.	Spartanburg, Spartanburg	R	1987 1989 1991 1993 1995
Wesson, Ruby G.	Spartanburg, Spartanburg	D	1959
Whipper, Lucille Simmons	Mt. Pleasant, Charleston	D	1985* 1987 1989 1991 1993 1995

White, Juanita M.	Hardeeville, Jasper	D	1979* 1981 1983 1985 1987 1989 1991 1993 1995
Williams, Ruth	Charleston, Charleston	D	1963
Wofford, Sandra S.	Ladson, Berkely	R	1989 1991 1993 1995
Young, Annette D.	Summerville, Dorchester	R	1991 1993 1995

*Notes:
Burch, Kimberly — Elected Oct. 15, 1991 (Burch)
Byrd, Dr. Alma W. — Elected June 25, 1991 (Mcbride)
Cork, Holly A. — Elected Oct. 11, 1989 (Cork), resigned March 17, 1992, elected to Senate
   (Waddell)
Council, Brenda — Elected Jan. 28, 1992 (McCain)
Crocker, Virginia L. — Elected May 9, 1978 (Holland)
Goggins, Juanita W. — Resigned Jan. 8, 1980
Hearn, Joyce C. — Elected Dec. 2, 1975 (Lafitte)
Johnson, Harriet F. — Elected Feb. 6, 1945 (Mills)
Manly, Sarah Gillespie — Elected Dec. 6, 1988
Martschink, Sherry Shealy — Elected April 21, 1987 (Ravenel)
Mason, Thomasine Grayson — Elected 1967 for a two year term
McDermott, Emma Jane — Elected July 1953 (Erwin)
Meacham, Rebecca D. — Elected Dec. 6, 1988 (Nesbitt)
Neilson, Denny Woodall — Elected Nov. 7, 1984 (Gardner)
Patterson, Elizabeth Johnston — Elected Dec. 4, 1979 (Stephens), resigned Nov. 7, 1986
Shissias, June Strother — Elected Jan. 7, 1992 (Burriss)
Smith, Nell Whiteley — Elected Nov. 19, 1981 (Smith)
Taylor, Levola S. — Elected June 5, 1991 (Favor)
Waites, Candy Y. — Elected June 14, 1988 (Toal)[F]
Whipper, Lucille Simmons — Elected Aug. 5, 1986 (Woods)
White, Juanita M. — Elected April 8, 1980 (Sauls)

SOUTH DAKOTA (1923–1995)

South Dakota women gained school suffrage in 1887 and full suffrage by constitutional amendment in 1918. Women first voted in state elections in 1920. Gladys Pyle (R–Huron, Beadle), became the first female legislator when she was elected in 1922.

State elections are held every two years for 70 representatives and 35 senators who serve two year terms. State legislative service is limited to four consecutive two year terms. Vacancies are filled by governor's appointment.

78 women have served in the South Dakota State Legislature:
   21 in the Senate
   64 in the House
   (7 in the House and Senate)

Women as Percentage of South Dakota Legislators

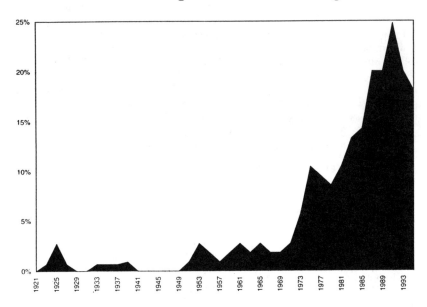

Senate
2 Year Terms

Name	City, County	Party	Legislative Year
Dunn, Rebecca J.	Sioux Falls, Minnehaha	D	1993 1995
Everist, Barbara	Sioux Falls, Minnehaha	R	1995
Green, Sharon V.	Rapid City, Pennington	D	1993
Kelley, Jacquie	Pierre, Hughes	D	1989
Kellogg, Dorothy M.	Watertown, Codington	D	1987 1989 1991
Kelm, Marilyn	Sioux Falls, Minnehaha	D	1975*
Lamont, Frances S.	Aberdeen, Brown	R	1975 1977 1979 1981 1983 1985 1987
Maicki, Carol	Black Hawk, Meade	D	1991
McCart, Elaine L.	Sioux Falls, Minnehaha	D	1975*
McCure, Mary	Redfield, Spink	R	1975 1977 1979 1981 1983 1985 1987 1989
Mickelson, Grace	Rapid City, Pennington	D	1971* 1973 1975
Miner, Doris	Gregory, Gregory	D	1979 1981 1983 1985 1987 1989 1991
Morford-Burg, Joann	Wessington Springs, Jerauld	D	1991 1993 1995
Muenster, Karen	Sioux Falls, Minnehaha	D	1985 1987 1989 1991

Nelson, Pamela A.	Sioux Falls, Minnehaha	D	1989 1991 1993 1995
Olson, Judith R.	Rapid City, Pennington	D	1989 1991
Rasmussen, Roberta A.	Hurley, Turner	D	1991 1993 1995
Sanders, Jessie E.	Hisega, Pennington	D	1937
Saukerson, Eleanor	Chamberlain, Brule	R	1991 1993
Stensland, Linda L.	Sioux Falls, Minnehaha	D	1991 1993
Wagner, Mary K.	Brookings, Brookings	R	1989 1991

House
2 Year Terms

Name	City, County	Party	Legislative Year
Anderson, Debra Rae	Sioux Falls, Minnehaha	R	1977 1979 1981 1983 1985 1987 1989*
Anderson, Eunice M.	Sioux Falls, Minnehaha	R	1965 1967 1969 1971
Barker, Linda K.	Sioux Falls, Minnehaha	D	1993 1995
Beckers, Florence J.	Rapid City, Pennington	R	1951 1953 1955
Beddow, Jean T.	Mitchell, Davison	D	1987 1989 1991
Biever, Violet S.	Oelrichs, Fall River	D	1975 1977 1979 1981
Bliss, Ellen F.	Sioux Falls, Minnehaha	R	1953 1955 1957 1959 1961 1963 1965 1967 1969*
Cruse, Peggy	Pierre, Hughes	D	1987
Davis, Kay	Sioux Falls, Minnehaha	D	1995
Duniphan, J. P.	Rapid City, Pennington	R	1995
Edelen, Mary Beaty	Vermillion, Clay	R	1973 1975 1977 1979 1983 1985 1987 1989 1991
Eidsness, Pat	Brookings, Brookings	R	1995
Eidy, Jean E.	Sioux Falls, Minnehaha	R	1983 1985
Everist, Barbara	Sioux Falls, Minnehaha	R	1993
Fiegen, Kristie K.	Sioux Falls, Minnehaha	R	1993 1995
Fischer-Clemens, Deb	Mitchell, Davison	D	1995
Fitzgerald, Carol E.	Rapid City, Pennington	R	1993 1995
Good, Janet R.	Long Valley, Jackson	D	1991
Greseth, Mona	Claire City, Roberts	R	1991
Halleen, Shirley K.	Sioux Falls, Minnehaha	D	1981 1983
Halling, Beverly	Spear Fish, Lawrence	R	1973 1975 1977
Hassard, Helena B.	Hot Springs, Fall River	R	1995
Hillard, Carole	Rapid City, Pennington	R	1991 1993
Hodges, Joyce E.	Lake Preston, Kingsbury	R	1987 1989 1991 1993
Humphrey, Louise B.	White River, Bennett	R	1959 1961
Hunking, Loila	Sioux Falls, Minnehaha	D	1973 1975
Ingalls, Marie C.	Mud Butte, Meade	R	1987 1989 1991
Johnson, Bernice Carter	Sioux Falls, Minnehaha	R	1977
Johnson, Carol Ann	Frankfort, Spink	R	1989* 1991
Jorgensen, Kay S.	Spearfish, Lawrence	R	1979 1981 1983 1993 1995

South Dakota House, continued

Name	City, County	Party	Legislative Year
Kelley, Celia M.	Mitchell, Davison	R	1925
Kellogg, Dorothy M.	Watertown, Codington	D	1981 1983
Kenner, Patricia E.	Rapid City, Pennington	D	1975 1977
Kotrba, Mary E.	Mitchell, Davison	D	1927
Kuhler, Deborah G.	Huron, Beadle	R	1987 1989
Kumm, Doris	Watertown, Codington	R	1979 1981 1983 1985 1987
Kundert, Alice	Mound City, Campbell	R	1991 1993
Larsen, Henrietta Mateer	Wessington Springs, Jerauld	R	1939
Lewis, Ann M.	Sioux Falls, Minnehaha	R	1985
Lloyd, Alma	Platte, Mix	D	1959*
Lockner, Joanne	Wessington, Beadle	D	1993 1995
Madden, Cheryl	Rapid City, Pennington	R	1993 1995
McKay, Alyce R.	Rapid City, Pennington	R	1983 1985 1987
Miller, Linda Lea *see* Viken	Sioux Falls, Minnehaha	D	1973 1975
Miner, Doris	Gregory, Gregory	D	1977
Moodie, Mabel	Burbank, Union	D	1925
Nelson, Pamela A.	Sioux Falls, Minnehaha	D	1987
Nepstad, Dorothy	Mitchell, Davison	R	1969 1971 1973 1975 1977
Nicolay, Janice K.	Sioux Falls, Minnehaha	R	1983 1985 1987 1989 1991 1993 1995
Olson, Christine	Sioux Falls, Minnehaha	R	1925
Perrigo, Kathleen A.	Rapid City, Pennington	D	1971
Pilcher, Patricia	Sioux Falls, Minnehaha	D	1989 1991
Pyle, Gladys	Huron, Beadle	R	1923 1925
Sanders, Jessie E.	Hisega, Pennington	D	1933 1935
Schreiber, Lola F.	Gettysburg, Potter	R	1987* 1989 1991 1993 1995
Sieh, Edna	Herrick, Gregory	R	1985*
Stensland, Linda L.	Sioux Falls, Minnehaha	D	1987 1989
Sullivan, Agnes C.	Lemmon, Perkins	R	1961 1963 1965
Van Gerpen, Louise	Avon, Bon Homme	R	1983*
Van Wagner, Evelyn	Aberdeen, Brown	R	1953
Vanderlinde, Mary	Sioux Falls, Minnehaha	D	1985 1987 1989 1991 1993
Viken, Linda Lea Miller *see Miller*	Rapid City, Pennington	D	1989 1991
Wagner, Mary K.	Brookings, Brookings	R	1981 1983 1985 1987
Wishard, Della M.	Prairie City, Perkins	R	1985 1987 1989 1991 1993 1995
Wofford, Marion G.	Sioux Falls, Minnehaha	R	1979 1981 1983 1985 1987

*Notes:
Anderson, Debra Rae — Resigned March 6, 1989
Bliss, Ellen F. — Resigned Jan. 23, 1969
Johnson, Carol Ann — Appointed April 27, 1989 (Heidepriem)
Kelm, Marilyn — Resigned Nov. 1975 (McCart)[F]
Lloyd, Alma — Appointed Feb. 9, 1960 (Lloyd)
McCart, Elaine L. — Appointed Nov. 19, 1975 (Kelm)[F]
Mickelson, Grace — Appointed Nov. 25, 1972 (Wallahan)
Schreiber, Lola F. — Appointed Nov. 20, 1987 (Christensen)
Sieh, Edna — Appointed Oct. 20, 1986 (Sieh)
Van Gerpen, Louise — Appointed Nov. 4, 1983 (Van Gerpen)

TENNESSEE (1921–1995)

Tennessee women gained presidential suffrage by legislative enactment in 1919 and state suffrage when the Tennessee state legislature became the final state to ratify the Nineteenth Amendment in 1920. On January 25, 1921, Anna Lee Worley (D–Bluff City, Sullivan County) won a special election to fill the senate seat vacated by the death of her husband. Although her husband had voted against ratification of the Nineteenth Amendment in the Tennessee

Women as Percentage of Tennessee Legislators

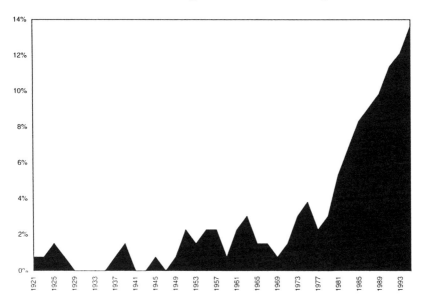

Senate, Anna Lee Worley introduced and won passage of Senate Bill No. 737 to "make women eligible to hold public office in Tennessee." In the next state elections in 1922, Marion Scudder Griffin (D–Memphis, Shelby County) was elected to the House for a full term.

State elections are held every two years for 99 representatives who serve two year terms. Senators served two year terms until 1968 when four year staggered terms were implemented for 33 senators. Odd numbered senate districts were up for re-election in 1994. Vacancies are filled by appointment and special election.

55 women have served in the Tennessee General Assembly:
    12 in the Senate
    47 in the House
    (4 in the House and Senate)

Senate
4 Year Terms (Before 1968, 2 Year Terms)

Name	City, County	Party	Legislative Year
Agee, Tommye	Nashville, Davidson	D	1975*
Anderson, Mary M.	Nashville, Davidson	D	1967
Ashe, Martha H.	Knoxville, Knox	R	1975*
Crow, Norma J.	Lyles, Hickman	R	1981*
Harper, Thelma	Nashville, Davidson	D	1991 1993 1995
Hughes, Mabel Williams	Arlington, Shelby	D	1951 1953 1955
Lashlee, Mildred Louella	Camden, Benton	D	1945
Montgomery, Ruth C.	Kingsport, Sullivan	R	1989 1991
O'Brien, Anna Belle Clement	Crossville, Cumberland	D	1977 1979 1981 1983 1985 1987 1989 1991 1993 1995
Rice, Carol	Clarksville, Montgomery	R	1993 1995
Scott, Lillian Neblitt	Memphis, Shelby	D	1957
Worley, Anna Lee	Bluff City, Sullivan	D	1921*

House
2 Year Terms

Name	City, County	Party	Legislative Year
Anderson, Mary M.	Nashville, Davidson	D	1963 1965 1973
Beavers, Mae	Mt. Juliet, Wilson	R	1995
Bell, Sharon	Knoxville, Knox	R	1979 1981

Bowers, Kathryn I.	Memphis, Shelby	D	1995
Brooks, Henri E.	Memphis, Shelby	D	1993 1995
Brown, Dr. Dorothy L.	Nashville, Davidson	D	1967
Brown, Tommie F.	Chattanooga, Hamilton	D	1993 1995
Brown, Wilma Harrison	Centerville, Hickman	D	1939*
Bushing, Jan Sullivan	Nashville, Davidson	D	1987
Chivers, Stephanie H.	Memphis, Shelby	R	1973*
Chumney, Carol J.	Memphis, Shelby	D	1991 1993 1995
Clark, Sandra	Knoxville, Knox	R	1973 1975
Davis, Anne M.	Knoxville, Knox	R	1925
Davis, Betty Coulter	Kingston, Roane	D	1955 1957 1959 1961 1963
DeBerry, Lois M.	Memphis, Shelby	D	1973 1975 1977 1979 1981 1983 1985 1987 1989 1991 1993 1995
Doyle, Frances	Nashville, Davidson	D	1969 1971
Draper, Maria Peroulas see Peroulas	Knoxville, Knox	R	1991 1993
Duer, Shirley Powell	Crossville, Cumberland	R	1981 1983 1985 1987 1989 1991 1993 1995
Eckles, Mary Ann	Murfreesboro, Rutherford	D	1995
Fleming, Gwen	Bristol, Sullivan	D	1971 1973
Frazier, Sarah Ruth	Chattanooga, Hamilton	D	1927
Gaia, Pam	Memphis, Shelby	D	1975 1977 1979 1981 1983 1985 1987 1989
Griffin, Marian Scudder	Bolivar, Shelby	D	1923
Halteman, Beth	Nashville, Davidson	R	1989 1991 1993 1995
Hassell, Joyce Barnett	Memphis, Shelby	R	1983 1985 1987 1989 1991 1993 1995
Jones, Sherry Stoner	Nashville, Davidson	D	1995
Knight, Peggy Steed	Clarksville, Montgomery	D	1991 1993
Langster, Edith Taylor	Nashville, Davidson	D	1995
Lowe, Joan	Lewisburg, Marshall	D	1981*
McMillan, Kim A.	Clarksville, Montgomery	D	1995
Miller, Elizabeth Lea	Bolivar, Hardeman	D	1925
Montgomery, Ruth C.	Kingsport, Sullivan	R	1981 1983 1985 1987
Moore-Patterson, Dana E.	Bristol, Sullivan	D	1983 1985
O'Brien, Anna Belle Clement	Crossville, Cumberland	D	1975
O'Dell, Ruth Webb	Carson Springs, Cocke	R	1937 1939
Owenby, Mae Stamey	Maryville, Blount	D	1993
Peroulas, Maria see Draper	Knoxville, Knox	R	1985 1987 1989
Pruitt, Mary J.	Nashville, Davidson	D	1985* 1987 1989 1991 1993 1995

Tennessee House, continued

Name	City, County	Party	Legislative Year
Robinson, Ruth M.	Jonesborough, Washington	R	1981* 1983 1985 1987 1989 1991
Scott, Lillian Neblitt	Memphis, Shelby	D	1951 1953 1955
Shadow, Mary	Decatur, Meigs	D	1949 1951
Shook, Katherine C.	Knoxville, Knox	D	1961 1963
Strong, Joan F.	Memphis, Shelby	D	1961 1963 1965
Taylor, Maude T.	Hermitage, Davidson	D	1957
Tullos, Edna H.	Memphis, Shelby	R	1991
Turner, Brenda Kaye	Chattanooga, Hamilton	D	1983* 1985 1987 1989 1991 1993 1995
Williams, Karen R.	Memphis, Shelby	R	1983 1985 1987 1989 1991 1993
Wolfe, Robbie T.	Savannah, Hardin	R	1989*

*Notes:
Agee, Tommye — Elected Nov. 1974 to unexpired term (Agee)
Ashe, Martha H. — Resigned Jan. 7, 1975 (Ashe)
Brown, Wilma Harrison — Elected Jan. 1939 (Brown)
Chivers, Stephanie H. — Appointed Dec. 1972
Crow, Norma J. — Appointed Aug. 24, 1981 (Crow)
Lowe, Joan — Elected March 4, 1981 (Low)
Pruitt, Mary J. — Elected Oct. 15, 1985 (Pruitt)
Robinson, Ruth M. — Appointed Jan. 25, 1982 (Robinson)
Turner, Brenda K. — Elected Nov. 4, 1983 (Davis)
Wolfe, Robbie T. — Appointed Feb. 20, elected May 30, 1989 (Wolfe)
Worley, Anna Lee — Elected Jan. 25, 1921 (Worley)

TEXAS (1923–1995)

Texas women gained primary suffrage by legislative enactment in 1918 and state suffrage on August 26, 1920. Women first voted in state elections in 1920. Women first ran for the state legislature in the state elections in 1922 and Edith E. Wilmans (D–Dallas, Dallas) won a house seat.

State elections are held every two years for 150 representatives who serve two year terms and 31 senators who serve four year terms. Vacancies are filled by special election.

79 women have served in the Texas State Legislature:
    11 in the Senate
    70 in the House
    (2 in the House and Senate)

Women as Percentage of Texas Legislators

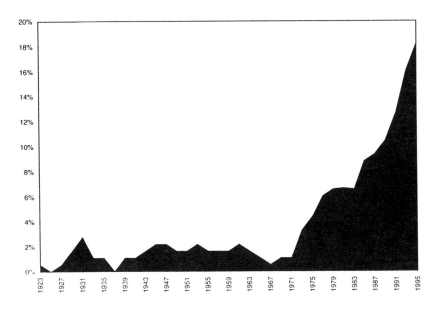

Senate
4 Year Terms

Name	City, County	Party	Legislative Year
Andujar, Betty	Fort Worth, Tarrant	R	1973 1975 1977 1979 1981
Colson, Neveille H.	Navasota, Grimes	D	1949 1951 1953 1955 1957 1959 1961 1963 1965
Johnson, Eddie Bernice	Dallas, Dallas	D	1987 1989 1991*
Jordan, Barbara	Houston, Harris	D	1967 1969 1971
Krier, Cynthia Taylor	San Antonio, Bexar	R	1985 1987 1989 1991
Neal, Margie	Carthage, Panola	D	1927 1929 1931 1933
Nelson, Jane	Lewisville, Denton	R	1993 1995
Rosson, Margaret Ann	El Paso, El Paso	D	1991 1993 1995
Shapiro, Florence	Plano, Collin	R	1993 1995
Stewart, Maribelle	Houston, Harris	D	1947*
Zaffirini, Judith	Laredo, Webb	D	1987 1989 1991 1993 1995

House
2 Year Terms

Name	City, County	Party	Legislative Year
Bailey, Kay	Houston, Harris	R	1973 1975
Banfield, Myra	Rosenberg, Fort Bend	D	1961 1963
Blair, Anita	El Paso, El Paso	D	1953
Bode, Mary Jane	Austin, Travis	D	1977* 1979
Cofer, Lanell	Dallas, Dallas	D	1977* 1979 1981
Colson, Neveille H.	Navasota, Grimes	D	1939 1941 1943 1945 1947
Combs, Susan	Austin, Travis	R	1993 1995
Conley, Karyne Jones	San Antonio, Bexar	D	1989 1991 1993 1995
Cooper, Anne	San Marcos, Hays	R	1985 1987
Danburg, Debra	Houston, Harris	D	1981 1983 1985 1987 1989 1991 1993 1995
Davila, Diana	Houston, Harris	D	1993 1995
Davis, Yvonne	Dallas, Dallas	D	1993 1995
Delco, Wilhelmina R.	Austin, Travis	D	1975 1977 1979 1981 1983 1985 1987 1989 1991 1993
Delisi, Dianne White	Temple, Bell	R	1991 1993 1995
Denny, Mary	Aubrey, Denton	R	1993 1995
Denton, Betty	Waco, McLennan	D	1977 1979 1981 1983 1985 1987 1989 1991 1993
Duff, Virginia	Ferris, Ellis	D	1951 1953 1955 1957 1959 1961
Dukes, Dawnna	Austin, Travis	D	1995
Ehrhardt, Harryette	Dallas, Dallas	D	1995
Farenthold, Frances	Corpus Christi, Nueces	D	1969 1971
Farrar, Jessica	Houston, Harris	D	1995
Fenley, Florence	Uvalde, Uvalde	D	1945
Files, Ray *see Still*	Waxahachie, Ellis	D	1941 1943 1945
Flores, Yolanda Navarro	Houston, Harris	D	1993
Giddings, Helen	Dallas, Dallas	D	1993 1995
Glossbrenner, Ernestine	Alice, Wells	D	1977 1979 1981 1983 1985 1987 1989 1991
Gordon, Margaret Harris	Waco, McLennan	D	1939
Gray, Patricia	Galveston, Galveston	D	1991* 1993 1995
Greenberg, Sherri	Austin, Travis	D	1991 1993 1995
Guerrero, Lena	Austin, Travis	D	1985 1987 1989 1991*
Gurley, Dorothy	Del Rio, Valverde	D	1951 1953
Hairgrove, Sue	Lake Jackson, Brazoria	D	1967*
Hamric, Peggy	Houston, Harris	R	1991* 1993 1995

Name	Location	Party	Years
Hawley, Judy	Portland, San Patrico	D	1995
Henderson, Persis	Groesbeck, Limestone	D	1949*
Hernandez, Christine	San Antonio, Bexar	D	1991 1993 1995
Hill, Anita	Garland, Dallas	D	1979 1981 1983 1985 1987 1989 1991
Hill, Patricia	Dallas, Dallas	R	1983 1985 1987 1989
Hughes, Sarah T.	Dallas, Dallas	D	1931 1933 1935
Isaacks, Maud	El Paso, El Paso	D	1953* 1955 1957 1959 1961 1963 1965
Johnson, Eddie Bernice	Dallas, Dallas	D	1973 1975 1977
Linebarger, Libby	Manchaca, Travis	D	1989 1991 1993
Luna, Vilma	Corpus Christi, Corpus Christi	D	1993* 1995
McBee, Susan Gurley	Del Rio, Valverde	D	1975 1977 1979 1981
McDonald, Nancy	El Paso, El Paso	D	1983* 1985 1987 1989 1991 1993 1995
McKenna, Jan	Arlington, Tarrant	R	1983 1985
Miller, Chris	Fort Worth, Tarrant	D	1973 1975 1977
Moffat, Nancy	Southlake, Tarrant	R	1993 1995
Moore, Helen	Texas City, Galveston	D	1929 1931 1935
Mowery, Anna	Fort Worth, Tarrant	R	1987* 1989 1991 1993 1995
Negley, Laura Burleson	San Antonio, Bexar	D	1929
Park, Carolyn	Bedford, Tarrant	R	1989 1991 1993 1995
Polk, Mary	El Paso, El Paso	D	1979 1981 1983
Rangel, Irma	Kingsville, Kleburg	D	1977 1979 1981 1983 1985 1987 1989 1991 1993 1995
Reyna, Elvira	Mesquite, Dallas	R	1993* 1995
Robinson, Phyllis Marie	Gonzales, Gonzales	D	1983 1985 1987 1989
Romo, Sylvia	San Antonio, Bexar	D	1993 1995
Rountree, Frances M.	Bryan, Brazos	D	1931
Rusling, Barbara	China Spring, McLennan	R	1995
Schechter, Sue A.	Houston, Harris	D	1991 1993
Shea, Gwyn Clarkston	Irving, Dallas	R	1983 1985 1987 1989 1991
Still, Ray Files see Files	Waxahachie, Ellis	D	1947 1949
Strong, Cora G.	Slocum, Anderson	D	1931*
Suiter, Elizabeth	Winnsboro, Wood	D	1943 1945 1947
Sutton, Lou Nelle	San Antonio, Bexar	D	1975* 1977 1979 1981 1983 1985 1987
Thompson, Senfronia	Houston, Harris	D	1973 1975 1977 1979 1981 1983 1985 1987 1989 1991 1993 1995
Van De Putte, Leticia	San Antonio, Bexar	D	1991 1993 1995

Texas House, continued

Name	City, County	Party	Legislative Yea
Weddington, Sarah Ragle	Austin, Travis	D	1973 1975 1977*
Wilmans, Edith E.	Dallas, Dallas	D	1923
Wohlgemuth, Arlene	Burleson, Burleson	R	1995
Woolley, Beverly	Houston, Harris	R	1995

*Notes:
Bode, Mary Jane—Elected Dec. 10, 1977 (Weddington)[F]
Cofer, Lanell—Elected Nov. 29, 1977 (Johnson)[F]
Gray, Patricia—Elected Nov. 3, 1992 (Collazo)
Guerrero, Lena—Resigned Jan. 4, 1991 (Maxey)
Hairgrove, Sue—Elected May 26, 1968 (Hairgrove)
Hamric, Peggy—Elected March 9, 1991 (Connelly)
Henderson, Persis—Elected April 13, 1949 (Henderson)
Isaacks, Maud—Elected March 6, 1954 (father, Isaacks)
Luna, Vilma—Elected May 1, 1993 (Cavasos)
McDonald, Nancy—Elected April 28, 1984 (Polk)[F]
Mowery, Anna—Elected May 7, 1988 (Leonard)
Reyna, Elvira—Elected Nov. 39, 1993 (Blackwood)
Stewart, Maribelle—Elected April 19, 1947 (Stewart)
Strong, Cora G.—Elected 1930 (Strong)
Sutton, Lou Nelle—Elected Aug. 7, 1976 (Sutton)
Weddington, Sarah Ragle—Resigned Sept. 9, 1977 (Bode)[F]

UTAH (1897–1995)

Utah women gained suffrage by territorial legislative enactment in 1870. Women voted in all elections and ran for local offices, but the political parties declared women ineligible for nomination to state legislative and executive offices. The U.S. Congress disenfranchised the women of Utah territory with the Edmund-Tucker Act of 1887 in an attempt to break Mormon political power before granting statehood. By 1894 the U.S. Congress passed an Enabling Act allowing for Utah statehood if an acceptable constitution was approved by the voters. The newly formed Republican and Democratic territorial parties included suffrage for women in their convention planks, but the Democrats also included eligibility for all political offices. The 1895 Constitution approved overwhelmingly by the male voters included full political equality for women. In the next state elections in 1896, women voted and ran for the state legislature. The first female state senator in the United States, Dr. Martha Hughes Cannon (D–Salt Lake City, Salt Lake County), was elected to the Senate and Eurithe LaBarthe (D–Salt Lake City, Salt Lake County) and Sarah Elizabeth N. Anderson (D–Ogden, Weber County) were elected to the House.

State elections are held every two years for 75 representatives who serve two year terms and 25 senators who serve four year terms. State legislative service is limited to twelve consecutive years beginning January 1995. Vacancies are filled by governor's appointment.

124 women have served in the Utah State Legislature:
    15 in the Senate
    115 in the House
    (6 in the Senate and House)

Women as Percentage of Utah Legislators

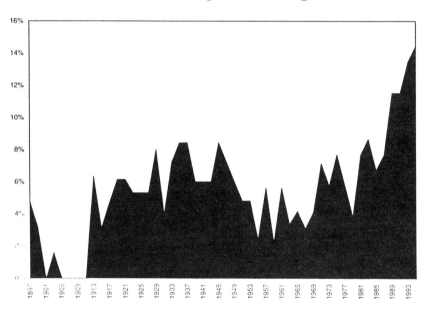

Senate
4 Year Terms

Name	City, County	Party	Legislative Year
Baird, Delpha A.	Salt Lake, Salt Lake	R	1991 1993
Cannon, Martha Hughes	Salt Lake, Salt Lake	D	1897 1899
Erickson, Edna E.	Salt Lake, Salt Lake	D	1941* 1943 1945
Farley, Frances	Salt Lake, Salt Lake	D	1977 1979 1981 1987 1989
Hayward, Elizabeth A.	Salt Lake, Salt Lake	D	1919 1921

Utah Senate, continued

Name	City, County	Party	Legislative Year
Jack, Nellie	Salt Lake, Salt Lake	D	1957*
Jensen, Cleo Lund	Sandy, Salt Lake	D	1939* 1949* 1951
Jensen, Vivian N.	Sandy, Salt Lake	D	1981*
Kinney, Antoinette B.	Salt Lake, Salt Lake	R	1921 1923
Lund, Cornelia	Salt Lake, Salt Lake	D	1937*
Musser, Elise Furer	Salt Lake, Salt Lake	D	1933 1935
Peterson, Millie M.	West Valley, Salt Lake	D	1991 1993 1995
Shepherd, Karen F.	Salt Lake, Salt Lake	D	1991
Stewart, Otella E.	Salt Lake, Salt Lake	D	1935 1937
Wayment, Dona	Clinton, Utah	R	1981* 1983 1985

House
2 Year Terms

Name	City, County	Party	Legislative Year
Abbott, Delila M. Richards	Salt Lake, Salt Lake	R	1957
Aird, Emily D.	Provo, Utah	D	1935 1937
Airey, Dr. Grace Stratton	Salt Lake, Salt Lake	Pro	1917; D 1919
Allen, Daisy C.	Salt Lake, Salt Lake	Pro	1917
Allen, Sheryl	Bountiful, Davis	R	1993* 1995
Anderson, Sarah Elizabeth N.	Ogden, Weber	D	1897
Anderson, Sunday C.	Salt Lake, Salt Lake	D	1951
Atwood, Genevieve	Salt Lake, Salt Lake	R	1975 1977 1979
Baca, Loretta	Salt Lake, Salt Lake	D	1995
Ballif, Algie E.	Provo, Utah	D	1959 1961
Bearnson, Margaret	Salt Lake, Salt Lake	D	1945
Bernard, Milly Oberhansly *see Oberhansly*	Kearns, Salt Lake	D	1973 1975
Blakely, Delora W.	Salt Lake, Salt Lake	D	1919
Bodell, Elizabeth Miller	Salt Lake, Salt Lake	D	1941*
Bosone, Reva Beck	Helper, Carbon	D	1933* 1935
Bradshaw, Afton B.	Salt Lake, Salt Lake	R	1985 1987 1989 1991 1993 1995
Brandt, Jo	Salt Lake, Salt Lake	D	1981
Buffmire, Judy Ann	Salt Lake, Salt Lake	D	1993 1995
Burns, Emma May Copper	Bountiful, Davis	D	1943* 1945
Cahoon, Matilda W.	Salt Lake, Salt Lake	R	1931
Cannon, Anne Wells	Salt Lake, Salt Lake	R	1913
Carlisle, Emily Stevenson M.	Murray, Salt Lake	D	1929
Carlisle, Vervene	Salt Lake, Salt Lake	D	1971* 1975 1977

Carlson, Mary	Salt Lake, Salt Lake	D	1993 1995
Cazier, Edna	Nephi, Juab	D	1949 1951 1953 1955 1957
Christensen, Lois	Provo, Utah	R	1947
Clegg, Cloa	Salt Lake, Salt Lake	R	1921
Conover, Eva W.	Ferron, Emery	D	1963 1965
Cooper, Grace Avery	Price, Carbon	D	1929
Coulter, Mary Anna C. Geigus	Ogden, Weber	R	1903
Cullimore, Odessa	Provo, Utah	D	1949
Dahl, Donna M.	Salt Lake, Salt Lake	R	1981 1983 1985
Davis, May Belle Thurman	Salt Lake, Salt Lake	R	1921
Dillree, Marda	Farmington, Davis	R	1993 1995
Dorman-Ligh, Wyllis	Salt Lake, Salt Lake	D	1977
Dunyon, Lillian F.	Salt Lake, Salt Lake	R	1923 1925
Erickson, Edna E.	Salt Lake, Salt Lake	D	1933
Eubanks, Sara	Salt Lake, Salt Lake	D	1993
Evans, Beverly Ann	Altamont, Duchesne	R	1987 1989 1991 1993 1995
Fanning, Faye B.	Ogden, Weber	D	1961
Florez, Bobby Valdez	Salt Lake, Salt Lake	D	1981* 1983 1985
Forsberg, Sophronia N. C.	Salt Lake, Salt Lake	R	1947
Fox, Christine R.	Lehi, Utah	R	1987* 1989 1991 1993 1995
Garff, Thelma	Salt Lake, Salt Lake	D	1937 1939
Gibson, Rhoda	Helper, Carbon	D	1933* 1935
Graham, Mary McIntosh	Salt Lake, Salt Lake	R	1923 1925
Griffin, Nethella King	Boulder, Garfield	D	1957
Gubler, Darlene	Salt Lake, Salt Lake	R	1995
Hales, Janette C.	Provo, Utah	R	1987* 1989
Halverson, Dionne P.	Ogden, Weber	D	1989* 1991
Harris, Minnie V.	Salt Lake, Salt Lake	D	1933
Hayward, Elizabeth A.	Salt Lake, Salt Lake	Pro	1915 1917
Horne, Alice Merrill	Salt Lake, Salt Lake	D	1899
Jack, Nellie	Salt Lake, Salt Lake	D	1939 1941 1943 1945 1947 1949 1953 1967 1969 1971 1973
Jacob, Maud B.	Provo, Utah	D	1937 1939 1941
Jarman, Beth S.	Bountiful, Davis	D	1975
Jarvis, Clara L.	Salt Lake, Salt Lake	D	1943* 1945
Jensen, Josephine Scott	Salt Lake, Salt Lake	D	1935 1937 1939 1941
Jensen, Lucinda P.	Bear River, Boxelder	R	1929
Jensen, Shirley V.	Sandy, Salt Lake	R	1993 1995
Jensen, Vivian N.	Sandy, Salt Lake	D	1983
Johnson, Henrietta B.	Brigham City, Box Elder	D	1937

Utah House, continued

Name	City, County	Party	Legislative Year
Johnson, Mary L.	Salt Lake, Salt Lake	D	1973 1975
Julander, Paula F.	Salt Lake, Salt Lake	D	1989 1991
Kanig, Lavinia L.	Spanish Fort, Utah	R	1983
Kimball, Margot	Salt Lake, Salt Lake	D	1971*
King, Ann Holden	Salt Lake, Salt Lake	R	1913
LaBarthe, Eurithe K.	Salt Lake, Salt Lake	D	1897
Larson, Patricia B.	Ogden, Weber	D	1991* 1993 1995
Lockman, Sue	Salt Lake, Salt Lake	R	1995
Loveridge, Della L.	Provo, Utah	D	1943 1945 1959 1961 1963 1965 1967 1969
Lowe, Mildred P.	Salt Lake, Salt Lake	R	1927 1931
Lowe, Rozello	Weber, Weber	R	1953*
Lund, Cornelia	Salt Lake, Salt Lake	D	1933
Lyman, Amy Brown	Salt Lake, Salt Lake	R	1923
Lyon, Nancy S.	Bountiful, Davis	R	1989 1991 1993
Maeser, Zelila M.	Logan, Cache	D	1935
Marchant, Beatrice	Salt Lake, Salt Lake	D	1969 1971
Masur, Dorothea E.	Ogden, Weber	R	1981
McGean, Madge	Salt Lake, Salt Lake	D	1941*
Merrill, Frances H.	Salt Lake, Salt Lake	R	1983 1985
Milner, Joanne R.	Salt Lake, Salt Lake	D	1987 1989 1991
Mitchell, Ivie	Sandy, Salt Lake	D	1947* 1949
Mulhall, Alla	Salt Lake, Salt Lake	D	1965
Murdock, Jean Z.	Bountiful, Davis	D	1943*
Nalder, Rebecca A.	Layton, Salt Lake	D	1971 1975
Nix, Pat	Orem, Utah	R	1987 1989
Oberhansley, Milly see Bernard	Kearns, Salt Lake	D	1967 1969 1971
Pastore, Ched	Salt Lake, Salt Lake	D	1981*
Paxman, Achsa Eggertson	Provo, Utah	R	1925 1927
Peterson, Georgia Bodell	West Valley, Salt Lake	R	1969* 1971 1973 1975 1977 1979*
Peterson, Sandra	Salt Lake, Salt Lake	D	1971*
Piercey, Anna Thomas	Salt Lake, Salt Lake	D	1919 1929
Purser, Martha	Magna, Salt Lake	D	1929
Pyne, Ethel	Orem, Utah	R	1947
Read, Edyth E.	Salt Lake, Salt Lake	R	1913
Rich, Mildred F.	Salt Lake, Salt Lake	D	1933
Rose, Janet	Salt Lake, Salt Lake	D	1987 1989 1991
Shumway, Naomi M.	Bountiful, Davis	R	1983
Skolfield, Jane W. Manning	Salt Lake, Salt Lake	R	1913
Smart, Julia	Salt Lake, Salt Lake	R	1925 1927
Smedley, Ann T.	Bountiful, Davis	R	1991*
Smith, Frances B.	Linwood, Dagget	R	1945
Smith, Karen Ann B.	Centerville, Davis	R	1993 1995

Smith, Susan Alice	Linwood, Dagget	R	1943
Stephens, Nora B.	Sunset, Davis	R	1993 1995
Stewart, Otella E.	Salt Lake, Salt Lake	D	1929
Tanner, Laura W.	Salt Lake, Salt Lake	R	1927 1931
Taylor, Lucille	Spanish Fork, Utah	D	1979*
Turner, Joan Redford	Salt Lake, Salt Lake	R	1979*
Urie, Rita Marie	Salt Lake, Salt Lake	D	1973
Vance, Elizabeth	Ogden, Weber	D	1951 1953 1955 1957 1961 1963 1965
Walker, Olene S.	Salt Lake, Salt Lake	R	1981 1983 1985 1987
White, Beverly J.	Tooele, Tooele	D	1971* 1973 1975 1977 1979 1981 1983 1985 1987 1989
Williams, Faye Eliza	Morgan, Morgan	R	1947
Wolstenholme, Lily C.	Salt Lake, Salt Lake	Pro	1915
Woolsey, Nathella Griffen *see Griffen*	Boulder, Garfield	D	1961

Progressive Utah Party: Airey, Allen and Hayward were Democrats, Wolstenholme was a Republican.

*Notes:
Allen, Sheryl—Appointed July 1994 (Burningham)
Bodell, Elizabeth Miller—Appointed March 5, 1941 (Bodell)
Bosone, Reva Beck—Resigned July 1933 (Gibson)[F]; moved to Salt Lake City where she was elected in 1934
Burns, Emma May Copper—Appointed July 1944 (Murdock)[F]
Carlisle, Vervene—Appointed July 1971 (Peterson)[F]
Erickson, Edna E.—Appointed Jan. 20, 1941 (Weggeland)
Florez, Bobby Valdez—Appointed Dec. 10, 1980 (Florez)
Fox, Christine R.—Appointed Aug. 19, 1987 (Fox)
Gibson, Rhoda—Appointed July 1933 (Bosone)[F]
Hales, Janette C.—Appointed July 5, 1988 (Call)
Halverson, Dionne P.—Resigned Feb. 1, 1991 (Larson)[F]
Jack, Nellie—Resigned Nov. 1958 (Jenkins)
Jarvis, Clara L.—Appointed March 1944 (Reed)
Jensen, Cleo Lund—Appointed Nov. 11, 1938 (Lund)[F]; appointed Feb. 14, 1949 (Bailery)
Jensen, Vivian N.—Appointed Dec. 15, 1980 (Jensen)
Kimball, Margot—Appointed Feb. 10, 1972 (Grundfossen)
Larson, Patricia B.—Appointed Feb. 11, 1991 (Halverson)[F]
Lowe, Rozello—Appointed Feb. 27, 1953 (Lower)
Lund, Cornelia—Resigned 1938 (C.Jensen)[F]
McGean, Madge—Appointed 1942 (McGean)
Mitchell, Ivie—Appointed Jan. 13, 1947 (Greenwood)
Murdock, Jean Z.—Died June 12, 1944 (Burns)[F]
Pastore, Ched—Appointed Dec. 15, 1982 (Williams)–Jan. 1, 1983
Peterson, Georgia Bodell—Appointed 1970 (Warnick), resigned March 12, 1979 (Turner)[F]
Peterson, Sandra—Resigned July 19, 1971 (Carlisle)[F]
Smedley, Ann T.—Appointed Jan. 14, 1991
Taylor, Lucille—Appointed March 1979 (Money)
Turner, Joan Redford—Appointed Dec. 11, 1979 (Peterson)[F]
Wayment, Dona—Appointed June 26, 1981 (Wayment)
White, Beverly J.—Appointed March 8, 1971 (Halliady)

VERMONT (1921–1995)

Vermont women gained suffrage on August 26, 1920. Women first voted in state elections in 1920. Women first ran for the state legislature in the state elections in 1920 and elected Edna Beard (R–Orange, Orange County) to the House.

State elections are held every two years for 150 representatives who serve two year terms and 30 senators who serve four year terms. The Vermont House was reduced from 246 to 150 members in the 1966 reforms. Vacancies are filled by governor's appointment.

532 women have served in the Vermont General Assembly:
  46 in the Senate
  515 in the House
  (29 in the House and the Senate)

Women as Percentage of Vermont Legislators

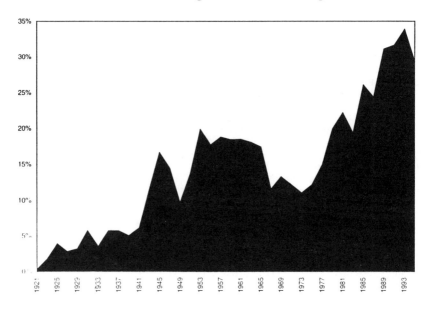

Senate
4 Year Terms

Name	City, County	Party	Legislative Year
Ankeney, Jean B.	Williston, Chittenden	D	1993 1995
Backus, Jan	Brattleboro, Windham	D	1989 1991 1993
Bartlett, Susan	Hyde Park, Lamoille	D	1993 1995
Beard, Edna	Orange, Orange	R	1923
Bickford, Luella F.	Bradford, Orange	R	1933
Brault, Mildred A.	St. Albans, Franklin	D	1959 1961
Bromley, Bernice V.	Weathersfield, Windsor	R	1959
Carlson, Mary Ann	Arlington, Bennington	D	1989 1991 1993
Chard, Nancy I.	Brattleboro, Windham	D	1995
Clark, Geraldine L.	Addison, Addison	R	1955 1957 1959
Conrad, Sally Y.	Burlington, Chittenden	D	1985 1987 1989 1991
Coutts, Flora Jane	Newport, Orleans	R	1937 1939
Drown, Susan T.	Sharon, Windsor	R	1951 1953
Ferraro, Betty M.	Rutland, Rutland	R	1993 1995
Franco, Helen M.	Barre Town, Washington	D	1965
Gardner, Jane Kendall	Arlington, Bennington	D	1983 1985
Gear, Sara M.	Burlington, Chittenden	R	1993 1995
Hammond, Margaret B.	Baltimore, Windsor	R	1967 1969 1971
Harvie, Ruth	Chester, Windsor	R	1995
Harwood, Madeline B.	Manchester Center, Bennington	R	1969 1971 1973 1977 1979 1981 1983
Hayden, Mildred C.	Berlin, Washington	R	1947 1949 1951 1953 1955
Hurley, Kathleen W.	St Albans, Franklin	D	1945
Keeler, Pearl Isabel	Barton, Orleans	R	1959 1961 1963
Kroger, Althea P.	Essex Junction, Chittenden	D	1991 1993
Laird, Nelly Cox	Montpelier, Washington	R	1929
Mallary, Gertrude Robinson	Fairlee, Orange	R	1957
McCaffrey, Rita	Rutland, Rutland	D	1989
Northrop, Consuelo B. see Bailey	Burlington, Chittenden	R	1931
Ready, Elizabeth Mary	Bristol, Addison	D	1989 1991 1993 1995
Riehle, Helen S.	Burlington, Chittenden	R	1993 1995
Rivers, Cheryl P.	Bethel, Windsor	D	1991 1993 1995
Robillard, Florence	Mendon, Rutland	D	1985 1987
Shea, Dorothy P.	Montpelier, Washington	R	1967 1969 1971 1973
Skeels, Helena H.	Isle La Motte, Grand Isle	R	1933
Skinner, Mary Just	Montpelier, Washington	D	1979 1981 1983 1985 1987 1989 1991
Smith, Elsie C.	Cambridge, Lamoille	R	1935
Sorrell, Esther Hartigan	Burlington, Chittenden	D	1973 1975 1977 1979 1981
Soule, Elizabeth W.	Fairfield, Franklin	R	1947
Soule, Sarah Sallie	Charlotte, Chittenden	D	1981 1983

Vermont Senate, continued

Name	City, County	Party	Legislative Year
Stephany, Judith B.	Burlington, Chittenden	D	1983*
Stoddard, Blanche Manning	Royalton, Windsor	R	1961 1963
Sweetser, Susan W.	Essex, Chittenden	R	1993 1995
Tudhope, Katherine R.	North Hero, Grand Isle	R	1947
Ward, Aline H.	Moretown, Washington	R	1961 1963
Westphal, Esther G.	Lake Elmore, Lamoille	R	1975*
Wills, Hazel M.	Bennington, Bennington	R	1961

House
2 Year Terms

Name	City, County	Party	Legislative Year
Ackert, Julia B.	Mt. Tabor, Rutland	R	1961 1963
Adams, Alice	Eden, Lamoille	R	1935
Adams, Carrie T.	West Haven, Rutland	R	1929 1935
Adams, Margaret	Marlboro, Windham	R	1953
Alexander, Doris S.	Irasburg, Orleans	R	1961 1963 1965 1967 1969
Allen, Alice B.	Chelsea, Orange	R	1951
Allen, Dorothy Coulter	Ferrisburg, Addison	R	1939 1941
Almy, Linda L.	Underhill Center, Chittenden	D	1987 1989 1991 1993 1995
Arnold, Shirlee Ann	Whiting, Addison	R	1983* 1985 1987
Ashcroft, Mary C.	Bellows Falls, Windham	D	1979* 1981
Auld, Susan D.	Worcester, Washington	R	1977* 1979 1981 1983 1985
Austin, Helen M.	Granby, Essex	R	1943
Babcock, Carmel Ann	Burlington, Chittenden	R	1975* 1977 1979 1981 1983 1985 1987 1989 1991 1993 1995
Bailey, Consuelo Northrop *see* *Northrop*	South Burlington, Chittenden	R	1951 1953
Baird, Rose	Newark, Caledonia	D	1965
Baird, Sandy L.	Burlington, Chittenden	D	1993 1995
Baird, Sara W.	Chittenden, Rutland	R	1945
Baker, Cleona Tatro	Concord, Essex	R	1957 1959 1965
Ball, Mary M.	West Fairfield, Franklin	R	1953
Ballard, Ruth	Canaan, Essex	R	1947
Barber, Georgia	Sheffield, Caledonia	R	1933
Barlow, Ada	Grafton, Windham	R	1925
Barnes, Ina F.	Andover, Windsor	R	1965*
Barrup, Doris Gray	Morgan, Orleans	R	1957 1959 1967 1969

Bartlett, Lucy	Bloomfield, Essex	D	1957 1959
Bartlett, Maedean C.	Richford, Franklin	D	1971 1973 1975*
Bartlett, Ruth G.	Richford, Franklin	R	1959 1961 1963
Bassett, Alice Cook	Burlington, Chittenden	D	1983 1985 1987 1989 1991
Bates, Mayolyn H.	Chester, Windsor	R	1979 1981 1983
Batten, Anne K.	East Hardwick, Caledonia	R	1981 1983 1985 1987
Bauer, Edith J.	Landgrove, Bennington	R	1959 1961 1963 1965
Bean, Candace	Westfield, Orleans	R	1965
Beard, Edna	Orange, Orange	R	1921
Beattie, Catherine M.	Danville, Caledonia	D	1965
Beattie, Deborah M.	Northfield, Washington	D	1967
Beattie, Mildred Boyce	Maidstone, Essex	R	1955 1957
Beaulieu, Jeanne C.	Westfield, Orleans	R	1963*
Belden, Nellie E.	Benson, Rutland	R	1929*
Belknap, Katherine M.	Rockingham, Windham	R	1945
Bellows, Elizabeth G.	Fairfax, Franklin	R	1941
Bemis, Grace E.	Athens, Windham	R	1935
Bentley, Florence W.	Sandgate, Bennington	R	1933
Bentley, Maria	Sandgate, Bennington	R	1929
Betts, Emily W.	Chelsea, Orange	R	1987*
Bickford, Luella F.	Bradford, Orange	R	1931
Blackmer, Ruth C.	Stockbridge, Windsor	R	1959*
Blackmer, Winona L.	Stockbridge, Windsor	R	1951 1953
Blaisdell, Flora G.	Fairfax, Franklin	R	1943
Bohi, Lynn White	River Junction, Windsor	D	1989 1993 1995
Book, Agnes E.	W. Haven, Rutland	R	1931
Bragg, Erlene	Waitsfield, Washington	R	1959
Breed, Mabel I.	Victory, Essex	R	1939
Bright, Louvenia Dorsey	South Burlington, Chittenden	D	1989 1991 1993
Bromley, Bernice V.	Weathersfield, Windsor	R	1951 1953 1955 1957
Bronson, Gwendolyn T.	Shelburne, Chittenden	R	1981 1983 1985 1987 1989 1991
Brown, Dorothy R.	Essex, Chittenden	R	1951 1953 1955 1957 1961
Brown, Eather Hill	Vergennes, Addison	R	1953*
Brown, Lula	Hancock, Addison	R	1947
Brown, Mabel C.	Williston, Chittenden	R	1935
Bryant, Blanche B.	Springfield, Windsor	R	1927
Buck, Catherine E.	Wheelock, Caledonia	R	1923
Buckley, Lilla Wilkie G.	Barton, Orleans	R	1935*
Bullis, Helen L.	Grand Isle, Grand Isle	R	1955
Burbank, Mildred J.	Waitsfield, Washington	R	1959 1961
Butson, Alfarata M.	Athens, Windham	R	1945 1947 1951
Camisa, Kathleen K. see Keenan	St. Albans, Franklin	D	1989* 1991
Cargill, Kate B.	Morgan, Orleans	R	1943 1945
Carlisle, Lillian B.	Burlington, Chittenden	D	1969
Carpenter, Fannie W.	Fletcher, Franklin	R	1941

Vermont House, continued

Name	City, County	Party	Legislative Year
Carpenter, Flora S.	Cabot, Washington	R	1957
Carpenter, Gila D.	Elmore, Lamoille	R	1937
Carpenter, Thelma M.	Washington, Orange	R	1961 1963
Carr, Harriet L.	Canaan, Essex	R	1957 1959; D 1965
Casavant, Dominique	Winooski, Chittenden	D	1979
Casavant, Lucille	Winooski, Chittenden	D	1989 1991 1993 1995
Cassidy, Ethel G.	Highgate, Franklin	R	1953 1955 1961
Chandler, Grace M.	St. Albans, Franklin	R	1959 1961
Charboneau, Elaine M.	Burlington, Chittenden	D	1981 1983 1985 1987 1989 1991
Chard, Nancy I.	Brattleboro, Windham	D	1991 1993
Chedel, Alice K.	Gaysville, Windsor	R	1959
Child, Etta B.	Middlebury, Addison	R	1959 1961
Chioffi, Nancy B.	Burlington, Chittenden	D	1991 1993*
Christopher, Nancy B.	Alburg, Grand Isle	D	1991 1993
Christowe, Margaret	West Dover, Windham	R	1975
Clapp, Elsie	Montgomery, Franklin	R	1935*
Clark, Elsie L.	Concord, Essex	R	1945
Clark, Geraldine L.	Addison, Addison	R	1951 1953
Clark, Hattie L.	Athens, Windham	R	1931 1939 1949
Cleveland, Eva	Coventy, Orleans	R	1941*
Cleveland, Lynne	Pittsford, Rutland	D	1993 1995
Cobb, Mable Ruggles	Westford, Chittenden	R	1953 1955 1957
Cobb, Velma B.	Morgan, Orleans	R	1961 1963
Cobleigh, Bertha P.	Concord, Essex	R	1941
Cochran, Theresa	Orange, Orange	R	1949 1953
Cohen, Esther H.	Burlington, Chittenden	D	1967 1969 1971 1973
Colby, Carrie V.	Burke, Caledonia	R	1953
Cole, Malvina	Stratton, Windham	R	1955
Cole, Ruth A.	Sunderland, Bennington	R	1955 1957 1967 1969
Coleman, Evelyn L.	Jamaica, Windham	R	1955
Collins, Kenalene J.	Readsboro, Bennington	R	1963 1965 1971 1973
Conant, Gloria	Colchester, Chittenden	R	1979 1981
Conant, Joan A.	Colchester, Chittenden	R	1989 1991 1993 1995
Conant, Myrtle M.	Richmond, Chittenden	R	1955
Condon, Marie Powers	North Bennington, Bennington	D	1981 1983 1985
Connor, Helen F. S.	Middlesex, Washington	D	1951
Cooke, Isabelle T.	Bridgeport, Addison	D	1959 1961 1963 1965
Cookson, Mary	Woodbury, Washington	I	1961 1963
Cooper, Flora	Engram Wells, Rutland	R	1923
Corey, Mary Lou	Franklin, Franklin	R	1993 1995
Coutts, Flora Jane	Newport, Orleans	R	1961 1963 1965 1967 1969 1971
Covell, Annie E.	Lemington, Essex	R	1945
Covell, Belle H.	Williamstown, Orange	R	1937
Cowles, Elsie A.	Thetford, Orange	R	1953 1955 1957 1959
Cragen, Florence H.	Bristol, Addison	R	1945 1947

Cree, Dorothy M	Wheelock, Caledonia	R	1931
Cree, Joyce B.	Wheelock, Caledonia	R	1943
Crispe, Pamela Simson	Putney, Windham	R	1989
Crocker, Patricia C.	Woodstock, Windsor	D	1993 1995
Crosby, Marie Goodwin	Mount Tabor, Rutland	R	1943 1945 1947
Cross, Hattie J.	Worcester, Washington	R	1937*
Crowe, Alice S.	Sheldon, Franklin	D	1953; R 1955
Cutting, Mildred Perry	Concord, Essex	R	1951* 1953 1955
Daily, Catherine	Hartford, Windsor	R	1959*
Daniels, Florence K.	Woodbury, Washington	R	1947 1949
Daniels, Gertrude	Grafton, Windham	R	1931 1933
Darling, Frances D.	Woodbury, Washington	R	1959
Davenport, Amy M.	Montpelier, Washington	D	1985 1987 1989
Davis, B. Olga	Burke, Caledonia	D	1965
Davis, Marion K.	Duxbury, Washington	R	1949
Day, Harriet Mary	Sheffield, Caledonia	R	1959
Dean, Nancy	Norwich, Windsor	R	1977
Decker, Melba A.	Shaftsbury, Bennington	R	1959*
Delair, Frances	Montpelier, Washington	R	1965 1967 1969*
Deos, Mary A. E.	Wheelock, Caledonia	D	1945
Deppman, Elizabeth	Middlebury, Addison	R	1979* 1981
Devereux, Maude E.	Mount Holly, Rutland	R	1967 1969 1971
Dickinson, Lillian	Orange, Orange	R	1955
Dimario, Judy	Waitsfield, Washington	D	1991 1993
Dimock, Annette	Topsham, Orange	R	1925
Doe, Marjorie G.	Westmore, Orleans	R	1951 1953
Dolan, Lillian M.	Berkshire, Franklin	D	1949
Dow, Bessie R.	Middlebury, Addison	R	1951
Dow, Jessie Del	Topsham, Orange	D	1923
Doyle, Marjorie	Arlington, Bennington	R	1965
Drennan, Flora	Woodbury, Washington	R	1931
Drew, Edith P.	Richford, Franklin	D	1953
Drown, Susan T.	Sharon, Windsor	R	1943 1945 1947 1949
Duell, Gretta M.	St. George, Chittenden	R	1957 1961
Duffy, Jean Anne	Milton, Chittenden	D	1983 1985 1987
Dunsmore, Elizabeth J.	Swanton, Franklin	D	1973 1975 1979 1981 1983 1985
Durgin, Maud Ann	Newport, Orleans	R	1989 1991 1993
Durkee, Irene H.	Rutland, Rutland	D	1979 1981
Dwyer, Martha Lang	Wheelock, Caledonia	R	1935
Dwyer, Ruth	Thetford Center, Orange	R	1995
Eastman, Lillian	Topsham, Orange	R	1965
Eastment, Juliane B.	Barre, Washington	R	1971
Eaton, Blanch M.	Hancock, Addison	R	1931
Eddy, Ethel A.	Stratton, Windham	R	1957 1959 1961
Edwards, Elizabeth	Middlebury, Addison	R	1979* 1983 1985
Ellsworth, Florence B.	Johnson, Lamoille	R	1953
Emery, May E.	Eden, Lamoille	R	1937 1939 1941*
Emmons, Alice M.	Springfield, Windsor	D	1983 1985 1987 1989 1991 1993 1995
Erkson, Pamela J.	Burlington, Chittenden	D	1979 1981

Vermont House, continued

Name	City, County	Party	Legislative Year
Evelti, Mary M.	Burlington, Chittenden	D	1975 1977 1979 1981 1983 1985 1987 1989
Everest, Ethel W.	Milton, Chittenden	R	1953 1955
Farnsworth, Marguerite	Waltham, Addison	R	1955
Farr, Amber	Bradford, Orange	R	1949
Farr, M. Zoe	Monkton, Addison	R	1931
Farr, Shirley	Brandon, Rutland	R	1945 1947
Farrar, Alli R.	Chester, Windsor	D	1989 1991 1993 1995
Fay, Josie J.	Williston, Chittenden	R	1925
Feeley, Theresa G.	Colchester, Chittenden	D	1977 1979 1981
Ferraro, Betty M.	Rutland, Rutland	R	1991
Field, Katharine C.	Waltham, Addison	R	1945
Field, Mary W.	Charlotte, Chittenden	D	1955 1957 1959
Fish, Della K.	Ira, Rutland	R	1937*
Fish, Etta H.	Ira, Rutland	R	1939 1945
Fisher, Jessie F.	Panton, Addison	R	1945
Fisher, Josephine	Stafford, Orange	D	1965
Foote, May M.	Charlotte, Chittenden	R	1947
Forbes, Madge E.	St. George, Chittenden	R	1945
Fortin, Viola	Burlington, Chittenden	D	1967 1969 1971
Fortna, Lixi	Warren, Washington	R	1983 1985 1987 1989
Foster, Bertha	Westford, Chittenden	R	1965
Fox, Sally G.	Essex Junction, Chittenden	D	1987 1989 1991 1993 1995
France, Elnora Elizabeth	Woodford, Bennington	D	1947*
Franco, Helen M.	Barre Town, Washington	D	1967 1969 1971
French, Irene	Stratton, Windham	R	1953
Frink, Evelyn R.	Charlotte, Chittenden	R	1943
Gaborsky, Dorothy B.	St. Johnsbury, Caledonia	R	1971*
Gallup, Gertrude P.	Woodford, Bennington	R	1949 1951
Gardner, Beatrice L.	South Hero, Grand Isle	D	1947
Gardner, Jane Kendall	Arlington, Bennington	D	1975 1977 1979 1981
Garland, Myrle L.	Lincoln, Addison	R	1943
Gear, Sara M.	Burlington, Chittenden	R	1985 1987 1989 1991
George, Esther S.	Sharon, Windsor	D	1963
Geprags, Dora Emma	Hinnesburg, Chittenden	R	1937
Gifford, Ethel B.	Sherburne, Chittenden	R	1939
Glidden, Ira C.	Franklin, Franklin	R	1949 1953
Glitman, K. Micque	Burlington, Chittenden	D	1985 1987 1989
Goddard, Florence A.	Stockbridge, Windsor	R	1945
Goodwin, Mary W.	Rutland, Rutland	R	1979 1981
Gorham, Flora B.	Kirby, Caledonia	R	1951 1953 1955 1957 1959
Gould, Myra B.	Elmore, Lamoille	R	1949 1951
Graham, Gladys	Brunswick, Essex	D	1963

Graham, Lorraine Hunt	Burlington, Chittenden	D	1967 1969 1971 1973 1975 1977 1979 1981
Gray, Carrie J.	Holland, Orleans	R	1951 1955 1957 1959 1961 1965
Gray, Helen S.	Fairfax, Franklin	R	1953
Gray, Jennie E.	Eden, Lamoille	R	1947 1955 1957
Grimes, Barbara L.	Burlington, Chittenden	D	1985 1987 1989 1991 1993*
Hall, Alice	Stannard, Caledonia	R	1963
Hallowell, Ann	Burlington, Chittenden	D	1993 1995
Hammond, Margaret B.	Baltimore, Windsor	R	1945 1947 1949 1951 1953 1955 1957 1959 1961 1963 1965
Harding, Ethel C.	Vershire, Orange	R	1933 1949
Harrington, Blanche	Shelburne, Chittenden	D	1935
Harroun, Ann P. Biron	Essex Junction, Chittenden	D	1981 1985 1987 1989
Harte, Helen C.	Charlotte, Chittenden	D	1965*
Harwood, Madeline B.	Manchester Center, Bennington	R	1989 1991
Hastings, Adah R.	Concord, Essex	R	1947 1949
Hawkins, Mary M.	Shaftsbury, Bennington	D	1935
Hayden, Mildred C.	Berlin, Washington	R	1943 1945 1965 1969
Hayes, Mary E.	Guildhall, Essex	R	1963* 1965
Heath, Martha	Westford, Chittenden	D	1993 1995
Heitman, Kathryn J.	Shoreham, Addison	R	1963 1965 1967 1969 1971 1973
Hill, Ethel Winifred	Plymouth, Windsor	R	1951 1953 1955 1957 1961
Hise, Elizabeth B.	Bristol, Addison	R	1989*
Hockert, Barbara	Burlington, Chittenden	D	1985 1987 1989
Hoffman, May Lucille	Salisbury, Addison	R	1955* 1957 1959
Holbrook, Lillian M.	Bloomfield, Essex	R	1947 1949
Holbrook, Mabel	Lemington, Essex	R	1943 1947 1949 1953
Hood, Louise B.	Windsor, Windsor	R	1979 1981 1983 1985 1987
Hook, Mildred J.	Brunswick, Essex	D	1957
Hooker, Cheryl Mazzariello	Rutland, Rutland	D	1993
Hopson, Iris R.	Wells, Rutland	R	1951 1953
Houston, Constance T.	Vergennes, Addison	R	1993 1995
Hoyt, Irene P.	Weathersfield, Windsor	R	1959 1961
Hromada, Mirth E.	Stratton, Windham	R	1943 1945 1947
Hubbard, Estella F.	Guildhall, Essex	R	1953
Hudson, Helen E.	Haven, Essex	D	1961 1963
Hudson, Ruth	Newark, Caledonia	D	1943
Hull, Charlotte M.	Shoreham, Addison	R	1931
Hutchins, Vera P.	Stannard, Caledonia	R	1945

Vermont House, continued

Name	City, County	Party	Legislative Year
Jacobs, Ethel R.	Guilford, Windham	R	1943*
James, Marjorie B.	Weybridge, Addison	R	1949
Jarrett, Evelyn L.	Burlington, Chittenden	D	1967 1969 1971 1973 1975 1977
Jeffrey, Nellie T.	Groton, Caledonia	R	1945
Jennett, Rose Mary	Grantville, Addison	R	1955 1957
Johnson, Edith Ann	Vershire, Orange	R	1945 1955
Johnson, Shirley	Vershire, Orange	R	1955 1957 1959 1963 1965
Jones, Charlotte T.	Rutland, Rutland	R	1967 1969 1971
Jones, June F.	Goshen, Addison	R	1945*
Jones, Nathalie H.	Johnson, Lamoille	R	1961
Just, Anne	Warren, Washington	D	1977 1979 1981
Keeler, Pearl Isabel	Barton, Orleans	R	1953 1955
Keenan, Kathleen see Camisa	St. Albans, Franklin	D	1993 1995
Kehaya, Barbara M.	Winooski, Chittenden	D	1983 1985 1987 1989
Kehler, Carolyn S.	Woodstock, Windsor	D	1993 1995
Kehoe, Kathy B.	Moretown, Washington	D	1993 1995
Kelton, Winifred L.	Athens, Windham	R	1955 1957 1959 1961 1963 1965
Kennedy, Jeanne Bonneau	South Burlington, Chittenden	D	1981 1985
Kent, Alberta S.	Panton, Addison	R	1951 1955
Kimball, Maude B.	Elmore, Lamoille	R	1945*
Kittredge, Kate S.	Walden, Caledonia	R	1953 1961 1963
Kitzmiller, Karen B.	Montpelier, Washington	D	1991 1993 1995
Kroger, Althea P.	Essex Junction, Chittenden	D	1977 1979 1981 1983
Kunin, Madeleine May	Burlington, Chittenden	D	1973 1975 1977
Kurt, Kerry	Colchester, Chittenden	D	1993 1995
Ladd, Arlene C.	Walden, Caledonia	R	1957 1959
Ladd, Lucia T.	Worcester, Washington	R	1953 1955 1957
Ladeau, Christine B.	Plainfield, Washington	R	1963 1965
Lafayette, Karen Moran	Burlington, Chittenden	D	1993* 1995
Lafreniere, Bertha	Bolton, Chittenden	R	1961 1963 1965
Laird, Nelly Cox	Montpelier, Washington	R	1927
Lamb, Mattie	Pittsfield, Rutland	R	1945*
Lamorder, Clara C.	Leicester, Addison	R	1953 1963
Lamorder, Flora	Warren, Washington	R	1925
Lancaster, Virginia M.	Woodstock, Windsor	R	1981
Landon, Alice C.	New Haven, Addison	R	1953 1955 1957 1959 1961 1963 1965
Lane, Amy R.	Newark, Caledonia	R	1941 1945
Lantman, Elizabeth L.	Hinnesburg, Chittenden	R	1945
Lawrence, Marion B.	Stamford, Bennington	R	1951

Leach, Ruth A.	Enosburg, Franklin	R	1951
Leamy, Margaret L.	W. Rutland, Rutland	D	1957 1959*
Leonard, Mabel Clara	Shoreham, Addison	R	1937
Lincoln, Eva K.	W. Rutland, Rutland	R	1959
Lindamood, V. Joyce	Springfield, Windsor	R	1985
Lingelbach, Doris	Thetford, Orange	D	1985 1987 1989 1991 1993
Livingston, Judith	Manchester, Bennington	R	1995
Locke, Esther S.	Topsham, Orange	R	1943
Long, Edna B.	Waitsfield, Washington	R	1951
Lucier, Grace C.	Jay, Orleans	D	1961 1963
Luginbuhl, Vi Larimore	South Burlington, Chittenden	R	1987 1989 1991
Lund, Doris V.	Victory, Essex	R	1943
Lund, Maude N.	Granby, Essex	R	1963
Lyon, Josephene H.	Highgate, Franklin	R	1941 1943 1945 1947
MacAuley, Della Sargent	Norwich, Windsor	R	1937 1939
MacDonald, Barbara	Williamstown, Orange	D	1983*
Macomber, Loula I.	Westford, Chittenden	R	1943
Madkour, Mary Mcgarey	Bennington, Bennington	R	1993 1995
Maher, Mary Barbara	South Burlington, Chittenden	D	1975 1977 1979 1981
Mallary, Gertrude Robinson	Fairlee, Orange	R	1953 1955
Maloney, Katherine	Jericho Center, Chittenden	D	1961
Manahan, Madeline	Enosburg Falls, Franklin	D	1995
Manning, Madelyn	Morristown, Lamoille	D	1965*
Marshia, Marion B.	Underhill, Chittenden	R	1945
Martell, Arlene J.	Georgia, Franklin	D	1969 1971
Martin, Elisa S.	Barre, Washington	R	1989 1991 1993 1995
Martin, Margaret F.	Middlebury, Addison	D	1987 1989 1991 1993 1995
Mason, Georgina B.	Brunswick, Essex	D	1943
Mason, Nina A.	Pawlet, Rutland	R	1931
Masten, Leah M.	Victory, Essex	R	1963 1965
Maxham, Bernice M.	Middlesex, Washington	R	1953 1955 1957 1959
McClintock, Bernice	Newbury, Orange	R	1961*
McCuin, Minetta E.	Belvidere, Lamoille	R	1943 1947
McLam, Alida	Thetford, Orange	R	1945
McMahon, Bessie	Stowe, Lamoille	D	1935*
Meech, Leoline A.	Monkton, Addison	R	1923
Mendicino, Jane A.	Essex Junction, Chittenden	R	1985 1987 1989 1991 1993
Milkey, Virginia A.	Brattleboro, Windham	D	1991 1993 1995
Miller, Alice M.	Westfield, Orleans	R	1953*
Miller, Mary P.	West Rutland, Rutland	D	1963
Millington, Sue H.	Peru, Bennington	R	1935*
Milne, Marion C.	Barre, Washington	R	1995

Vermont House, continued

Name	City, County	Party	Legislative Year
Mills, Maud L.	Stockbridge, Windsor	R	1949
Molinaroli, Lucille C.	Barre, Washington	R	1967 1969 1971 1973 1975 1977 1979
Moloney, Annie J.	Rutland, Rutland	D	1929
Moore, Edna M.	Derby, Orleans	R	1945 1947
Moore, Karen J.	Rutland, Rutland	D	1995
Morse, Eva M. *see* Morse-Sayers	Calais, Washington	R	1971 1973 1975
Morse, Gretchen B.	Charlotte, Chittenden	R	1977 1979 1981 1983 1985*
Morse, Muriel	Jay, Orleans	D	1965
Morse-Sayers, Eva M. *see Morse*	Calais, Washington	R	1977 1979
Mosher, Katherine M.	Bridgewater, Windsor	R	1957
Moulton, Elizbeth M.	Derby, Orleans	R	1931
Moulton, Grace C.	Panton, Addison	R	1953 1957
Munn, Dorothy D.	West Fairlee, Orange	R	1945 1947
Munn, Kathleen M.	Fairlee, Orange	R	1931 1951
Murphy, Margaret A.	Lowell, Orleans	D	1957 1959 1961 1963 1965
Myers, Daisy L.	Woodford, Bennington	R	1959 1961 1963 1965
Neely, Noel Anne	Woodstock, Windsor	R	1977 1979 1981
Newton, Ada M.	Vernon, Windham	R	1927 1929 1931
Nichols, Mary B.	Braintree, Orange	R	1941
Nifong, Susanna W.	Benson, Rutland	R	1929*
Niles, Ina R.	Derby, Orleans	R	1925
Norris, Janet L.	Newport Town, Orleans	R	1953 1955
Northrop, Frederika B.	Fairfield, Franklin	I	1953
Nuovo, Betty A.	Middlebury, Addison	D	1981 1983 1985 1987 1989
Nye, Mary G.	Berlin, Washington	R	1939*
Ogden, Mary	Landgrove, Bennington	R	1943*
O'Meara, Lettie T.	Topsham, Orange	R	1959
O'Neil, Lisa M.	White River Junction, Windsor	R	1991 1993
O'Neil, Mildred H.	Montpelier, Washington	R	1967
Paige, Helen L.	Westford, Chittenden	R	1959 1961 1963
Parizo, Mary Ann	Essex Junction, Chittenden	D	1991 1993 1995
Parker, Belle M.	Chittenden, Rutland	R	1943
Patno, Pearl Aleath	South Hero, Grand Isle	R	1957
Patridge, Bertha Mae	Victory, Essex	R	1955 1957
Paul, Concetta M.	Rutland, Rutland	R	1973 1975
Paul, Madeline R.	West Fairlee, Orange	R	1959 1961 1965
Paull, Mary S.	Newport, Orleans	R	1985 1987
Peaslee, Janice L.	Guildhall, Essex	R	1989 1991 1993 1995
Pelkey, Frances B.	Highgate, Franklin	D	1963 1965
Perry, Carrie E.	Ira, Rutland	R	1949 1951
Petersen, Hazel K.	N. Hero, Grand Isle	R	1963

Peterson, Julie A.	Brattleboro, Windham	D	1983 1985 1987 1989
Pike, Gladys D.	Searsburg, Bennington	R	1955* 1957
Pingert, Christina M.	Colchester, Chittenden	R	1983 1985
Poeter, Emma R.	Goshen, Addison	R	1957 1959
Pollard, Annie M.	Baltimore, Windsor	R	1933 1935 1937 1939 1941 1943
Pollard, Erminie Lois	Cavendish, Windsor	R	1951
Porter, Patiricia L.	Colchester, Chittenden	R	1985 1987*
Potter, Lula Fletcher	Hyde Park, Lamoille	R	1945 1947 1957 1959 1961 1963
Potvin, Jane B.	South Hero, Grand Isle	D	1985 1987 1989 1991
Pratt, Mary T.	Shrewsbury, Rutland	R	1949
Price, Megan D.	Fair Haven, Rutland	R	1987 1989 1991
Prindle, Hazel	Charlotte, Chittenden	R	1985* 1987* 1989 1991 1993
Puffer, Erma E.	Vernon, Windham	R	1959 1961 1963 1965 1967 1969 1985
Pugh, Ann D.	South Burlington, Chittenden	D	1993 1995
Putnam, Jessie M.	Worcester, Washington	R	1927
Ranney, Mabel F.	Pittsfield, Rutland	R	1943 1945*
Ranney, Zilpah Fay	Pittsfield, Rutland	R	1961 1963 1965
Redfield, Marion	Barton, Orleans	R	1957 1959
Reed, L. Mae Wynne	Vergennes, Addison	R	1937
Reuschel, Barbara A.	Burlington, Chittenden	D	1979 1981
Rice, Doris B.	Searsburg, Bennington	R	1959 1961 1963 1965
Richardson, Lillian	Orange, Orange	R	1925
Ricker, Addie E.	Groton, Caledonia	R	1943 1953
Riehle, Helen S.	Burlington, Chittenden	R	1983* 1985 1987 1989 1991
Rivero, Marilyn Keith	Milton, Chittenden	D	1991 1993 1995
Roberts, Grace Esther	Barnard, Windsor	R	1957 1959 1963 1965
Robillard, Florence	Mendon, Rutland	D	1973
Robinson, Ann Mae	Hartford, Windsor	R	1957*
Robinson, Mehitable Crawford	W. Rutland, Rutland	R	1927 1929
Rock, Mary R.	Ludlow, Windsor	D	1939*
Rogenski, Marion M.	White River Junction, Windsor	D	1991
Rogers, Elizabeth	Orange, Orange	R	1951
Rogers, Mary Louise C.	Cabot, Washington	R	1945
Rosenstreich, Judy P.	Waterbury Center, Washington	R	1973 1975
Rowland, Polly	Burlington, Chittenden	D	1979 1981
Roy, Gladys B.	Barnet, Caledonia	R	1953 1955 1957
Roy, Katie Cook	Bradford, Orange	R	1951*
Royal, Blanche Mildred	Lemington, Essex	R	1955 1957 1959
Rule, Della	Waltham, Addison	R	1963*
Russell, Lois P.	Shrewsbury, Rutland	R	1951
Rutledge, Ruth	Fairlee, Orange	R	1943

Vermont House, continued

Name	City, County	Party	Legislative Year
Sanford, Edith Irene	Stamford, Bennington	R	1935* 1937 1939 1941 1943 1945 1947 1949 1953 1955
Sargeant, Marion T.	Granville, Washington	R	1963 1965
Sargent, Theresa M.	Jay, Orleans	R	1941 1943 1945 1947
Savage, Stella R.	Bloomfield, Essex	R	1939 1941 1943 1945 1961 1963 1965
Savery, Bertha Lane	Wallingford, Rutland	R	1957
Sawyer, Ruth C.	Waitsfield, Washington	R	1953
Schaefer, Ingeborg G.	Colchester, Chittenden	R	1987* 1989 1991 1993
Scribner, Ellen K.	Calais, Washington	R	1963
Seibert, Ann	Norwich, Windsor	D	1987* 1989 1991 1993 1995
Seward, Ella	Wallingford, Rutland	R	1925
Shampeny, Mildred E.	Rochester, Windsor	R	1951
Shea, Dorothy P.	Montpelier, Washington	R	1959 1961 1963
Sheltra, Nancy J.	Derby, Orleans	R	1989 1991 1993 1995
Shiman, Gail	Milton, Chittenden	D	1975
Shonio, Tenie C.	Elmore, Lamoille	R	1947
Shores, Edna H.	Granby, Essex	R	1947
Shores, Lillian D.	Granby, Essex	R	1941
Silsby, Fannie Jordan	Lunenberg, Essex	R	1957 1959 1961 1963 1965
Simpers, Mary P.	Colchester, Chittenden	R	1983 1985 1987 1989 1991 1995
Simpson, Jean W.	Craftsbury, Orleans	R	1945 1947 1951
Simpson, Mary T.	Craftsbury, Orleans	R	1925
Sisco, Leonora W.	Bradford, Orange	R	1943
Skeels, Helena H.	Isle La Motte, Grand Isle	R	1931
Small, Millie	Quechee, Windsor	R	1981
Smith, Cathleen W.	Norton, Essex	R	1965
Smith, Elsie C.	Cambridge, Lamoille	R	1925
Smith, Fannie A.	Panton, Addison	R	1941
Smith, H. Ione	Sandgate, Bennington	R	1937 1941
Smith, Irene Durkee	Rutland, Rutland	D	1977
Smith, Lillian	Vershire, Orange	R	1953
Smith, Minnie Rose	Athens, Windham	R	1927
Smith, Ruth Helen	Shrewsbury, Rutland	R	1945
Smith, Ruth R.	Barre, Washington	R	1987 1989 1991 1993
Soule, Sarah Sallie	Charlotte, Chittenden	D	1977 1979
Spaulding, Alda Lailn	Newport Town, Orleans	R	1947
Spencer, Marion W.	Vergennes, Addison	R	1975 1977 1979 1981
Spring, Edith B.	Stannard, Caledonia	R	1947
Stagg, Evelyn W.	Bomoseen, Rutland	D	1983 1985 1987 1989
Stanion, Theresa D.	Essex Junction, Chittenden	D	1975 1977 1979 1985
Stearns, Doris R.	Johnson, Lamoille	R	1945

Steele, Karen K.	Waterbury, Washington	R	1983 1985 1987 1989 1991 1993 1995
Stephany, Judith B.	Burlington, Chittenden	D	1977 1979 1981 1983*
Stevens, Flora G.	Sutton, Caledonia	R	1953 1955
Stigers, Marie H.	Andover, Windsor	R	1961 1963 1965*
Stockwell, Janet	Waterbury, Washington	R	1939*
Stoddard, Blanche Manning	Royalton, Windsor	R	1957 1959
Stokes, Ruth S.	Williston, Chittenden	R	1985 1987 1989 1991
Stone, Harriet R.	Sunderland, Bennington	R	1959 1961 1963 1965
Stufflebeam, E. May	Bakersfield, Franklin	R	1943
Sullivan, Mable	St. Johnsbury, Caledonia	R	1971*
Sullivan, Mary M.	Burlington, Chittenden	D	1991 1993 1995
Sumner, Julia R.	Danby, Rutland	R	1941 1943 1945 1949 1951
Swainbank, Louise R.	Johnsbury, Caledonia	R	1971 1973 1975 1977 1979
Syri, Amy	Concord, Essex	R	1975
Taisey, Laura B.	Troy, Orleans	R	1951 1953 1955
Tanner, Alma R.	Putney, Windham	R	1955
Tassie, B. Leola	Woodbury, Washington	R	1951
Taylor, Annie Roberts	Brunswick, Essex	R	1937 1939
Taylor, Florence E.	Brunswick, Essex	R	1945 1947
Taylor, Katie Elizabeth	Somerset, Windham	R	1925 1927 1929 1931 1933 1935 1937
Taylor, Winifred A.	Brunswick, Essex	R	1941
Thayer, Velma B.	Barnard, Windsor	R	1947 1949 1951 1953
Thompson, Dorothy	St. George, Chittenden	R	1953
Thurber, Mary D.	Charlotte, Chittenden	R	1967 1971
Tosh, Elizabeth D.	Barre, Washington	D	1985
Towle, Ellen G.	Franklin, Franklin	R	1937*
Towne, Ruth H.	Montpelier, Washington	R	1977 1979 1983 1985 1987 1989 1991 1993 1995
Tudhope, Iva M.	North Hero, Grand Isle	R	1957 1959 1961
Tudhope, Katherine R.	North Hero, Grand Isle	R	1945
Tuttle, Vivian G.	Stratton, Windham	R	1963 1965
Utley, Blanche Drennan	Woodbury, Washington	R	1953 1955 1957
Vaughn, Charlotte	Thetford, Orange	D	1927 1929
Vincent, Val	Waterbury, Chittenden	D	1991 1993 1995
Voyer, Cathy	Morrisville, Lamoille	R	1995
Wakefield, Helen W.	Randolph, Orange	R	1973 1975 1977 1979
Walbridge, Ruth T.	Rutland, Rutland	R	1981
Waldbridge, Frances C.	Cabot, Washington	R	1961
Walter, Gertrude	East Haven, Essex	R	1935
Ward, Aline H.	Moretown, Washington	R	1947 1953 1969*
Ward, Florence Miles	Moretown, Washington	R	1955 1957
Warren, Mabel R.	Kirby, Caledonia	R	1935 1943
Washburn, Florence E.	Haven, Essex	R	1933
Waterbury, Janice Wright	Ripton, Addison	R	1957 1959 1961

Vermont House, continued

Name	City, County	Party	Legislative Year
Way, Genia Martha Moore	North Hero, Grand Isle	R	1939
Webb, Susan Howard	Plymouth, Windsor	R	1973 1975 1977 1979
Webster, Elizabeth W.	Whiting, Addison	R	1951 1953 1955
Weed, Marion	Sutton, Caledonia	R	1961 1963 1965
Weeks, Jennie B.	Norton, Essex	I	1943
Welch, Kathleen	Hancock, Addison	D	1961
Welch, Patricia L.	Springfield, Windsor	R	1991
Wells, Gertrude W.	Cabot, Washington	D	1933
White, Bernice D.	Topsham, Orange	R	1949
White, Sadie Lucy	Burlington, Chittenden	D	1967 1969 1971 1973 1975 1977 1979 1983
Whitehill, Grace	Morgan, Orleans	R	1965
Whitney, Mabel E.	Peru, Bennington	R	1947
Whittier, Belva Cox	Hancock, Addison	R	1939
Wilbur, Melba R.	Tinmouth, Rutland	R	1947 1949
Wilcox, Ann Brown	Plymouth, Windsor	R	1941 1945
Wilcox, Esther Elizabeth	Arlington, Bennington	R	1953* 1955
Williams, Alice A.	Craftsbury, Orleans	D	1949
Williams, Daisy	Charlotte, Chittenden	R	1935
Williams, Lucina	St. George, Chittenden	R	1947
Wilson, Arlene Lois	Rutland, Rutland	D	1967* 1969*
Winch, Rev. Mabel	Sunderland, Bennington	R	1925
Wing, Gloria A.	Morrisville, Lamoille	R	1987 1989
Winship, Edna E.	Windham, Windham	R	1945* 1953 1955 1957 1959
Wood, Barbara C.	Bethel, Windsor	R	1981 1983 1985 1987 1989 1991 1993
Wood, Violet P.	East Haven, Essex	R	1955
Wright, Ruth E.	Colchester, Chittenden	R	1943* 1947 1951
Wright, Sylvia B.	Rupert, Bennington	R	1945 1947
Yarnell, Carolyn	Colchester, Chittenden	D	1987 1989 1991 1993 1995
Young, Lillie	Guilford, Windham	R	1949
Young-Price, Toby	Putney, Windham	D	1981* 1983 1985 1987 1989

*Notes:

Arnold, Shirlee Ann—Appointed Oct. 3, 1983
Ashcroft, Mary C.—Appointed Aug. 15, 1979 (Stack)
Auld, Susan D.—Appointed June 1978
Babcock, Carmel Ann—Appointed Oct. 14, 1975 (Kennedy)
Barnes, Ina F.—Appointed Jan. 4, 1965 (Stigers)[F]
Bartlett, Maedean C.—Died April 28, 1975
Beaulieu, Jeanne C.—Appointed Jan. 27, 1964 (Stevenson)

Belden, Nellie E.—Appointed Feb. 2, 1929 (Nifong)[F]
Betts, Emily W.—Appointed March 10, 1987 (Betts)
Blackmer, Ruth C.—Appointed Jan. 12, 1960 (Pratt)
Brown, Eather Hill—Appointed Dec. 22, 1952 (Brown)
Buckley, Lilla Wilkie G.—Appointed Dec. 21, 1935 (Buckley)
Camisa, Kathleen Keenan—Appointed April 1989 (father, Keenan)
Chioffi, Nancy B.—Resigned June 30, 1993 (Lafayette)[F]
Clapp, Elsie—Appointed Jan. 14, 1935 (Clapp)
Cleveland, Eva—Appointed Sept. 10, 1941 (Goss)
Cross, Hattie J.—Appointed Jan. 7, 1937 (Cross)
Cutting, Mildred Perry—Appointed Jan. 6, 1951 (Cutting)
Daily, Catherine—Appointed Jan. 6, 1960 (Daily)
Decker, Melba A.—Appointed Jan. 27, 1960 (Decker)
Delair, Frances—Appointed Feb. 24, 1969 (Thorp)
Deppman, Elizabeth—Appointed Aug. 6, 1979 (Deppman)
Edwards, Elizabeth—Appointed Aug. 6, 1979
Emery, May E.—Appointed Sept. 10, 1941 (Hayford)
Fish, Della K.—Appointed Jan. 7, 1937 (Fish)
France, Elnora Elizabeth—Appointed March 18, 1947 (Knapp)
Gaborsky, Dorothy B.—Appointed Feb. 26, 1971 (Sullivan)(F)
Grimes, Barbara L.—Resigned Nov. 5, 1993 (McNamara)
Harte, Helen C.—Appointed March 22, 1965 (Harte)
Hayes, Mary E.—Appointed Nov. 18, 1963 (Hayes)
Hise, Elizabeth B.—Appointed Nov. 1, 1989
Hoffman, May Lucille—Appointed March 21, 1955 (Hoffman)
Jacobs, Ethel R.—Appointed March 15, 1944 (Clark)
Jones, June F.—Died 1946 (Hayes)
Kimball, Maude Boardman—Died Nov. 25, 1944 (Gay)
Lafayette, Karen Moran—Appointed July 1, 1993 (Chioffi)[F]
Lamb, Mattie—Appointed Sept. 25, 1946 (Ranney)[F]
Leamy, Margaret L.—Died 1958 (Sutokoski)
MacDonald, Barbara—Died April 19, 1983 (MacDonald)
Manning, Madelyn—Appointed Jan. 28, 1965 (Manning)
McClintock, Bernice—Appointed April 26, 1961 (Cobb)
McMahon, Bessie—Appointed Jan. 10, 1935 (McMahon)
Miller, Alice M.—Appointed April 9, 1952 (Miller)
Millington, Sue H.—Resigned Dec. 10, 1935 (Larkin)
Morse, Gretchen B.—Resigned Jan. 1985 (Prindle)(F)
Nifong, Susanna W.—Resigned 1929 (Belden)[F]
Nye, Mary G.—Appointed July 20, 1940 (Carver)
Ogden, Mary—Appointed March 15, 1944 (J. Thompson)
Pike, Gladys D.—Appointed Jan. 25, 1955 (Pike)
Porter, Patricia L.—Resigned 1988 (Schaefer)(F)
Prindle, Hazel—Appointed Jan. 9, 1985 (G. Morese)(F); appointed Jan. 5, 1988
Ranney, Mabel F.—Died 1946 (Lamb)[F]
Riehle, Helen S.—Appointed Feb. 13, 1983 (Riehle)
Robinson, Ann Mae—Appointed Dec. 18, 1956 (Wright)
Rock, Mary R.—Appointed July 24, 1940 (Rock)
Roy, Katie Cook—Appointed Jan. 31, 1951 (Roy)
Rule, Della—Appointed March 6, 1963 (Rule)
Sanford, Edith Irene.—Appointed Dec. 10, 1935 (Sanford)
Schaefer, Ingeborg G.—Appointed Feb. 18, 1988 (Porter)(F)
Seibert, Ann—Appointed Jan. 5, 1988 (Stout)
Stephany, Judith B.—Resigned Jan. 28, 1983(MacLellan), elected to Senate
Stigers, Marie H.—Died Nov. 7, 1964 (Branes)[F]
Stockwell, Janet—Appointed July 24, 1940 (Stockwell)
Sullivan, Mable—Resigned Jan. 1971 (Gaborsky)(F)

Vermont, continued

Towle, Ellen G. — Appointed Jan.7, 1937 (Towle)
Ward, Aline H. — Appointed March 3, 1969 (Eurich)
Westphal, Esther G. — Appointed April 14, 1976 (Westphal)
Wilcox, Esther Elizabeth — Appointed Dec. 22, 1952 (Walsh)
Wilson, Arlene Lois — Appointed Aug. 1, 1967 (Payne); appointed Feb. 13, 1969 (Gallagher)[F]
Winship, Edna E. — Appointed Sept. 25, 1946 (Stowell)
Wright, Ruth E. — Appointed Jan. 7, 1943 (Thompson)
Young-Price, Toby — Appointed March 9, 1981 (Edwards)

VIRGIN ISLANDS,
Territory of (1953–1995)

Women in the Virgin Islands gained full suffrage in the 1936 Organic Act passed by the U. S. Congress. Ann Christian Abramson (R–St. Croix) was the first woman elected to the Virgin Islands Territorial Legislative Assembly in 1953. In 1955, Lucinda A. Mullin (D–St. Thomas) was the first woman elected to the Virgin Islands Territorial Unified Legislature.

Women as Percentage of
Virgin Islands Territorial Legislature

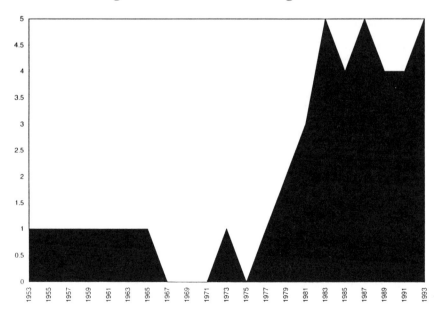

The Organic Act of 1936 established three districts for the election of members to three Municipal Councils that convened as a Legislative Assembly. In 1954 the Congress revised the Organic Act and established a Unified Legislature with state elections held every two years for 15 senators who serve two years terms in the unicameral legislature.

13 women have served in the Virgin Islands Territorial Legislature.

Senate
2 Year Terms

Name	City, County	Party	Legislative Year
Abramson, Ann Christian	St. Croix	R	1953 1957*
Berry, Lorraine L.	Charlotte Amalie, St. Thomas	D	1983 1985 1993 1995
Boschulte, Bertha C.	St. Thomas	D	1965
Gomez, Judy M.	St. Thomas	D	1993 1995
Hansen, Alicia	Christiansted, St. Croix	I	1987 1993 1995
Hodge, Cleone Creque see Maynard	St. Thomas	D	1977 1979
James, Alicia Torres	St. Croix	D	1987 1989
Maynard, Cleone Creque see Hodge	St. Thomas	D	1983 1985 1987
Mullin, Lucinda A.	St. Thomas	D	1955 1957 1959 1961 1963
O'Neal, Lilliana Bellardo de	Christiansted, St. Croix	R	1981 1983 1985 1987 1991 1993 1995
Pickard, Mary Ann	St. Croix	D	1993
Rouss, Ruby M.	St. Croix	D	1973 1975 1979 1981 1983 1985
Simmonds, Ruby	Charlotte Amalie, St. Thomas	D	1981 1983
Williams, Stephenie Scott	Charlotte Amalie, St. Thomas	D	1991

*Notes:
Abramson, Ann Christian—Appointed 1958 (Merwin).

VIRGINIA (1924–1995)

Virginia women gained suffrage August 26, 1920. Women first voted in state elections in 1923. Women first ran for the Virginia General Assembly in the

1923 state elections when Sarah Lee Fain (D–Norfolk) and Helen Timmons Henderson (D–Council, Russell County) were elected to the House of Delegates. Helen Ruth Henderson (D–Russell County) was elected to her mother's seat in 1927.

State legislative elections are held in odd years for 100 delegates who serve two year terms and 40 senators who serve four year terms. Vacancies are filled by special election.

49 women have served in the Virginia General Assembly:
    8 in the Senate
    45 in the House
    (4 in the House and Senate)

Women as Percentage of Virginia Legislators

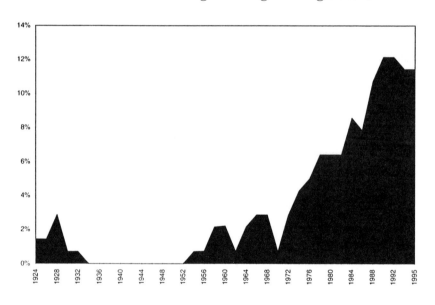

Senate
4 Year Terms

Name	City, County	Party	Legislative Year
Dalton, Edwina P. *see*			
Phillips	Richmond, Henrico	R	1988
Hailey, Evelyn M.	City Of Norfolk	D	1982*
Howell, Janet D.	Reston, Fairfax	D	1992 1994

Lucas, L. Louise	Portsmouth, Portsmouth	D	1992 1994
Miller, Emilie F.	Merrifield, Fairfax	D	1988 1990
Miller, Yvonne B.	City Of Norfolk	D	1986* 1988 1990 1992 1994
Phillips, Edwina Dalton *see Dalton*	Richmond, Henrico	R	1990
Scott, Eva Mae	Amelia, Amelia	R	1980 1982
Woods, Jane H.	Fairfax, Fairfax	R	1992 1994

House
2 Year Terms

Name	City, County	Party	Legislative Year
Baker, Inez	Portsmouth, Portsmouth	D	1958 1966
Booker, Sallie C.	Henrico, Henrico	D	1926 1928
Byrne, Leslie L.	Falls Church, Fairfax	D	1986 1988 1990 1992*
Caldwell, Vinnie	Galax,	D	1928
Christian, Mary T.	City Of Hampton	I	1986 1988 1990 1992 1994
Cody, Gwendalyn F.	Annandale, Fairfax	R	1982* 1984
Connally, Julia A.	Arlington, Arlington	D	1992 1994
Cooper, Shirley F.	Yorktown, York	D	1982* 1984 1986 1988 1990 1992 1994
Crittenden, Flora D.	City of Newport News	D	1992* 1994
Crouch, Joyce Knoles	City Of Lynchburg	R	1990 1992 1994
Cunningham, Jean W.	Richmond, Henrico	D	1986* 1988 1990 1992 1994
Darner, L. Karen	Arlington, Arlington	D	1990 1992 1994
Fain, Sarah Lee	City Of Norfolk	D	1924 1926 1928
Galland, Marion	City Of Alexandria	D	1964 1966 1968
Giesen, Charlotte C.	Radford, Montgomery	R	1958 1960
Hailey, Evelyn M.	City Of Norfolk	D	1974 1976 1978 1980
Harrison, Edythe C.	City Of Norfolk	D	1980 1982*
Heinz, Elise B.	Arlington, Arlington	D	1978 1980
Henderson, Helen Ruth	Council, Russell	D	1928
Henderson, Helen Timmons	Council, Russell	D	1924
Jones, Joan Shepherd	City of Lynchburg	D	1974 1976 1978 1980
Keating, Gladys B.	Franconia, Fairfax	D	1978 1980 1982 1984 1986 1988 1990 1992 1994
Marshall, Mary A.	Arlington, Arlington	D	1966 1968 1972 1974 1976 1978 1980 1982 1984 1986 1988 1990

Virginia House, continued

Name	City, County	Party	Legislative Year
McDiarmid, Dorothy Shoemaker	Vienna, Fairfax	D	1960 1964 1966 1968 1972 1974 1976 1978 1980 1982 1984 1986 1988
Miller, Yvonne B.	City Of Norfolk	D	1984 1986*
Munford, Joan H.	Blacksburg, Montgomery	D	1982 1984 1986 1988 1990 1992
Orebaugh, Phoebe M.	Broadway, Rockingham	R	1982* 1984 1988 1990
Paul, Bonnie L.	Shenandoah Valley, Harrisburg	R	1976 1978
Puller, Linda T.	Mt. Vernon, Fairfax	D	1992 1994
Putney, Lacey E.	Bedford, Bedford	I	1984
Rhodes, Anne G.	Richmond, Henrico	R	1992 1994
Rollins, Linda M.	Leesburg, Loudoun	R	1988 1990
Scott, Eva Mae	Amelia, Amelia	I	1972 1974 1976 1978
Sheppard, Eleanor Parker	Richmond, Henrico	D	1968 1970 1972 1974 1976
Sherwood, Beverly	Winchester, Frederick	R	1994*
Smith, Julie L.	City Of Virginia Beach	D	1982*
Squyres, Nora A.	Falls Church, Fairfax	D	1982*
Stafford, Barbara M.	Pearisburg, Bland, Giles	R	1990*
Stone, Kathryn H.	Arlington, Arlington	D	1954 1956 1958 1960 1962 1964
Terry, Mary Sue	Stuart, Patrick	D	1978 1980 1982 1984
Van Landingham, Marian A.	City Of Alexandria	D	1982 1984 1986 1988 1990 1992 1994
Wallace, Linda M.	Leesburg, Loudoun	R	1992
Watts, Vivian E.	Annandale, Fairfax	D	1982 1984
White, Emma Lee	Gloucester County	D	1930 1932
Woods, Jane H.	Fairfax, Fairfax	R	1988 1990

*Notes:

Byrne, Leslie L. — Resigned, elected to U.S. Congress Nov. 1992
Cody, Gwendalyn F. — Elected Nov. 1981, lost reapportionment election Nov. 1982, re-elected Nov. 1983
Cooper, Shirley F. — Elected reapportionment election 1982
Crittenden, Flora D. — Elected Nov. 1992 (Maxwell)
Cunningham, Jean W. — Elected Jan. 1986 (Lambert)
Hailey, Evelyn M. — Elected Nov. 1981, did not run in reapportionment election Nov. 1982
Harrison, Edythe C. — Lost reapportionment election Nov. 1982
Miller, Yvonne B. — Resigned 1987, elected to Senate (Babalas)
Orebaugh, Phoebe M. — Elected reapportionment election Nov. 1982
Sherwood, Beverly — Elected Jan. 24, 1994 (Schoonover)
Smith, Julie L. — Elected reapportionment election Nov. 1982
Squyres, Nora A. — Elected reapportionment election Nov. 1982
Stafford, Barbara Jo Morris — Elected Nov. 6, 1990 (Stafford)

WASHINGTON (1911–1995)

Washington women first gained suffrage by territorial legislative enactment in 1883 and voted in the 1894 and 1896 elections, then lost the privilege by a state Supreme Court decision. In 1887 they tried again, but lost again in a state Supreme Court ruling. School suffrage for women was enacted in 1890. Women finally gained full suffrage after statehood in a 1910 constitutional amendment. Women first voted in state elections in 1912 and elected Frances C. Axtell (R–Bellingham, Whatcom County) and Dr. Nena Jolidon Croake (Progressive–Tacoma, Pierce County) to the house. Lulu Haddon and her daughter, Frances Haddon Morgan both served in the House and Senate representing Ketsap County. Audrey Lindgren Gruger's mother, Mable Lindgren (Nonpartisan–Minot, Ward County), served in the North Dakota House 1929-30.

State elections are held every two years for 98 representatives who serve two year terms and 49 senators who serve four year terms. State legislative service is limited for the house to six out of twelve years and for the senate for eight out of fourteen years. Limitation years began in November 1992. Vacancies are filled by governor's appointment and special election.

Women as Percentage of Washington Legislators

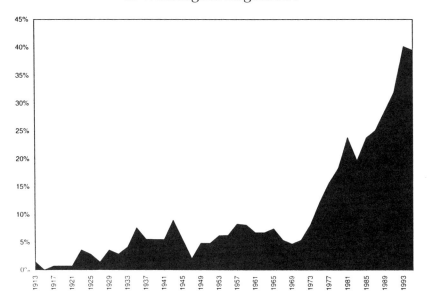

190 women have served in the Washington State Legislature:
   50 in the Senate
   168 in the House
   (28 in the House and Senate)

Senate
4 Year Terms

Name	City, County	Party	Legislative Year
Anderson, Ann	Bellingham, Whatcom	R	1987 1989 1991 1993 1995
Buffington, Nancy	Seattle, King	R	1975 1977
Craswell, Ellen	Bremerton, Kitsap	R	1981 1983 1985 1987 1989 1991
Drew, Kathleen	Issaquah, King	D	1993 1995
Fairley, Barbara	Seattle, King	D	1995
Farquharson, Mary U.	Seattle, King	D	1935 1937 1939 1941
Forbus, Lady Willie	Seattle, King	D	1943 1945
Franklin, Rosa	Tacoma, Pierce	D	1993* 1995
Fraser, Karen	Lacey, Thurston	D	1993 1995
Gehrman, Agnes M.	Raymond, Pacific	R	1941 1943
Gould, Susan	Edmonds, Snohomish	R	1975 1977 1979 1981
Granlund, Barbara	Port Orchard, Kitsap	D	1983 1985*
Haddon, Lulu B.	Bremerton, Kitsay	D	1937 1939 1941*
Hale, Patricia	Kennewick, Benton	R	1995
Hankins, Shirley W.	Richland, Benton	R	1989*
Happy, Majorie B.	Spokane, Spokane	R	1961*
Haugen, Mary Margaret	Camano Island, Snohomish	D	1993 1995
Hayner, Jeanette C.	Walla Walla, Walla Walla	R	1977 1979 1981 1983 1985 1987 1989 1991
Hurley, Margaret	Spokane, Spokane	D	1979* 1981 1983
Hurn, Reba J.	Spokane, Spokane	R	1923 1925 1927 1929
Johnson, Gertrude L.	Rolling Bay, Kitsap	D	1943*
Kohl, Jeanne	Seattle, King	D	1995
Kreidler, Lela	Olimpia, Thurston	D	1991*
Lee, Eleanor	Burien, King	R	1977* 1979 1981 1983 1985 1987 1989
Long, Jeanine H.	Mill Creek, Snohomish	R	1995
Loveland, Valoria H.	Pasco, Franklin	D	1993 1995
Malstrom, Katherine E.	Tacoma, Pierce	D	1933 1935 1939 1941 1943
McAuliffe, Rosemary	Bothell, King	D	1993 1995
Monohon, Carol A.	Raymond, Pacific	D	1977*
Morgan, Frances Haddon	Bremerton, Kitsap	D	1961 1963 1965 1967
Murray, Patty	Seattle, King	D	1989 1991*

Niemi, Janice	Seattle, King	D	1987* 1989 1991 1993
North, Lois	Seattle, King	R	1975 1977 1979*
Prentice, Margarita	Seattle, King	D	1993 1995
Rasmussen, Marilyn	Eatonville, Pierce	D	1993 1995
Reid, Katherine	Spokane, Spokane	D	1979*
Ridder, Ruthe B.	Seattle, King	D	1973* 1975 1977 1979 1981
Rinehart, Nita	Seattle, King	D	1983 1985 1987 1989 1991 1993 1995
Roach, Pamela N.	Auburn, King	R	1991 1993 1995
Sheldon, Betti L.	Bremerton, Kitsap	D	1993 1995
Skratek, Sylvia P.	Kent, King	D	1991* 1993
Smith, Linda A.	Vancouver, Clark	R	1987* 1989 1991 1993 1995
Spanel, Harriet A.	Bellingham, Whatcom	D	1993 1995
Stratton, Lois J.	Spokane, Spokane	D	1985 1987 1989 1991
Vozenilek, Beverly	Tacoma, Pierce	R	1979*
Wanamaker, Pearl A.	Coupeville, Snohomish	D	1935* 1937 1939*
Winsley, Shirley J.	Fircrest, Pierce	R	1993 1995
Wojahn, Lorraine R.	Tacoma, Pierce	D	1977 1979 1981 1983 1985 1987 1989 1991 1993 1995
Wood, Jeanette	Woodway, Snohomish	R	1995
Woody, Dianne	Woodinville, King	D	1977* 1979 1981 1983

House
2 Year Terms

Name	City, County	Party	Legislative Year
Allen, Katherine Y.	Edmonds, Snohomish	R	1983 1985 1987*
Anderson, Eva	Chelan, Chelan	R	1949 1951 1953 1955 1957 1959
Axtell, Frances C.	Bellingham, Whatcom	R	1913
Ballasiotes, Ida	Mercer Island, King	R	1993 1995
Becker, Mary Kay	Bellingham, Whatcom	D	1975 1977 1979 1981
Behm, Georgiana	Everett, Snohomish	D	1943
Belcher, Jennifer	Olympia, Thurston	D	1983 1985 1987 1989 1991
Berleen, Jeanette	Seattle, King	R	1981
Boede, Violet P.	Orcas Island, San Juan	D	1935 1937 1941 1943 1945 1949
Bowman, Rose	Centralia, Lewis	R	1989 1991
Bradford, Gene	Snohomish, Snohomish	D	1937
Brekke, Joanne J.	Seattle, King	D	1977* 1979 1981 1983 1985 1987 1989 1991
Brough, Jean Marie	Federal Way, King	R	1983 1985 1987 1989 1991 1993
Brown, Lisa J.	Spokane, Spokane	D	1993 1995

Washington House, continued

Name	City, County	Party	Legislative Year
Cantwell, Maria	Mountain Terrace, Snohomish	D	1987 1989 1991
Casada, Sarah M.	Puyallup, Pierce	R	1991 1993 1995
Clocksin, Virginia	Port Ludlow, Mason	R	1967
Cochran, Pat	Richland, Benton	D	1975
Cody, Eileen	Seattle, King	D	1995
Cohen, A. Lou	Seattle, King	D	1935
Cole, Grace	Seattle, King	D	1981* 1983 1985 1987 1989 1991 1993 1995
Colwell, Anna K.	Marysville, Snohomish	R	1919* 1921
Cooke, Suzette	Kent, King	R	1993 1995
Costa, Jeralita	Marysville, Snohomish	D	1995
Cothern, Barbara S.	Bothell, King	D	1993
Coughlin, Margaret	Seattle, King	D	1937
Craswell, Ellen	Bremerton, Kitsap	R	1977 1979
Croake, Nena J.	Tacoma, Pierce	Pro	1913
Dickerson, Mary I.	Seattle, King	D	1995
Doty, Shirley L.	Yakima, Yakima	R	1985 1987 1989
Edlund, Lenea L.	Seattle, King	D	1935
Edmondson, Betty L.	Yakima, Yakima	R	1991 1993
Eide, Tracey	Federal Way, King	D	1993
Ellis, Jerry	Yakima, Yakima	D	1983
Epton, Kathryn	Spokane, Spokane	D	1957 1959 1961 1965
Erickson, Phyllis K.	Tacoma, Pierce	D	1973 1975 1977 1979 1981*
Fancher, Helen	Tonasket, Oknogan	R	1977 1979 1981
Fisher, Ruth	Tacoma, Pierce	D	1983 1985 1987 1989 1991 1993 1995
Flint, Sally	Pierce County	R	1979*
Fogg, Kathryn	Seattle, King	D	1939
Forner, Elmira	Kent, King	R	1989* 1991 1993
Fortson, Eleanor A.	Camano Island, Snohomish	D	1973 1975 1977
Franklin, Rosa	Tacoma, Pierce	D	1991 1993*
Fraser, Karen	Lacey, Thurston	D	1989 1991
Galloway, Shirley A.	Vancouver, Clark	D	1979 1981 1983
Gehrman, Agnes M.	Raymond, Pacific	R	1947
Gleason, Marian C.	Tacoma, Pierce	D	1957 1959 1961 1963
Granlund, Barbara	Port Orchard, Kitsap	D	1979 1981
Gruger, Audrey Lindgren	Seattle, King	D	1977 1979 1981*
Haddon, Lulu B.	Bremerton, Kitsap	D	1933 1935
Hankins, Shirley W.	Richland, Benton	R	1981 1983 1985 1987 1989* 1995
Hansen, Julia Butler	Cathlamet, Wahkiakum	D	1939 1941 1943 1945 1947 1949 1951 1953 1955 1957 1959

Harman, Emma	Renton, King	D	1943
Taylor *see Taylor*			
Haskell, Frances M.	Tacoma, Pierce	R	1919
Haugen, Mary Margaret	Camona Island, Snohomish	D	1983 1985 1987 1989 1991
Hayner, Jeanette C.	Walla Walla, Walla Walla	R	1973 1975
Henry, Mildred E.	White Salmon, Benton	D	1957* 1959 1961 1963
Hine, Lorraine Ann	Des Moines, King	D	1981 1983 1985 1987 1989 1991 1993
Holm, Barbara	Olympia, Thurston	D	1987 1993
Houchen, Joan	Camona Island, Snohomish	R	1979 1981
Hurley, Margaret	Spokane, Spokane	D	1953 1955 1957 1959 1961 1963 1965 1967 1969 1971 1973 1975 1977 1979*
Hutchinson, Mary	Tacoma, Pierce	R	1929 1931
Hymes, Cheryl	Mt. Vernon, Skagit	R	1995
Johnson, Doris J.	Kennewick, Benton	D	1965 1967 1971 1973
Johnson, Gertrude L.	Rolling Bay, Kitsap	D	1943*
Johnson, Linda Sue	Bothell, King	D	1993
Johnson, Margaret L.	Shelton, Mason	R	1991
Johnson, Peggy	Shelton, Mason	R	1995
Jones, Matilda	Seattle, King	R	1949 1951 1955
Karahalios, Sue M.	Oak Harbor, Island	D	1993
Kastner, Jessie B.	S. Tacoma, Pierce	F-L	1923
Keen, Marie F.	Longview, Cowlitz	R	1935
Kehoe, Agnes	Spokane, Spokane	D	1939 1941 1943 1945
Kelley, Grace	Aberdeen, Grays Harbor	D	1949
Kessler, Lynn	Hoquiam, Grays Harbor	D	1993 1995
King, Majorie	Seattle, King	D	1965*
Kirk, Gladys	Seattle, King	R	1957 1959* 1961 1963 1965 1967 1969 1971
Kohl, Jeanne	Seattle, King	D	1993
Lambert, Kathy	Redmon, King	R	1995
Lane, Jay	Seattle, King	R	1981*
Lanz, Ester M.	Tacoma, Pierce	D	1933
Lecocq, Mary	Lynden, Whatcom	R	1953
Lee, Eleanor	Burien, King	R	1975 1977*
Leonard, June	Seattle, King	D	1985 1987 1989 1991 1993
Leonard, Margaret J.	Spokane, Spokane	R	1981
Linville, Kelli	Bellingham, Whatcom	D	1993
Lisk, Barbara	Zillah, Yakima	R	1991 1993 1995
Long, Jeanine H.	Mill Creek, Snohomish	R	1983 1985 1993
Lux, Mary Stuart	Olympia, Thurston	D	1965 1967
Lynch, Majorie	Yakima, Yakima	R	1963 1965 1967 1969 1971
Mason, Dawn	Seattle, King	D	1995

Washington House, continued

Maxie, Peggy Joan	Seattle, King	D	1971 1973 1975 1977 1979 1981
May, Catherine D.	Yakima, Yakima	R	1953 1955 1957
McCaffree, Mary Ellen	Seattle, King	R	1963 1965 1967 1969
McCormick, Geraldine	Spokane, Spokane	D	1969 1971 1973 1975 1977 1979 1981
McMahan, Lois	Gig Harbor, Pierce	R	1995
McMorris, Cathy	Colville, King	R	1993* 1995
McQuesten, Ida	Tacoma, Pierce	R	1929 1931
Meddins, Winnifred C. P.	Tacoma, Pierce	D	1943
Meyers, Florence W.	Colfax, Whitman	D	1933 1935 1937
Miller, Louise	Woodinville, King	R	1983 1985 1987 1989 1991 1993*
Miller, Mabel I.	Everett, Snohomish	R	1923 1925
Mitchell, Maryanne	Federal Way, King	R	1991 1995
Monohon, Carol A.	Raymond, Pacific	D	1977* 1979 1981 1983
Morgan, Frances H.	Bremerton, Kitsap	D	1959
Morgen, Gladys	Spokane, Spokane	R	1975*
Morris, Betty Sue	Vancouver, Clark	D	1989 1991 1993 1995
Mulliken, Joyce	Ephrata, Grant	R	1995
Myers, Holly M.	Vancouver, Clark	D	1989 1991 1993
Niemi, Janice	Seattle, King	D	1983 1985 1987*
North, Frances	North Bend, King	D	1973 1975 1977 1979 1981
North, Lois	Seattle, King	R	1969 1971 1973
Nutley, Busse	Vancouver, Clark	D	1985 1987 1989
O'Donnell, Ann T.	Seattle, King	D	1959* 1961 1963 1965*
Ogden, Val	Vancouver, Clark	D	1991 1993 1995
Osterman, Leona S.	Shelton, Mason	D	1975*
Parker, Adela	Seattle, King	D	1935
Patterson, Julia	Seattle, King	D	1993 1995
Pearsall, Cathy	Tacoma, Pierce	D	1977
Pennick, Blanche	Montesano, Pacific	D	1945
Phillips, Gladys	Aberdeen, Grays Harbor	R	1951
Powers, Carolyn	Port Orchard, Kitsap	D	1983
Prentice, Margarita	Seattle, King	D	1987* 1989 1991
Radcliff, Renee	Mulkiteo, Island	R	1995
Rasmussen, Marilyn	Eatonville, Pierce	D	1987 1989 1991
Rayburn, Margaret	Grandview, Yakima	D	1985 1987 1989 1991 1993
Rector, Shirley	Spokane, Spokane	D	1989
Reeves, Belle Culp	Wenatchee, Chelan	D	1923 1925 1931 1933 1935 1937*
Regala, Diane	Tacoma, Pierce	D	1995
Ridgway, Emma Abbott	Sedro Woolley, Skagit	D	1945 1949 1951 1953 1955

Rinehart, Nita	Seattle, King	D	1979* 1981
Roland, Judi D.	Auburn, King	D	1991 1993
Romero, Sandra S.	Olympia, Thurston	D	1993 1995
Rosbach, Wilma	Chehalis, Lewis	D	1979 1981
Rust, Nancy S.	Seattle, King	D	1981 1983 1985 1987 1989 1991 1993 1995
Schmidt, Karen	Bainbridge, Kitsap	R	1981 1983 1985 1987 1989 1991 1993 1995
Scott, Patricia	Everett, Snohomish	D	1983* 1985 1987 1989 1991 1993 1995
Sherman, Marion Kyle	Maple Valley, King	D	1975 1977 1979 1981
Silver, Billie Jean	Spokane, Spokane	R	1983 1985 1987 1989 1991 1993 1995
Skinner, Mary	Yakima, Yakima	R	1995
Smith, Linda A.	Vancouver, Clark	R	1983* 1985 1987*
Smith, Nettie Luella	Seattle, King	D	1943* 1945
Sommers, Helen	Seattle, King	D	1973 1975 1977 1979 1981 1983 1985 1987 1989 1991 1993 1995
Spanel, Harriet A.	Bellingham, Whatcom	D	1987 1989 1991
Stevens, Val	Arlington, Snohomish	R	1993 1995
Stratton, Lois J.	Spokane, Spokane	D	1979* 1981 1983
Swayze, Frances G.	Gig Harbor, Pierce	R	1953 1955 1957 1959 1961 1963 1965*
Sweetman, Maude	Seattle, King	R	1923 1925 1927 1929
Talcott, Gigi	Tacoma, Pierce	R	1993 1995
Taylor, Emma see Harman	Renton, King	D	1941
Testu, Jeanette	Seattle, King	D	1943 1949 1951 1953 1955 1957 1959 1961
Teutsch, Delores E.	Kirkland, King	R	1979 1981
Thibaudeau, Pat	Seattle, King	D	1993 1995
Thomas, Linda Craig	Gig Harbor, Pierce	R	1985
Thrasher, Pearl	Seattle, King	D	1945
Twidwell, Vivien	Aberdeen, Grays Harbor	D	1957 1959
Unsoeld, Jolene	Olympia, Thurston	D	1985 1987
Valle, Georgette W.	Seattle, King	D	1965 1973 1975 1977 1979 1981 1985 1987 1989 1991 1993 1995
Veloria, Velma R.	Seattle, King	D	1993 1995
Walker, Sally	Tacoma, Pierce	R	1985 1987 1989*
Wanamaker, Pearl A.	Coupeville, Snohomish	D	1929 1931 1933 1935*
Williams, Ina P.	N. Yakima, Yakima	Pro	1917
Wilson, Karla	Lake Stevens, Snohomish	D	1985 1987 1989

Washington House, continued

Name	City, County	Party	Legislative Year
Winsley, Shirley J.	Fircrest, Pierce	R	1973* 1977 1979 1981 1985 1987 1989 1991
Wintler, Ella	Vancouver, Clark	R	1939 1943 1947 1951 1953 1955 1957 1959 1961 1963
Wojahn, Lorraine R.	Tacoma, Pierce	D	1969 1971 1973 1975
Wolfe, Cathy	Olympia, Thurston	D	1993 1995
Wood, Jeanette	Woodway, Snohomish	R	1987* 1989 1991 1993
Wynne, Linda	Benton County	R	1977*

*Notes:

Allen, Katherine Y.—Died June 7, 1988 (Wood)[F]
Brekke, Joanne J.—Appointed Feb. 6, 1978 (Williams)
Cole, Grace—Appointed Jan. 11, 1982 (Gruger)[F]
Colwell, Anna K.—Appointed March 20, 1920 (Gorham)
Erickson, Phyllis K.—Resigned May 1, 1981 (Kaiser)
Flint, Sally—Appointed Jan. 9, 1980 (Haley)
Forner, Elmira—Appointed Jan. 8, 1990 (Patrick)
Franklin, Rosa—Resigned Jan. 25, 1993, appointed to Senate (Rasmussen)
Granlund, Barbara—Resigned Sept. 1, 1985 (W.Granland)
Gruger, Audrey Lindgren—Resigned Jan. 10, 1982 (Cole)[F]
Haddon, Lulu B.—Resigned Dec. 4, 1942 (Klinefelter)
Hankins, Shirley W.—Resigned Sept. 19, 1990, elected to Senate (Benizt)
Happy, Majorie B.—Appointed 1962 (Happy)
Henry, Mildred E.—Appointed Jan. 24, 1957 (Olson)
Hurley, Margaret—Resigned Nov. 6, 1979, elected to Senate (Reid)[F]
Johnson, Gertrude L.—Appointed Nov. 17, 1942 (Klinefelter), resigned Nov. 22, 1943, appointed to Senate (Klinefelter)
King, Majorie—Appointed Sept. 2, 1965 (O'Donnell)[F]
Kirk, Gladys—Appointed & Elected June 1959 (Moriaty)
Kreidler, Lela—Appointed Jan. 14, 1991 (Kreidler)
Lane, Jay—Appointed Jan. 14, 1981 (Taller)
Lee, Eleanor—Resigned Nov. 1977, elected to Senate (Rohrbach)
McMorris, Cathy—Elected Jan. 1994 (Morton)
Miller, Louise—Resigned Jan. 3, 1994 (Backlunds)
Monohon, Carol A.—Resigned March 14, 1977, appointed to Senate (Bailey)
Morgen, Gladys—Appointed Jan. 25, 1976 (Luders)
Murray, Patty—Resigned Nov. 1992, elected U.S. Senate
Niemi, Janice—Resigned Sept. 18, 1987 (Anderson), appointed to Senate (McDermott)
North, Lois—Resigned Dec. 31, 1979 (Bradburn)
O'Donnell, Ann T.—Appointed Mar. 3, 1959 (Dore), died May 25, 1965 (King)[F]
Osterman, Leona Savage—Appointed 1976 (father, Savage)
Prentice, Margarita—Appointed May 31, 1988 (Lux)
Reeves, Belle Culp—Resigned Feb. 1938, appointed Secretary of State
Reid, Katherine—Appointed Aug. 13, 1979 (Keefe), resigned Nov. 6, 1979 (Hurley)[F]
Ridder, Ruthe B.—Elected July 19, 1973 (Lux)
Rinehart, Nita—Appointed Nov. 6, 1979 (Douthwaite)
Scott, Patricia—Appointed Jan. 4, 1984 (Martinis)
Skratek, Sylvia P.—Elected Nov. 6, 1990

Smith, Linda A. — Elected Nov. 8, 1983 (Rostibem), resigned Dec. 4, 1987 (Butterfield) elected
    to Senate (Tanner), resigned Nov. 1994, elected to US Congress
Smith, Nettie Luella — Appointed Dec. 1942 (Smith)
Stratton, Lois J. — Appointed Jan. 3, 1980 (Hurley)[F]
Swayze, Frances G. — Resigned Sept. 29, 1965 (son, Thomas Jr.)
Vozenilek, Beverly — Appointed Aug. 2, 1979 (Newschwander)
Walker, Sally — Resigned Sept. 28, 1990 (Broback)
Wanamaker, Pearl A. — Resigned Jan. 1937, appointed to Senate (Tewksbury), resigned
    Dec. 7, 1940 (Bargren)
Winsley, Shirley J. — Appointed April 12, 1974 (Kelley)
Wood, Jeanette — Appointed July 29, 1988 (Allen)[F]
Woody, Dianne — Appointed Sept. 27, 1977 (Woody)
Wynne, Linda — Appointed June 8, 1978 (Boldt)

WEST VIRGINIA (1923–1995)

West Virginia women gained suffrage on August 26, 1920. Anna Johnston
Gates (D–Charleston, Kanawha County) became West Virginia's first woman
lawmaker when she was elected to the House of Delegates in 1922.

Women as Percentage
of West Virginia Legislators

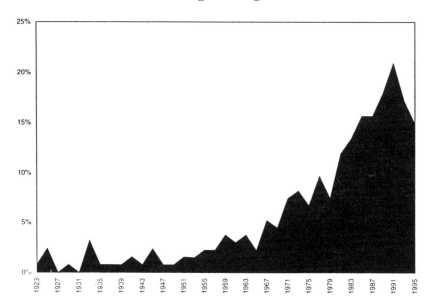

State elections are held every two years for 100 delegates who serve two year terms and 34 senators who serve four year staggered terms. Vacancies are filled by governor's appointment.

122 women have served in the West Virginia State Legislature:
    17 in the Senate
    111 in the House
    (6 in the House and Senate)

Senate
4 Year Terms

Name	City, County	Party	Legislative Year
Baker, Bettie H.	Moorefield, Hardy	D	1965* 1967
Blatnik, Thais Shuler	Wheeling, Ohio	D	1989 1991 1993 1995
Boley, Donna J.	St. Mary's, Pleasants	R	1985* 1987 1989 1991 1993 1995
Chase, Jean Scott	Weston, Lewis	D	1981 1983
Dice, Jane	Greenbrier County	D	1939*
Herndon, Judith A.	Wheeling, Ohio	R	1973* 1975 1977 1979 1981
Hyre, Hazel Edna	Ripley, Jackson	D	1933*
Leonard, Louise	Harpers Ferry, Jefferson	R	1971 1973
Lucht, Sondra Moore	Martinsburg, Berkeley	D	1983* 1985 1987 1989 1991 1993
Marchand, Mary O.	Morgantown, Monongalia	D	1957*
Minear, Sarah M.	Parsons, Tucker	R	1995
Pritt, Charlotte J.	Charleston, Kanawha	D	1989 1991
Rundle, Juliet Walker	Pineville, Wyoming	D	1989 1991*
Spears, Ursula Jae	Elkins, Randolph	D	1981 1983 1985 1987 1989 1991
Walker, Martha Yeager	Charleston, Kanawha	D	1993 1995
Wehrle, Martha G.	Charleston, Kanawha	D	1989* 1991 1993
White, Rebecca I.	Jane Lew, Harrison	D	1995

House
2 Year Terms

Name	City, County	Party	Legislative Year
Andrews, Eudora Catherine	Charleston, Kanawha	D	1959
Baker, Betty C.	Huntington, Cabell	D	1963*
Belcher, Mae S.	Pineville, Wyoming	D	1959 1963
Blatnik, Thais Shuler	Wheeling, Ohio	D	1977 1981 1983 1985

Bledsoe, June	Charleston, Kanawha	D	1981 1983
Boiarsky, Barbara	Charleston, Kanawha	D	1971*
Bolling, Helen B.	Harrison County	D	1967*
Bradley, Patricia Mastrantoni *see* Mastrantoni	Weirton, Hancock	D	1989*
Brown, Bonnie S.	Charleston, Kanawha	D	1983 1985 1987 1991 1993
Brum, Brenda	Parkersburg, Wood	D	1991 1993
Burke, Marjorie	Glenville, Gilmer	D	1977* 1981 1983 1985 1987 1989 1995
Calvert, Ann	Charleston, Kanawha	R	1991 1995
Caperton, Dee	Charleston, Kanawha	D	1987
Cerra, Ramona Gail	Charleston, Kanawha	D	1989 1991
Cole, Phyllis	Weston, Grant	D	1989*
Compton, Mary Pearl	Union, Monroe	D	1989 1991 1993 1995
Cook, Delores W.	Ridgeview, Monroe	D	1989 1991 1993
Cooke, Hannah W. Alexander	Charlestown, Jefferson	D	1925*
Craig, Michele Prestera *see Prestera*	Huntington, Cabell	D	1977
Crandall, Ethel L.	Huntington, Cabell	D	1963 1967 1969 1971 1977 1979 1981 1983 1985 1987
Crookshanks, Betty Dorsey	Rupert, Greenbrier	D	
Davis, Elizabeth A.	Montgomery, Fayette	R	1925
Davis, Sue A.	Huntington, Cabell	D	1981 1983 1985
Douglas, Vicki V.	Martinsburg, Berkeley	D	1991 1993 1995
Drewry, Elizabeth Simpson	Northfork, McDowell	D	1951 1953 1955 1957 1959 1961 1963
Edgar, Betsy J.	Hillsboro, Pocahontas	D	1971*
Evans, Frances	Logan, Logan	D	1949
Facemyer, Karen L.	Ripley, Jackson	R	1993 1995
Flannery, Mildred	Logan, Logan	D	1957*
Fleischauer, Barbara Evans	Morgantown, Monogalia	D	1995
Garrett, Linda Nelson	Curtin, Webster	D	1985 1987
Gates, Anna Johnston	Charleston, Kanawha	D	1923
Gillispie, Lucille E.	Clendenin, Kanawha	R	1973
Given, Kelly	Hurricane, Putnam	R	1995
Given, Phyllis E.	Charleston, Kanawha	D	1971 1973 1975 1981 1985 1987 1989
Goldsmith, Ruth	Charleston, Kanawha	R	1981 1991
Hall, Fannie A.	New Martinsville, Wetzel	D	1925*
Hallanan, Elizabeth V.	Charleston, Kanawha	R	1957*
Harman, Pearl Theressa	Yukon, McDowell	R	1933
Harper, Minnie Buckingham	Keystone, McDowell	R	1927*
Hartman, Patricia Ogden	Huntington, Cabell	D	1977 1979 1981 1983 1987
Hatfield, Barbara A.	Charleston, Kanawha	D	1985 1987 1989

West Virginia House, continued

Name	City, County	Party	Legislative Year
Hathaway, Grace M.	Grantsville, Calhoun	R	1945*
Herndon, Judith A.	Wheeling, Ohio	R	1969* 1971 1973*
Holt, Helen	Weston, Lewis	R	1955*
Holt, Jean S.	Charleston, Kanawha	R	1973
Holt, Katherine	Hinton, Summers	D	1983*
Hubbard, Susan	Huntington, Cabell	D	1995
James, Bianca M.	Jefferson County	D	1975*
Johnson, Katie B.	Sutton, Braxton	D	1945*
Jones, Dr. Harriet B.	Glendale, Marshall	R	1925
Kessel, Nancy	Charleston, Kanawha	D	1991 1993
Kurtz, Virginia Reay	Weston, Lewis	R	1939*
Lane, Charlotte R.	Charleston, Kanawha	R	1979 1985 1991
Leach, Margarette	Huntington, Cabell	D	1993 1995
Leary, Shelby Bosley	Blacksville, Monongalia	D	1983 1985 1987
Long, Lydia D.	Pt. Pleasant, Mason	D	1989
Maple, Erma	Folansbee, Brooke	D	1969*
Martin, Elizabeth M.	Morgantown, Monongalia	D	1981 1983 1985
Mastrantoni, Patricia *see Bradley*	Weirton, Hancock	D	1985 1987
Mathis, Maxie	Wayne, Wayne	D	1965
McCallister, Joan	Winfield, Putnam	D	1983
Meadows, Lucille	Fayetteville, Fayette	D	1991*
Merow, Florence L.	Morgantown, Monongalia	D	1985 1989
Merritt, Mary Martha	Beckley, Raleigh	D	1971 1973
Metheney, Twila S.	Morgantown, Monongalia	D	1987 1989
Miller, Peggy	Charleston, Kanawha	R	1989 1991 1993 1995
Mills, Opaldene	Welch, McDowell	D	1957*
Neal, Sarah Lee	Rainell, Greenbrier	D	1973 1975 1977 1979 1981 1983 1985 1987
Osborne, Elizabeth	Princeton, Mercer	D	1995
Paul, Freda Nobel	Huntington, Cabell	D	1965 1967 1971
Payne, Jessica	Huntington, Cabell	R	1957
Pettit, Tamara	New Cumberland, Hancock	D	1989* 1991 1993 1995
Phillips, Deborah F.	Scott Depot, Putnam	D	1985 1987 1989 1991 1993
Pickett, Shirley	Kyle, McDowell	D	1969*
Pitsenberger, Julia Lockridge	Elkin, Randolph	D	1975 1977
Potts, Louise Gowdy	Grafton, Taylor	R	1943*
Presley, Phyllis A.	Raleigh County	D	1979*
Prestera, Michele Craig *see Craig*	Huntington, Cabell	D	1973 1975
Price, Lucy Montgomery S.	Scarbro, Fayette	D	1933 1935
Pritt, Charlotte J.	Charleston, Kanawha	D	1985 1987

Proctor, Allie Dickerson	Cliffton, Fayette	D	1935*
Radenbaugh, Frances Irving	Parkersburg, Wood	R	1929
Reed, Pat	Beckley, Raleigh	D	1991 1993
Richards, Evelyn E.	Huntington, Cabell	R	1979 1985 1989 1991 1993
Rogers, Sandy	Vienna, Wood	R	1981 1983 1985 1987
Rotgin, Helaine	Charleston, Kanawha	D	1977
Rutledge, Phyllis J.	Charleston, Kanawha	D	1969 1971 1973 1989 1991 1993*
Schupbach, Evelyn	New Martinsville, Wetzel	D	1965* 1967
Sharp, Jane Price	Pocahontas County	D	1989*
Shuman, Pamela Sue	Wellsburg, Brooke	D	1973* 1975 1977 1979 1981
Sims, Barbara W.	Parkersburg, Wood	R	1991
Smirl, Jody Guthrie	Huntington, Cabell	R	1967 1969 1971 1973 1985 1995
Snyder, Carolyn M.	Charles Town, Jefferson	D	1977*
Spears, Ursula Jae	Elkins, Randolph	D	1975 1977 1979
Spencer, Sharon	Charleston, Kanawha	D	1983 1987 1989 1991 1993
Starcher, Virginia Jollifeer	Ripley, Jackson	D	1987 1989
Strite, Lucille Scott	Berkeley Springs, Morgan	D	1931*
Suddarth, Eddie M.	Grafton, Taylor	D	1933
Theiling, Jane H.	Charleston, Kanawha	D	1981 1983
Thornhill, Lucille	Bluefield, Mercer	D	1965* 1969
Tsapis, Callie	Weirton, Hancock	D	1959 1961 1963 1967
Van Sickler, Mary	Lewisburg, Greenbrier	D	1945*
Walker, Martha Yeager	Charleston, Kanawha	D	1991
Walker, Nell W.	Winona, Fayette	D	1937 1939 1941 1943 1945 1947 1949 1951 1953 1955 1959 1961
Warner, Barbara A.	Bridgeport, Harrison	D	1989 1991 1993 1995
Wehrle, Martha G.	Charleston, Kanawha	D	1975 1977 1979 1981 1983
White, Patricia Holmes	Poca, Putnam	D	1985 1987 1989 1991 1993
Williams, Margaret Potts	Jefferson County	D	1941*
Withrow, Jackie	Beckley, Raleigh	D	1961 1963 1965 1967 1969 1971 1973 1975 1977
Woods, Winifred Davis	Williamsville, Ritchie	R	1941*
Yeager, Emily W.	Welch, McDowell	D	1993* 1995
Yoho, Pearle	Marshall County	D	1961*

*Notes:

Baker, Bettie H.—Appointed Jan. 11, 1965 (Baker)
Baker, Betty C.—Appointed Jan. 7, 1964 (Baker)
Boiarsky, Barbara—Appointed April 13, 1971 (Boiarsky)
Boley, Donna J.—Appointed May 14, 1985 (White)
Bolling, Helen B.—Appointed June 27, 1968 (Marstiller)
Bradley, Patricia Mastrantoni—Resigned Nov. 1, 1989 (Pettit)(F)
Burke, Marjorie—Appointed April 13, 1978 (Burke)
Cole, Phyllis—Appointed Oct. 23, 1989 (Harmon)
Cooke, Hannah W. Alexander—Appointed Jan. 27, 1926 (Cooke)
Dice, Jane—Appointed Dec. 26, 1939 (Jasper)
Edgar, Betsy J.—Appointed April 18, 1972 (Edgar)
Evans, Frances—Appointed May 16, 1949 (Trent)
Flannery, Mildred—Appointed March 19, 1958 (Flannery)
Hall, Fannie A.—Appointed April 2, 1926 (Hall)
Hallanan, Elizabeth V.—Resigned July 1, 1957
Harper, Minnie Buckingham—Appointed Jan. 19, 1928 (Harper)
Hathaway, Grace M.—Appointed Nov. 7, 1945 (Hathaway)
Herndon, Judith A.—Appointed June 2, 1970 (Campanion), resigned July 3, 1974,
  appointed to Senate
Holt, Helen—Appointed Feb. 17, 1955 (Holt)
Holt, Katherine—Appointed Aug. 20, 1984 (Holt)
Hyre, Hazel Edna—Appointed March 12, 1934 (Hyre)
James, Bianca M.—Appointed Oct. 11, 1976 (Snyder)[F]
Johnson, Katie B.—Appointed March 7, 1945 (Johnson)
Kurtz, Virginia Reay—Appointed Dec. 26, 1939 (Kurtz)
Maple, Erma—Died July 1969 (Schwertfeger)
Marchand, Mary O.—Appointed June 17, 1958 (Marchand)
Mathis, Maxie—Appointed Dec. 16, 1965 (Mathis)
Meadows, Lucille—Appointed Dec. 11, 1990 (Hatcher)
Mills, Opaldene—Appointed June 19, 1958 (Mills)
Pettit, Tamara—Appointed Dec. 1, 1989 (Bradley)[F]
Pickett, Shirley—Appointed July 9, 1969 (Wooten)
Potts, Louise Gowdy—Appointed Dec. 18, 1943 (Potts)
Presley, Phyllis A.—Appointed Jan 16, 1979 (Stacy)
Proctor, Allie Dickerson—Appointed June 13, 1936 (Procter)
Rundle, Juliet Walker—Resigned Dec. 31, 1990 (Bailey)
Rutledge, Phyllis J.—Resigned March 31, 1994
Schupbach, Evelyn—Appointed Sept. 20, 1965 (Schupbach)
Sharp, Jane Price—Appointed Oct. 23, 1989 (Helmick)
Shuman, Pamela Sue—Appointed Jan. 30, 1974 (D'Aurora)
Snyder, Carolyn M.—Resigned Oct. 11, 1977 (James)[F]
Strite, Lucille Scott—Appointed Sept. 1931 (Scott)
Thornhill, Lucille—Appointed Oct. 28, 1965 (Holroyd)
Van Sickler, Mary—Appointed Feb. 27, 1945 (Van Sickler)
Wehrle, Martha G.—Appointed Sept. 5, 1989 (Holmes)
Williams, Margaret Potts—Appointed Nov. 19, 1941 (Alexander)
Woods, Winifred Davis—Appointed March 19, 1941 (Woods)
Yeager, Emily W.—Appointed March 10, 1993 (Whitley)
Yoho, Pearle—Appointed Sept. 14, 1961 (Pastilong)

WISCONSIN (1925-1995)

Wisconsin women gained school suffrage in 1900, presidential suffrage by legislative enactment in 1919 and state suffrage on August 26, 1920. Women first voted in state elections in 1920 and first ran for the state legislature in the state elections in 1922. Three women were elected to the House in 1924, Mildred Barber (R–Marathon, Marathon County), Hellen M. Brooks (R–Coloma, Green Lake County), and Helen F. Thompson (R–Park Falls, Price Lake County).

State elections are held every two years for 99 representatives who serve two year terms and 55 senators who serve four year staggered terms. Even numbered senate districts were elected in 1992 and odd numbered districts in 1994. Vacancies are filled by special election.

74 women have served in the Wisconsin State Legislature:
    13 in the Senate
    70 in the Assembly
    (9 in the Assembly and Senate)

Women as Percentage of Wisconsin Legislators

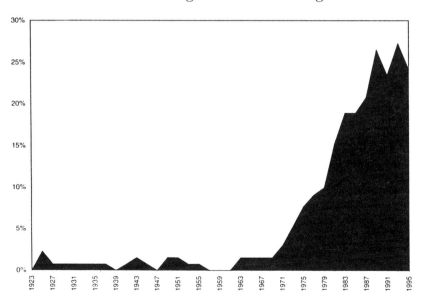

Senate
4 Year Terms

Name	City, County	Party	Legislative Year
Buettner, Carol A.	Oshkosh, Winnebago	R	1987* 1989 1991 1993 1995
Clausing, Alice	Colfax, Dunn	D	1993 1995
Darling, Alberta	River Hills, Milwaukee	R	1993 1995
Engeleiter, Susan Shannon *see Shannon*	Menomonee, Dunn	R	1979* 1981 1983 1985 1987 1989
Farrow, Margaret A.	Elm Grove, Waukesha	R	1991 1993 1995
Huelsman, Joanne B.	Waukesha, Waukesha	R	1989* 1991 1993 1995
Lorman, Barbara	Fort Atkinson, Sinnissippi	R	1979* 1981 1983 1985 1987 1989 1991 1993
Moore, Gwendolynne	Milwaukee, Milwaukee	D	1993 1995
Morrison, Kathryn M.	Platteville, Grant	D	1975 1977
Panzer, Mary E.	West Bend, Washington	R	1993* 1995
Radosevich, Michele G.	Hudson, St. Croix	D	1977 1979
Rosenzweig, Peggy A.	Wauwatosa, Milwaukee	R	1993* 1995
Ulichny, Barbara L.	Milwaukee, Milwaukee	D	1985 1987 1989 1991

Assembly
2 Year Terms

Name	City, County	Party	Legislative Year
Albers, Sheryl K.	N. Freedom, Sauk	R	1991* 1993 1995
Baldwin, Tammy	Madison, Dane	D	1993 1995
Barber, Mildred	Marathon, Marathon	R	1925
Beal, Polly W.	Milwaukee, Milwaukee	R	1993
Bell, Jeannette	West Allis, Milwaukee	D	1983 1985 1987 1989 1991 1993 1995
Blanchard, Carolyn J.	Edgerton, Rock	R	1963* 1965 1967 1969
Brooks, Hellen M.	Coloma, Green Lake	R	1925
Buettner, Carol A.	Oshkosh, Winnebago	R	1983 1985 1987*
Charbonneau, Agnes	Douglas County	R	1931
Coggs, Marcia P.	Milwaukee, Milwaukee	D	1977 1979 1981 1983 1985 1987 1989 1991
Darling, Alberta	River Hills, Milwaukee	R	1989* 1991
Donoghue, Julia Sheehan	Merrill, Marathon	R	1973 1975 1977 1979 1981 1983
Doughty, Esther S. *see Luckhardt*	Horicon, Dodge	R	1963 1965 1967
Doyle, Ruth B.	Madison, Dane	D	1949 1951
Duren, Joanne M.	Cazenovia, Richland	D	1971 1973 1975 1977 1979 1981

Engeleiter, Susan Shannon *see* *Shannon*	Menomonee, Dunn	R	1977 1987
Farrow, Margaret A.	Elm Grove, Waukesha	R	1989
Goodrich, Patricia A.	Berlin, Marquette	R	1975 1977 1979 1981 1983
Gronemus, Barbara	Whitehall, Trempealeau	D	1983 1985 1987 1989 1991 1993 1995
Hanson, Doris J.	Mcfarland, Dane	D	1993 1995
Harsdorf, Sheila E.	River Falls, Pierce	R	1989 1991 1993 1995
Hinkfuss, Rosemary	Green Bay, Brown	D	1989 1991 1993
Hough, Maxine	East Troy, Walworth	D	1991
Hubler, Mary	Rice Lake, Barron	D	1985 1987 1989 1991 1993 1995
Huelsman, Joanne B.	Waukesha, Waukesha	R	1983 1985 1987 1989*
Jaronitzky, June	Iron River, Barsfield	R	1981 1983
Kelso, Carol	Green Bay, Brown	R	1995
Klusman, Judith A.	Oshkosh, Winnebago	R	1989 1991 1993 1995
Krosnicki, Kathleen A.	Muskego, Waukesha	R	1993
Krug, Shirley	Milwaukee, Milwaukee	D	1985 1987 1989 1991 1993 1995
Krusick, Margaret Ann	Milwaukee, Milwaukee	D	1983* 1985 1987 1989 1991 1993 1995
Kryszak, Mary Olszewski	Milwaukee, Milwaukee	D	1929 1933 1935 1937 1941 1943 1945*
Ladwig, Bonnie L.	Racine, Racine	R	1993 1995
Lahn, Jacquelyn J.	Osseo, Trempealeau	R	1989
Lautenschlager, Peggy A.	Fond Du Lac, Fond Du Lac	D	1989 1991
Lazich, Mary A.	New Berlin, Waukesha	R	1993 1995
Lewis, Margaret	Jefferson, Jefferson	R	1985 1987 1989
Linton, Barbara J.	Highbridge, Ashland	D	1987 1989 1991 1993 1995
Luckhardt, Esther Doughty *see* *Doughty*	Horicon, Dodge	R	1969 1971 1973 1975 1977 1979 1981 1983
Magnuson, Sue R. *see* *Rohan*	Horicon, Dodge	D	1985 1987
Manders, Verna M.	Milwaukee, Milwaukee	D	1967*
Metz, Sharon K.	Green Bay, Brown	D	1975 1977 1979 1981 1983 1985
Mielke, Janet Soergel	Madison, Dane	D	1971 1973
Miller, Majorie M.	Madison, Dane	D	1971 1973 1975 1977 1979 1981 1983
Moore, Gwendolynne	Milwaukee, Milwaukee	D	1989 1991
Morris-Tatum, John-nie	Milwaukee, Milwaukee	D	1993 1995
Munts, Mary Lou	Madison, Dane	D	1973 1975 1977 1979 1981 1983
Nelsen, Betty Jo	Shorewood, Milwaukee	R	1979* 1981 1983 1985 1987 1989*

Wisconsin Assembly, continued

Name	City, County	Party	Legislative Year
Notestein, Barbara	Milwaukee, Milwaukee	D	1985 1987 1989 1991 1993 1995
Owens, Carol	Oshkosh, Winnebago	R	1993 1995
Panzer, Mary E.	West Bend, Washington	R	1979* 1981 1983 1985 1987 1989 1991 1993*
Plache, Kimberly M.	Racine, Racine	D	1989 1991 1993 1995
Plous, Lois	Milwaukee, Milwaukee	D	1979* 1981 1983
Potter, Rosemary	Milwaukee, Milwaukee	D	1989* 1991 1993 1995
Raihle, Sylvia H.	Chippewa Falls, Chippewa	R	1949 1951 1953 1955
Robson, Judith B.	Beloit, Rock	D	1987* 1989 1991 1993 1995
Rohan, Sue Magnuson see *Magnuson*	Monona, Dane	D	1989 1991
Rosenzweig, Peggy A.	Wauwatosa, Milwaukee	R	1983 1985 1987 1989 1991 1993*
Schneiders, Lolita	Menomonee Falls, Dunn	R	1981 1983 1985 1987 1989 1991 1993 1995
Seratti, Lorraine M.	Florence, Florence	R	1993 1995
Shannon, Susan see *Engeleiter*	Menomonee, Dunn	R	1975
Smith, Patricia Spafford	Shell Lake, Washburn	D	1979 1981 1983
Tesmer, Louise M.	Milwaukee, Milwaukee	D	1973* 1975 1977 1979 1981 1983 1985 1987 1989*
Thompson, Helen F.	Parks Fall, Price	R	1925 1927
Ulichny, Barbara L.	Milwaukee, Milwaukee	D	1979 1981 1983
Van Dreel, Mary Lou E.	Green Bay, Brown	D	1987 1989 1991
Varda, Margaret P.	Iron County, Iron	I	1943
Vergeront, Susan B.	Cedarburg, Washburn	R	1985 1987 1989 1991 1993
Wagner, Mary K.	Salem, Racine	D	1979 1981
Walling, Esther K.	Neenah, Winnebago	R	1983 1985 1987 1989
Williams, Annette Polly	Milwaukee, Milwaukee	D	1981 1983 1985 1987 1989 1991 1993 1995
Young, Rebecca	Madison, Dane	D	1985 1987 1989 1991 1993 1995
Zeuske, Cathy Susan	Shawano, Shawano	R	1983 1985 1987 1989

*Notes:
Albers, Sheryl K.—Elected Dec. 10, 1991 (Schultz)
Blanchard, Carolyn J.—Elected April 2, 1963 (Blanchard)

Buettner, Carol A.—Resigned April 7, 1987, elected to Senate
Darling, Alberta—Elected May 1, 1990 (Nelson)[F]
Engeleiter, Susan Shannon—Elected April 28, 1980 (Murphy)
Huelsman, Joanne B.—Resigned June 2, 1989, elected to Senate (Davis)
Krusick, Margaret Ann—Elected June 28, 1983 (Andrea)
Kryszak, Mary Olszewski—Died July 16, 1945
Lorman, Barbara—Elected Dec. 2, 1980 (Bear)
Manders, Verna M.—Elected Oct. 10, 1967
Nelsen, Betty Jo—Elected July 10, 1979 (Johnston), resigned Jan. 12, 1993 (Darling)[F]
Panzer, Mary E.—Elected Jan. 31, 1980 (Lewis), resigned Sept. 21, 1993, elected to Senate (Stitt)
Plous, Lois—Elected April 29, 1980 (Wahner)
Potter, Rosemary—Elected Oct. 17, 1989 (Tessmer)[F]
Robson, Judith B.—Elected June 9, 1987 (Weeden)
Rosenzweig, Peggy A.—Resigned April 6, 1993, elected to Senate
Tesmer, Louise M.—Resigned Aug. 1, 1989 (Potter)[F]

WYOMING (1911–1995)

Wyoming women gained full suffrage and political rights by territorial legislative enactment in 1869, and the statehood constitution in 1890. Women first voted in state elections in 1890.

Women as Percentage of Wyoming Legislators

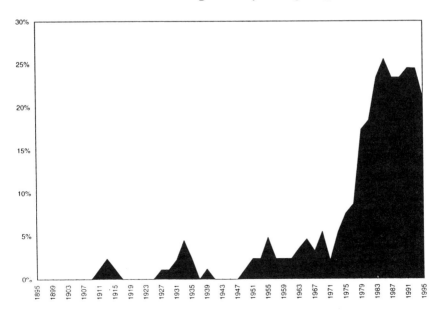

Women first ran on minor party tickets for the Territorial Legislature in 1873 and 1888, and after statehood for the state legislature in 1892, 1894, 1898 and 1908. The first major party legislative nominees were in the 1910 election and Mary G. Bellamy (D–Laramie, Albany County) won a house seat.

State elections are held every two years for 60 representatives who serve two year terms and 30 senators who serve four year staggered terms. State legislative service is limited for the house to three terms in any twelve year period and for the senate to three terms in any twenty-four year period. Vacancies are filled by governor's appointment.

72 women have served in the Wyoming State Legislature:
   14 in the Senate
   67 in the House
   (9 in the House and Senate)

Senate
4 Year Terms

Name	City, County	Party	Legislative Year
Anderson, Susan	Casper, Natorna	R	1993*
Boyle, June	Laramie, Albany	D	1973 1975 1977 1979 1981 1983
Byrd, Harriett Elizabeth	Cheyenne, Laramie	D	1989 1991
Corbitt, Willa Wales	Riverton, Fremont	D	1965
Cubin, Barbara L.	Casper, Natorna	R	1993 1995*
Herbst, Della	Sheridan, Sheridan	D	1987 1989 1991
Hickey, Winifred	Cheyenne, Laramie	D	1981 1983 1985 1987 1989
Kinney, Lisa	Laramie, Albany	D	1985 1987 1989 1991 1993
Kunz, April Brimmer	Cheyenne, Laramie	R	1993 1995
Lummis, Cynthia M.	Cheyenne, Laramie	R	1993
MacGuire, Mary C.	Casper, Natrona	D	1993*
McGrath, Dora	Thermopolis, Hot Springs	R	1931 1933
Parks, Catherine M.	Weston, Campbell	R	1979 1981 1983
Wilkins, Edness Kimball	Casper, Natorna	D	1967 1969

House
2 Year Terms

Name	City, County	Party	Legislative Year
Anderson, Susan	Casper, Natorna	R	1991
Arnold, Sheila	Laramie, Albany	D	1979 1981 1983 1985 1987 1989 1991

Barker, Wende	Laramie, Albany	D	1993 1995
Beherns, Mary	Casper, Natorna	R	1987
Bellamy, Mary G.	Laramie, Albany	D	1911
Birleffi, Lynn	Cheyenne, Laramie	D	1985 1987
Bodine, Janice M.	Evanston, Uinta	R	1991
Boice, Shirley	Cheyenne, Laramie	R	1951 1953 1955
Boyle, June	Laramie, Albany	D	1963 1965 1967 1969 1971
Brown, Margaret	Rawlins, Carbon	R	1983 1985
Burton, R. M. "Johnnie"	Casper, Natorna	R	1983 1985 1987
Byrd, Harriett Elizabeth	Cheyenne, Laramie	D	1981 1983 1985 1987
Campbell, Lettie D.	Lincoln, Lincoln	R	1931
Connaghan, Lucille	Riverton, Fremont	D	1933 1935
Crowley, Ellen	Cheyenne, Laramie	R	1973 1977 1979 1981 1985 1987
Cubin, Barbara L.	Casper, Natorna	R	1987 1989 1991
Devin, Irene K.	Laramie, Albany	R	1993 1995
Dickey, Lynn	Sheridan, Sheridan	D	1983 1985 1987 1989
Dobos, Barbara M.	Casper, Natorna	D	1983 1985
Edelman, Ruth Nelson	Sheridan, Sheridan	R	1939
Enterline, Madge	Casper, Natorna	R	1949 1951
Eskens, Esther	Casper, Natorna	R	1975 1977 1979 1981
Fagan, Josephine W.	Lusk, Niobrara	D	1933
Gams, Sylvia S.	Cowley, Big Horn	R	1989 1991 1993 1995
Garcia, Edith	Cheyenne, Laramie	D	1991
Hansen, Matilda	Laramie, Albany	D	1975 1977 1979 1981 1983 1985 1987 1989 1991 1993
Hendricks, La Verna	Glenrock, Converse	D	1983
Herbst, Della	Sheridan, Sheridan	D	1983 1985
Humphrey, Shirley J.	Cheyenne, Laramie	D	1983 1985 1987 1989 1991
James, Verda I.	Casper, Natorna	R	1955 1957 1959 1961 1963 1965 1967 1969
Kunz, April Brimmer	Cheyenne, Laramie	R	1985 1991
Law, Clarene	Jackson, Teton	R	1991 1993 1995
Lummis, Cynthia M.	Cheyenne, Laramie	R	1979 1981 1985 1987 1989 1991
MacMillan, Patti L.	Laramie, Albany	R	1979 1981 1983 1985 1987 1989 1991 1993 1995
Mathews, Mable	Sundance, Crook	R	1929
McConigley, Nimi	Casper, Natrona	R	1995
Meldrum, Helen S.	Lovell, Big Horn	R	1977
Miller, Anna B.	Larmie, Albany	D	1913
Mockler, E. Jayne	Cheyenne, Laramie	D	1993 1995

Wyoming House, continued

Name	City, County	Party	Legislative Year
Murphy, Nyla A.	Casper, Natorna	R	1979 1981 1983 1985 1987 1989
Nagel, Patricia J.	Casper, Natorna	R	1993 1995
Odde, Mary	Shoshoni, Fremont	R	1981 1983 1985 1987 1989
Parks, Catherine M.	Weston, Campbell	R	1973 1975 1977
Paseneaux, Carolyn	Casper, Natorna	R	1993 1995
Perkins, Dorothy A.	Casper, Natorna	R	1983 1985 1987 1989 1991 1993 1995
Peternal, Nancy F.	Kemmerer, Lincoln	D	1971 1975
Phelan, Elizabeth B.	Cheyenne, Laramie	D	1969 1973 1977 1979 1981 1983
Rochelle, Kathleen Ogden	Lusk, Niobrara	D	1927 1933 1935
Ryckman, Louise	Green River, Sweetwater	D	1985 1987 1989 1991 1993 1995
Schwope, Mary K.	Cheyenne, Laramie	D	1975 1979 1981 1983 1985 1987 1989 1991
Session, Kathryn L.	Cheyenne, Laramie	D	1993 1995
Shreve, Peg	Cody, Park	R	1979 1981 1983 1985 1987 1989 1991 1993 1995
Simons, Marlene J.	Beulah, Crook	R	1979 1981 1983 1985 1987 1989 1991 1993 1995
Spielman, Alice	Gilette, Campbell	R	1953 1955
Stark, Glenda F.	Casper, Natorna	R	1993 1995
Strand, Ann	Rock Springs, Sweet Water	D	1979 1981 1983 1985
Taylor-Horton, Pamela S.	Cheyenne, Laramie	D	1995
Truax, Nettie	Sundance, Crook	D	1913
Tugman, Pat	Cheyenne, Laramie	R	1979
Vlastos, Carol Jo	Casper, Natorna	R	1989 1991
Wallace, Nancy G.	Evanston, Uinta	R	1969 1971
Watson, Carol	Cheyenne, Laramie	D	1989 1991
Wilkins, Edness Kimball	Casper, Natorna	D	1955 1957 1959 1961 1963 1965 1973 1975 1977 1979
Wood, Morna	Alva, Crook	D	1915
Wooldridge, Sherri L.	Cheyenne, Laramie	D	1993 1995
Wright, Virginia L.	Sheridan, Sheridan	R	1989 1991 1993
Zanetti, Kenilynn S.	Rock Springs, Sweet Water	D	1995

*Notes:
Anderson, Susan — Resigned Sept, 1993 (MacGuire)[F]
Cubin, Barbara L. — Resigned Nov. 1994, elected U.S. Congress
MacGuire, Mary C. — Appointed Sept. 1993 (Anderson)[F]

Appendix A

Women State Legislators Statistics, 1895–1995

Year	Senate	House	Democrat	Republican	Independent*	Total Women**	Legislature***	% Women
1895	0	3	0	3	0	3	155	1.9
1897	1	5	3	1	2	6	220	2.7
1899	1	7	4	2	2	8	290	2.8
1901	0	1	0	0	1	1	290	.3
1903	0	2	1	1	0	2	304	.7
1905	0	0	0	0	0	0	307	0
1907	0	0	0	0	0	0	308	0
1909	0	2	1	1	0	2	322	.6
1911	0	5	4	1	0	5	328	1.5
1913	1	10	4	6	1	11	590	1.9
1915	3	6	6	1	2	9	916	1
1917	1	11	6	3	3	12	1108	1.1
1919	2	23	12	13	0	25	1314	1.9
1921	5	34	11	27	1	39	3743	1
1923	7	92	37	55	7	99	7045	1.4
1925	10	131	38	99	4	141	7396	1.9
1927	13	115	36	86	6	128	7413	1.7
1929	15	135	42	100	8	150	7557	2
1931	13	139	54	92	6	152	7577	2
1933	14	122	68	62	6	136	7608	1.8
1935	14	125	80	56	3	139	7592	1.8
1937	17	130	81	64	2	147	7515	2
1939	14	136	65	81	4	150	7485	2
1941	9	145	75	78	1	154	7496	2.1
1943	12	188	82	115	3	200	7502	2.7
1945	15	221	94	142	0	236	7454	3.2

Continued

Year	Senate	House	Democrat	Republican	Independent*	Total Women**	Legislature***	% Women
1947	19	197	58	158	0	216	7480	2.9
1949	18	202	94	126	0	220	7479	2.9
1951	23	219	84	156	2	242	7497	3.2
1953	21	278	90	206	3	299	7539	4
1955	23	289	118	190	4	312	7566	4.1
1957	29	288	109	206	2	317	7615	4.2
1959	34	307	167	172	2	341	7752	4.4
1961	36	289	138	183	4	325	7773	4.2
1963	33	311	139	201	4	344	7835	4.4
1965	37	340	183	189	5	377	7854	4.8
1967	49	271	160	154	6	320	7616	4.2
1969	49	266	145	165	5	315	7638	4.1
1971	46	300	169	174	3	346	7606	4.5
1973	64	380	222	219	3	444	7563	5.9
1975	91	518	385	221	3	609	7565	8.1
1977	108	595	433	265	5	703	7562	9.3
1979	108	668	446	326	4	776	7482	10.4
1981	137	775	508	397	7	912	7482	12.2
1983	174	818	589	397	6	992	7438	13.3
1985	196	905	600	492	9	1101	7461	14.8
1987	223	948	680	481	10	1171	7461	15.7
1989	261	1007	743	516	9	1268	7461	17
1991	300	1059	817	533	9	1359	7461	18.2
1993	343	1184	930	585	12	1527	7424	20.6
1995	340	1195	845	674	16	1535	7424	20.7

*Independent includes Independents, Non-Partisan, and minor parties. All North Dakota included until 1937; Minnesota until 1973; Nebraska after 1937.

**Total number based on women serving in spring of odd years and does not include those who may have resigned before April or those who were appointed or elected after April. Totals do not include non-voting delegates in Maine or territorial legislatures.

***Constitutional totals for state legislatures are added as women became eligible to run for state legislature. Forty-eight states included by 1929. Alaska and Hawaii added in 1959.

First Women Legislators of States and Territories

(Listed Chronologically)

COLORADO **1895** *House* Clara Cressingham, R–Denver, Arapahoe; Carrie Clyde Holly, R–Pueblo, Pueblo; Frances S. Klock, R–Denver, Arapahoe

UTAH **1897** *Senate* Dr. Martha Hughes Cannon, D–Salt Lake, Salt Lake. *House* Sarah Elizabeth N. Anderson, D–Ogden, Weber; Eurithe K. LaBarthe, D–Salt Lake, Salt Lake

IDAHO **1899** *House* Clara L. Campbell, R–Boise City, Ada; Hattie F. Noble, D–Idaho City, Boise; Mary A. Wright, Populist–Rathdrum, Kootenai

WYOMING **1911** *House* Mary G. Bellamy, D–Laramie, Albany

WASHINGTON **1913** *House* Frances C. Axtell, R–Bellingham, Whatcom; Dr. Nena Jolidon Croake, Progressive–Tacoma, Pierce

ARIZONA **1915** *Senate* Frances Willard Munds D–Prescott, Yavapai. *House* Rachel Emma A. Berry, D–St. Johns, Apache

OREGON **1915** *Senate* Kathryn Clarke, R–Glendale, Douglas. *House* Marian B. Towne, D–Phoenix, Jackson

MONTANA **1917** *House* Margaret Smith Hathaway, D–Stevensville, Ravalli; Emma S. Ingalls, R–Kalispell, Flat Head

CALIFORNIA **1919** *House* Esto B. Broughton, D–Modesto, Stanislaw; Grace S. Dorris, R–Bakersfield, Kern; Elizabeth Hughes, R–Oroville, Butte; Anna L. Saylor, R–Alameda, Alameda

KANSAS **1919** *House* Minnie Tamar Johnson Grinstead, R–Liberty, Seward

NEVADA **1919** *House* Sadie D. Hurst, R–Reno, Washoe

NEW YORK **1919** *House* Mary M. Lilly, D–New York, New York; Ida B. Sammis, R–Huntington, Suffolk

CONNECTICUT **1921** *House* Emily Sophie Brown, R–Naugatuct, New Haven; Rev. Grace I. Edwards, I–New Hartford, Litchfield; Lillian M. S. Frink, R–Canterbury, Windham; Mary M. Hooker, R–Hartford, Hartford; Helen A. Jewett, D–Tolland, Tolland

INDIANA **1921** *House* Julia D. Reynolds Nelson, R–Muncie, Delaware

MICHIGAN **1921** *Senate* Eva McCall Hamilton, R–Grand Rapid, Kent

NEW HAMPSHIRE **1921** *House* Jessie Doe, R–Rollinsford, Strafford; Dr. Mary L. R. Farnum, D–Boscawen, Merrimack

NEW JERSEY 1921 *House* Margaret B. Laird, R–Newark, Essex; Jennie C. Van Ness, R–East Orange, Essex

NORTH CAROLINA 1921 *House* Lillian E. Clement, D–Black Mountain, Buncombe

OKLAHOMA 1921 *Senate* Lamar Looney, D–Hollis, Greer-Harmon. *House* Bessie S. McColgin, R–Rankin, Roger Mills

TENNESSEE 1921 *Senate* Anna Lee Worley, D–Bluff City, Sullivan

VERMONT 1921 *House* Edna Beard, R–Orange, Orange

ARKANSAS 1922 *House* Frances Hunt, D–Jefferson County

KENTUCKY 1922 *House* Mary Elliott Flanery, D–Catlettsbury, Boyd

MARYLAND 1922 *House* Mary E. W. Risteau, D–Forest Hill, Harford

ALABAMA 1923 *House* Harriet Hooker Wilkins, D–Selma, Dallas

GEORGIA 1923 *House* Bessie Kempton, D–Atlanta, Fulton; Viola Ross Napier, D–Macon, Bibb

ILLINOIS 1923 *House* Lottie Holman O'Neill, R–Downers Grove, Dupage

MAINE 1923 *House* Dora Pinkham, R–Fort Kent, Aroostook

MASSACHUSETTS 1923 *House* M. Sylvia Donaldson, R–Brockton, Plymouth; Susan W. Fitzgerald, D–Jamaica Plains, Suffolk

MINNESOTA 1923 *House* Myrtle Cain, Farm Labor–Minneapolis, Hennepin; Sue Metzger Dickey Hough, R–Friberg, Otter Tail; Hannah Jensen Kempfer, I–Minneapolis, Hennepin; Mabeth Hurd Paige, I–Minneapolis, Hennepin

MISSOURI 1923 *House* Mellcene T. Smith, D–University, St. Louis; Sarah Lucille Turner, D–Kansas City, Jackson

NEW MEXICO 1923 *House* Bertha M. Paxton, D–Las Cruces, Dona Ana

NORTH DAKOTA 1923 *House* Minnie D. Craig, R–Esmond, Benson; Nellie Doughterty, D–Minot, Ward

OHIO 1923 *Senate* Nettie B. Loughead, R–Cincinnati, Hamilton; Maude C. Waitt, R–Cleveland, Cuyahoga. *House* Nettie M. Clapp, R–Cleveland, Cuyahoga; Lulu T. Gleason, R–Toledo, Lucas; Adelaide Ott, R–Youngstown, Mahoning County; May M. Van Wye, R–Clifton Hamilton

PENNSYLVANIA 1923 *House* Alice M. Bentley, R–Meadville, Crawford; Rosa S. DeYoung, R–Philadelphia, Philadelphia; Sarah McCune Gallaher, R–Ebensburg, Cambia County; Helen Grimes, R–Pittsburgh, Allegheny; Sarah Gertrude MacKinney, R–Chicora, Butler; Lillie H. Pitts, R–Philadelphia, Philadelphia; Martha S. Speiser, R–Philadelphia, Philadelphia; Martha G. Thomas, R–Whitford, Chester

RHODE ISLAND 1923 *House* Isabella Ahearn ONeill, D–Providence, Providence

SOUTH DAKOTA 1923 *House* Gladys Pyle, R–Huron, Beadle

TEXAS 1923 *House* Edith E. Wilmans, D–Dallas, Dallas

WEST VIRGINIA 1923 *House* Anna Johnston Gates, D–Charleston, Kanawa

MISSISSIPPI 1924 *Senate* Carrie Belle Kearney, D–Flora, Madison. *House* Nellie Nugent Somerville, D–Greenville, Washington

VIRGINIA 1924 *House* Sarah Lee Fain, D–Norfolk; Helen T. Henderson, D–Council, Russell

DELAWARE 1925 *House* Florence M. Hanby, R–Holly Oak, New Castle

HAWAII, Territory 1925 *House* Rosalie Keliinoi, R–Kapana, Kaual

NEBRASKA 1925 *House* Mabel A. Gillespie, D–Gretna, Sarpy; Clara C. Humphrey, R–Mullen, Hooker; Sarah T. Muir, R–Lincoln, Lancaster

WISCONSIN 1925 *House* Mildred Barber, R–Marathon County; Hellen M. Brooks, R–Coloma, Green Lake; Helen F. Thompson, R–Park Falls, Price Lake

FLORIDA **1929** *House* Edna Giles Fuller, D–Orlando, Orange
IOWA **1929** *House* Carolyn Campbell Pendray, D–Maquoketa, Jackson
SOUTH CAROLINA **1929** *Senate* Mary G. Ellis, D–Coosawhatch, Jasper County
PUERTO RICO **1933** *House* Maria Luisa Arcelay de la Rosa, Union Republicana–
  Mayaguez
LOUISIANA **1936** *Senate* Doris Lindsey Holland, D–Greensburg, St. Helena
ALASKA, Territory **1937** *House* Nell Scott, D–Sedvia
GUAM **1947** *House* Rosa Aguigui Reyes, Merizo
AMERICAN SAMOA **1953** *House* Mabel C. Reid, Maoputasi; Zilpher Jennings,
  Swains Island
VIRGIN ISLANDS **1953** *Senate* Ann Christian Abramson, D–St. Croix
ALASKA **1959** *Senate* Irene E. Ryan, D–Anchorage. *House* Helen Fischer, D–An-
  chorage; Blanche L. McSmith, D–Anchorage; Doris M. Sweeney, D–Juneau
HAWAII **1959** *House* Dorothy L. Devereux, R–Honolulu, Oahu; Eureka B. Forbes,
  R–Honolulu, Oahu
NORTHERN MARIANAS **1979** *House* Serafina King, D–Tinian; Felicidad Ogu-
  moro, R–Saipan

Appendix C
First Women State Legislators of Parties

REPUBLICANS

STATE LEGISLATORS:
Colorado Elections November 1894, House of Representatives:
Clara Cressingham, Denver, Arapahoe County, 1895-96
Carrie Clyde Holly, Vineland, Pueblo County, 1895-96
Frances S. Klock, Denver, Arapahoe County, 1895-96

STATE SENATE:
Colorado Elections November 1916, Senate:
Agnes L. Riddle, Denver, Denver County, 1915–1918

DEMOCRATS

STATE LEGISLATORS:
Utah Elections November 1896, House of Representatives:
Sarah Elizabeth N. Anderson, Ogden, Weber County, 1897–1898
Eurithe K. LaBarthe, Salt Lake City, Salt Lake County, 1897-98

STATE SENATE:
Utah Elections November 1896, Senate:
Dr. Martha Hughes Cannon, Salt Lake City, Salt Lake County, 1897–1900

POPULIST

STATE LEGISLATOR:
Colorado Elections November 1896, House of Representatives:
Evangeline Heartz, Denver, Arapahoe County, 1897-98, 1899–1900

NONPARTISAN

STATE LEGISLATORS:
Colorado Elections November 1896, House of Representatives:
Martha A. B. Conine, Denver, Arapahoe County, 1897-98

PROGRESSIVE

STATE LEGISLATORS:
Washington Elections November 1912, House of Representatives:
Dr. Nena Jolidon Croake, Tacoma, Pierce County, 1913-14

INDEPENDENT

STATE LEGISLATORS:
Connecticut Elections, November 1920, House of Representatives:
Rev. Grace I. Edwards, New Hartford, Litchfield County, 1921-22

FARM-LABOR

STATE LEGISLATORS:
Minnesota Elections, November 1922,
   House of Representatives:
Myrtle Cain, Minneapolis, Hennepin
   County, 1923-24
Washington Elections, November
   1922, House of Representatives:
Jessie B. Kastner, Tacoma, Pierce
   County, 1923-24

SOCIALIST

STATE LEGISLATORS:
Pennsylvania Elections November,
   1930, House of Representatives
Lilith M. Wilson, Reading, Berks
   County, 1931-32

First Women State Legislators in Leadership Roles

CAUCUS SECRETARY, 1895:
  Colorado
Clara Cressingham, Denver, Arapahoe County, Republican Majority Caucus Secretary, 1895-96, in the Colorado House of Representatives

CAUCUS CHAIR, 1899:
  Idaho
Mary A. Wright, Rathdrum, Kootenai County, Populist Minority Caucus Chair, 1899–1900, in the Idaho House of Representatives

MINORITY LEADER, 1921:
  Montana
Margaret Smith Hathaway, Stevensville, Ravalli County, Democratic Minority Leader, 1921-22, Montana House of Representatives

MAJORITY LEADER, 1935:
  Utah
Reva Beck Bosone, Salt Lake City, Salt Lake County, Democratic Majority Leader, 1935-36, Utah House of Representatives

MAJORITY WHIP, 1941:
  New Mexico
Concha De Ortiz Y Pino, Galisteo, Santa Fe County, Democratic Majority Whip, 1941-42, New Mexico House of Representatives

SPEAKER, 1933:
  North Dakota
Minnie D. Craig, Esmond, Benton County, Non Partisan League (Republican), Speaker 1933-34 in the North Dakota House of Representatives

SENATE CAUCUS CHAIR, 1931:
  New Hampshire
Edgar Maude Ferguson, Bristol, Grafton County, Republican Majority Chair, 1931-32, New Hampshire Senate.

SENATE PRO TEM, 1931:
  New Mexico
Louise Holland Coe, Carrizozo, Lincoln County, Democrat, Senate Pro Tem 1931-32 and 1935-36, New Mexico Senate

SENATE PRESIDENT, 1955:
  Vermont
Consuelo Northrop Bailey, Burlington, Chittenden County, Republican, Senate 1931-32, House of Representatives 1951–1954, Speaker 1953-54, Lieutenant Governor and President of the Senate 1955-56

Appendix E

First Women State Legislators by Ethnic Background

NATIVE AMERICAN
STATE LEGISLATOR:

Michigan elections November 1924
Cora Belle Reynolds Anderson, a Republican from L'Anse, Baraga County
was the first woman elected to the House where she served 1925-26. She
was La Pointe Band, Chippewa. After graduating from the Graves Normal
School in Michigan and the Haskell Indian Nations Institute in Kansas, she
returned to her home in northern Michigan to teach before her service.

Montana elections November 1932
Dolly Lucille Smith Cusker Akers, a Democrat, from Roosevelt County
served 1933-34 in the Montana House of Representatives. She was Day Eagle
Woman of the Assiniboine Tribe and in 1960 was elected the first woman member of the Assiniboine Tribal Council.

AFRICAN AMERICAN
STATE LEGISLATOR:

West Virginia Governor appointed January 10, 1929
Minnie Buckingham Harper, a Republican from Keystone, McDowell County
was appointed to succeed her deceased husband in the West Virginia House of
Delegates.

Pennsylvania elections November 1938
Crystal Dreda Bird Fauset, a Democrat from Philadelphia, Philadelphia County
served in the Pennsylvania House of Representatives until she resigned to
accept appointment in Pennsylvania with the WPA in the fall of 1939.

HISPANIC AMERICAN
STATE LEGISLATOR:

New Mexico elections November 1930
Fedelina Lucero Gallegos, a Republican from Wagon Mound, Mora County
served in the New Mexico House of Representatives 1931-32.

Porfirria Hidalgo Saiz, a Democrat from Mangas, Catron County, New
Mexico served in the New Mexico House of Representatives 1931-32.

ASIAN AMERICAN
STATE LEGISLATOR:

Hawaii elections November 1962
Patsy Takemoto Mink, a Democrat from Honolulu, Oahu, served in the
Hawaii State Senate 1963-64. She previously served in the Territorial
House of Representatives in 1957 and the Territorial Senate in 1959. She is
presently serving her ninth term in the United States Congress.

Appendix F
Length of Service

Brynhild Haugland, 1939–1990, North Dakota
A Republican from Minot, Ward County was first elected to the North Dakota House of Representatives in 1938. She served for twenty-six two year terms until she retired in 1990.

Edwynne C. Polly Rosenbaum, 1949–1994, Arizona
A Democrat from Globe, Maricopa County was appointed in 1949 to the Arizona House of Representatives to fill the unexpired term of her husband after his death. She won twenty-two subsequent elections for two year terms before she lost in 1994.

Selected Bibliography

Rosters of Women State Legislators by Election Year

1894

"On the Eve of the Election," *The Woman's Journal*, Nov. 10, 1894, pp. 535–34.
"Women Office-Holders in Colorado and Wyoming," *The Woman's Journal*, Jan. 12, 1895, p. 10.
"The Three Who Came First," by Elizabeth M. Cox in *State Legislatures*, Nov. 1994, vol. 20, no. 11, pp. 12–19.

1896

"Women in Utah Legislature," *The Woman's Journal*, Feb. 6, 1897, p. 46.
"Gentle Persuaders, Utah's First Women Legislators," by Jean Bickmore White in *Utah Historical Quarterly*, Winter, 1970, pp. 31–49.

1898

"Colorado's Women Legislators," *The Woman's Journal*, Dec. 24, 1898, p. 409.
"Idaho's Women Legislators," *The Woman's Journal*, Jan. 28, 1899, p. 32.
"Utah," *The Woman's Journal*, March 25, 1899, p. 96.
"Colorado Women Legislators," *The Woman's Journal*, Aug. 19, 1899, p. 26 from "Woman Suffrage in the West," by Ella S. Stewart in the *Union Signal*.
"'Women Will Have a Hand in Such Matters From Now On' Idaho's First Women Lawmakers," by Elizabeth M. Cox in *Idaho Yesterdays, Journal of Idaho and Northwest History*, vol. 38, no. 3, Fall, 1994, pp. 2–9.

1900

"Colorado's Women Citizens," *The Woman's Journal*, Oct. 5, 1901, p. 317.
"In Colorado Legislature," *The Woman's Journal*, Feb. 16, 1901, p. 53.

1906

"Colorado Women Legislators," by Phoebe Reeve in *The Modern World*, April 1907, vol. 7, no. 4, pp. 210–11.

1908

"More Testimony from Idaho," *The Woman's Journal*, Sept. 25, 1909, p. 153.
"Mrs. Lafferty's Bill Went Through" (Colorado), *The Woman's Journal*, July 2, 1910.

1910

"First in Wyoming," *The Woman's Journal*, Nov. 5, 1910.
"Four Women Legislators" (Colorado), *The Woman's Journal*, Nov. 19, 1910, p. 205.
"A Woman Legislator" (Colorado), *The Woman's Journal*, April 8, 1911, p. 106.

1912

"Chooses First Woman Senator" (Colorado), *The Woman's Journal*, Dec. 7, 1912, p. 385.
"Woman at Work as Legislators" (Washington), *The Woman's Journal*, Jan. 25, 1913, p. 25.
"Women Succeed in Legislature" (Colorado), *The Woman's Journal*, May 3, 1913, p. 137.
"Representative Truax, Wyoming Woman's Record," *The Woman's Journal*, July 26, 1913, p. 233.
"A Woman Solon, Woman Leads Reform in Wyoming," *The Woman's Journal*, Aug. 9, 1913, p. 249.

1914

"Several Women in Legislature," *The Woman's Journal*, Nov. 14, 1914, p. 302.
"A Woman Legislator" (Wyoming), *The Woman's Journal*, Feb. 6, 1915, p. 40.
"Wyoming Woman in Legislature," *The Woman's Journal*, Feb. 13, 1915, p. 54.
"Woman Rises to Crisis" (Oregon), *The Woman's Journal*, Apr. 10, 1915, p. 117.
"My Work as a Woman Senator" (Arizona), *The Woman's Journal*, Apr. 24, 1915, p. 134.

1916

"Mothers of Men as Legislators of State," *National Suffrage News*, vol. 111, No. 3, Apr. 1917, pp. 7–9. NAWSA Collection [Manuscript Division, Library of Congress, Wash., DC].

1918

"Women in State Legislatures," *The Woman Citizen*, Dec. 7, 1918, p. 568.
"Women in State Legislatures of 1920," *The Woman Citizen*, Feb. 14, 1920, p. 871.

1920

"Women Elected to State Legislatures," Press Release, National American Woman Suffrage Association, Nov. 23, 1920, LWV, Series I, Box 68, File Suffrage Papers Apr. 27–Nov. 23, 1920. [Manuscript Division, Library of Congress, Wash., DC].
"Women Elected to State Legislatures" (State Legislature Chart 1920). *The Woman Citizen*, Nov. 27, 1920, p. 717.
"Woman Legislators," *The Woman Citizen*, Jan. 8, 1921, p. 873.
"Women Elected," *The Woman Citizen*, Nov. 19, 1921, p. 20.
"Women Elected," *The Woman Citizen*, Jan. 28, 1922, p. 20.
"More Election News," *The Woman Citizen*, Feb. 25, 1922, p. 20.

1922

"Women Entries in the Election Races" (State Legislature Candidate Chart 1922), *The Woman Citizen*, November 4, 1922, p. 12–13, 29–30.
"Women Who Won," *The Woman Citizen*, Nov. 18, 1922, p. 8–10, 29.

"More Women Who Won," *The Woman Citizen*, Dec. 2, 1922, pp. 10–11, 27.

"Election News Still Comes," *The Woman Citizen*, Dec. 30, 1922, p. 22.

"Legislators Elected 1922" (State Legislature Chart 1922), *The Woman Citizen*, Sept. 8, 1923, p. 23.

"Some Election Results," *The Woman Citizen*, Nov. 17, 1923, p. 22.

"Kentucky's Legislators," *The Woman Citizen*, Jan. 26, 1924, p. 23.

"A Correction," *The Woman Citizen*, Feb. 23, 1924, p. 22.

1924

"Nominees for State Senate and House of Representatives" (State Legislature Candidate Chart 1924), *The Woman Citizen*, Nov. 1, 1924, p. 10, 28–30.

"Women Who Won," *The Woman Citizen*, Nov. 15, 1924, p. 11, 30.

"Women Who Won" (State Legislature Chart 1924), *The Woman Citizen*, Nov. 29, 1924, p. 22–23.

"Election Corrections," *The Woman Citizen*, Dec. 13, 1924, p. 25.

"Election News, Still," *The Woman Citizen*, Dec. 27, 1924, p. 22.

"Some Election Returns," *The Woman Citizen*, Dec. 1925, p. 33.

1926

"Women Who Won" (State Legislature Chart 1926), *The Woman Citizen*, Dec. 1926, p. 35–36.

"December Update," *The Woman Citizen*, Jan. 1927, p. 35.

"March Update," *The Woman Citizen*, March 1927, p. 36.

"Women Elected," *The Woman Citizen*, May 1928, p. 30.

1928

"Women Who Won" (State Legislature Chart 1928), *The Woman Citizen*, Jan. 1929, p. 30.

"Final Election Returns," *The Woman Citizen*, Feb. 1929, p. 31.

"Still More Elected," *The Woman Citizen*, April 1929, p. 30.

"Women Elected in 1929," *The Woman Citizen*, Dec. 1929, p. 30.

"We Counted Wrong," *The Woman Citizen*, March 1930, p. 28.

1930

"World News" (State Legislature Chart 1930), *The Woman Citizen*, Jan. 1931, p. 46–48.

"Women Who Won," *The Woman Citizen*, Jan. 1931, p. 7.

"Women Who Won," *The Woman Citizen*, Feb. 1931, p. 7, 32.

1932

"A Survey of Women in Public Office." Compiled by Press Department, National League of Women Voters, Oct. 1933, revision.

1936

"Women in State Legislatures, 1937," by Bernice T. Van Der Vries in *State Government*, vol. 10, no. 10, Oct. 1937, pp. 203–215.

1948

"Women Serving in 1949 State Legislatures." Compiled by the Women's Bureau, U.S. Department of Labor, Wash., DC, April 1949.

340 SELECTED BIBLIOGRAPHY

"Women in 1949 State Legislatures" in *Women in Politics: A Practical Guide for Women* by Louise M. Young (NY: Pellegrine and Cudahay, 1950), pp. 310–321.
"Democratic Women Elected to State Offices in 1948 Elections." Compiled by the Women's Division, Democratic National Committee, Wash., DC, 1949.

1950
"Women Serving in 1951 State Legislatures." Compiled by the Women's Bureau, U.S. Department of Labor, Wash., DC, 1951.

1956
Women in the Public Service, 1957. Compiled by the Women's Division, National Republican Party (Wash., DC, 1957).

1958
Women in the Public Service, 1959. Compiled by the Women's Division, National Republican Party (Wash., DC, 1959).

1960
Women in State Government, 1961. Compiled by the Women's Bureau, U.S. Department of Labor (Wash., DC, June 1961).

1964
Women in State Elective Offices, 1965. Compiled by the Women's Bureau, U.S. Department of Labor (Wash., DC, June 1965).

1966
Republican Women in State Legislatures. Compiled by the Women's Division, National Republican Party (Wash., DC, Nov. 1966).
Democratic Women State Legislators. Compiled by the Women's Division, Democratic National Committee (Wash., DC, Nov. 1966).

1968
Women in State Elective Offices. Compiled by the Women's Bureau, U.S. Department of Labor (Wash., DC, June 1969).

1970
Women in the Public Service 1971. Compiled by the Women's Division, National Republican Party (Wash., DC, 1971).
"Women State Legislators 1972." Compiled by the Center for the American Woman and Politics. (Eagleton Institute of Politics, Rutgers University: January 1972).

1972
"Women in the State Legislature, 1973," in *Women's Rights Almanac* by Nancy Gager (Bethesda: Elizabeth Cady Stanton Pub. Co., 1974).

1974
Women in Public Office: A Biographical Directory and Statistical Analysis. Compiled by Center of the American Woman and Politics, Eagleton Institute of Politics,

Rutgers University. Sara B. Chrisman, Project Director. (New York: R. R. Bowker Co., 1976).

1976

Women in Public Office: A Biographical Directory and Statistical Analysis. Compiled by Center of the American Woman and Politics, Eagleton Institute of Politics, Rutgers University. Kathy Stanwick, Project Staff, and Marilyn Johnson, Statistical Research Director. (New Jersey: Scarecrow, 1978).

1978

"Women State Legislators." Compiled by the Women's Education Fund (Wash., DC, Nov. 1978)

1980 to Present

National Directory of Women Elected Officials 1981. Compiled by the National Women's Political Caucus (New York: Phillip Morris, Companies Inc.). 1981—Present (biennially—odd years).

National Legislative Rosters

The Book of the States (Lexington: The Council of State Governments), 1935 to Present (biennially).

State Elected Officials and Legislatures (Lexington: The Council of State Governments), 1949 to Present (biennially).

Taylor's Encyclopedia of Government Officials, Federal and State (Texas: Political Reseach, Inc., 1967), 1967 to Present (biennially).

State Yellow Book (Wash., DC: Leadership Directories, Inc.), 19-- to Present (biennially).

Election Results Directory (Denver: National Conference of State Legislatures) 1993–Present (annually, identifies gender).

National Political Directories and Biographies

Who's Who in American Politics, 1967–68, eds. P. A. Thais and E. L. Henshaw. (New York: Bowker, 1967) 1967 to Present (biennially).

Black Elected Officials, 1971: A National Register. Compiled by the Joint Center Research Staff (Wash., DC: Joint Center for Political and Economic Studies, 1971) 1971 to Present (biennially).

Latino Elected Officials 1985 edited by National Association of Latino Elected Officials (Wash., DC and New York City: National Association of Latino Elected Officials, 1985) 1985 to Present (biennially).

Sources in the Fifty States and Territories

State Manuals, Directories, Registers, Red, Brown, Blue Books
House and Senate Journals

Session Laws
Newspapers

Rosters of Women State Legislators by State and Historical Rosters of State Legislatures

The *History of Women Suffrage* by Susan B. Anthony, Elizabeth Cady Stanton, Matilda Gage, and Ida Husted Harper first published 1902–22 and republished by Arno Press of New York in 1969, is most valuable for an overview of each state and the drive for suffrage. State reports to headquarters are printed chronologicially. These reports eventually included a section on women in office that provides some information about the early women legislators, see volumes IV, V, VI.

ALABAMA
"Women in the Alabama Legislature, 1922–1990" in "Stepping Out of the Shadows, Women in the Alabama Legislature, 1922–190" by Joanne Varner Hawks in *Stepping Out of the Shadow, Alabama Women, 1819–1990*, ed. Mary Martha Thomas (University of Alabama Press, 1995), pp. 174–75.
"A Select Few: Alabama's Women Legislators 1922–1983" by Joanne Varner Hawks. *Alabama Review*, Volume XXXVIII, No. 31 (July, 1985), pp. 175–201.

ALASKA
"A Tribute to Women Elected to the Alaska Legislature: Women Members 1936–1983," in *Profiles in Change: Names, Notes and Quotes For Alaskan Women* by Ginna Brelsford. (Alaska Commission on the Status of Women, 1983), Appendix.
Alaska Legislature, Roster of Members 1913–1991. (State of Alaska Legislative Affairs Agency, December, 1991, Juneau, AK).
Who's Who in Alaskan Politics: A Biographical Dictionary 1884–1974. Compiled by Evangeline Atwood and Robert N. DeArmond (Portland: Binford and Mort for Alaska Historical Commisssion, 1977).

AMERICAN SAMOA
"Women in the American Samoa Legislature." Compiled by Kereti Mata' Utia, Legislative Reference Bureau, 1991.

ARIZONA
"Women in the Arizona State Legislature 1912–1993" in *Arizona Legislative Data, 1949–1993.* Compiled by Rita Mae Kelly, Director, and Diane Jezek-Powell, Research Assistant, Gender Opportunities Leadership Development Forum. (Tempe: Arizona State University, School of Justice Studies, 1993).
"Women Who Have Served in the Arizona State Legislature 1920–1990." Compiled by the Arizona Order of Women Legislators, pp. 7–15.
"Women in the Arizona State Legislature 1912–1987," Appendix A, pp. 145–148 and "Arizona Women and the Legislature" by Rita Mae Kelly, Jayne Burgess and Katie Kaufmann in *Women and the Arizona Political Process*. Rita Mae Kelly, ed., Womens Studies Program, Arizona State University. (Lanham, MD: University Press of America, Inc., 1987).

"Senate and House Membership List 1949–1993" in *Arizona Legislative Data, 1949–1993*. Compiled by Rita Mae Kelly, Director, and Diane Jezek-Powell, Research Assistant, Gender Opportunities Leadership Development Forum. (Tempe: Arizona State University, School of Justice Studies, 1993).

ARKANSAS
"Women Members of the Arkansas Legislature 1922–1980." Compiled by Legislative Council, 1981.
"Arkansas Historical Session Rosters" in *Historical Report of the Secretary of State, 1986*. (Little Rock: Secretary of State, 1986), pp. 387–430.

CALIFORNIA
"Roster of Women by Year" in *California Legislature 1986* by James D. Driscoll, Chief Clerk of the Assembly (Center for California Studies, California State University, December 1986).
"Women Legislators in California (1849–1971)." Compiled by Vera Nicholas, California State Library, State Information and Reference Center.
Black Elected Officials in California by Fisher Serthard (San Francisco: R&E Associates, 1978).
List of Constitutional Officers, Congressional Representatives, Members of the California State Legislature, and Members of the Supreme Court, 1849–1985. Compiled by James D. Driskoll, Chief Clerk of the Assembly and Darryl R. White, Secretary of the Senate. (Sacramento: 1985).

COLORADO
"Women Who Have Served in the Colorado General Assembly 1895–1991." Compiled by Legislative Council of the Colorado General Assembly. (Denver, 1991).
"Women Who Have Served in Elective Positions in Colorado, Past and Present" in *See How She Runs*, compiled by the Committee on Promotion of Qualified Women for Elective and Appointive Offices (Pueblo: Colorado Commission on Status of Women, 1972), Appendix C, pp. 18–19.

CONNECTICUT
"Women Members of the Connecticut General Assembly 1921–1993" in *Connecticut Register and Manual 1993–94*. (Hartford: Secretary of State, 1993), pp. xi–xxii.
"Women Who Have Served in the Connecticut Legislature 1941–1969." Compiled by the Women in the Connecticut State Library Law/Legislative Reference Unit, December 1991.
"Connecticut Women Holding Legislative or Official Positions 1921–31." Compiled by Legislative Reference, State Library, March 23, 1931.

DELAWARE
"Delaware Women Legislators 1924–1989." Legislative Council, Division of Research (Hand written, no authorship).

FLORIDA
A Changing Pattern: Women in the State Legislature by Allen Morris, Historian Office of the Florida House of Representatives (Tallahassee: Oct. 1991), 4th ed., rev.

"Creating a Different Pattern: Florida's Women Legislators 1928–1986" by Mary Carolyn Ellis and Joanne Varner Hawks, *Florida Historical Quarterly*, July 1987, pp. 68–83.
The People of Lawmaking in Florida 1822–1993. Compiled by John B. Phelps (Tallahassee: Florida House Of Representatives, 1993).

GEORGIA
"Georgia General Assembly Women, 1923–1989." Compiled by the staff of the *Georgia Official and Statistical Register*, 1989.
"Women Legislators and Congressional Representatives from Georgia 1923–1969." Compiled by Dr. Cynthia C. Thompson, Office of Legislative Counsel, Legislative Services Committee.
"Historical Roster of Members of the State Senate and House by County 1800–1992" in the *Georgia Official and Statistical Register 1977–79* (Atlanta: Department of Archives and History, 1971). "1979–1989" in *Georgia Official and Statistical Register 1985–1988*.

GUAM
"Biographical Information on Women in the Congress of Guam." Compiled by Cecilia A. Q. Morrison, Guam Legislature Archives, 1994.
"Historical Session Roster of the Guam Legislature 1950–1994." Compiled by Cecilia A. Q. Morrison, Guam Legislature Archives, 1993.

HAWAII
" Women Legislators in Hawaii 1933–1993." Compiled by Commission on the Status of Women, Honolulu, 1993.

IDAHO
"Women in the Idaho Legislature 1899–1983" in *Who's Who of Idaho Women in the Past* by Betty Penson-Ward (Boise: Idaho Commission on Women's Programs, 1981). Appendix, pp. 46–48.
Ladies of the House (and Senate), History of Idaho Women Legislators by Gladys Rae Swank (Sune St. Hood, ID, 1978).
"Historical Roster 1890–1990" in *Idaho Blue Book, 1989* (Boise: Secretary of State, 1990), pp. 161–180.

ILLINOIS
"Illinois Women in Congress and the General Assembly." *Research Response* (Legislative Reference Bureau, File 10-5054, Nov. 2, 1993).
"Illinois Women Legislators 1923–1971." Compiled by Patricia Coughlin, Legislative Reference Bureau, 1991.
"Legislative Roster, 1818–1994" in *Illinois Blue Book 1993* (Springfield: Secretary of State, 1993), pp. 480–525.

INDIANA
"Women Legislators in the Indiana General Assembly" in *The Centennial History of Indiana, 1816–1978* by Justine E. Walsh. (Indianapolis: Select Committee of the Indiana General Assembly and the Indiana Historical Bureau, 1987), vol. 2, Appendix A, Table 16, pp. 725–27.

A Century of Achievement: Black Hoosiers in the Indiana General Assembly by Alan Frank January (Indianapolis: 1986).

Biographical Directory of the Indiana General Assembly 1900–1984, ed. Justin E. Walsh (Indianapolis: Select Committee on the Centennial History of the Indiana General Assembly and Indiana Historical Bureau, 1984), vol. 2.

IOWA
"Iowa Women Legislators, Their Party, and Their Terms," in *Legislators and Politicians: Iowa's Women Lawmakers* by Suzanne O'Dea Schenken (Ames: Iowa State University Press, 1995), pp. xvii–xviii.

"Iowa Women State Legislators 1929–1993." Compiled by the Legislative Service Bureau, Legislative Librarian, 1991.

The Iowa General Assembly: Our Legislative Heritage, 1846–1980 by Francis J. Stork and Cynthia A. Clingan (Des Moines: Iowa State Senate, 1980).

KANSAS
"Women Legislators in Kansas 1919–1994." Compiled by Legislative Reference, State Library, 1993.

KENTUCKY
"Women Who Served in the Kentucky General Assembly 1922–1990." Compiled by Leslie Cummins, Legislative Research Commission, 1991.

Kentucky Women Legislators 1922–1996, Biographical Sketches by Lindsay Campbell, Executive Director (Frankfort: Kentucky Commission on Women, 1995).

Kentucky General Assembly Membership, 1948–1992. Compiled by the Legislative Research Council. (Frankfort: Legislative Research Council, 1994).

LOUISIANA
"Women in the Louisiana Legislature 1992–96." Compiled by the Legislative Research Library, Baton Rouge, LA, 1991.

Women of the Louisiana Legislature by St. Rep. Louise Johnson (Farmerville, La.: Greenbay Publishing, 1986).

Louisiana Legislative Council Directory 1936–1962. Compiled by the Legislative Council (Baton Rouge: Legislative Council, 1963).

MAINE
"Women Members in the Maine Legislature 1923–1978." Compiled by the Law and Legislative Reference Library.

MARYLAND
"Women State Legislators of the General Assembly of Maryland, 1921–1994." Compiled Lynda C. Davis, Director Department of Legislative Reference. Library and Information Services, Annapolis, MD, 1991.

Archives of Maryland, New Series I, an Historical List of Public Officials of Maryland, ed., Edward C. Papenfuse (Annapolis: Maryland State Archives, 1990), vol. 1.

MASSACHUSETTS
"Number of Women in the Massachusetts General Court, 1923–1991." Compiled by the Massachusetts State Library, George Fingold Library, Boston, 1991.

MICHIGAN
Women in the Michigan Legislature 1921–1994 by St. Rep. Mary C. Brown (Lansing: House of Representatives, second edition, 1994).
"Historical Roster 1983–1992" in *Michigan State Manual, 1993*, pp. 336–341.

MINNESOTA
"Women in the Minnesota Legislature 1923–1991." Compiled by Marilyn Cathcart, Director Legislative Reference Library, 1991.
"Women in the Minnesota Legislature, 1923–1977" by Arvonne S. Fraser and Sue E. Holbert in *Women of Minnesota*, eds., Barbara Stahler and Gretchen Kreuter (St. Paul: Minnesota Historical Society, 1977), pp. 280–81.
Minnesota Congressmen, Legislators and Other Elected State Officials, An Alphabetical Checklist 1849–1971. Compiled by W. F. Toensing. (St. Paul: Minnesota State Historical Society, 1971).

MISSISSIPPI
Women of the Mississippi Legislature 1922–1980. Compiled by Mississippi Library Commission, Information Services Department, Jacqueline P. Payne with University of Mississippi Professors Dr. Joanne Varner Hawks and Dr. Carolyn Ellis, and Law Student J. Byron Morris.
"Women in the Mississippi Legislature (1924–1981)," by Joanne Varner Hawks, M. Carolyn Ellis, and J. Byron Morris. *The Journal of Mississippi History*, Volume XLIII, No. 4, November, 1981, pp. 266–292.

MISSOURI
Historical Listing of the Missouri Legislature 1820–1988. Compiled by Thomas D. Shriver (to 1930), Secretary of State James C. Kirkpatrick (1940–76) and Roy D. Blunt (1976–88), (Jefferson City: Office of the Secretary of State, 1988).

MONTANA
"Women in the Montana Legislative Assembly, 1917–1979," Table 5 in *Montana Legislators 1864–1979* by Ellis Waldron. (Missoula: Bureau of Government Research, University of Montana, 1980), p. 20.
Montana Legislators 1864–1979 by Ellis Waldron. (Missoula: Bureau of Government Research, University of Montana, 1980).

NEBRASKA
Nebraska Women in History: Women Senators from 1925–1981. Compiled by the Nebraska Commission on the Status of Women (Lincoln: 1981).
"Nebraska Legislators 1855–1989" in *Nebraska Blue Book 1988–89*. (Lincoln: Clerk of the Legislature, 1988), pp. 300–378.

NEVADA
Women in the Nevada Legislature, 1919–1995, Background Paper 91–51. Compiled by Danna R. Bennett, Senior Research Analyst, Research Division, Legislative Council Bureau. (Carson City: Research Division, Legislative Council Bureau, 1995).
"Lady Lawmakers 1919–1981." Compiled by Legislative Counsel Bureau, Research Division, 1981.
Nevada Legislators, 1861–1993. Compiled by Pat Lancaster. (Carson City: Research Division, Legislative Counsel Bureau, revised 1993).

NEW HAMPSHIRE
New Hampshire Women Legislators 1921 to 1971 by Leon W. Anderson (Concord: The Evans Printing Company, 1971).

"Historical Senate Roster" in *New Hampshire Manual for the General Court 1991*, pp. 63–74.

NEW JERSEY
"Women Members of the New Jersey Legislature 1845–1994." Compiled by Elizabeth L. Cox, Department of Community Affairs, Nov. 1994.

"New Jersey Assemblywomen, 1921–1995" in *Equality Deferred, Women Candidates for the New Jersey Assembly, 1920–1993* by Richard P. McCormick and Katheryne C. McCormick (NJ: Center on American Women in Politics, Eagleton Institute of Politics, Rutgers University, 1994), pp. 47–48.

"Historical List by County of the General Assembly 1845–1953," *New Jersey Legislative Manual 1953–54*. (By Authority of Legislature: S. Kinder Srauss Associates, 1952), pp. 167–209.

"Historical List by County of the General Assembly 1948–1993," *New Jersey Legislative Manual 1993–94*. (By Authority of Legislature: S. Kinder Srauss Associates, 1994), pp. 281–297.

NEW MEXICO
"Women Legislators From 1912 to 1991." Compiled by the Legislative Council Service, 1991.

"Historical Sessions Roster 1912–1926" in *New Mexico Blue Book 1927* (Santa Fe: Secretary of State, 1928), pp. 38–45.

NEW YORK
Lawmakers: Biographical Sketches of the Women of the New York State Legislature 1918–1988. Compiled by St. Rep. Helene E. Weinstein, Chairwoman, Legislative Women's Caucus. (Albany: Assembly, 1988).

"Historical Roster New York Assembly 1896–1989," *New York Red Book 1989–90*. (Albany: N.Y. Legal Publishing Co., 1989), pp. 172–192, 349–394.

NORTH CAROLINA
"Women Who Have Served in the North Carolina General Assembly 1921–91." Compiled by the Legislative Service Office Library, 1991.

"Historical Roster of the General Assembly by Counties" in *North Carolina Government 1583–1979*, ed., John L. Cheney, Jr. (Raleigh: Secretary of State, 1981), pp. 1041–1319.

NORTH DAKOTA
"North Dakota Women Legislators 1923–1991." Compiled by Legislative Council Staff.

"North Dakota Women Legislators, by Session, 1923–1989" in *Lady, If You Go Into Politics: North Dakota's Women Legislators 1923–1989* by Ann Rathke (University of North Dakota, 1991), Appendix B.

"Historical Sessions Roster 1889–1989," *North Dakota Centennial Blue Book, 1989* (Bismarck: Secretary of State, 1989).

NORTHERN MARIANA ISLANDS
"Women in the Northern Mariana Islands Legislature." Compiled by Michael S. Majors, Legislative Assistant, Office of State Senator Atalig, 1994.

OHIO
"Ohio Women as Elected Officials: An Overview 1923–1993." Compiled by Ohio Women's Policy Research Commission, 1993.
"Ohio Women Legislators 1923–1979." Compiled by the Ohio Women's Information Center, 1978.
Ohio House of Representatives Membership Directory 1803–1965. Compiled by Carl Guess, Chief Clerk of the House. (Columbus: Columbus Blank Co., 1966).

OKLAHOMA
"Oklahoma Women in Elective Office." Compiled by Betty Jean Mathis, Oklahoma Department of Libraries, 1988.
"Historical Roster by Session, 1907–1991," *Directory and Manual of the State of Oklahoma, 1991–1992.* (Oklahoma City, 1991), pp. 128–172.

OREGON
"Women of the Oregon Legislature, 1915 – Present." Compiled by Laurie Wimmer, Executive Director, Oregon Commission for Women, Feb. 1994.
"Chronological List of Women in the Oregon Legislatures, Showing Length of Service and City of Residence at Time in Office" in *Alphabetical List of Oregon's Legislators.* Compiled by Cecil L. Edward, (Salem: Legislative Administrative Committee, 1993).
Alphabetical List of Oregon's Legislatures. Compiled by Cecil L. Edward, (Salem: Legislative Administrative Committee, 1993).
Chronological List of Oregon's Legislatures. Compiled by Cecil L. Edward, (Salem: Legislative Administrative Committee, 1993).

PENNSYLVANIA
Women in the Pennsylvania Legislature, 1921–1984. Compiled by Carol Blake Yulick and Robert L. Cable, Legislative Reference Bureau, Dec. 1984.
"Historical List of Members of the General Assembly 1890–1954," *Pennsylvania State Manual, 1953–54,* pp. 454–499.
"Historical List of Members of the General Assembly 1950–1989," *Pennsylvania State Manual, 1989–90,* pp. 283–295.

PUERTO RICO
"Senadoras 1937–1992" in *Senado de Puerto Rico 1917–92.* (San Juan: Secretary of Senate, 1992), p. 18.
Miembros y Funcionarios de la Asamblea Legislativa de Puerto Rico 1900–1972. (San Juan: Secretary of Senate, 1972).
Elecciones y Partidos Politicos de Puerto Rico 1900–1980.
Senado de Puerto Rico 1917–92. (San Juan: Secretary of Senate, 1992).

RHODE ISLAND
"Chronological List of Women Legislators 1923–1983," in *The Elect: Rhode Island's Women Legislators 1922–1990* by Emily Stier Adler and Stanley Lemons. (League of Rhode Island Historical Societies, 1990), pp. 245–50.

SOUTH CAROLINA

"Women of the South Carolina General Assembly" in *Legislative Update, March 21, 1989,* (Charleston: Legislative Council of the General Assembly, 1989).

"Ladies in the Gentleman's Club: South Carolina Women Legislators 1928–1984" by Carolyn Ellis and Joanne Varner Hawks in *Proceedings of the South Carolina Historical Association,* (Aiken: South Carolina Historical Association, 1986) pp. 17–32.

"Historical Session Lists 1692–1973" in *Biographical Directory of South Carolina House of Representatives* compiled by House Research Committee. (Columbia: University of South Carolina Press, 1986), vol. 1.

Biographical Directory of the South Carolina Senate 1776–1985 by N. Louise Bailey, Mary L. Morgen, Carolyn R. Taylor (Columbia: University of South Carolina Press, 1986, 3 vols.).

SOUTH DAKOTA

"South Dakota Women Legislators 1925–1993." Compiled by Legislative Research Council, 1993.

Biographical Directory of the South Dakota Legislature, 1889–1989. (Pierre: Legislative Research Council, 1989), 2 vols.

Historical Listing of South Dakota Legislators, 1862–1993. (Pierre: Legislative Research Council, 1993).

TENNESSEE

"Women Who Have Served in the Tennessee General Assembly 1921–1987." Compiled by the Office of Legislative Services, Office of Legal Services, Revision and update of 1973 edition by Barbara Langley, Bud Gangwer, and Julie McCown, October, 1987.

Biographical Directory of the Tennessee General Assembly . Compiled by Illene J. Cornwell (Nashville: Tennessee State Library and Archives, 1988), vol. III 1901–1931, vol. IV 1931–1951, vol. V 1951–1971, vol. VI 1971–1991.

TEXAS

"Women Members of the Texas Legislature 1923–1993." Compiled by the Texas Legislative Reference State Library, 1993.

"Women Who Have Served in the Texas Legislature 1923–1985" in *Texas Women, a Pictorial History* by Ruth Winegarten (Austin: Eakin Press, 1986) p. 163.

Members of the Texas Congress 1836–1845, Members of the Texas Legislature 1846–1992. (Austin: Texas Legislative Council, 1992).

UTAH

Women Legislators in Utah 1896–1993. Compiled by St. Rep. Delila M. Abbott, Sept. 1974, Revised and Updated by St. Rep. Beverly White, 1992 (Salt Lake: Governor's Commission for Women and Families, January, 1993).

"Women Legislators in Utah 1933–1986." Compiled by Utah Governor's Commission for Women. (Salt Lake: 1986).

Women Legislators in Utah 1896–1976. Compiled by St. Rep. Delila M. Abbott, Sept. 1974 (Salt Lake: Utah Order of Women Legislators, 1976).

VERMONT

"Vermont Women in the Legislature 1921, 1925, 1935, 1945, 1955, 1965, 1967, 1969,

1971, 1973, 1975, 1977." Compiled by the Robert L. Hagerman, Assistant Editor of State Papers, 1981.

VIRGIN ISLANDS

"Women in the Virgin Island Legislature." Compiled by Eunice Francis, Office of the Legislative Council, 1991.

"Women Legislators" in *History of the Legislature of the United States Virgin Islands*. Compiled by John Collins. (St. Croix: Legislature of the Virgin Islands, 1984), pp. 46–50.

"Historical Roster by Session, 1937–1983" in *History of the Legislature of the United States Virgin Islands*. Compiled by John Collins. (St. Croix: Legislature of the Virgin Islands, 1984), pp. 3–5, 15, 19–24.

VIRGINIA

"Women in the General Assembly 1924–1991." Compiled by Legislative Services.

"A Roll Call of Women Legislators in the Virginia General Assembly, 1924 to 1988" in *The Almanac of Virginia Politics* by Flora Crater, Muriel Smith, and Anne Donley, 6th Edition, 1988 Supplement, pp. 36–40.

"A Bicentennial Register of the Members" in *The General Assembly of the Commonwealth of Virginia, 1619–1978*. Compiled by Cynthia Miller Leonard. (Richmond: Virginia State Library, 1978).

The General Assembly of the Commonwealth of Virginia 1919–1936, A Biographical Dictionary by Edward Griffith Dodson (Richmond: State Publisher, 1961).

WASHINGTON

Political Pioneers, The Women Lawmakers by Elected Washington Women. (Olympia, October, 1983).

"Demographic Data on Washington State's Women Legislators" in *Women in the Washington State Legislature 1913–1983* by Babara Gooding, Senior Thesis Evergreen State College, August 1983, Appendix C. Updated to 1994 by Gayle Palmer, Western Division, Washington State Library.

Washington Women in State Government. Compiled by Earl Coe, Secretary of State (Olympia: Secretary of State, 1952).

Members of the State Legislature by Districts from 1889 to 1991. Revised by Gordon A. Golob and Alan Thpmson. (Olympia: Washington State Legislature, 1991).

WEST VIRGINIA

"Women Members of the West Virginia State Legislature 1920 – 1995." Compiled by West Virginia Women's Commission.

"Historical Roster of Members of the Senate and Assembly, 1893–1989" in *West Virginia Blue Book 1989*, (Charlestown, 1989), pp. 347–387.

WISCONSIN

"Wisconsin Women Legislators — A Historical List." Compiled by A. Peter Cannon, Research Analyst, Library Research Division, Legislative Reference Bureau in *Wisconsin Briefs*, January 1991. Update, December 1994.

"Members of the Wisconsin Legislature 1848–1991" in *Wisconsin Blue Book, 1991–92*, (Madison: Wisconsin Reference and Library Section, Legislative Reference Bureau, 1991), pp. 257–710.

WYOMING

"Wyoming Women in Legislature 1890 to 1990," in *Wyoming Blue Book, 1989* (Cheyenne: Secretary of State, 1989), pp. 218–19.

"Historical List of the Members of the State Legislature" in *Wyoming Blue Book, 1974*, 3 vols. Virginia Cole Trenholm, ed. (Cheyenne: State Archives and Historical Dept., 1974), vol. 2, 1890–1943, pp. 253–278; vol. 3, 1945–1974, pp. 52–90.

Name Index

Cherry, Gwendolyn Sawyer 90, 92
Chesky, Evelyn G. 154
Chesley, Ruby A. 192
Chestnut, Cynthia Moore 90
Child, Etta B. 286
Childs, Peggy 94
Chinn, Jennie 171
Chinoy, Kathy Geller 90
Chioffi, Nancy B. 286, 297
Chisholm, Mary E. 137
Chisholm, Shirley 224
Chivers, Stephanie H. 271, 272
Chizmar, Nancy L. 138
Chonko, Lorraine N. 138
Chowning, Vonne Stout 184
Christensen, Joan 224
Christensen, Lois 279
Christenson, Linda 233
Christian, Mary T. 301
Christiansen, Marie A. 192
Christianson, Donna 163, 166
Christie, Augusta K. 137, 139
Christopher, Nancy B. 286
Christopherson, Chris 233
Christowe, Margaret 286
Chronic, Betty 69, 72
Chronister, Rochelle Beach 126
Chuinard, Fritzi 247
Chumney, Carol J. 271
Chun, Connie 102
Chun, Suzanne N. J. 102
Church, Grace N. 139
Churilla, Mildred Kopack 117
Ciarlo, Flora L. 111
Cid, Irene Birch 192
Cierpiot, Connie 171
Cinelli, Adele P. 219; see also Hundley
Clagett, Virginia P. 146
Clapp, Elsie 286, 297
Clapp, Nettie M. 238, 239, 330
Clapprood, Majorie A. 154
Clark, Barbara M. 224
Clark, Betty Jean 94, 122
Clark, Cynthia M. 192
Clark, Elsie L. 286

Clark, Geraldine L. 283, 286
Clark, Hannah E. 75; see also Russell
Clark, Harriet L. 75
Clark, Hattie L. 286
Clark, Janet 163
Clark, Karen 163
Clark, Margaret Pruitt 139
Clark, Martha Fuller 192
Clark, Mary V. 75
Clark, Matilda F. Tann 168
Clark, Nancy Randall 137, 139
Clark, Pauline Alston 168
Clark, Rita 251
Clark, Ruth B. 69
Clark, Ruth H. 75
Clark, Sandra 271
Clark, Shirley M. 192
Clark, Vivian R. 192
Clarke, Alyce Griffin 168, 169
Clarke, Hilda S. 75
Clarke, Kathryn 245, 246, 249, 329
Clarno, Beverly A. 247
Clary, Debbie A. 229
Clausing, Alice 318
Clay, Alberta Z. 192
Clayton, Verna L. 111
Cleary, Audrey 233
Clegg, Cloa 279
Clement, Lillian E. 226, 229, 329
Clements, Floy 111
Clements, Hannah C. 192
Clemons, Jane A. 192
Clemons, Thomasina 76
Cleveland, Connie L. 233
Cleveland, Eva 286, 297
Cleveland, Lynne 286
Cleven, Carol C. 154
Cline, Nellie 104, 124, 126; see also Steenson
Clocksin, Virginia 306
Clouchek, Emma 105
Clough, Ruth Thorndike 137, 139
Cobb, Hazel Warner 130, 132
Cobb, Kay 167
Cobb, Mable Ruggles 286
Cobb, Reba L. 126
Cobb, Velma B. 286
Cobb-Hunter, Gilda Yvette 263

Cobleigh, Bertha P. 286
Cocchiarella, Vicki 177
Cocco, Jacqueline M. 76
Cochran, Deborah R. 154
Cochran, Pat 306
Cochran, Theresa 286
Cochrane, Betsy Lane 227, 229
Coderre, Elaine A. 260
Cody, Dorothy A. 177
Cody, Eileen 306
Cody, Gwendalyn F. 301, 302
Coe, Alice Lee 76
Coe, Blanche M. 76
Coe, Elizabeth W. 76
Coe, Louise Holland 219, 334
Coes, Betsy A. 192
Cofer, Lanell 274, 276
Coffey, Barbara J. 139
Coffin, Alice Walker 93, 96
Coggs, Marcia P. 318
Cogswell, Charlotte P. 192, 211
Cohen, A. Lou 306
Cohen, Esther H. 286
Cohen, Gertrude S. 122
Cohen, Joyce 246, 247
Cohen, Lita Indzel 251
Cohen, Naomi K. 76
Coker, Lynda 94
Colberg De Rodriquez, Blanca E 256
Colburn, Marjorie D. 192
Colby, Carrie V. 286
Cole, Dorothy 168
Cole, Grace 306, 310
Cole, Helen G. 243
Cole, Malvina 286
Cole, Martha 192
Cole, Phyllis 313, 316
Cole, Ruth A. 286
Coleman, Carolyn S. 243
Coleman, Donna 171
Coleman, Evelyn L. 286
Coleman, Linda 168
Coleman, Mary H. 168, 169
Coleman, Sharon L. 163
Collins, Barbara Rose 159
Collins, Beatrice S. 76
Collins, Earlean 110
Collins, Elna Jan 243
Collins, Kenalene J. 286
Collins, Mayne A. 146

Edwards, Lydia Justice 105, 108
Edwards, Marilyn A. 172, 174
Edwards, Mary 105, 108
Edwards, Norma Dee 159
Egeland, Leona H. 65
Egenes, Sonja 122
Ehrhardt, Harryette 274
Eide, Tracey 306
Eidsness, Pat 267
Eidy, Jean E. 267
Eisenstadt, Pauline B. 220
Eldredge, Jane M. 125
Eliot, Geraldine 57
Ellingson, Nettie E. 233
Ellingwood, Ruth A. 139
Elliot, Isabel M. 122
Elliott, Daisy 159
Ellis, Anna M. 247
Ellis, Etta L. 195
Ellis, Jerry 306
Ellis, Mabel S. 57, 59
Ellis, Mary Gordon 262, 263, 331
Elloitt, Geraldine 77
Ellsworth, Florence B. 287
Elrod, Rena 111
Emerson, Bessie 195
Emery, Julia 77
Emery, May E. 287, 297
Emmons, Alice M. 287
Emmons, Joanne G. 158, 159
Emmons, Linda N 77
Emmons, Marie P. 77
Emons, Imogene V. 195
Empson, Cindy 126
Engeleiter, Susan Shannon 318, 319, 321; see also Shannon
Enget, June Y. 233
Engle, Barbara L. 117
Engle, Lavinia 147
Engler, Colleen House 159; see also House
English, Jerry F. 214, 217
English, Karen L. 55, 57
Engram, Beverly Leigh 93
Engstrom, Thelma Catherine 49
Enterline, Madge 323
Enz, Catherine 172
Epps, Mary Ellen 69
Epton, Kathryn 306
Erb, Lillian 77, 85

Erickson, Edna E. 277, 279, 281
Erickson, Phyllis K. 306, 310
Erk, Anna P. 77
Erkson, Pamela J. 287
Ervin, Susan G. 229
Erwin, Judy 111
Erwin, Phyllis R. 139
Escott, Sundra E. 47, 48; see also Russell
Escutia, Martha M. 65
Eskens, Esther 323
Eskesen, Ruth E. 57
Espinola, Joan E. 195
Esposito, Theresa H. 229
Estenson, Jo Ellen 177
Estrada, Sharon 176
Eu, March K. Fong 65
Eubanks, Sara 279
Evans, Beverly Ann 279
Evans, Ernestine D. 220
Evans, Faith P. 102
Evans, Frances 313, 316
Evans, Geri 163
Evans, Jan 184
Evans, Marilyn Bailey 90
Evans, Martha W. 227, 229
Evans, Nancy 154
Evanson, Barbara 232
Evarts, Katharine A. 77
Evelti, Mary M. 288
Everest, Ethel W. 288
Everhart, Denise 126
Everist, Barbara 266, 267
Eylar, Calla K. 220; see also Wolfe
Eylar, Elma R. 243
Ezzard, Martha M. 67, 69, 72

Faatz, Jeanne 69
Facemyer, Karen L. 313
Facey, Florence Kerr 177
Fadeley, Nancie Peacocke 247
Fagan, Josephine W. 323
Fagan, Veronica Barrett 260, 261
Fahey, Marcella C. 73
Fahey, Mary Q. 77
Fahrbach, Ruth C. 77
Fahrenkamp, Bettye 51
Faiks, Jan 51

Fain, Sarah Lee 300, 301, 330
Fair, Patricia A. 195
Fairley, Barbara 304
Fallin, Mary 243
Fallon, Tina 87, 88
Falls, Sharon 94
Falvey, Catherine E. 154
Falvey, Katherine M. 122, 124
Fancher, Helen 306
Fanning, Faye B. 279
Fantasia, Mary E. 154
Fantin, Arline M. 111
Farenthold, Frances 274
Farese, Orene 167, 168
Farhat, Debbie 159
Farley, Frances 277
Farmer, Annette 247, 249
Farmer, Elaine F. 251
Farmer, Marjorie Dilley 73, 77
Farmer, Nancy 172
Farnsworth, Marguerite 288
Farnsworth, Susan 139
Farnum, Mary L. R. 187, 195, 329
Farquharson, Mary U. 304
Farr, Amber 288
Farr, M. Zoe 288
Farr, Shirley 288
Farr, Thelma W. 168, 169; see also Baxter
Farragher, Clare M. 215, 217
Farrar, Alli R. 288
Farrar, Jessica 274
Farris, Carol 177
Farrow, Margaret A. 318, 319
Farve, Naomi W. 134
Faulise-Boone, Dorothy 77
Faulkner, Ellen 195
Faulkner, Patricia Anne 147
Fauset, Crystal Bird 251, 254, 335
Favreau, Irene B. 77
Fawcett, Charlotte D. 252
Fawell, Beverly J. 110, 111
Fay, Josie J. 288
Fay, Marguerite R. 139
Fay, Wilma J. 117, 119

Lee, Dorothy McCullough 246, 247, 249
Lee, Eleanor 304, 307, 310
Lee, Fern E. 234
Lee, Frances S. 70
Lee, Janis K. 125
Lee, Judy 233
Lee, Lena K. 148
Lee, Rebecca E. 200
Lee, Shirley W. 233
Leeper, Gertrude B. 58, 59
Legasse, Dorothy L. 200
Lehto, Arlene I. 164
Leiby, Mary E. 252
Leidy, Ella A. 141
Leising, Jean 116
Lemaire, Patricia 141
Lemay, Mary S. 200
Leonard, Elizabeth M. 79
Leonard, June 307
Leonard, Louise 312
Leonard, Mabel Clara 291
Leonard, Margaret J. 307
Leopold, Alice K. 79
Leppik, Peggy 164
Lesewski, Arlene J. 162
Lesher, Lois M. 87
Leslie, Anne 200
Lester, Helen M. 79
Letendre, Evelyn S. 200
Leuck, Claire M. 118
Levesque, Mary E. 260
Levi, Connie M. 164
Lewis, Ann M. 268
Lewis, Clara Wentworth M. 80
Lewis, Helen E. 80
Lewis, Jacqueline 155
Lewis, Jean L. 246, 247
Lewis, Joyce 141
Lewis, Leslie 247
Lewis, Margaret 319
Lewis, Margaret Russell 134, 135
Lewis, Marian V. 91
Lewis, Marilyn S. 252
Lewis, Mary Ann 200
Lewis, Maryanne 155
Lewitz, Loretta 80
Lilly, Mary M. 222, 225, 329
Lima, Charlene 260
Linard, Sharlyn 220
Linck, Alaska S. 50
Lincoln, E.Louise 141

Lincoln, Eva K. 291
Lincoln, Georgianna 51, 52
Lindamood, V. Joyce 291
Lindeman, Anne 55, 58
Lindgren, Mabel 231, 234, 235, 303
Lindner, Patricia Reid 112
Lindquist, Robin 247
Linebarger, Libby 275
Lingelbach, Doris 291
Lint, Janis R. 200
Linton, Allie Mae 131
Linton, Barbara J. 319
Linville, Kelli 307
Lipman, Wynona M. 214
Lipman-Brown, Lori 184
Lipschutz, Gerdi E. 225, 226
Lipsey, Triette E. 160, 161
Lipsky, Joan 122
Lisk, Barbara 307
Liss, Sophie G. 80
Little, Eleanor H. 80
Little, Patricia L. 185
Little, Suzanne R. 51
Little, Teena S. 227
Littler, Kathleen P. 70
Livingston, Judith 291
Llovet Diaz, Josefina 256, 257
Lloyd, Alma 268, 269
Lloyd, Daisy R. 118
Lloyd, Mary Ellen 104, 107, 108
Lloyd, Ruth 240
Lloyd-Jones, Jean 121, 123
Lock, Selma 70, 72
Locke, Esther S. 291
Locke, Stephainie 141
Lockman, Sue 280
Lockner, Joanne 268
Lockton, Janet K. 80
Lockwood, Lorna E. 58, 59
Loder, Suzanne K. 200
Logan, Cecilia M. 118
Logee, Edith C. 259
Loizeaux, Suzanne 188, 200
Lojzim, Ruth E. 80
Lokan, Jane 248
Lonergan, Joyce 123
Long, Beth 172, 175
Long, Betty Jane 168
Long, Dee 164
Long, Edna B. 291

Long, Jeanine H. 304, 307
Long, Linda D. 200
Long, Lydia D. 314
Long, Martha A. 200
Long, Martha E. 70
Long, Paula A. 148, 151
Longley, Susan W. 137
Longstaff, Marion Lee 141
Look, Theone F. 141
Looney, Lamar 242, 243, 329
Loose, Katherine 148, 151
Lopes, Maria J. 260
Lord, Evelyn M. 86
Lord, Florence S. 80
Lord, Hazel C. 137, 141
Lord, Marion M. 200
Lorman, Barbara 318, 321
Loughead, Nettie B. 238, 330
Lourey, Becky 164
Love, Ida Viola 220
Love, Lucille A. 260
Love, Mary Ann 148, 151
Love, Minnie C. T. 15, 70
Lovejoy, Lynda Morgan 220; see also Morgan
Lovejoy, Marian E. 200
Lovejoy, Virginia K. 201
Loveland, Valoria H. 304
Loveridge, Della L. 280
Lovett, Glenys P. 141
Lowden, Sue 184
Lowe, Bettye 95, 97
Lowe, Joan 271, 272
Lowe, Mabel Leota 118
Lowe, Mildred P. 280
Lowe, Rozello 280, 281
Lowenthal, Margaret Welsh 134
Lown, Elizabeth D. 201
Lozeau, Donnalee M. 201
Lubbers, Teresa S. 116
Lucas, Jeanne Hopkins 227, 231
Lucas, June H. 240
Lucas, L. Louise 301
Lucht, Sondra Moore 312
Lucier, Grace C. 291
Luckhardt, Esther Doughty 319; see also Doughty
Lucy, Irene M. 201
Ludwig, Margaret G. 137
Luginbuhl, Vi Larimore 291

Taichert, Ruth 221
Taisey, Laura B. 295
Talcott, Gigi 309
Tally, Lura Self 228, 230
Talmadge, Quilla E. 217
Tamposi, R. Betty 208, 212
Taneszio, Theresa 83
Tanger, Winifred A. 83
Tanner, Alice J. 174
Tanner, Alma R. 295
Tanner, Gloria Travis 68, 71, 72
Tanner, Laura W. 281
Tanner, Sally 66
Tansey, Marie 241
Tarpley, Nancy L. 208
Tarr, Gail H. 143
Tarrant, Harriet B. 208
Tartaglione, Tina 251
Tassie, B. Leola 295
Tate, Joan C. 208
Tate, Margaret 167, 169
Tatibouet, Jane B. 102
Tavares, Charletta B. 241
Tavarres, Charlotte 241
Taylor, Ada C. 208, 212
Taylor, Annie Roberts 295
Taylor, Arie P. 71
Taylor, Bessie H. 83
Taylor, Dorothy Mae Delavallade 135
Taylor, Edith 107, 108
Taylor, Elinor Z. 253
Taylor, Emma 309; see also Harman
Taylor, Florence E. 295
Taylor, Jackie 248
Taylor, Katie Elizabeth 295
Taylor, Levola S. 264, 265
Taylor, Lila V. 179
Taylor, Lucille 281
Taylor, Maretta Mitchell 96
Taylor, Maude T. 272
Taylor, Mildred Frick 225
Taylor, Priscilla G. 143
Taylor, Rena Mary 68, 71
Taylor, Virginia F. 208
Taylor, Winifred A. 295
Teaford, Jane 123
Teagan, Linda 156
Teague, Sharon Beasley 96
Tebedo, Mary Anne 68, 71, 72

Tedesco, Jane J. 83
Telek, Leona Lee 253
Telford, Edna B. 156, 157
Temkin, Zena H. 83
Tempest, Carol 71
Ten Eyck, Maude E. 225
Tennille, Margaret 230
Ter Kuile, Barbara J. 83
Teregeyo, Ana S. 237
Terninko, Maggie Boyle 208, 212
Terrell, Ethel 160
Terry, Joan E. 208
Terry, Mary Frances 169
Terry, Mary Sue 302
Tesmer, Louise M. 320, 321
Testu, Jeanette 309
Teutsch, Delores E. 309
Thaler, Daisy Wigginton 130
Thayer, Velma B. 295
Theiling, Jane H. 315
Thibaudeau, Pat 309
Thielen, Cynthia 103
Thode, Edna Blowden 56, 59
Thomas, Betty Dorton 230, 231
Thomas, Ellen E. 143
Thomas, Linda Craig 309
Thomas, Louphenia 47, 48
Thomas, Mable Able 96
Thomas, Martha G. 250, 253, 330
Thomas, Nadine 94, 96
Thomas, Paula H. 264
Thomas, Regina 96
Thomas, Rhonda 59
Thomas, Virginia M. 150
Thompson, Agnes Mavourneen 143
Thompson, Anne M. 71
Thompson, Barbara Cooper 208
Thompson, Carolyn Ann 244
Thompson, Doris L. 208
Thompson, Dorothy 295
Thompson, Eliza Jennings 54
Thompson, Elizabeth H. 62
Thompson, Helen F. 317, 320, 331
Thompson, Isabelle N. 100

Thompson, Lila W. 217
Thompson, Lillian B. 221
Thompson, Lizzie Price 135
Thompson, Majorie J. 128
Thompson, Marianne H. 208
Thompson, Mary L. 221
Thompson, Norma 62
Thompson, Patricia L. 123
Thompson, Rose Mary 123, 124
Thompson, Ruth 160
Thompson, Senfronia 275
Thompson, Sharon A. 230
Thompson, Sylvia Alexander 248
Thomson, Glyneta B. 208
Thornhill, Lucille 315, 316
Thornton, Jarushia 47, 48
Thornton, Jean T. 84
Thorp, Norma 128, 129
Thrasher, Pearl 309
Thresher, Irene K. 156
Thropp, May A. 217
Thurber, Mary D. 295
Thurman, Karen L. 89
Thurston, Florence H. 143
Tibbetts, Thelma P. 208
Tierney, Marie 233
Tiffany, Sandra 185
Tignor, Beatrice 145, 150, 151
Tillotson, Carolyn 125
Tilton, Elmira F. 208
Tingley, Helen C. 150, 151
Tinker, Carol W. 221
Tinsman, Maggie 121
Tippin, Barbara 84
Tischer, Mae 52
Titcomb, Bonnie L. 137
Titus, Constandina 184
Toal, Jean Hoefer 264
Tobin, Joan T. 174
Tobin, Marjorie 132
Tobin, Mary Ann 132
Todd, Jane Hedges 226
Toelkes, Dixie E. 128
Toll, Rose 253
Tolman, Janet 208
Tomboulian, Alice 160
Tomlin, Frances F. 230
Tompkins, Eileen 165
Toohey, Cynthia D. 52
Toomey, Kathryn W. 208
Tootell, Lucy Rawlings 261

NAME INDEX 397

Wilson, Arlene Lois 296, 298
Wilson, Betty 217
Wilson, Constance K. 228, 230, 231
Wilson, Cynthia Randolph 132
Wilson, Esther M. 119
Wilson, Helen Francis 210
Wilson, Hestia 68, 72
Wilson, Ida R. 119
Wilson, Jean T. 254
Wilson, Karla 309
Wilson, Lenna G. 210; see also Perry
Wilson, Lilith M. 254, 333
Wilson, Lori 90
Wilson, Mary E. 71
Wilson, Peggy Ann 230, 231
Winch, Rev. Mabel 296
Wines, Hazel Bell 182, 186
Wing, Gloria A. 296
Winikow, Linda 223, 226
Winkler, Cheryl J. 241
Winkler, Lenny T. 84, 85
Winkley, Noreen D. 210
Winn, Cecelia L. 210
Winn, Julie 143
Winn, Neita McCargo 169
Winner, Leslie 228
Winship, Edna E. 296, 298
Winsley, Shirley J. 305, 310, 311
Winslow, Karyl 179
Winter, Elizabeth A. 254
Winters, Barbara 210
Wintler, Ella 310
Wirth, Sandra Lee 226
Wisdom, Jane A. 186
Wise, Dr. Helen D. 254
Wiseman, Myrtle Lura Belle 230
Wiser, Betty H. 231
Wishard, Della M. 268
Wiswell, Marguerite H. 210
Witeck, Kate 181
Witherspoon, Dorothy K. 71
Withrow, Jackie 315
Wofford, Marion G. 268
Wofford, Sandra S. 265
Wohlgemuth, Arlene 276

Wojahn, Lorraine R. 305, 310
Wojcik, Kathleen L. 114
Wojewodzki, Catherine 88
Wojtas, Joyce A. 84
Wolchick, Ruth 132
Wolcott, Olga Doran 123
Wolf, Katie L. 116, 119
Wolf, Sarah Margaret 119
Wolfe, Calla K. Eylar 221; see also Eylar
Wolfe, Cathy 310
Wolfe, Jan Johnson 176; see also Johnson
Wolfe, Robbie T. 272
Wolstenholme, Lily C. 281
Womacks, Martha A. 119
Won Pat-Borga, Judith 98
Wong, Norma 103
Wood, Barbara C. 296
Wood, E. Sharon 150, 151
Wood, Elizabeth A. 84
Wood, Gertrude P. 84
Wood, Jeanette 305, 310, 311
Wood, Jo An E. 107
Wood, Lucille T. 210
Wood, Marie W. 143
Wood, Morna 324
Wood, Violet P. 296
Woodard, Wilma C. 228, 231
Woodbridge, Cora 66
Woodbury, Marjorie S. 210
Woodford, Majorie M. 84
Woodhouse, Janet 71
Woodman, Louisa K. 210
Woodruff, Marian D. 210
Woods, Deborah L. 210
Woods, Harriett 171
Woods, Jane H. 301, 302
Woods, Josie Alma 186
Woods, Loretta Cooper 241
Woods, Phyllis L. 210
Woods, Winifred Davis 315, 316
Woodson, Mariene E. 90
Woodward, Ellen Sullivan 169
Woodward, Lucille M. 84
Woodward, Maud L. 84
Woodward, Neila P. 210, 212

Woodward, Sarah J. 210
Woody, Dianne 305, 311
Wooffendale, Lucille 119
Wooldridge, Sherri L. 324
Woolley, Beverly 276
Woolridge, Martha C. 186
Woolsey, Nathella Griffen 281; see also Griffen
Wooten, Cynthia 249
Worcester, Georgie E. 210
Word, Alrene 62
Workman, Betty 150
Worley, Anna Lee 269, 270, 272, 329
Worman, Marna Jo 119
Worthen, Dorothy M. 210
Worthen, Sandra 88
Wright, Barbara 217
Wright, Cathie 64, 66
Wright, Delores C. 221
Wright, Harriet G. R. 71
Wright, Joan C. 88
Wright, Joan M. 217
Wright, Julia T. 85
Wright, Mary A. 22, 104, 107, 329, 334
Wright, Patricia 56, 59
Wright, Ruth 71
Wright, Ruth E. 296, 298
Wright, Sylvia B. 296
Wright, Virginia L. 324
Wrynn, Lucie 85
Wuelper, Marion 210
Wyatt, Diana E. 179
Wyatt, Margaret L. 119
Wylie, Fannie B. 181, 182
Wylie, Sharon 249
Wyman, Nancy S. 85
Wynd, Elisabeth S. 254
Wynia, Ann J. 165
Wynne, Linda 310, 311
Wynot, Retha Deal 48

Yacavone, Muriel T. 85
Yancy, Barbara 167, 169
Yantis, Effie E. 210
Yarnell, Carolyn 296
Yatman, Marion F. 261
Yeager, Emily W. 315, 316
Yearian, Emma R. 107
Yenger, Sue 121
Yennaco, Carol A. 210
Yerrington, Lillian L. 85
Yih, Mae 246, 249
Yoh, Donna 128
Yoho, Pearle 315, 316